"AN EXTRAORDINARY BOOK!"
—*Newsday*

"A riproaring story of sex, murder, hijinks and lowjinks and the whole dripping with money, drugs and plots of all sorts."

—*Natchez Democrat*

"COMPELLING! . . . The language gives a bite to reality and keeps us reading . . . giving us the details we crave in this kind of True Crime genre."

—*The Los Angeles Times*

"IT'S SUPERB . . .

fast moving and riveting. It is reeled out just like the murder mystery it is—except this time it's true."

—*The Sacramento Union*

"HERE IS SENSATIONALISM WITH A CAPITAL 'S'!"
—*Publishers Weekly*

GARY CARTWRIGHT

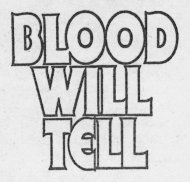

BLOOD WILL TELL

The Murder Trials of
T. Cullen Davis

PUBLISHED BY POCKET BOOKS NEW YORK

POCKET BOOKS, a Simon & Schuster division of
GULF & WESTERN CORPORATION
1230 Avenue of the Americas, New York, N.Y. 10020

Copyright © 1979, 1980 by Gary Cartwright

Published by arrangement with Harcourt Brace Jovanovich, Inc.
Library of Congress Catalog Card Number: 78-22246

ISBN: 0-671-83343-X

First Pocket Books printing July, 1980

10 9 8 7 6 5 4 3 2 1

POCKET and colophon are trademarks of Simon & Schuster.

Printed in the U.S.A.

For Phyllis,
with love and appreciation

Contents

WHEN
THE OLD MAN
DIED

1

THE RICHEST MAN
EVER TRIED
FOR MURDER

149

THE OPERA
AIN'T OVER TILL
THE FAT LADY SINGS

313

EPILOGUE

457

Author's Note

The high stakes and the rich excitement of the plot first drew me to the story of Cullen and Priscilla Davis. It has those ingredients in abundance. It also has something to think about: how the legal system works when the man accused is a multimillionaire, can afford the best lawyers, and cannot be bankrupted by the need to defend himself.

I do not mean to imply that justice miscarried. Cullen has consistently maintained his innocence of the crimes he has been tried for; in one case he was acquitted and in the other the jury was unable to agree on a verdict. Cullen's lawyers did establish reasonable doubt in the first trial, and until a verdict is reached in the second case, Cullen rightly enjoys a presumption of innocence. That's as it should be. The facts are the facts, and I have stuck to them. But had the facts been exactly the same and had the accused been poor, would the trials' outcomes have been different? And would that have been as it should be?

Many people helped me write *Blood Will Tell*. Attorneys for both sides were available for interviews. So were Cullen and Priscilla. Many others gave generously of their time. Some asked not to be named, and rather than list those I can, I would like to thank them all anonymously: they know who they are. My editors at *Texas Monthly* deserve a special thank you, as do Tom Stewart for a splendid editing job and Sidney Brammer for typing the manuscript and helping me maintain sanity at the end.

G. C.

WHEN
THE OLD MAN
DIED

My grandfather's clock
was too large for the shelf
so it stood ninety years
on the floor

It was taller by half
than the old man himself,
yet it weighed
not a pennyweight more.

It was bought on the morn
of the day that he was born
and was always his treasure and pride.
But it stopp'd
short,
never to go again,
when the old man died.

—"My Grandfather's Clock"
AMERICAN CHILDREN'S SONG

In the beginning no one thought of it as a mansion, much less *The Mansion*. That would come later, as the empire that financed it was shaking at the roots. To the thousands who drove by it every day, wondering but never knowing who was up there or what was happening, the big house off Hulen Boulevard looked more like a museum than a mansion.

It stood alone on the knob of a hill, its 181 acres of manicured lawn bordered to the north by the Clear Fork of the Trinity River and to the south and west by the Colonial Country Club golf course. A quiet residential lane named Mockingbird came to a dead end at the mansion's southeast gate, which was technically the main entrance but always seemed like the rear entrance to the estate. Hulen Boulevard, a major artery connecting the old silk stockings area called Arlington Heights with the newer pocket of upward mobility known as Tanglewood, ran for nearly a half-mile along the western edge of the mansion grounds. Old-timers sometimes referred to the land as "the old dairy," though it hadn't been used as a dairy since well before the early 1940s when Fort Worth oil millionaire Kenneth W. Davis, Sr., purchased the tract from the heirs of one Mitilda Burford. A few who knew that the land belonged to the Ken Davis family called it "the old Davis farm," but again it had been years since cattle grazed under the tall pecans and ancient oaks.

In late 1968 a gang of workers appeared with bulldozers and backhoes and enough equipment and supplies to build a shopping center. A foundation was poured over thousands of feet of high ground. Gradually and without fanfare, the eye-popping sprawl of trapezoids and parallelograms and oddly sloping white

3

walls that would come to be called The Mansion appeared and took life. And still nobody thought to call it a mansion. Except for the "Private Drive" signs fixed unobtrusively to the heavy iron gates on Mockingbird and Hulen, the place might have been some sort of avant-garde institution, an academy for the advancement of arts and science, perhaps. It had that look about it, cool and impersonal and unassimilable, institutionally awkward as though its design had been compromised many times; but permanent as any structure was likely to be in Fort Worth, Texas. There had been mansions in Fort Worth since the days of the great cattle drives and, after that, the West Texas oil boom, towers of leaded glass and imported stones that appeared along the Clear Fork of the Trinity, as dramatically and convulsively as new volcanoes erupting from the ocean floor. Almost without exception they had been demolished and their memories buried in yellowing archives. In their own time the mansions of Burk Burnett and Tom Waggoner, who hunted wolves with President Teddy Roosevelt along the Trinity in 1905, must have impressed passersby in the way that the mansion at 4200 Mockingbird did seventy years later, as something impregnable, like a Moorish fortress, something that might stand for a thousand years.

It was said that the mansion covered 19,000 square feet, though that figure was probably exaggerated, and was constructed at a cost of $6 million. That figure included the lavish furnishings and collection of paintings, bronzes, and gold and jeweled knickknacks, but not the land itself. It was difficult to calculate the true value of 181 privately owned acres along the river just southwest of downtown Fort Worth. The area just beyond the Davis estate included not only Colonial Country Club and its magnificent golf course, but the campus of Texas Christian University, the TCU Stadium and Field House, Forest Park, the city zoo, and the Botanic Gardens. The Davis estate was without question the largest tract of unimproved, privately owned land in the best section of Fort Worth. It wasn't the size or cost of the mansion that made it such a showpiece, but the

4

fact that it was so highly visible, located as it was on the highest knoll of the choicest piece of land. To the heavy flow of traffic along Hulen, the mansion appeared to protrude from the trees like something other-worldly—like a phantom ocean liner, landlocked by some mysterious force.

What sort of person would build such a home? People found it hard to imagine. Obviously, someone who wanted to call attention to himself: to those who knew the story, this was the strangest part of all. The mansion at 4200 Mockingbird was the carefully planned, meticulously supervised dream home of Kenneth Davis's middle son, T. Cullen Davis, a man who, until the moment he moved in, was lost in the shadows of his family name.

Although the Davises had lived in Fort Worth for almost fifty years and were counted among the richest families in town, the name was so obscure that no society editor or gossip columnist was likely to recognize it, much less accord it any special meaning. There were many rich and ostentatious families in Fort Worth, third- and fourth-generation oil and cattle people, but the Davises weren't among them. The *Fort Worth Star-Telegram*, founded by the city's patron booster Amon Carter, knew so little about the Davis family that it hadn't even bothered to maintain a separate file on the family in the reference room. Alice Bound Davis, wife of the oilman and mother of his three sons, had donated the money to construct the Noble Planetarium at the Fort Worth Children's Museum but had intentionally allowed people to forget her contribution by naming it for Miss Charlie Noble, longtime astronomy instructor. Ken Davis, Sr., was a contemporary of Sid Richardson, Clint Murchison, Amon Carter, and other legendary Texas wheeler-dealers, but hardly anyone below the rank of bank president thought of him that way, or thought of him at all. He was known, not affectionately, as Stinky Davis. "He was a short, robust man, no more than five-six," a longtime business acquaintance explained. "But he wasn't the sort of man you'd call Shorty." No one used his nickname in his presence, of course, but the mere mention of Stinky Davis caused quakes and tremors in the boardrooms of a number of large financial institutions.

Stinky Davis raised his three boys, Kenneth Jr., Cullen, and Bill, to be frugal, protective, diligent, hard-nosed business types. All three graduated from Arlington Heights High School and Texas A & M. They were sent to Texas A & M because, as a family friend put it, "it was the cheapest, hardest place the old man could find." In those days, the late 1940s and the first half of the 1950s, Texas A & M was sometimes called "West Point on the Brazos," referring to the river that cut through that isolated part of central Texas where the institution was located, and to the compulsory military training that the all-male student body had to endure. Aggies were a breed apart, the dirt and guts and finger-nails of higher education in Texas.

When the old man died in August of 1968, the three sons took over the family-owned conglomerate known as Kendavis Industries International, Inc. The old man had literally built it from nothing, starting with four employees in 1929 and expanding it in his lifetime until it had thousands of employees and offices and subsidiaries all over the world. Yet hardly anyone, not even the old man's most trusted advisers—perhaps not even the sons themselves—had a true concept of Stinky Davis's net worth. What the old man left his sons was an equal and undivided share of a business worth in excess of $300 million. In the ten years after the old man's death, Kendavis Industries (sometimes known by its logo, Kiii) quadrupled in value, and still only a handful of people had any real concept of its reach and wealth. This was because Stinky Davis had doggedly refused to sell shares of his companies to the public. With one exception, all the companies under the Kiii umbrella were wholly owned by the old man and later his sons. It was and is without question one of the largest privately held conglomerates in the United States—it has been estimated that fewer than 5 percent of *all* companies in this country are as large. By 1977

6

combined sales of the eighty-plus Kiii companies exceeded $1.03 billion.

It was not apparent at the time, but the wall of secrecy that Stinky Davis so carefully constructed around his empire began to crumble on August 29, 1968, the day he died. It was also the day that T. Cullen Davis, his middle son, married Priscilla Lee Wilborn, a sexy, twice-married platinum blonde who came from so far on the other side of the tracks it wasn't even the same railroad. Though the date of the death and the marriage appeared to be coincidental, it had a strategic value. Since Cullen's brothers were both divorced, it was agreed that the newlyweds would move into the old family home on Rivercrest in Arlington Heights. Thus Cullen Davis, who had just inherited an equal share of the family fortune, became a little more than equal. No one knew it at the time, but Cullen was already drafting plans for his mansion.

To say that the marriage shocked Fort Worth society would be to overestimate the esteem in which Cullen was held back in 1968. But the wedding did cause some tongues to waggle. People who had never paused a moment to consider Cullen considered him now and asked *why her?* Priscilla was an outsider and went out of her way to show it. She was a tiny, striking figure with a cascade of silver-blonde hair and an affinity for gowns cut spectacularly low. At Cullen's urging, one of Priscilla's first expenditures as a member of the Davis family was for silicone breast implants. She came to the marriage with, as they say in Forth Worth, "a good balcony," and after the breast implants she snapped heads every time she walked through the lobby of the Colonial or River Crest Country Club. Cullen's first wife, Sandra, had been known among the social set as a plain, unadorned woman who made her own dresses and kept her place, but Priscilla knew little and cared less about such places: in her experience, women who knew how to operate sewing machines were likely to spend their whole life behind one. Priscilla's notion of a fine gown required a bare minimum of material, yet she thought nothing of spending $20,000 a month on clothes. Her favorite piece of jewelry was a gold necklace that spelled out RICH BITCH.

Once so formal and reserved that even his father complained that Cullen dressed like "some kinda popinjay," Cullen now lived vicariously through Priscilla. He began to shun high society in favor of discos and classy honky-tonks, and he squandered huge sums of money on indulgences that must have had the old man spinning in his grave. Not the least of these was the $6-million mansion. It was hardly the place Stinky Davis would have built, but of course that was the point.

It was said that Cullen built the mansion to immortalize his marriage to Priscilla, and maybe in the beginning this was true. But other forces played just below the surface. For whatever reason, the marriage was not as solid as the mansion. Although Cullen adopted Priscilla's oldest daughter, Dee, and gave her his family name, Dee Davis and her new stepfather were far from compatible. Dee wasn't accustomed to harsh discipline, but Priscilla said Cullen whipped her frequently and sometimes severely. On one occasion when Dee forgot to lock the kitchen door, Cullen broke her nose and slammed her kitten on the floor until it was dead. Priscilla's other children, Jack Wilborn, Jr., and Andrea Wilborn, continued to live with their father and visited the mansion only occasionally. Andrea, a tender and sensitive girl, came to fear Cullen and finally refused to visit the mansion at all. Priscilla, too, seemed to bring out a dark side of Cullen Davis. Priscilla complained to friends that Cullen demanded either too much or too little; the couple couldn't seem to find a happy medium. Cullen accused her of having illicit affairs, and when she denied the affairs, he broke her nose and on another occasion her collarbone. Other times he snubbed her or humiliated her in public. In the early years of the marriage Cullen and Priscilla traveled extensively to Europe and South America, but gradually Cullen started traveling alone, and when he did, Priscilla's alleged affairs became more than a figment of Cullen's imagination.

In August 1974, almost exactly six years after the

death of Kenneth Davis, Sr., and the simultaneous and shocking marriage of his second son to an overt outsider, Priscilla filed for divorce and Cullen moved out of the mansion and into a motel. It was to be a bitter, protracted divorce struggle. Each side hurled charges of deceit and treachery, and each time they seemed close to a settlement, one or the other found a reason to delay the final resolution. At the same time something else was happening that upset the equilibrium of the family fortune. Three months after Priscilla filed her divorce papers, the youngest brother, Bill Davis, filed suit against his two older brothers, charging that they were conspiring to squeeze him out of his inheritance. There had been numerous disagreements among the brothers, but two things in particular inflamed Bill Davis. First was Cullen Davis's "extravagant and wasteful business expenditures and investments" in the management of Cummins Sales and Service, one of the major Kiii subsidiaries that Cullen headed. Second, Bill objected to "the use of the [company] personnel, banking relations, deposits and credit . . . to obtain [personal] loans for T. Cullen Davis." According to Bill Davis, Cullen had turned Cummins from a moneymaking concern into a business that was $46 million in debt. What is more, Bill Davis charged, Cullen had run up personal debts of at least $16 million since the death of their father. Perhaps the most damning part of the suit was the charge that Cullen and Ken Jr. manipulated stock in Stratoflex, the only major Kiii stock available to the public, for the purposes of tax fraud. This last charge smacked of criminal intent and threatened to provoke an investigation by the Securities and Exchange Commission.

As the months wore on and the battle raged between husband and wife, and among brothers, Cullen settled in for a long fight. He had a new girlfriend, an attractive young divorcée named Karen Master, and instead of in a motel he now lived in her home in the Edgewood section of Fort Worth.

Priscilla, too, was finding it unpleasant to live alone and invited a strange procession of people unknown to

Fort Worth society to share the mansion. The first was a former motorcycle racer named W. T. Rufner. Priscilla started seeing Rufner several months before she filed for divorce, and when Cullen moved out of the mansion, Rufner and a consortium of his friends moved in and stayed for six months or longer. T-man, as Rufner was known in the Fort Worth drug world, eventually wore out his welcome and was forcibly evicted from the mansion. At the same time Priscilla began carrying on with a six-foot-nine former TCU basketball player named Stan Farr. By the spring of 1975, Farr was sharing not only the mansion but the master bedroom.

After many delays the divorce trial was finally scheduled to begin on July 30, 1976, but again there were problems. This was Priscilla's thirty-fifth birthday and she was a nervous wreck. Her lawyers once again filed a motion to delay the divorce trial, using a letter from Priscilla's doctor as evidence that she was in no condition to endure a trial. Domestic Relations Court Judge Joe Eidson promised to rule on the motion in a few days.

Three days later, on Monday, August 2, Cullen and Ken Jr. and their chief financial adviser, Walter Strittmatter, were meeting with attorneys to discuss the lawsuit brought by Bill Davis. As Strittmatter recalled, they were sitting in the fifth-floor executive room of the Mid-Continent Building when word reached corporate headquarters that Judge Eidson had granted Priscilla's request. Eidson not only granted another delay in the divorce proceedings; he also ordered Cullen to pay a lump sum of $52,000 for maintenance and attorneys' fees and increased support payments from $3,500 to $5,000 a month. It was claimed that Cullen took this latest bad news in stride, but Ken Jr. was upset and said so in no uncertain terms. It wasn't the money. What galled everyone at the meeting was the continuing problem of having to go through Judge Eidson in order to make any sort of corporate transaction. Judge Eidson reserved for himself the right to tell Cullen how to run his business. What chapped Cullen was still another

10

order by Eidson, this one prohibiting him from visiting the mansion or otherwise hassling his estranged wife. Cullen no longer pretended that he built the house for Priscilla. It was *his* mansion. "She's just a guest there," he snapped. Cullen claimed that just prior to the marriage Priscilla had signed a prenuptial agreement disclaiming any right to the family fortune.

Cullen worked until nearly 8:00 P.M. on August 2. For the next four or five hours his whereabouts were unknown.

It was about midnight on that hellish August night when Priscilla and Stan Farr returned to the mansion. Someone had tampered with the security system, but Priscilla dismissed the warning as she moved through the kitchen turning out lights. Andrea was spending the night, and Priscilla speculated that her twelve-year-old had carelessly deactivated the security system. If so, it was the last thing Andrea ever did: the girl lay dead in a basement utility room, a bullet hole through her chest and her eyes open as though death had come before she could blink. As Priscilla walked to the stairs leading to the master bedroom, a man in black stepped from the laundry room, said "Hi," and shot her once through the chest. Stan Farr raced downstairs and the killer shot him four times, then dragged Farr's enormous body down the hallway to the kitchen, toward the basement where Andrea's body was hidden. Terrified, clutching at the bleeding wound in her chest, Priscilla escaped through the courtyard and down the hill to the home of a neighbor she had never met. She banged on the door, screaming: "My name is Priscilla Davis. I live in the big house in the middle of the field off Hulen. I am very wounded. Cullen is up there killing my children. He is killing everyone. . . ."

Stinky Davis enjoyed reminding folks that he didn't pick all that money off trees. He was a champion of the work ethic, a staunch defender of free enterprise, and a believer in the principle that money talks. Above all he was a family man, a procreator of his own image and style. It must have given him comfort to know that when he died, his empire would pass down "equal and undivided" to his three boys. Surely his own experience suggested it would not remain that way.

The old man consciously fostered a fierce sense of competition among his sons, assigning them menial tasks and then personally inspecting the jobs in the manner of a drill instructor. A family friend recalled: "Stinky would tell the boys, 'Go down to the lake and repair that old piling. When you get done, I'll come down and show you how it should have been done.'" He was constantly giving his sons advice such as "Keep your mind 100 percent on your work" and "If you're *talking,* you're not *listening.*" The boys would have to take him at his word: there was no way they could know how hard it had been.

Ken Jr., the old man's firstborn and namesake, was Stinky's favorite and, in a sense, his spiritual heir. Born at the beginning of the depression, when the old man was just starting his oil field supply business in Fort Worth, Ken Jr. was the only one of the boys who had any feeling for hard times, other than the hard times that were part of the family regimen. Ken Jr. was short and willow-built like his father (for obvious reasons no one ever called him Little Ken) and the blazer of the trail that Cullen would follow four or five years later. Bill was the baby, gentle and less pragmatic, more like his adoring mother. Alice Bound Davis loved all three

12

of her sons, but Bill was her blessing. Cullen was the quietest, most distant, and least outgoing of the three—"the weak one" some said, not exactly supine but painfully uncertain of himself. And yet, of the three, Cullen probably most admired the old man and suffered to emulate him. All of the boys were no doubt conscious of their inheritance, but they weren't ostentatious about it. The old man kept a tight grip on their life-styles by keeping a tight grip on their pocketbooks. Cullen was expected to mow the lawn of the enormous family home on Rivercrest Drive the same as Ken Jr. had and Bill would—and for the same wages, twenty-five cents. The old man never played favorites where money was concerned.

Stinky was constantly reminding his wife and sons that their wealth should not be taken for granted. One Christmas when he apparently forgot to buy a gift for his beloved wife, he handed her a note written on the back of an envelope: "My Dearest Alice: Let us all remember that people without too much are usually happier. Since we are all blessed with so much in the way of good health, good looks and wealth we should dedicate this day to another happy Christmas."

Growing up as he had in a time of jingoistic hard-assing and black gold, Stinky took as his own the oil field virtues of self-reliance and piety. You would hardly call Stinky Davis a fun lover—in his favorite parable of the ant and the grasshopper he clearly came down on the side of diligence—but the charge of the times that drove him to the top was every bit as manic as that experienced by the hapless grasshopper. When the old man gave his sons advice, as he did frequently, it was the same sound advice he gave himself: don't get caught napping. Friends recalled an occasion years ago, when times were still relatively lean, that Stinky sent Ken Jr. to summer camp. It was a first-class summer camp, but a problem developed. A camp counselor wrote Mr. Davis a letter complaining that Ken Jr. and his friends were unmercifully harassing one of the lesser boys in camp. Stinky snapped off a letter by return mail, demanding an explanation from both his son and the counselor. Ken Jr. replied that "the reason we nag the boy is because he is filthy and a sissy." The counselor acknowledged that this was an accurate assessment and added that the boy was also "incompetent." Friends thought Stinky would accept this as a resolution and be pleased, but he was not.

"Is that right? Was the boy incompetent?" Mr. Davis asked his son.

"Yes, sir," Ken Jr. said.

"Then you were wasting your time," the old man reprimanded him.

After Cullen was born, Stinky built his own camp at his retreat on Eagle Mountain Lake. The only three boys who ever went there were his sons. Maybe because he never had as much time to spend with Cullen as he did with Ken Jr., Stinky sometimes treated his second son with an almost condescending patience. Not that he pampered Cullen, he just went out of his way to make certain that his discipline had a clear object. Cullen did not do well in arithmetic in grade school, and this portended bad for a boy who was going to Texas A & M for an engineering degree. Cullen recalled with a certain fondness the time his father backhanded him off a stool for repeatedly giving the wrong answer to a homework problem. After that, Cullen became a serious student of math.

It was as though Ken Jr. inherited a disproportionate share of the old man's talent for self-reliance, leaving Cullen with the scraps. Just as he named his oldest son for himself, Stinky named Cullen after the man he respected second—the legendary Houston oil millionaire and philanthropist Hugh Roy Cullen. Known as "the king of the Texas wildcatters," Hugh Roy Cullen had an almost mystic power to find oil where others had failed. He practiced what old-timers called "creekology," following the earth's clues down river and creek beds and dry streams, studying rock formations, pondering and puzzling seemingly insignificant cretaceous outcrops until the formations of the earth below seemed to spread out like a map in his mind. It was a gift Stinky Davis never acquired, though he made a fortune selling

14

supplies to men like Hugh Roy Cullen. If the old man imagined that some of Hugh Roy Cullen's mystic qualities might rub off on his namesake, he was disappointed. T. Cullen Davis grew up as the most humorless and practical of men.

When Ken Jr. was in the army, he usually wrote home about amusing incidents in town involving himself and several old classmates. Cullen wrote home half sick about his assignment as stock supervisor at a naval supply depot in Indiana. Cullen complained that the bachelor officers' quarters were drafty and lonesome, there being only himself and one other ensign in the whole BOQ. What's more, he'd been overlooked for promotion and wanted his father's advice.

Stinky dictated the following reply: "Dear Cullen: It all sounds like you have gotten the break anyone should be looking for. . . . If I were you, I would project my plans to take advantage of this situation. . . . My advice is to keep in good standing with anyone directly over you. Work hard, keep right on studying and learn the habits of getting along. Don't 'bitch'! The fact that you are one of only two ensigns in the BOQ gives you an opportunity to be the head man with very little competition. Possession usually has some influence, [and] the [BOQ] will not always be unoccupied. I'm sure your comment about being 'at the end of the world' is a pun, son."

In a postscript he added that Cora Williams, the longtime family maid, had read Cullen's letter and commented: "What does that Cullen 'killer diller' expect—a blonde, brunette, and redhead in every vacant room?"

Born in Pennsylvania in 1895, Kenneth W. Davis, Sr., came of age in that wondrous time when Americans were first realizing that petroleum was something more than a handy substitute for whale oil. Ransom Olds had perfected the internal combustion engine, and Henry Ford had devised a method to mass-produce a simple, reliable machine that was already revolutionizing and shrinking the world. The first significant oil strikes had come in the fields of Pennsylvania, and, as

15

the saying went, "when the sparrows begin disappearing from the streets of New York, you'll know oil is here to stay." Ken Davis was playing semipro baseball and working in a steel mill, but he was restless to see firsthand the wild frontier of opportunity that he kept reading about. In the buzz of activity that preceded World War I, he saw his chance. Davis took flying lessons, and when war was declared, he immediately enlisted in the U.S. Army Air Service. He was assigned to one of the three flying fields that the Royal Canadian Flying Corps had established a few years earlier on the great prairie of North Texas, near the booming town of Fort Worth. After the war, Davis returned to Pennsylvania, but he couldn't get the scent of the frontier out of his nostrils.

Fort Worth was a young town that had survived by appreciating new ideas. Established by Maj. Gen. Jenkins Worth in 1849 as the northernmost in a chain of forts, the mission of the fort was to protect such blossoming villages as Dallas from attacks by Comanches and Kiowas. General Worth ordered the fort built at the juncture of two forks of the Trinity, on a bluff where the Tarrant County Courthouse now stands. In those days the Trinity was clear and clean, a natural preserve for wild flowers, mustang, deer, turkey, bear, wolves, and small game.

The new town evolved as a place where life was austere and the law paid tribute to the customs of the migrating settlers. Some of the newcomers were from Missouri and the old Northwest Territory, but the majority came from southern and border states where slavery was still an institution. There were few plantations in Fort Worth—so far as it's recorded, the largest owned only thirty-six slaves—but sentiment was strongly against abolition. Just as their descendants would fret over the menace of godless communism a hundred years later, those early settlers believed that civilization would end at the hands of the "Mystic Red," a code name for abolitionists who poisoned wells, fired towns, and incited riots among slaves. For such infidels justice was harsh and quick. One such unfortunate was the

Rev. Anthony Buley who was hanged from a large pecan tree where you would now find the intersection of White Settlement Road and Northwest Highway, then carted to the roof of a store near the courthouse where his body was hanged a second time and left to dangle until it was nothing but a skeleton rattling on a rotting rope.

Fort Worth might have wilted and blown away like many other frontier towns except for its good fortune to be located on a river. As rivers go, the Trinity was never much, but in the 1870s it became a major stop on the cattle trail leading to the northern markets. Fort Worth was the last village of any consequence where a trail hand could reprovision and enjoy a final fling before striking out for Indian Territory.

With the coming of the railroad in the 1870s new settlers poured into town. Every second one seemed to be a merchant. Land prices skyrocketed and property changed hands with each deal of the cards. In the dust of the trail herds, the railroad, the telegraph, and the merchants came a yeasty crowd of cowboys, professional gunmen, buffalo hunters, gamblers, dance hall girls, and, of course, lawyers. Already there was a burgeoning rivalry with the village of Dallas, thirty miles to the east. Even way back then, citizens of Dallas looked on Fort Worth as a bewildering paradox. It was wild and mean, and yet a reporter for the *Dallas Herald* claimed to have visited Fort Worth and found the place so drowsy that a live panther was sleeping in the middle of Main Street. Significantly, citizens of Fort Worth found this allusion attractive and adopted the nickname Panther City. For years many Fort Worth business firms (and the local baseball team) chose to use the sobriquet *panther*. There are still eight or nine Panthers in the Fort Worth phone book—Panther City Elks, Panther Chemicals, Panther Mobile Homes, and so forth. It was reported in the January 25, 1873, edition of the *Fort Worth Democrat* that "the live panther at the Keg Saloon scalped a man yesterday evening."

People in Fort Worth were not pleased when the riotous, blasphemous, take-it-to-hell-and-back frontier began to exhaust itself, but that's what was happening: by the 1890s the town had a reformer for every merchant and a church for every gambling saloon. The butcher wagon still plied the narrow, rutted streets with its hanging slabs of bear, buffalo, venison, and prairie chicken, but the village of 7,000 was taking on a permanent look. Soon, quiet, tree-lined streets would appear. Young men in straw boaters escorted young ladies in white lace to the dances on the roof garden of the Wheat Building, and the city's first mansions imposed themselves on Quality Hill on the western edge of what is now downtown Fort Worth. Families like the Waggoners, Burnetts, and Van Zandts set the character for all that followed. And yet a special gun-and-knife club charm existed then and continues to exist today. The White Elephant Saloon, where Longhair Jim Courtright was shot down two decades before, became a hangout for high rollers and serious drinkers after the turn of the century. Iron Jawn McGraw, who brought his New York Giants to Fort Worth for spring training, put his boots on the brass rail at the White Elephant and downed many a mug of beer, as did such notables as James J. Corbett, John L. Sullivan, and sports promoter Tex Rickard. Then as now the main sports in Fort Worth were fighting and gambling (golf would soon follow), and the White Elephant provided free telegraphic sports returns along with its nickel beer and upstairs gambling parlor.

Just before the turn of the century there was an economic crisis of sorts when northern markets began to boycott Texas cattle, claiming that the lank and rangy longhorns that had kept Fort Worth bustling were infested by ticks. Once again the enterprising leaders of the city found a solution both practical and lasting. If carcasses rather than live animals were shipped to the north and east, someone reasoned, ticks would not be a factor. So it was that the first of a number of stockyards and packinghouses were established across the river from the courthouse, in that section now known as the North Side. The Southwestern Exposition and Fat Stock Show, which along

18

with the Colonial Country Club golf tournament is still one of the social highlights in Fort Worth, was inaugurated in 1896. Between the years of 1900 and 1910, the city's population exploded from 27,000 to 73,000.

But the boom that brought Kenneth Davis back to town and made Fort Worth what it is today was due not to the foresight of a civic leader but to pure geographic and geophysic luck. As World War I was winding down in Europe, someone was drilling a hole in a drought-stricken, seemingly worthless prairie about fifty miles west of Fort Worth. Oil in quantities never dreamed of came gushing up near the little town of Ranger. In the years just after the Armistice new oil fields were discovered all around Fort Worth—in Eastland, Cisco, and Brekenridge to the west, in Burkburnett to the north. In a godforsaken patch of scrub called Hogtown, oil gushed so profusely that the only street through town became, literally, a lake of fine crude. Never in the history of man had so much oil come out of the ground so fast. And square in the middle of this basin of gushers sat Fort Worth, the city where Kenneth Davis had already earned his wings as a pilot and would earn them again in the new and specialized business of trafficking in oil.

In the mid-1920s when Ken Davis returned to Texas for good, the place for a young man to learn the business was in the oil fields. He worked as a roustabout and a driller and a tool dresser, but what caught his eye and influenced his thinking was the oil field supply business. Any fool with enough money to secure a lease and buy equipment could drill for oil, and it must have occurred to Ken Davis that there were many more fools than potential oil wells. Every smelly, dusty boomtown had some sort of supply store where the operators hung out, trading rumors and leases and sad tales of the dusters that broke men's hearts and spending vast sums to buy equipment to go out and try again. The oil field supply business was both safe and profitable, but more than that, it was an education into the many and varied ways that oil could be exploited.

19

While Ken Davis was working as a clerk in an oil field supply store he heard about a tiny, struggling company in Fort Worth called Mid-Continent Supply. Davis and his wife moved to Fort Worth and with a few thousand dollars that they had saved bought the company or, more accurately, bought the *name*. Mid-Continent was a mere shell of a company when Davis took over in 1929. But Fort Worth was the hub, the gateway to the fields of North and West Texas. It was headquarters for major oil companies and a concentration point for oil operators of all shades and persuasions. The lobby of the Westbrook Hotel a few blocks north of the Mid-Continent Building was the boomtown version of the stock exchange, and on a good day the action was so heavy it spilled out onto the sidewalk. At the corner of 4th and Main, people stood in line to buy phony leases from men they had never seen before. A lot of people were getting rich, but a lot more were getting poor. From rags to riches and back again was an amazingly short trip. Sid Richardson and his Dallas pal, Clint Murchison, Sr., made several millions each in 1919–20, were totally wiped out in 1921 when oil dropped to one dollar a barrel, got it back with some to spare in 1929, went broke again in 1930 when the East Texas fields came in and oil nosedived to ten cents a barrel, and skyrocketed to the top again by 1935.

Stinky Davis's fortune went nowhere but up. Fewer than seven years after he took over Mid-Continent, Davis began to diversify. In 1936 he bought Great Western Drilling, from which grew six additional companies. Ten years after that he bought Loffland Brothers, soon to become the world's largest drilling contractor and the parent of ten new subsidiary companies. Then came Cummins Sales and Service and its six offspring, and then Stratoflex, which spawned seven more companies throughout the world. Stinky Davis drilled an occasional oil well, but he was a speculator only in the sense that he speculated on the industry. There were finally so many companies that Davis had to invent a new one to take care of them, and thus was born the umbrella company called Kendavis Industries International, Inc. (Kiii). By now the old man could close his eyes, point to a globe, and almost certainly put his finger on a country where a Kiii company was located—Norway, Germany, Scotland, the Netherlands, Austria, Turkey, Morocco, Bolivia, Venezuela, Iran, India, Mexico, Australia, Taiwan, Malaysia, South Africa, Nigeria, Canada. Nearly every company operating under the Mid-Continent or Kiii logo was the largest or among the largest in its field. And, with some minor exceptions, Ken Davis owned it all, down to the last rig and pencil sharpener.

Davis might have made a huge profit if he had gone public and sold some of his stock to outsiders, but then he didn't like outsiders. There was no one he trusted the way he trusted himself. He didn't want to answer to a gaggle of shareholders and explain why he chose to pour profits into research and development rather than into stock dividends. By holding it all tightly to his vest, the old man could take it where he pleased, even if it meant absorbing losses for ten years or longer. He built his empire, and his indomitable will would tolerate no dissent. Shares of Stratoflex were occasionally traded over the counter, but there was little threat of outside interference. The mystery was why he allowed Stratoflex to go public. People who didn't know him well wondered if Stinky Davis was going soft, but those closer to the old man believed he was merely experimenting with human nature. It was the nature of humans to be both greedy and foolhardy, or that had been his experience. There was a saying in the oil fields that any man who whistles coming out of a gambling hall is likely to wind up face down in the mud with his pockets turned inside out. But Stinky Davis was just obstinate enough to try it. Maybe that's what he was doing . . . whistling . . . just to see if there were any takers. One analyst told *Fort Worth Star-Telegram* business writer Judith Curtis: "The old man wanted to take the stock public to see if he could sell it for more than it was worth. It was a very popular type of business. It was apparently price motivated because his follow through [with subsequent stock offerings] was negligible." Or maybe the old man was just creating some perks for company executives and loyal employees, a little something for their declining years. Whatever the case, very little Stratoflex stock ever got out of the Mid-Continent Building.

Other Texas oil moguls shunned publicity, but none with the passion of Stinky Davis. The only place anyone recognized him was inside the Mid-Continent Building. A former employee who edited the company newspaper recalled, "There was a standing rule that his picture had to appear on every page." And yet never once in forty years did his picture appear in Amon Carter's *Fort Worth Star-Telegram*. Ten years after Ken Davis's death, a clerk in the *Star-Telegram* could locate only three small clippings in the paper's files, one of them his obituary. A two-paragraph item in 1949 shed some light on his character. It was an article about Stinky successfully defending his horseshoe-pitching championship at the annual Exchange Club picnic. When asked to what he attributed his prowess at horseshoes, Stinky said he always relaxed in his hammock at his Eagle Mountain Lake retreat an hour prior to the tournament. Then, while his opponent looked on, he pitched his first horseshoe with his eyes closed. "That first horseshoe is usually a ringer," he said, "and it has the desired effect on your opponent." It galled and confounded Amon Carter that Davis had no interest in civic affairs. Carter, who was such a Fort Worth chauvinist that he refused to visit Dallas without a sack lunch, once asked Ken Davis to support some pet project for the betterment of Fort Worth, and Davis gave him the cold cackle. When the powerful publisher let it be known that Fort Worth wouldn't look kindly on this sort of pettiness, Stinky snapped: "Tell you what, Amon. You take Fort Worth and I'll take the rest of the world."

He was just as brash with the rest of the world. A longtime acquaintance told of an important international business meeting in New York, arranged by the State Department to negotiate a multi-million-dollar oil deal with the government of Venezuela: "It was a very touchy diplomatic situation in which the State Department was attempting to persuade Loffland to grant Venezuela credit for the drilling operation. Before they could even get around to the protocol of formal introductions, Stinky slammed his fist on the table and demanded three million dollars up front. Otherwise, no deal. . . . Loffland wouldn't move its rigs a single inch. The ambassador from Venezuela turned the color of a chili pepper, and the guy from State said: 'Mr. Davis, don't you realize you're dealing with the government of Venezuela?' Stinky said: 'You damn right I do! That's why I want three million up front!' "

Ten years after Ken Davis's death, employees and former employees of Mid-Continent still spoke his name in reverence. The old man admired, in fact demanded, loyalty and obedience, but he also rewarded it. He terrified secretaries and clerks with his mere presence, and in the tradition of great tyrants indulged his idiosyncrasies. Male employees of Mid-Continent didn't dare walk out of the building without a hat on their heads, and those who wore taps on their shoes or green neckties were summarily dismissed. Attendance at the annual company picnic was compulsory. It was said, too, that he used to stand by the front door and determine for himself exactly what time each employee arrived at work; given his abhorrence of wasted seconds, this, if it happened, probably didn't happen often. But he paid better than average salaries, and those employees who endured his tyranny retired content and secure. Earl Barber, an elderly gentleman who lives now in Shreveport, Louisiana, worked twenty-three years at Mid-Continent and still refers to the founder as "Mr. Davis." A few years before Barber retired, the old man called him into his office and said, "Earl, gimme $75," which Barber forked over without a question. In return, Davis gave Barber an interest in a well that had already proved out. For the next twenty years the well paid Earl Barber $300 a month, and it was still producing when he sold his interest for $15,000. Barbara Coontz, Davis's private secretary and

23

longtime companion, left Mid-Continent shortly after his death, apparently secure financially. So did many others.

Stinky Davis was a private man who preferred to deal one-on-one. It was that way with Earl Barber; it was that way with Barbara Coontz. It was that way with a wealthy landowner named Mrs. Floyd J. Holmes. In the early 1920s Mrs. Holmes was a controversial figure in a sensational murder case: her oilman husband shot and killed another oil millionaire in downtown Fort Worth one block from the Mid-Continent Building, which was known back then as the Floyd J. Holmes Building. Holmes claimed the other oilman was fooling around with his wife and won a quick acquittal. Holmes died a year before Stinky Davis moved to Fort Worth, but Davis and Mrs. Holmes became friends and business associates. Until her strange suicide in 1942, Mrs. Holmes was apparently the only stockholder and director of Mid-Continent Supply Company other than Stinky Davis himself. She still owned the Mid-Continent Building in fact. Stinky Davis didn't acquire the building that housed his empire until 1948, six years after Mrs. Holmes wrapped a coat hanger around her fur coat and jumped out of a tenth-floor window in the Forest Park Apartments.

In 1965 Stinky Davis was partially crippled by a stroke. It impaired his ability to walk or use his right arm, but apparently his iron determination to rule all that was his went undeterred. Paradoxically, what finally humiliated the old man was his vanity. He couldn't stand for people to see him in that condition. "The man was extremely prideful," his private physician, Dr. E. Ross Kyger, recalled. Instead of coming to the office, the old man had himself driven to the Mid-Continent Building. An elevator operator summoned Barbara Coontz, who reported to his car to take dictation, deliver mail, and fetch the people he wanted to see that day. Ken Jr. explained that his father refused to come to the office because "he figured that after a certain lapse of time, he would be over his ailment and he would be able to come back to work looking just as he

24

did before the stroke." Stinky Davis was particularly vain about his penmanship. Barbara Coontz recalled: "He had beautiful handwriting [before the stroke]. He practiced diligently to improve his handwriting after the stroke. I would say he practiced every day. He kept a little book. Sometimes he would write instructions. Sometimes he wrote the alphabet."

But the old man got worse, not better. When he could no longer come downtown, Barbara Coontz delivered his work to the family home on Rivercrest. Alice Bound Davis had been dead for several years by this time, and except for Barbara Coontz the old man was alone. He saw his sons occasionally. Ken Jr. had moved to Tulsa to assume command of that end of the family empire. Cullen and Bill Davis, who shared the operations in Fort Worth, had dinner once a week, on Tuesday evening, at the family home. Sometimes Bill would bring along his girlfriend, Mitzi, but she would usually stay in the kitchen with the family maid, Cora Williams. It's not clear if the old man knew near the end that Sandra had filed for divorce and that Cullen was dating Priscilla Lee Wilborn. If he did, it must have hurt because the old man put great store in his family. When he could go on no longer, Kenneth Davis, Sr., died.

By the time Kenneth and Alice Davis bought a home and began raising their sons in Arlington Heights, the pattern of Fort Worth was firmly established. It was Cowtown . . . "the place where the West begins." Future leaders downplayed the cowboy image and busted their vests attempting to picture Fort Worth as a modern mecca of technology and urban sophistication, and for a while in the years after World War II future generations believed them, but the twin themes of cowboys and outlaws were never far from the surface. People in Fort Worth are proud of their bawdy past and take pains to convince outsiders that here is "the most Texan of Texas cities." The characters have changed, but the predominant image of Fort Worth today is the same as it was in the 1930s—Amon Carter presenting the traditional ten-gallon hat to a visiting general, and Burk Burnett astride his prancing palomino leading Comanche Chief Quanah Parker and thirty-eight domesticated Indians in the Fat Stock Show parade down Main Street. Box seats at the rodeo have been in the same families for years.

On the southeast corner of downtown Fort Worth where the ultramodern Tarrant County Convention Center now stands, there flowered at one time a community of rogues unmatched anywhere in the West. They called it Hell's Half Acre. As an entity it was demolished about the time of World War I, but the city still celebrates its spirit. One of the most popular histories of Fort Worth, written by Leonard Sanders and Ronnie Tyler and published under the auspices of the Amon Carter Museum of Western Art, devotes a large part of its text to Hell's Half Acre. It was here in the White Elephant Saloon that Luke Short gunned down Marshal Longhair Jim Courtright, a onetime outlaw himself. Around the turn of the century Fannie Porter's house of ill repute became the hideout of Butch Cassidy (aka Jim Lowe, aka George Leroy Parker), Harry Longbaugh (The Sundance Kid), Harvey (Kid Curry) Logan, Blackjack Tom Ketchum, Elza Lay and Deaf Charley Hanks, who together were known as the Hole in the Wall Gang (aka The Wild Bunch). It was in Hell's Half Acre that Etta Place (aka Katharine Ross) met Butch and Sundance and took off on a spree of robbing and shooting in South America. It is said that Etta Place eventually returned to Cowtown, where for the next forty-something years she operated one of Fort Worth's most prosperous whorehouses, the infamous Waco Hotel on East 15th. Delbert Willis, longtime city editor of the *Fort Worth Press,* spent years researching Etta Place and believes that she became Eunice Gray, who died in 1962 when her whorehouse burned to the ground.

Hell's Half Acre attracted the city's most spectacular reformer, the Rev. J. Frank Norris, who went on to become pastor of Fort Worth's First Baptist Church and one of the first evangelists to recognize the advantages of radio. In 1911 he split the city apart by announcing from the pulpit the names of the owners of eighty whorehouses. Eight of them turned out to be men prominent and influential in both civic and religious affairs. In the years that followed there were a number of attempts on the preacher's life, but he continued to prosper. So did the spirit of Hell's Half Acre, which had moved out North Main, near the stockyards. The old Right Hotel, which still stands on Exchange Street a half block off North Main, was one of the burrows where Machine Gun Kelly, Pretty Boy Floyd, Bonnie Parker, and Clyde Barrow hid out in the 1930s. In the gray days of the depression, heroes were at a premium, so it's not surprising to recall that many an occupant of the bread line looked on the notorious bandits as messengers of the people. In Fort Worth they are still regarded as a proud part of the city's heritage. Old-timers recall with nostalgia how Bonnie once recited a poem of her own composition, a poem addressing iself not to good and evil but to economic inequities of society and the social havoc such inequities were sure to foster. She mailed the poem to Amon Carter.

In the early 1950s when Cullen Davis was attending Arlington Heights High School, nearly every hotel on the south end of downtown Fort Worth was a whorehouse. They ran wide open. Every cop in town knew it, and so did every schoolboy. In those days, a quickie at the Stewart Hotel cost $3.50. For another $1.50 you got what they called an around-the-world. Through the 1950s there was gambling and gang warfare all over Tarrant County. These weren't highly organized, eastern-style gangs but small cliques of hometown boys who took to crime as naturally as others did to football and baseball. The descendants of Hell's Half Acre had moved out to the Jacksboro Highway where a neon stream of honky-tonks and nightclubs ran all the way to Lake Worth. Some of the better clubs, like the Casino and Jacks and the Skyliner, catered to students, particularly upper-middle-class kids from Arlington Heights who could be counted on to have money and transportation. In the late 1950s when much of the country still thought marijuana was something Mexicans and Chinamen shot in their arms, students from Arlington Heights were scoring it easily in the dives and alleys along the Jacksboro Highway.

This intermingling of the best and worst of society may not have been exclusive to Fort Worth, but in Texas Fort Worth had no rival. Honky-tonk Saturday Night—it was a tradition, and tradition was not taken lightly in Cowtown. Fort Worth police never did get around to cleaning up the Jacksboro Highway, but, like time's healing river, it cleaned itself. In the mid- and late 1950s several dozen local hoods were executed gangland-style and their bodies stashed in narrow graves around Lake Worth. The last of the desperadoes was Gene Paul Norris, who finally made the fatal mistake of robbing the Carswell Air Force Base payroll in 1957. Several dozen Fort Worth cops, state troopers, and Texas Rangers chased Gene Paul to a field outside town where, with quick due process, he was cut down in a blizzard of bullets. Many in Fort Worth were relieved to learn of Gene Paul's fate, but many others looked on it sadly as the passing of an era.

Arlington Heights—the area in general and the high school in particular—has long been a microcosm of Fort Worth society, an easy blend of the richest and poorest segments of the city. Because the river formed a natural northern boundary, the city grew from downtown south, then southeast. West of downtown, Arlington Heights developed into a residential area only after World War I. Heights began as the dream of a most improbable speculator named H. B. Chamberlain. President of the worldwide YMCA, Chamberlain was actually a globe-trotting promoter who shortly after the turn of the century sold lots in west Fort Worth to people all over the world. The lots remained all but worthless

28

until 1917, when the army decided the area would be an ideal place to establish a large training camp. In the months that followed, more than 100,000 troops trained at Camp Bowie, and when the war ended just as the West Texas oil boom began, the leftover network of utility lines, roads, and trolley tracks made the area an ideal location for the hordes of new rich.

It was an area of natural beauty. The river forked just north of the courthouse, the West Branch running west and north toward Lake Worth, and the Clear Branch dipping southwest, carving bluffs and watering lush meadows of oaks, elms, and pecan trees. Forest Park, Botanic Gardens, TCU, Colonial Country Club, and large residential areas that would later be called Westover Hills, Ridglea, Tanglewood, and Benbrook grew between and around the two branches of the Trinity. In the middle of it all, bisected by a charming red-brick thoroughfare called Camp Bowie Boulevard, was Arlington Heights.

For years the only high school in west Fort Worth was AHHS. Its students were called "tea sippers" by teenagers from the rougher sections of town, but for pure machismo and fidelity to the cowboy mystique there wasn't a school that could match it. Maybe because most of their daddies could afford to pay for the damage, AHHS students were wilder and meaner than anyone had a right to be. They were a curious blend of bluebloods whose families had founded River Crest and later Colonial country clubs, poor white kids from the far west side, a few Mexican-Americans, air force brats from Carswell Air Force Base, and orphans from Lena Pope Home. No blacks and hardly any Jews lived or attended school in Arlington Heights when Cullen Davis was a student there. In most cases those who didn't already have a name like Van Zandt or Leonard Stripling or Davis would never be heard of again. There were exceptions: a scrawny misfit named Lee Harvey Oswald attended AHHS, as did John Deutschendorf, the son of an air force officer. Deutschendorf later was famous as John Denver. In 1976 a graduate of the class of '51, Tommy Thompson, became celebrated as the author of *Blood and Money,* a best-seller about murder in Houston high society, and one of Thompson's classmates, T. Cullen Davis, was accused of the most sensational murders in the city's history.

Even those who knew of his family's great wealth would not have predicted that T. Cullen Davis would take his place among the school's most celebrated alumni. In the months after the murders, a few who attended South Hi Mount Elementary School in the early 1940s remembered him as "that kid who came to school in a limousine," but they were probably confusing him with someone else. He was a shy, reticent boy, so ordinary and inoffensive that hardly anyone noticed. His grades were average and his social life private and oriented around his family. J. B. Smallwood, who grew up in a poorer section called White Settlement but became Cullen's friend at Stripling Junior High, recalled, "He looked like a person who needed people." Smallwood, who later became a professor of English at North Texas State University, remembered a time when he was home sick. The only person who visited him was Cullen, who rode over on his motorbike and brought Smallwood a stack of comic books. Cullen like to shoot pool and play shuffleboard and hang out at the ice cream parlor, but he participated in no organized sports or school activities, caused no trouble, and contributed nothing to the general weal. Chip Fairbanks went all the way through high school and college with Cullen; he recalled: "In one way Cullen was just like the old man. Both of them were tight as Dick's hatband. When Cullen got his first car, a Chevy Powerglide—that must have been Christmas of our senior year at Arlington Heights—he'd charge us a nickel to ride to the pool hall." Unlike his classmates, Cullen was never a drinker or hell raiser, and he seldom dated the same girl more than once or twice. In a school system where the standard dress for boys was boots, Levi's, and T-shirt, Cullen frequently wore suits and ties. At Texas A & M, Cullen took easily to the austere life of a cadet, and after he returned to Fort Worth from a tour with the navy, he customarily dressed in the style of a young executive applying for his first job at the bank. Even the old man complained that Cullen was stuffy and ordered his son several sport coats, but Cullen apparently never got around to wearing them.

If there was anything at all unconventional about Cullen Davis, it was his choice of women. One of the Van Zandt women, whose family founded the Fort Worth National Bank and who traced her bloodline back to the first families of Fort Worth, recalled that even before Cullen's first marriage to Sandra, a pattern had developed. "He had this Pygmalion thing," the Van Zandt woman said. "He dated girls from the other side of the track, so to speak. Good-looking girls, but girls without a lot of money or class. Sandra is a good example. She came from the other side of town. The carhop type, you might say. She was rough around the edges, but it wasn't long until she learned to cotton to what Cullen was doing. She learned to fit in and do whatever Fort Worth society wanted her to do."

Another woman with close ties to Fort Worth society explained, "Cullen always had a lot of girlfriends—he was always extremely good-looking, in a sort of old-fashioned way—but there were few important women in his life. The women that Cullen married were submissive, women he thought he could control." Those whose friendship with Cullen goes back a number of years believe that the most important woman in his life was Dana Campbell, an attractive, headstrong, blunt-spoken woman who was once married to Grayford Campbell, reputed at one time to be the toughest man in Fort Worth. Dana Campbell's relationship with Cullen began before his marriage to Sandra and continues even now, but no one seems surprised that they never married. "Cullen couldn't handle her," a friend observed. "She's too independent and self-assured. She's the type of woman that Cullen needs but can't allow himself to have."

When Cullen's marriage to Sandra began to sour in the spring of 1967, nobody was terribly surprised to see him take up with Priscilla Lee Wilborn, least of all the gossips around Ridglea Country Club. Priscilla spent

31

almost every afternoon on the tennis courts at Ridglea, a relatively new country club on the city's far west side. Members at Ridglea knew very little about Priscilla, only that she had married used-car dealer Jack Wilborn about eight years before, when she was eighteen and he was nearly forty. She had three children, two by Jack Wilborn and one by a previous marriage, but when she started spending most of her time at the country club, she stopped bringing her kids along. "Everyone saw her flirting and carrying on with the waiters and lifeguards," one member recalled. Not long before that, Priscilla had dyed her dark hair platinum blonde. She told friends that she did it to please Jack Wilborn—at his insistence, in fact. She'd even cried and said it hurt her feelings when Wilborn first asked her to wear a blond wig, then demanded she dye her hair. Not many believed her; it was the general opinion around the club that Priscilla was hell-bent on retaining her youth, and this included finding a new husband and bettering her position in life. If the new hair color didn't prove it, they pointed to the sexy tennis outfits she had lately adopted and to a new coterie of young friends who usually surrounded her.

Cullen first met Priscilla in May of 1967, one day before the start of Colonial's annual National Invitational Golf Tournament. They met on the tennis courts at Ridglea. Cullen was playing with Sandra, but there was no way he could keep his eyes off the sexy, full-chested blonde on the next court. Sandra and Priscilla knew each other slightly; they were part of the same group of women who played tennis regularly at Ridglea, and Sandra introduced her husband to Priscilla. Priscilla had never heard of Cullen Davis or Mid-Continent, but she was immediately attracted to him. Cullen had a nice, dry sense of humor, she thought, and he was handsome and smooth, like a ballroom dancer. Priscilla and a friend accepted Cullen's invitation to play doubles, and later they joined Cullen and Sandra for drinks in the clubhouse. Shortly, Jack Wilborn appeared at the bar and reminded Priscilla that her mother was watching the children; they had promised to be home early.

32

Everyone who is prominent in Fort Worth society, or aspires to be, makes a point of attending the annual golf tournament at Colonial. Few of them bother to watch the golfers; the best sport is in the clubhouse, the site of an annual five-day cocktail party. Priscilla was not surprised then to run into Cullen Davis the following day in the Terrace Room bar at Colonial. He was seated with a large group of people, and when he spotted Priscilla, he invited her to join them. What a strange, attractive man, Priscilla recalled thinking: almost painfully shy and polite, he nevertheless seemed to go out of his way to attract her attention. Cullen's close friend Dana Campbell had once observed how difficult it was for Cullen to meet new people. "He cannot ingratiate himself in a crowd," Dana had said. "He'll walk into a party and stand off by himself, wanting someone to recognize him." That's how he seemed to Priscilla that day at Colonial. Later, when she had excused herself and left the table, Cullen followed her. "Did I say anything to offend you?" he asked. This struck Priscilla as a strange question, but there was a certain charm in the way he said it. Still later, as Priscilla was talking to a friend in the country club lobby, Cullen deliberately walked between them. "Excuse me," he said, smiling at Priscilla. For a while, that was the end of it, but Priscilla had been around enough to know when someone was working up nerve to make a move.

The day the golf tournament ended, Cullen left the country, flying first to the Paris Air Show, then on to Moscow. While Cullen was out of the country, Sandra retained attorney Hershel Payne and filed for divorce. Close friends were certain that Sandra was bluffing, that she was demanding more attention and consideration, but those who were new to the group like Priscilla took Sandra at her word when she talked about the divorce. The following week, while Cullen was still out of the country, Sandra threw a party for some of her tennis friends at Ridglea. Priscilla had the impression that Sandra was showing off for a certain tennis pro known to the women regulars as "Mr. Popular." Priscilla complained later: "When Sandra invited everyone, she distinctly said it was casual, but she wore a brown crepe cocktail dress. If that's not showing off, I don't know what is!"

On June 13, at almost exactly the same time that Sandra filed for divorce, Jack Wilborn brought suit against Priscilla. She wasn't surprised. She knew their marriage was on the rocks. She was already looking for a job. "The age difference is too much," Priscilla confided to friends. "I've asked Jack why we can't just be friends, but he's being unreasonable." Wilborn wanted the house in Ridglea and custody of the three children, Jackie and Andrea, born from his marriage with Priscilla, and Dee, Priscilla's daughter by her first marriage. "He's using the children as leverage," Priscilla said. "He knows that the children are the only hold he has on me."

During a hearing to decide on a temporary settlement, Priscilla was awarded the house and the children. But it was apparent to her that things would get nasty before long, and she hired the best attorney she could afford. His name was Tolly Wilson, and ironically he later served as one of the assistant district attorneys assigned to prosecute Cullen Davis for murder. The divorce hearing got nastier than anyone had anticipated. A baby-sitter who worked for the Wilborns testified that she never saw Priscilla feed her children a hot meal, and when she did feed them, it was on the floor. "What did she expect!" Priscilla protested. "The only time the baby-sitter was there was when we were going out. I always fixed the kids a picnic on the floor in front of the TV." The baby-sitter's mother told the divorce court that Priscilla ran around the house scantily clad —she was apparently referring to Priscilla's lacy tennis outfits—and a maid testified that Priscilla used foul language in front of the children and was seldom at home. Priscilla hotly denied using foul language, but it was true that she spent a good part of almost every day at the country club.

In the heat and bitterness of the charges, Priscilla reported to Tolly Wilson that Wilborn stopped by the house to pick up some clothes and ended up raping her.

"If it happens again," the attorney told her, "we'll report it." A week later Priscilla reported another rape, and the lawyer so advised the court. The judge ordered Wilborn to stay away from his estranged wife and set the divorce trial for January 1968.

Priscilla hadn't seen Cullen Davis since the golf tournament in May, but that August she telephoned him at Mid-Continent. "Do you remember me?" she asked in her little girl's voice. She was sure he would. She asked if Cullen could get her tickets for the Dallas Cowboys–Green Bay Packers exhibition game. "Your chances of getting tickets to that game are slim to none," Cullen told her. Priscilla thanked him and hung up, but a few hours later Cullen called back: that night Cullen and Priscilla met for the first time at a small, out-of-the-way barbecue and beer place. They began seeing each other regularly after that.

Cullen's own divorce with Sandra was moving slowly through the legal process, and for this reason he was careful to meet Priscilla someplace where they wouldn't be recognized. They attended Cowboys football games in the fall of 1967, but Cullen arranged for them to sit on opposite sides of the Cotton Bowl and meet later at a jazz club in North Dallas. At this point Sandra knew nothing about Cullen carrying on with Priscilla Lee Wilborn. More important, neither did Cullen's father. A rumor circulated Fort Worth that the old man threatened to disinherit Cullen if he married Priscilla, but a rumor is all it was: Stinky Davis never met Priscilla and probably never knew she existed. Cullen's friends knew, however. Most of them understood, or claimed to. After all, Cullen was thirty-four years old and legally separated from his wife. It was time he sampled some of the forbidden pleasures most people in Arlington Heights took for granted. One of the few who believed that Cullen would marry Jack Wilborn's estranged wife was Dana Campbell. In the beginning it was nothing more than a physical attraction. Dana felt; but as the divorce suit wore on, it because apparent to Dana that Cullen was determined to call Sandra's bluff.

Cullen was becoming more and more open about his

relationship with Priscilla. "Cullen is used to being in the background," Dana told friends. "Priscilla is his way of calling attention to himself." Dana liked Priscilla. Priscilla was flashy, but she was also gutsy. All parties had gone too far to turn back now. There was a period of several weeks that fall when Priscilla didn't hear from Cullen. But she had heard that he showed up at the annual Mid-Continent picnic with Sandra and their oldest son, little Cullen. Shortly after that, Cullen telephoned and told Priscilla that he and Sandra were attempting reconciliation.

"I hope it works out," Priscilla said, apparently not very convincingly.

"No, you don't," Cullen told her.

"How can you be so egotistical?" Priscilla said.

"Maybe we can have dinner."

"Not a chance," Priscilla told him and hung up. But she was not surprised a few weeks later when Cullen called and told her the reconciliation hadn't worked.

Priscilla moved to Dallas, where Cullen set her up with an apartment and an allowance. She began studying to earn a real estate broker's license. In December, Cullen telephoned Priscilla from New York and asked her to marry him as soon as the divorce was final. He asked her to give up the pursuit of her real estate license and wait for him to resolve his own problems with Sandra. Priscilla said she would think about it. She was still thinking about it when she learned that Cullen had taken Sandra and the two boys to the Davis home for a family Christmas gathering. Priscilla was furious.

"Sandra is trying to use Cullen's father to force him to come back to her," Priscilla told friends. "I know exactly what she's doing! Sandra told me herself that Mr. Davis always gives cash to his favorite daughter-in-law at Christmas." At this point in time, Sandra was the only daughter-in-law the old man had. Ken Jr. and Bill were both divorced, and though Bill was already living with his fiancée, Mitzi, they had been careful to conceal their cohabitation from the old man.

The day after Christmas, Cullen again telephoned Priscilla. He told her that the split with Sandra was complete and permanent and that Sandra was threatening him with Polaroid pictures of some furniture he had broken, threatening him, in effect, with his temper tantrums. He was angry and wanted to get out of town. The next day Cullen and Priscilla flew to Acapulco to celebrate the New Year. Except for their clandestine trips to Dallas, it was the first time they had traveled as a couple. Priscilla's own divorce trial was scheduled for the following week, and she looked forward to some time alone with Cullen.

Jack Wilborn may have been a good old boy, but his mama didn't raise a dummy: he knew what was going on, and he made certain that Sandra Davis did too. On January 2, 1968, as Cullen and Priscilla were sleeping in their room at the Green Oaks Inn in Fort Worth, recovering from the frenetic trip to Acapulco where Priscilla had caught flu, Wilborn's team of private investigators kicked down the door, sprayed the room with Mace, and took a lot of pictures. "I don't remember them breaking down the door," Priscilla recalled. "I had a high fever and was asleep. The first thing I knew, there were two men at the door and I felt something damp hitting my face. My first thought was, it's acid! I ran to the bathroom and slammed the door. I could hear Jack yelling, 'You son of a bitch, where's my wife?' and then I heard Sandra crying and telling Cullen he'd never see his kids again. Someone said, 'Come on, Jack, we've got enough pictures.' Then they left."

The following day Cullen called on Jack Wilborn and told him he intended to marry Priscilla.

"I want the house," Wilborn said icily. "And I want the kids."

Cullen and Priscilla were in no position to bargain. Once tempers subsided, Cullen felt certain, they would both be able to see their children. As for the house, Cullen told Priscilla of his plans to construct the mansion. He'd already commissioned Fort Worth architect Albert Komatsu. A few weeks later Priscilla's divorce was granted, but Cullen's frustrations continued. The judge again postponed proceedings and granted Sandra's request for increased support payments. Cullen was so angry he changed lawyers. "He wanted it over," Priscilla recalled. "He couldn't think of anything else." He had planned a business trip to South America and wanted it to be their honeymoon, but now he had to go alone. Nine days later Priscilla telephoned Cullen's office at Mid-Continent, and his secretary and girl Friday, Fern Frost, told her that Cullen was on his way home. "I don't know what you've done to him," Fern Frost supposedly told Priscilla, "but that's the shortest trip he's ever made to South America."

Priscilla found work as a clerk in an employment agency, but by spring she quit and spent most of her time with Cullen at the Green Oaks in Fort Worth. It had been a year since their first meeting at Ridglea, and now Cullen and Priscilla were seen openly in public, though their relationship was kept secret from Cullen's father. Another Colonial golf tournament came and went. The younger set that composed the golf tournament revelers didn't appear shocked to see the lovers together in the Terrace Room. In July, Cullen returned from a trip to Europe. Apparently he still wasn't certain about the outcome of his divorce because he brought home two leopard coats, one for Priscilla and the other for Sandra. He ended up giving them both to Priscilla for her twenty-seventh birthday on July 30. It was the first time in her life that anyone had ever given Priscilla furs, and for a week she slept under them both, with the air conditioner at the Green Oaks turned up high.

One Tuesday night after Cullen returned from his weekly dinner at the family home on Rivercrest, Cullen told Priscilla that his divorce would be final the next week. They set August 29 as their wedding date. They reserved a chapel and ordered flowers. Priscilla bought a new dress. Bill and Mitzi had agreed to be their witnesses. It's not clear what Cullen intended to tell his father, but of course he never had to tell him anything.

When Cullen returned to the Green Oaks on the evening of August 27, he gave Priscilla a document to sign. Cullen's attorneys would contend later that this was the alleged prenuptial agreement in which Priscilla waived all claims to the family fortune, but that wasn't how Priscilla remembered it. According to her, Cullen represented it as a document dealing with corporate taxes and appeared irritated when she questioned him. The document later played a part in both the divorce and the murder trial. Fern Frost testified at the murder trial that she personally took the papers to the Green Oaks and witnessed Priscilla's signature. Priscilla swears she never met Fern Frost until two days later, after the secretary called the Green Oaks and told them that the old man had been rushed to the hospital.

On the late afternoon of August, less than an hour after he was taken to the hospital, Stinky Davis was dead. They hadn't been able to reach Ken Jr., who was in Canada, but Cullen and Bill were with him at the end. Priscilla and Mitzi, who would soon marry into the family, waited outside with Cora Williams, Barbara Coontz, and Fern Frost.

When Cullen came out of the old man's hospital room, there were tears in his eyes, but he said nothing. They drove Cora Williams back to the house on Rivercrest—it was the first time Priscilla had ever been inside the family home. Cullen told the old servant about his wedding plans, and despite her grief Cora Williams gave her blessing and told him to go ahead. Bill agreed, and they proceeded to the chapel where the wedding ceremony was performed.

Cullen started changing the day he met Priscilla, but when they got married, he really took off. If Cullen's marriage vows were a covenant, it was more likely one with himself. Cullen had never seemed in control of his destiny, and this never seemed to bother him, but he emerged from his marriage to Priscilla controlling it with a passion. It was as though the species emerged from the cocoon and became a butterfly in one long continuous metamorphic spell—as though it skipped the worm stage entirely. It was not that Cullen cared less about form and propriety, he just seemed more interested in fun. Those around him were delighted that Cullen was becoming one of the boys.

Cullen traded his frugal Pontiac for a Cadillac and bought Priscilla a Continental, at her suggestion. He refused to wear the black leather suit that Priscilla ordered, but he relented to tweed sport coats and turtlenecks for weekends. He learned to mix business with pleasure and found it to his liking. He took up skiing and target shooting. It was during this early period of his marriage with Priscilla that Cullen got his first suntan.

Priscilla recalled that they spent the first year or so of their marriage "shopping and traveling all over the world." Cullen always enjoyed globe hopping, and now he liked traveling with Priscilla on his arm. On the spur of a moment he might grab Priscilla and whisk her off to Rome or Paris or Caracas or Rio de Janeiro. Contractors would soon start work on the mansion, and as Cullen and Priscilla traveled the markets of the world, he began to collect art and antiques. Once when an airline misplaced their luggage, Cullen made an instant decision to purchase his own Learjet.

"We met important people all over the world," Priscilla said. "One year we stood right there in the VIP section, right next to President Nixon and his daughters, watching Apollo Eleven lift off. I think that same day we had lunch with the president of General Motors —Ed and Dolly something."

In Priscilla's eyes, Cullen *was* a celebrity. Until their marriage she had had no real concept of wealth, and though she claimed many times the money didn't matter, she found enormous satisfaction in helping Cullen spend it. "It was like a dream," she said. "I could hardly believe we had really found it. Of course the money didn't hurt. What's the saying? 'I've been rich and I've been poor and believe me, rich is better'? It's like, winning isn't everything, but losing is nothing."

40

A Fort Worth socialite who knew Cullen and Priscilla in the early years of their marriage recalled that Cullen seemed to enjoy indulging his new bride. It was an experience watching Priscilla order from a restaurant menu. She ordered the choicest parts from three or four different dinners. Cullen seemed pleased by her extravagance and the delightful way she had of keeping the waiters hopping. "Neither of our husbands allowed us to smoke," the socialite remembered, "so Priscilla and I would sneak off to the ladies' room for a cigarette. Once when we were in the ladies' room, I asked Priscilla about the fantastic combination of food she'd ordered . . . the most expensive beef tenderloin, a stuffed potato that went with the escalopes de veau, asparagus that went with the capon, baked stuffed mushroom caps, and a salad that came with something else. Priscilla said: 'Let me tell you the two best things about being rich. You can order anything you like off a menu without looking at the price, and you can pick up a telephone and call anyone anywhere and talk as long as you damn please.' I couldn't help being touched by the way she said it."

It was difficult to determine if the change in Cullen Davis carried over to his life inside the cloistered walls of the Mid-Continent Building; hardly anyone except the three brothers and their top financial adviser, Walter Strittmatter, was privy to the upper levels of the conglomerate, and it was possible for the brothers to keep secrets from each other. Although each of them owned one-third of Kiii, control of individual subsidiaries was divided among them in the manner of autonomous fiefdoms. For example, Bill and Ken Jr. owned about 75 percent of Great Western Drilling, compared to Cullen's 24 percent. Cullen wasn't an equal in this company. But Stratoflex and Cummins Sales and Service were owned almost entirely by Cullen and Ken Jr. Each son had his own area of predominance. It was not practical, and perhaps not necessary, for them to work together on a day-to-day basis. On the throne once occupied exclusively by the old man sat Walter Strittmatter, vice-president of the Kendavis Management Company, conduit for all funds generated in the name of Kiii. Total sales for all the companies under the Kendavis umbrella exceeded $1 billion a year, and as the chief officer of the management company Strittmatter had the job of directing the flow of money among the various subsidiaries. In effect, the management company was a lending agency, empowered by the board of directors to shift money from company to company as need dictated. Thus, if anyone fully understood the overall picture at Kiii, it was more likely to be Strittmatter than any one of the three brothers. If Strittmatter foresaw the inevitable showdown, he kept his own counsel.

"Cullen and Ken have always been very secretive," one insider observed. "They operate all their business on a need-to-know basis. Cullen is personally that way. Almost every relation he has is one-to-one." Those who had been privy to the boardroom, or to Cullen's unadorned fifth-floor office at Mid-Continent, regarded him as highly disciplined and dedicated. "He was always totally prepared," said one executive. "He spoke with authority and came straight to the point. He wouldn't tolerate a vague answer. His single aim was to see the company improve its position." If there was any change in Mid-Continent after the old man's death, it was an intensification of Cullen's will to go forward. "He never doubted that he could improve the company's sales," the executive said. "And he had no patience for anyone who didn't believe what he believed." It was because of Cullen's dedication to the company that associates were shocked when he brought Priscilla to a board meeting a few days after the wedding. Within minutes every secretary and receptionist in the building was talking about Priscilla. The implication was clear: they could accept her, or they could take a long walk. No one talked about it, but it must have been apparent that Cullen was headed in new directions.

Cullen personally supervised the design and construction of the mansion. In this singular undertaking he not only refused to indulge Priscilla but in many instances didn't bother to consult her. When it was completed in 1972, the mansion consisted of twenty rooms, a gigantic indoor pool, a half-dozen balconies and fortresslike courtyards, a series of connecting hallways, and a basement of winding passages containing the intricate security and electronic systems that controlled every active part and portion of the mansion. Designed after a similar system at Fort Worth's Kimball Art Museum, the security was coordinated with the lighting system. A time clock in the basement was set to turn on dozens of outside lights at twilight and switch them off again at dawn. Magnetic switches fixed to each of the thirty-one entrances and exits were hooked to an alarm system, and photoelectric cells sensitive enough to detect the slightest movement were triggered to sound an alarm. Two central control panels, one upstairs in the master bedroom and one on the wall near the main entrance, activated 200 circuits: by dialing a three-digit code number, a person could activate or deactivate any lock on any door or window in the mansion, or even open or close the drapes. When the system was fully activated, thirty-one security bolts dropped into place like thirty-one hard steel soldiers, a sound like the sound of a prison locking up at night. It was a chilling sensation, listening to the bolts crash into place and maybe hearing the wind rustling the leaves of the great oaks outside. As one attorney observed later, the mansion was a perfect setting for a murder.

The only room in the mansion that Cullen did not personally supervise was Priscilla's enormous pink bathroom next to the master bedroom. Cullen had his own bath and dressing room, but the pink room with the three walls of twenty-foot floor-to-ceiling mirrors, the sunken marble tub, and the crystal chandelier was Priscilla's design. Right down to the cat box next to the bidet, it reflected her personality, not Cullen's.

Cullen had never expressed much interest in art before, but soon the mansion would house a fortune in jade, gold, marble, and bronze. Both modern and traditional sculpture lined the long, high-ceilinged parquet hallways and decorated the courtyards and balconies. Literally hundreds of paintings, mostly by nineteenth-century European artists, covered the walls in each of

43

the twenty rooms. Even the six bathrooms resembled the alcoves of an art gallery—a $400,000 Renoir hung in the guest bath near the den.

At first Cullen seemed baffled and hesitant as he pondered the enormous variety of paintings and sculptures from which he might choose, but later he bought works of art impulsively, almost as though he were buying them by the pound. Two Fort Worth artists, brothers Scott and Stuart Gentling, recalled a trip to New York with Cullen and Priscilla in 1971, a few months before the mansion was completed. Cullen invited the Gentlings along to help select works of art for his new home.

Stuart Gentling, who flew to New York with Priscilla and Cullen in the Learjet (Scott joined them later), remembered his first impressions: "Priscilla had this enormous mane of white platinum hair and oversized purple glasses, a white mantle or pullover, and purple pants. Cullen was wearing a silky greenish charcoal suit and narrow tie—I remember he laughed when I referred to him as the best-dressed man of *1962*. Priscilla did most of the talking. She seemed warm and honest. Cullen seemed . . . I guess you would call it impenetrable. He was polite and very pleasant, but you could feel this inner tension, this *held-in* attitude."

The following morning, a Saturday, the Gentling brothers directed Cullen and Priscilla to 57th Street and Madison Avenue and began to work their way uptown, visiting almost every gallery they passed.

"We started by asking what kind of art interested them," Stuart Gentling said. "Realism? Impressionism? Cubism? They didn't know. They knew nothing at all about art . . . *zippo*. But what impressed us was, they didn't pretend. They told us, 'Just show us what you think we'd like.' So we started uptown. We hit all the biggies, gallery after gallery. Cullen was inscrutable, absolutely no reaction. Priscilla would just say, 'I don't like it.' I found this lovely Matisse, but Priscilla said, 'I don't like it.' Scott found a Hellenistic philosophic head in white marble, dating to 325 A.D. and attractively priced at $1,800. Priscilla said, 'That would look good by my bathtub,' but for some reason they didn't buy it. We must have looked at the works of hundreds of different artists. Same reaction.

"By now it was late Saturday afternoon; most of the galleries were either closed or in the hands of caretakers. We had worked our way up to the Seventies when Cullen saw a painting in the window. I told him it was by Jean Dufy, the lesser-known brother. We went inside where I introduced Mr. and Mrs. Davis to the old black caretaker in charge. Priscilla was talking a blue streak, but Cullen still said nothing. After a long time Cullen pointed to the Dufy in the window, and to another Dufy, both in the $6,000 to $7,000 price range, and said, 'We'll take those two, and that one over there, and that other one.' I think he bought four or five in all for something like $30,000. The black caretaker turned white when Cullen whipped out his checkbook."

This was apparently the one and only time that Cullen sought advice in selecting works of art. But he continued to buy whatever caught his attention—a $350,000 jade pagoda; an $85,000 chess set with a black-and-white jade board inlaid with yellow and white gold; a white onionskin jade vase from the Ming Dynasty; a replica of the Taj Mahal made of solid gold with diamonds, rubies, emeralds, and sapphires sprinkled over the surface. On another trip to New York he spotted a painting in a gallery window on his way to the airport. He ordered the driver to stop, went inside, and bought everything the gallery had—*115 paintings and bronzes*. By 1974, when Priscilla filed for divorce and Cullen moved out, the value of the mansion's art treasure was conservatively estimated at $3 million. In the words of one critic, paintings hung on every wall "like certificates of stocks and bonds."

Yet when visitors entered the mansion's cool, impersonal living room, it was not the two Dufys or the silver display case of jade, ivory, and precious stones that snapped one about—it was a brilliantly lighted six-by-eight-foot portrait of Cullen and Priscilla that dominated the north wall. Cullen commissioned the portrait from Fort Worth artist Wayne Ingram. It looked like a poster for a tawdry movie. In the foreground Cullen

45

was portrayed in his dark business suit, seated in his chairman-of-the-board pose and smiling his thin, dry-ice smile. Less dominant, Priscilla was pictured suspended in space, her long platinum hair falling over her shoulders, and a maximum of breasts and thighs showing through her micromini dress. In the background floated ghost images of the master and mistress—of Cullen shooting pool, Cullen with his skis, Cullen in his tennis togs; the ghost images of Priscilla were hard set poses in gowns and short leather skirts. A European friend looking at the painting once remarked to Priscilla, "You look like something else Cullen did."

At the beginning of their marriage Priscilla made an effort to fit in with Fort Worth society, going out of her way to please and even patronize the society matrons. She assumed this was what Cullen wanted, and at first it was. For years the Davis family had been total strangers to the society pages, but after the mansion was completed, pictures and items about Cullen and Priscilla appeared regularly. The Opera Ball, the Jewel Charity Ball, the Steeplechase . . . Cullen in his midnight blue tux with the velvet lapels, Priscilla in an aqua gown cut to the navel. Easter Sunday at Rivercrest . . . Cullen in his ice cream coat, wide tie, and two-tone shoes, Priscilla and Dee in micromini skirts, looking more like sisters than mother and daughter. Priscilla holding hands with tennis stars Ron Holmberg and Rod Laver at a party welcoming them to Colonial. Priscilla serving tea to members of the Women's Board of the Fort Worth Children's Hospital, the majority of them posing tight-lipped and cheerless in front of the large Wayne Ingram portrait.

The mansion took center stage. It became a show-place, the likes of which Fort Worth had not seen since the days of the cattle barons. Like everyone else, society editors seemed unable to comprehend, much less describe, the mansion: one breathless writer for the *Star-Telegram* called it "a multifaceted house with an air of architectural lightness and serenity." The mansion was a monument, no question about it; but when studied at length, the structure appeared to celebrate not a perfect marriage but T. Cullen Davis. And yet it was a stupendous malaprop; it seemed so *out of character*. Sue Smith, a neighbor whose property backed up to the estate, recalled her astonishment the one and only time she met Cullen Davis: "It was so hard to connect this man with this place. He struck me as . . . I don't know exactly . . . it was like talking to a man who had worked very hard to overcome a speech impediment." Later, with the benefit of hindsight, Fort Worth society turned up its nose and called the mansion vulgar, but for a few years it was a stage on which the elite acted out chosen roles and wondered what was going on up there at night. Presumably, God's wrath would correct it. On one thing nearly everyone agreed: Priscilla went with the place.

Little by little Cullen and Priscilla descended from high society. Some thought Priscilla was pulling him down; others suspected Cullen was using her as a guide, trying to discover his lost youth, looking for Honkytonk Saturday Night. With Priscilla on his arm, Cullen became a fixture at the new night spots springing up along Camp Bowie Boulevard—the Old San Francisco Saloon, the Rangoon Racquet Club. They skipped the Steeplechase Ball and went skiing in Aspen. They were the stars of every party. While Priscilla paraded around the Colonial golf course in hip huggers and a halter top that did nothing except exaggerate her custom-made breasts, Cullen screened *Deep Throat* in the well-provided trailer that he'd ordered hoisted by crane onto the country club parking lot. People said that one night in a Dallas restaurant, without warning, Priscilla unzipped Cullen's fly and complimented his manhood. Priscilla denied the story, though she acknowledged that Cullen was constantly encouraging her to "be aggressive." In recognition of some occasion or other, Priscilla had her pubic hair dyed pink and shaped like a heart. Cullen loved it. Priscilla was his fix. Alone, he was inconspicuous. Priscilla made the difference—*Miss Rich Bitch*—he *loved* it.

Cullen had few close, lasting friends, but in the months after their marriage he and Priscilla made a number of new acquaintances. They began hanging around with David and Judy McCrory and Larry and Carmen Thomas. Cullen met David McCrory in a honky-tonk on Camp Bowie called the Pink Elephant. McCrory, son of a Fort Worth cop, grew up in a shabby section of northeast Fort Worth called Riverside. Riverside was about as far from Rivercrest as you could get. Old friends called him Little Moose, though, like Cullen, McCrory had few friends, old or new. Pat Burleson, a karate instructor who went to school with McCrory's older brother, Big Moose, recalled that Little Moose "had a talent for getting into trouble; it was getting *out* of trouble where he usually needed help." McCrory was a likable, hulkish, tenth-grade dropout who always seemed to be between jobs; he made pocket change hustling pool. Pool it was that brought Cullen and McCrory together and created, if not a friendship, at least a sort of mutual respect. As it turned out, Cullen was a better hustler than McCrory. While their wives nagged in the background and begged to go home, Cullen and McCrory played one against one until closing time. Later, McCrory bought the Pink Elephant "so we could play after hours." Priscilla became extremely close friends with both Judy McCrory and Carmen Thomas, and it was this connection that kept the couples close. They had dinner and drank and partied as a group and took occasional trips in Cullen's Learjet to Aspen, Colorado, and Acapulco.

There was another group with whom Cullen became more than casually acquainted and, to a surprising degree, intertwined. They were a group of men roughly his own age who shared a passion for Dallas Cowboys football games and pooled their resources to purchase a private box at the Cowboys' newly constructed home field, Texas Stadium. The group included Hershel Payne, the lawyer who had represented Cullen's ex-wife in the divorce suit; Buddy Young, an officer at the Fort Worth National Bank; and Roy Rimmer, Jr., a former stockbroker turned promoter. By 1970 the Dallas Cowboys were the hottest attraction in the Dallas–Fort Worth Metroplex. The team was owned by Clint Murchison, Jr., son of the legendary oilman who had been a peer, though not a friend, of Stinky Davis. The team epitomized the trend toward sophistication and computer technology that had captured the imagination of the National Football League. Texas Stadium, with its ring of upper-level private boxes decorated as suites, epitomized the affluence of Metroplex. It was Cullen's idea to buy the box at Texas Stadium. He purchased it in the name of Stratoflex, Inc., at a cost of $120,000, and paid to have it furnished and decorated. The other couples each chipped in $10,000. To their dismay, Cullen insisted that Priscilla take charge of the decor. She selected pink Pucci-print velvetine wallpaper, pink carpeting, floor-to-ceiling mirrors, a marble and wrought-iron bar and serving area, white leather armchairs, and a black dropped ceiling from which smaller mirrors dangled in indirect lighting. One of the wives thought it looked like "a French whorehouse," but what it really looked like was Priscilla's bathroom.

Cullen organized the football weekends. The group gathered at the mansion on Sunday mornings for brunch and Bloody Marys and traveled to the stadium in three cars. Cullen took it on himself to reserve tables at the Cowboy Club and later, after the game, at one of the better Dallas restaurants. No one objected that the group undertaking became Cullen's party.

Cullen's weekend companions were a prosperous, homogeneous group of business and professional men and their wives. They were in their late thirties or early forties. The men usually sat together and discussed football while the women chatted about hairdressers and Bill Blass designs. If the luminary of this group was Cullen Davis, its enigmatic shadow was Roy Rimmer, Jr. No one understood the curious bond between Cullen and Roy Rimmer, but it plainly existed. Until he became Cullen's best friend and constant companion, Rimmer appeared to be nothing more than a down-and-out stockbroker, hanging by the thread of whatever questionable deal he might have working. Rimmer had worked for a while in a stockbrokerage firm that went under. A Dallas investor claimed that Rimmer had once cost him a great

49

deal of money by convincing him to sell his stock in a company called Magellan Petroleum. According to the investor, Rimmer circulated a story that Magellan had drilled a dry hole. This turned out to be false. After the investor had sold his stock, he learned that Rimmer had bought it. Later, Rimmer formed his own company. True or not, stories like this were well traveled among Fort Worth investors and made the relationship between Rimmer and Cullen Davis even more inexplicable. A close acquaintance of both men explained: "If you told me Cullen Davis killed two people, I might believe you. But I'd never believe Cullen was involved in any sort of unethical or dishonest business dealing. It's just something he wouldn't do."

Rimmer first met Cullen Davis about 1969. Both men had taken their families skiing in Aspen, and their friendship developed so quickly that Rimmer flew back to Fort Worth in Cullen's Learjet, leaving his own family behind. There was a noticeable physical resemblance between the two men—same close-cropped hair, same delicate, aquiline facial features and slender build, same nervous eyes and thin smile, same preference in clothes. Over the next year or so they bought and sold a number of stock issues, losing money on almost all of them. Cullen estimated later that over the next eight years he lost more than $7 million through his investments with Rimmer. In a 1978 deposition, a remarkable pattern of trust emerged in which Cullen claimed that he had fronted Rimmer large sums of money that Rimmer inevitably lost.

In each of their deals, Cullen claimed that Rimmer acted as finder. Their first major investment was the acquisition of a small conglomerate based in Omaha, Nebraska, called AGC. When Rimmer found AGC, the conglomerate was on the verge of bankruptcy and needed money immediately to pay off its existing debts. Rimmer convinced Cullen to make two loans to AGC, one for $1.5 million and a second for almost $2 million. To raise the money, Cullen did something he had never done before—he arranged a personal loan from a Fort Worth bank, using Kendavis Industries' enormous assets as collateral. Rimmer received a finder's fee of $90,000 from AGC and later borrowed another $211,000 from Cullen to purchase controlling interest in the conglomerate. Rimmer took over as president of AGC, at a management fee of $8,000 a month, but two years later, in 1973, the conglomerate was still in deep financial trouble and Cullen had not recovered a cent on his investment of $3.5 million. In 1974 Cullen was forced to "roll over" his personal loan, borrowing money from the Fort Worth National Bank to repay the other loans. This time he used the stock from Mechanical Rubber, the only AGC subsidiary that was making money, as collateral. As a hedge, Cullen promised that Mid-Continent would purchase the stock of Mechanical Rubber in the event he defaulted on the loan, which he did. Cullen would ultimately admit that his entire investment "went down the drain."

Some months later, Rimmer approached Cullen with another deal. Cullen described it: "He worked out some deal with a bankruptcy court and with the stockholders of the company to acquire Republic Aluminum through another corporation he had set up called West Texas Corporation." Cullen loaned Rimmer $600,000 to complete this transaction. Later, according to Cullen: "I foreclosed on the note with Roy, took ownership in the company [Republic Aluminum] and operated it myself for a period, then sold it." Cullen sold it for $1 million, which appears to be a profit until you consider that the payment is spread over twenty years.

By now all the AGC subsidiaries had been sold or liquidated, but the deal hadn't been totally forgotten. The SEC had filed charges against Rimmer, claiming that he had sent out false proxy information on the conglomerate. Among other things, Rimmer was accused of listing Hershel Payne as a candidate for reelection to the board of directors of AGC without having obtained Payne's permission. The law requires that a person's consent must be received.

Although Cullen had already written off his $3.5 million loan to AGC as "bad luck," he pressed Rimmer to repay the $211,000 he had borrowed for the stock purchase. "He was apparently not capable of paying," Cullen said later. "He hadn't even paid interest in a long time." In an effort at least to pay interest, Rimmer worked out another deal. He arranged for AGC to purchase from Cullen's longtime friend, Dana Campbell, the rights to a patent on a polyvinylchloride sleeve used in oil exploration. AGC paid Dana Campbell $25,000 for the patent, then sold it for $165,00. Rimmer used some of the profit to pay interest on Cullen's original loan. The catch was that the purchaser of the patent was Stratoflex, one of Cullen's companies.

In 1974, the deposition continued, Rimmer came to Cullen with still another proposal. This time Cullen ponied up $400,000 for the purchase of Capital Building Systems, another company in bankruptcy. Again the debt wasn't paid, and again Cullen had to foreclose. In his deposition Cullen acknowledged that the value of Capital Building today "is not very much." Next, Cullen loaned Rimmer $2 million for the acquisition of a land development company, Beckland Resources. Again he used Kendavis Industries to secure the bank loan, and again the money was not repaid.

Then, Cullen claimed Rimmer set up a new company, Newcorp, and Cullen advanced him $250,000 so that Newcorp could purchase the stock of Beckland. By the fall of 1978 Cullen had not recovered a penny from either Beckland or Newcorp, though he still hoped to sell his interest in Beckland. But Rimmer wasn't through yet: he wanted to buy another bankrupt company, Hillcrest Carpets. This time Cullen didn't loan him the money, but he assumed a liability for $800,000. Hillcrest Carpets went out of business, and the liability still hadn't been paid by the fall of 1978.

The attraction of Cullen Davis to Roy Rimmer, Jr., was more than a business relation; it was a friendship, albeit one that defied logic and common experience. Neither man was known in the community for making and keeping friends, but in this case the trust seemed hopelessly one-sided. A man who knew them both speculated that "Rimmer is one of the few people who ever consented to be Cullen's friend," but this explanation didn't seem adequate. No one understood it—certainly not Bill Davis, who was becoming increasingly irate as large hunks of the family fortune disappeared down the hole. Cullen's outside activities could no longer be considered a personal matter. By his own admission, the ventures with Roy Rimmer had already cost $7.5 million. All this money was secured by the assets of Kiii, as was the $6 million Cullen had spent on the mansion, and later the staggering legal fees he had to pay. In certain cases Walter Strittmatter arranged for Cullen's bank loans. The Kiii companies that absorbed the weight of Cullen's dealings appeared to be the two that he controlled as president, Stratoflex and Cummins Sales and Service. Cullen could claim that his losses were a trifling sum compared to the value of the family-owned empire—after all, in the decade since the old man died, the total net income *after taxes* of all the Kendavis companies was nearly $200 million. Against such figures, a man might play loose and free for years without appreciable damage.

Bill Davis didn't share Cullen's estimates of what constitutes a trifling sum. Through the late part of 1972 and the early part of 1973, as Cullen and Priscilla were settling into the mansion and furnishing it in the manner of a sultan's palace, the arguments between the two brothers became increasingly heated and bitter. Bill and Mitzi were married now and had moved into the old family home on Rivercrest. Priscilla and Mitzi remained friends, but it hurt and baffled both to see the family being torn apart. Once when Priscilla casually mentioned one of Cullen's business deals in front of Mitzi, Cullen blew up and told her he didn't want her talking to Mitzi again. At first Ken Jr. seemed a neutral observer in the feud, but as rumors of the quarrel began to seep out and spread through the Mid-Continent Building, the older brother quickly sided with Cullen.

Inevitably, a few top-ranking Mid-Continent employees got caught in the powerplay. When Bill Davis sent out invitations to his annual Christmas party, a message circulated around the Mid-Continent Building that anyone who accepted would be fired. Executive

Jack George either didn't get the message or chose to ignore it. A respected and trusted employee who had put in twenty-five years of service at Mid-Continent, George attended Bill Davis's party. That same night Ken Jr. telephoned Cullen in Aspen and Jack George lost his job. The news settled on the Mid-Continent Building like a nameless virus; it was plainly a warning of what was to follow.

One of Bill Davis's primary objections was that Cullen had built his mansion on the choicest section of the 181 acres owned equally by the brothers. Ken Jr. and Cullen were able to compromise on this point, trading the younger brother the family property on Eagle Mountain Lake in return for his claim to part of the old Davis farm, but this failed to appease Bill Davis on his other, more serious objections. Bill contended that Cullen's wild and reckless spending habits had turned Cummins from a moneymaking concern "into a money-losing business with a backbreaking load of debts exceeding $48 million." According to Bill Davis, Cullen had run up *personal* debts in the neighborhood of $16 million, mainly because of the monies Cullen lavished on the mansion and his boondoggles with Roy Rimmer. Though the family empire continued to earn tens of millions of dollars per year, Bill charged that Ken Jr. and Cullen had "recklessly increased the indebtedness" of Kiii in excess of $150 million. Bill also contended that Cullen attempted to cover his wild spending sprees by arranging to use employee pension funds as collateral for his losing ventures. The older brothers might have dismissed allegations that they were squandering corporate funds —after all, they *owned* roughly two-thirds of the corporation—but the younger brother persisted with other charges that smacked of possible criminal violations. Bill contended that Cullen and Ken Jr. had manipulated stock in Stratoflex, the only major Davis stock available to the public, in a tax fraud scheme. The brothers denied it, but Bill Davis alleged that the tax fraud worked like this:

Cullen and Ken Jr. would order one or more of the other Kiii corporations to purchase shares of Stratoflex

54

in the open market, timing the purchase to coincide with recommendations of the stock by a stockbroker. This would have the effect of driving up the price of Stratoflex, at which time the brothers would donate some of the inflated stock to charity. They would then permit the stock to drop back to its original price. Thus the tax-deductible donations to charity would represent no real loss, except of course to the Internal Revenue Service and to the unwitting speculators who bought at the inflated price.

In August of 1973, when it became apparent that Bill Davis was no longer compatible with them, Ken Jr. and Cullen called a meeting of the board of directors and, by a vote of two to one, *fired* Bill Davis from all directorships in Kendavis Industries.

If Cullen thought this was the end of his troubles, he was badly mistaken. It was just the beginning.

Priscilla knew they were talking about her. She went out of her way to make sure they were. At heart Fort Worth was a small town, an introverted town, a town that viewed the world from a narrow perch and aspired to very little it hadn't created itself. People in Dallas always seemed to be flying off to New York or Los Angeles or London or Paris, but people in Fort Worth tended to look on exotic places as a plot against basic values. They didn't talk about new Broadway plays or R. D. Laing or luncheons at the Algonquin; they talked about each other, which meant they talked about sex— who was doing it, and with whom. They celebrated the double standard. Practically everyone who grew up in Arlington Heights had known the ex-Aggie who died a hero, fornicating with a cocktail waitress while his wife and mistress waited in their respective places for his call. The poor waitress was so humiliated that she dressed the corpse before calling an ambulance. If you took a poll at the Rangoon Racquet Club, nine out of ten males would say they preferred to go in the same manner. No one bothered much about Vietnam or Watergate when they could talk about next week's Cowboys game—or this week's story about Priscilla. One prominent socialite claimed that Priscilla had once been a hooker in Shreveport, Louisiana; though nobody had been able to offer a shred of proof, many believed her story. The stories that the men told were usually less malicious. The story of Priscilla unzipping Cullen's fly in the fancy restaurant in Dallas was told with considerable respect, as was the story about a dinner party at the mansion. In this accounting, Priscilla lifted a small, silver serving bell from the Steuben-glass-topped dining room table, held it up for her guests' careful inspection, then giggled: "I don't know what this is, but it keeps the niggers hopping." People in Fort Worth society did not regard the use of *nigger* as common; on the contrary, it demonstrated a social awareness in keeping with custom and tradition. Calling someone a nigger was like calling someone a Jew: it was intended less as a slur than as a code word identifying the speaker as one of the club.

The people who gossiped about Priscilla weren't just the wags at Colonial and River Crest, or the afternoon drunks and philanderers at the Rangoon Racquet Club; they were clerks at the dry cleaners, managers of supermarkets, delivery boys. Many didn't know her name, but they knew she was married to a rich man. They knew that she wore skimpy halters and tight pants and drove around in a Lincoln Continental. A Ridglea housewife who had a daughter Andrea's age claimed that Priscilla was so rich she had a washer and dryer for her dogs. Like much of the gossip, the story had a grain of truth—the truth being that Priscilla took in stray dogs and kept them in the laundry room. Stories like this delighted Priscilla and perhaps reinforced her self-image as the vamp who dragged her ermine coat

in the dust and wore the necklace that spelled out RICH
BITCH.

One thing did bother Priscilla. She resented being
thought of as a girl from the sticks who had hit it big.
"That's just not *true!*" she protested. "My background
is as good as anybody's. My mother always had a good
job. She majored in English as USC when we were living
in LA after my father . . . sort of wandered off. There
were always books around. I took piano lessons for four
years. I was a good student. I was very popular. I was a
member of the student council. Whatever the 'in' thing
was, that's what I was. If I wanted to be a cheerleader,
I knew I could get the votes. I had a *super* childhood.
My mother always took the time to see that we were
entertained. We had the only swing set and sandpile in
our neighborhood when we lived in Galena Park."

When Priscilla delivered one of her I'm-as-good-as-
anybody monologues, her eyes got watery and Galena
Park began to sound more like an Enchanted Forest
than what it was—a grimy, blue-collar community of
steel mills and petrochemical plants located near the
Houston Ship Channel. Priscilla could carry on for days
about the months she spent in Los Angeles. This was
while her mother was trying to overcome the shock of
being abandoned with three children. Priscilla loved the
image of herself at Hollywood High, but her roots were
in Galena Park. All she knew about her father was what
her mother told her: "If you ever met him, you'd like
him." She knew that her father had been a rodeo rider
and a spare-time "geologist," a name sometimes adopted
by oil field roughnecks who aspired to higher callings.

After her father split, it was her mother's brother,
Uncle Guy, who took responsibility for the family,
which also included Priscilla's two brothers, grand-
father, and grandmother. Uncle Guy was a blue-collar
worker for the giant Houston construction firm of
Brown & Root, and Priscilla used to tell classmates that
Uncle Guy built the Gulf Freeway. After she married
Cullen Davis, Priscilla moved her mother and Uncle
Guy to Fort Worth. She was proud of them, proud to
be descended from a line of sturdy survivors. "People

57

in Fort Worth," she said, "enjoy being big fish in a little pond"; at least she knew there was a world outside the geographical bounds of Arlington Heights.

It wasn't the petty gossip that bothered Priscilla, it was the omission of what she felt were her real accomplishments. No one, for example, ever mentioned her Brownie troop. Or the fact that she was PTA homeroom chairman. Or that she took ballet at TCU or logged twenty-three hours in flying lessons until she broke her ankle skiing. Later, in those surrealistic weeks after the murders of her lover and her twelve-year-old daughter, people laughed when they read that all Priscilla wanted from life was "a husband, babies, and a vine-covered cottage." It hurt Priscilla that no one took the time to know that it was true.

Priscilla saw herself as a simple, good-hearted woman. When a friend was down with the flu, Priscilla was the first one there with hot soup. "Good old practical mother Davis," she sometimes called herself. She was barely sixteen when she married Dee's father, Jasper Baker, a twenty-one-year-old ex-marine from Galena Park. The marriage lasted less than a year. Priscilla was eighteen when she met Jack Wilborn, a handsome, rakish used-car dealer from Fort Worth. Although Wilborn was nearly forty, he was a prime catch. He had money and didn't mind spending it, and his reputation as a card player enhanced his roguish charm. "I love to feel those cards in my hands," Wilborn told her. He owned a thriving used-car business in Fort Worth and was a member of the Petroleum Club and Ridglea Country Club. Shortly after their first meeting Priscilla married Jack Wilborn and moved to Fort Worth. A son, Jackie, was born a year later, when Priscilla was nineteen, and Andrea was born three years after that.

Andrea became the great prize in Jack Wilborn's life. For years Wilborn had wanted a daughter and had almost despaired of having one until he married Priscilla. He was so thrilled when Priscilla went to the hospital to deliver their firstborn that he bought his wife a new rose-pink Cadillac "to bring my daughter home." The daughter turned out to be a son, Jackie, but Priscilla recalled, "Jack never gave up wanting a girl. When Andrea was born three years later, there was never any doubt she would be her daddy's little girl." For a flint-eyed used-car dealer, Jack Wilborn could be surprisingly soft, even syrupy, on the subject of Andrea. "She was always the first one to kiss me good morning and the last to kiss me good night," he recalled. A beautiful, diffident girl with an impish grin at life, Andrea was one of those children that grown-ups naturally pamper and older children instinctively protect. "When Andrea told you good morning," a friend recalled, "she really meant it." On days when there was no school, Wilborn usually took her with him to his office or on out-of-town business trips. When an emergency room nurse telephoned Jack Wilborn in the early morning hours of August 3, 1976, and told him that his daughter had been shot, Wilborn did something he hadn't done since his own childhood: he prayed. In the unbearably painful days to come, he would pray many times.

Not long after Priscilla's marriage to Cullen, Wilborn allowed Dee to live with her mother and stepfather. Jackie and Andrea continued to live with their father. Although Wilborn was able to forgive Priscilla, he never pretended to like Cullen Davis and never encouraged Andrea to visit the mansion. "Andrea loved her mother," Wilborn said, "but they couldn't have a relationship because of Cullen. Cullen resented Andrea. She was passive. She'd do anything in the world to avoid a conflict. Cullen couldn't stand for things to be smooth. He humiliated her. He called her an idiot and said she was stupid." Andrea wasn't stupid, but in some ways she was awkward and slow. She lived in her own world and operated at her own pace. Dee's friend Bev Bass, who was six years older than Andrea and thought of the girl as her little sister, said that Andrea was easily distracted—a fallen leaf or a pattern of sunlight would catch her attention and hold it until someone called her back to reality. She would dally for hours over a seemingly simple homework assignment but seldom complete it. She loved to draw pictures of trees and animals and frequently gave friends hand-painted greeting cards, always signed "By Andrea Wilborn." Dee and Bev Bass assisted Andrea with her schoolwork, combed her hair, and even helped her dress—Andrea wasn't stupid, but her concept of time was at odds with the rest of the world's. Priscilla nicknamed Andrea Pussycat, a name Andrea later gave to one of her dogs. She called another dog Willie Nelson. Her closest friends were her pets—a bird named Cinnamon, a cat called Tiger, a baby alligator, a wild duck, a bat. "She was so gentle, so quiet," Priscilla said. "She was just like me—she loved to take in stray animals. She was the kind who could keep a cat and a canary in the same room." In the early years of the marriage, Cullen seemed attracted to Andrea and regarded her as a replica of her mother. He called them "my big white pig" and "my little white pig."

Though Andrea and Jackie never lived in the mansion and in fact spent little time there until after Priscilla and Cullen separated, Priscilla maintained individual bedrooms for all three of her children. Andrea's room was pink and lacy. A pink velvet heart with the words ANDREA'S ROOM was fixed to the door. By her twelfth and final birthday, Andrea had blossomed into a woman—she was five foot seven, 110 pounds, and at an age when most girls are still waiting for their first training bra, she wore a C cup.

Cullen was generous with the children, but he demanded absolute discipline and submission to his authority. He was intolerant of mistakes and failure and was as heavy-handed in dispensing punishment as his old man had been. Bev Bass told of an incident in the eighth grade when Dee defied Cullen. "We were playing outside. He came looking for her," Bass said. "He kicked her all the way up the stairs, and then he beat her. He hit her with a belt, then made her come downstairs and show us the welts." Cullen was absolute master of his household. Dinner was served at the appointed time, or it wasn't served. Once, when Priscilla and her three children were a few minutes late to the airfield where the Learjet was waiting to take the family on a holiday to Aspen, Cullen ordered the pilot to take off without them. At Cullen's insistence, Priscilla and the two girls learned to play chess. Of the three children, only Jackie, who hardly ever visited the mansion when Cullen was there, escaped his wrath.

Yet there were times when Cullen went out of his way to help Dee or Andrea with some problem, times when his patience seemed inexhaustible. About six months before Priscilla filed for divorce, Cullen insisted on helping Andrea with her math lesson. He kept her awake most of the night forcing her to memorize the work, and his despair at the girl's inability to grasp the fundamental problem seemed genuine. "I tried to tell him that Andrea was a slow learner, a dreamer, a girl with artistic instincts." Priscilla said. After that hard night's math lesson, Andrea told her father, "I don't want to go back there again." Priscilla testified that several months after the incident, Cullen demanded that she call Andrea and order her back to the mansion. Jack Wilborn was listening on an upstairs extension. "Cullen got on the phone and started using profanity," Wilborn said. "Andrea told him she had already made plans to spend the weekend with me, but Cullen got furious and told her to either visit the mansion or give back every single thing he'd ever given her. 'You'll never be welcome at this house again,' Cullen told her. After that there was no way I'd let Andrea go over there. She was terrified of the man."

Dee was more of a disciplinary problem than her younger sister. More outspoken and considerably less gentle than Andrea, Dee seemed to go out of her way to provoke Cullen. Priscilla told about the night Cullen broke Dee's nose and slammed her kitten on the floor until it was dead. Dee later described the incident: "I was asleep. Cullen woke me up and made me follow him downstairs to the kitchen. He said, 'Do you know what you've done wrong?' I said I didn't. He said, 'You left the door unlocked.' I told him I was sorry, I guess I forgot. He said, 'Why must you always be sure the door's locked?' Well, I didn't know, but I said, 'Because someone might steal your precious junk.' That's when he slapped me. He asked me again, and when I didn't answer, he hit me again."

Priscilla heard Dee scream and ran downstairs with a kitten in her arms.

"Dee's face was bloody. Her nose was broken," Priscilla said. "I said something and Cullen grabbed the kitten out of my hands and threw it on the floor. He picked it up and threw it again, then again . . . until the kitten was dead. Then he asked Dee to tell him why she should always lock the door. Dee told him because somebody might come in and steal precious valuables. That seemed to satisfy him. I was terrified. I called the police and called Bill and Mitzi, but Cullen went about his business like nothing happened."

A year or so after the incident with the kitten, Cullen again slapped Dee, and this time she ran away. The authorities located her, and when a social welfare worker asked Cullen what he planned to do, he said point-blank that it was his intention to take the girl home "and beat her severely."

Cullen rarely displayed his temper publicly, though on such occasions his tantrums made lasting impressions on witnesses. There were dozens of witnesses to a commonly cited incident one year at the Steeplechase Ball, Fort Worth's premier social event. A hard rain was falling as the elegantly attired guests tried to leave. Parking attendants were having a bad time getting all the cars up to the clubhouse entrance. Cullen got it in his head that they were taking too long getting his car, so he reached into the attendants' booth, grabbed the board of car keys, and flung it into the mud. A lot of very prominent folks went home in taxicabs that night.

Some fours years after their marriage, Cullen's ardor for Priscilla began to cool. Not long after they moved from the old family home on Rivercrest into the mansion, Priscilla began to suspect they had something less than a perfect marriage. By August of 1973, the same month that Ken Jr. and Cullen fired Bill Davis, the marriage was rapidly deteriorating. It was a strange time, one that Priscilla wasn't prepared to handle. Cullen seemed especially close to Bill at first, but now a mention of Bill or Mitzi was likely to set him off. Priscilla testified to the periodic beatings, the snubs, the temper tantrums, the growing impatience, the inexplicable chill in their love life. "He makes me feel like I'm being too aggressive, which is exactly the quality in me he used to love," Priscilla complained to her friends Judy McCrory and Carmen Thomas. Cullen used the slightest excuse to pick a fight, or so it seemed to Priscilla. She couldn't forget her shock one night when Cullen rebuffed her sexual advances, shouting, "Can't you keep your damn hands off me?" There was a night in Palm Springs in 1972 when Cullen "beat and kicked me until I was black and blue." This occurred after she accused Cullen of flirting with another woman. Priscilla told of the time in 1973, just after she broke her ankle skiing, when Cullen beat her with her own crutch. And the time in Marina Del Ray with Roy Rimmer and some friends when he broke her collarbone, and the night he knocked her across the pool table in the mansion and broke her nose. A girlfriend, Francine Gordan, witnessed the pool table fight. In fact, Francine Gordan was the cause of the fight—Cullen had it in his head that Francine had lured Priscilla into an encounter with two men at a bar called the Sea Hag. Cullen had a different version of the fight. He recalled: "I didn't strike her. I put her down on the floor and twisted her arm until she told me what I wanted to know." One would imagine that at some point Priscilla would have told Cullen to take a long walk off a short pier, but in fact it was Cullen who first mentioned divorce. As Priscilla remembered it, Cullen first confessed his infidelity, then said something like, "Well, I guess it's over."

The final straw, again according to Priscilla, came when Cullen locked all her jewelry in his office at Mid-Continent. Priscilla said: "I called him and said I would be there in fifteen minutes and he better have that jewelry waiting. He met me at the door with the jewelry in an envelope. We rode down the elevator together and this time *I* brought up the subject of divorce. Cullen said, 'OK, I've been there before.' I said, 'Oh, *no, you* haven't!' " Priscilla wrote a $1,500 check on her Master

Charge and marched to the office of Ronald Aultman and Jerry Loftin, two attorneys she picked more or less at random. It was several days after the two attorneys filed divorce papers that they began to realize the enormous stakes of the game.

This was July 1974, almost six years after the marriage and one year since Bill Davis had been fired. In November, Bill Davis filed his own suit, charging Cullen with recklessly squandering the family fortune and accusing him of criminal fraud against both his older brothers. This was a time of extreme frustration for Cullen Davis, a time of repeated setbacks and feelings of impotency. At first Priscilla seemed to leave the door to reconciliation slightly ajar. A few weeks after Cullen moved from the mansion into the Ramada Inn, Priscilla visited *him*. They watched the Cowboys football game on television and made love; then Priscilla came to the point. She needed a new Lincoln Continental Mark IV and wanted Cullen's approval, which she got. *Then* she slammed the door for good.

The case was routinely assigned to the court of Domestic Relations Judge Joe Eidson, a blunt-spoken man who, like most divorce judges in Texas, tended to sympathize with the poor housewife. In this case, of course, neither party was *poor,* but Eidson didn't immediately recognize this. He awarded temporary custody of the house, all its furnishings, and the new Lincoln Continental to Priscilla. He also gave Priscilla custody of Dee Davis and monthly support payments that would escalate as the suit dragged on and the extent of Cullen's vast holdings became clear. In addition, Judge Eidson issued a restraining order prohibiting Cullen Davis from visiting the mansion or otherwise bothering his estranged wife; this order would become pivotal in the district attorney's decision to file capital murder charges.

The ultimate frustration, the squeeze that trapped Cullen in a way he had never imagined being trapped, was Judge Eidson's order freezing his considerable assets. Ironically, Cullen's attorneys gave the judge little choice: their contention that Priscilla had signed a prenuptial agreement threw a shadow over the issue of community property. On November 8, just as Bill Davis was filing his suit, Cullen's attorneys petitioned Eidson's court for permission to sell 44,930 shares of his Western Drilling Company stock for $1,403,163, citing as a reason "the national credit crunch" and short-term loans to various banks in the amount of $14 million. The judge refused. Instead, he ordered Cullen to increase his monthly support payments from $2,500 to $3,500. In December 1974 the judge made Cullen pony up another $18,500 as an "advance on community property for trial expenses."

Subsequent hearings in Judge Eidson's court became increasingly bitter, as first one party and then the other were granted postponements. Eidson eventually set the date of July 30, 1976, for a final resolution, but once again Priscilla's attorneys petitioned for a postponement and once again Eidson agreed. The attorneys also asked that support payments be increased from $3,500 to $5,000 and that Priscilla be awarded an additional $52,000 for expenses and legal fees. The judge announced that he would consider the request over the weekend and make a ruling the following Monday.

On Monday, August 2, 1976, Eidson granted Priscilla's requests. And that night a man three eyewitnesses identified as Cullen Davis gained entrance to the mansion and murdered Andrea Wilborn and Stan Farr.

~~o • o~~

Nobody in Forth Worth society knew it at the time, but the party that Priscilla threw to celebrate Cullen's moving out of the mansion lasted throughout the fall of 1974 and most of the winter of 1975. From all accounts it was some party. The guest of honor was a highly improbable figure named W. T. Rufner who arrived at 4200 Mockingbird almost as soon as Cullen departed and stayed until Priscilla, with the help of some friends, evicted him six months later. In the meantime varying numbers of drifters, musicians, and drug dealers camped out at the mansion on a semipermanent basis. While there was enough drunken laughter, loud music, and backfiring motorcycles to terrorize a medium-sized town, hardly anyone in Arlington Heights, and least of all T. Cullen Davis, was aware that the mansion had gone underground.

Actually, Cullen had once met the guest of honor. He'd driven Rufner home from the airport. This was in March 1974, five months before Priscilla filed for divorce. David and Judy McCrory had moved to Boston, and Priscilla had flown up for a short visit. When she returned, Cullen met her at the airport. Priscilla was accompanied by a man with daffy green eyes, shoulder-length hair, and a scraggly beard. She introduced W. T. Rufner as a man she met on the airplane.

Though their marriage had already shown signs of floundering, Cullen had no reason then to suspect Priscilla was fooling around—and even if he was suspicious of Priscilla, he wouldn't have been suspicious of Rufner. He looked like a drug user, hardly the type with whom Priscilla would be having an affair. On the contrary, Cullen seemed to enjoy him. A compulsive talker who looks and talks a little like Kris Kristofferson, Rufner joked and told stories about his career as a professional motorcycle racer. It was almost three years later when Cullen learned the truth about Rufner—that he was Priscilla's lover, both before and after the separation. This was a segment of Priscilla's life that few people knew existed, a tumultuous period that she would deny repeatedly, even after the facts became apparent.

Priscilla claimed that she accidentally met Rufner while visiting the McCrorys in Boston and that she found him repugnant. There had been some sort of altercation that ended with Rufner and David McCrory slugging it out in a parking lot. On the way back to Fort Worth, Rufner and Priscilla stopped over for a night in Baltimore. Priscilla denied that she slept with Rufner in either Boston or Baltimore. She said that they had separate quarters at the McCrorys' and stayed in different hotel rooms in Baltimore. This wasn't how Rufner remembered it. According to him they shared a sofa in Boston. As for sleeping arrangements in Baltimore, he recalled shooting pool all night with some motorcycle friends. He couldn't remember where Priscilla was.

Priscilla continued to see Rufner all through the spring and summer of 1974. Rufner, known to his friends as T. or T-man, must have been a refreshing change from the man she had married six years earlier. It was as though Priscilla was retreating in time to a simpler and more fundamental point in her life. T-man's main interests were guns, knives, and motorcycles. Indeed, he had been a hot number on the professional motorcycle circuit before he got broken up a few years earlier. He was a union electrician, but that's not how he made all that money. If Priscilla was not clear on this point at the time of the Boston trip, she certainly understood it a few days later. On March 27 T-man and several of his associates were busted by state and federal narcotics agents. The list of illicit drugs uncovered in the raid on Rufner's house included marijuana, speed, cocaine, and an impressive number of other substances. The narcs also confiscated five pistols, two shotguns, and $2,645 in cash. Among those arrested that same day were Larry "Squint" Myers and his common-law wife, Sandy Guthrie Myers. Larry Myers later went to prison for his part in the dope ring, and the others pleaded guilty and accepted ten-year probated sentences.

The drug bust did nothing to disrupt Priscilla's relationship with Rufner. In June, while Cullen was out of town, she threw a birthday party for Rufner. Cullen's attorneys claimed later that Priscilla's birthday gift to Rufner was a gram of cocaine, an allegation she denied. The party was attended by twenty-five to thirty of Rufner's motorcycle friends and lasted three days.

On July 4, 1974, still several weeks before she filed for divorce, Priscilla rented a Winnebago mobile home to transport a group of family and friends to the annual Willie Nelson Picnic at College Station. The Willie Nelson Picnic had become something of a summer ritual in Texas, attracting more than 100,000 country music lovers to a Woodstock-type gathering. The event came to be called simply The Picnic. There had never been anything like it in Texas, or anywhere else: a literal melting pot of cosmic cowboys, college kids, motorcycle gangs, assorted freaks, authentic rednecks and kickers, politicians, writers, professional football players, and of course entertainers—Kris Kristofferson, Tom T. Hall, Leon Russell, Jerry Jeff Walker, Waylon Jennings, Steve Fromholtz, and Willie Nelson. For three days and nights the masses wallowed in the heat and dust, bombarded by the amplified sounds of progressive country music and inundated by amazing quantities and varieties of drugs, babble, and love and half-naked bodies swaying on the perimeter of sanity and sometimes far beyond it.

Typically, Priscilla was able to rationalize her role as that of a mother hen chaperoning her daughter Dee Davis and some other Arlington Heights teenagers. The group in the rented Winnebago did include sixteen-year-old Dee, her boyfriend, Tommy Brown, and two other teenagers, Becky Ferguson and Valerie Marazzi, but it also included drug offenders W. T. Rufner and Larry Myers and several other men and women old enough to be the teenagers' parents. Valerie Marazzi, whose father had managed Ridglea Country Club and who had known Dee and her family for a number of years, testified later that someone brought along a variety of drugs—"a white powdery substance, a brown powdery substance, a green leafy substance, and some pills"—which they spread out like a buffet on the kitchen counter of the Winnebago. Valerie Marazzi, though only seventeen at the time, was no novice to drugs. Even before the Winnebago trip to College Station, Valerie participated in several outings with Priscilla, Rufner, and Larry Myers in which a variety of illicit substances was readily available. Drugs were only a part of the hijinks in the Winnebago. That other virtue of the times—sex—was also in abundance. Marazzi testified that "W. T., Larry, Priscilla, that guy from Oklahoma City I didn't know, and his girlfriend" all got naked on the trip to College Station and indulged in some group sex. Valerie was no novice to group sex, either. At roughly that same period of time the pretty Arlington Heights teenager found herself in Larry Myers's bedroom with Myers, Rufner, and Priscilla. Valerie recalled that they were all naked in bed when Rufner suggested that the men switch partners. The switch was made, and Valerie and Rufner sat on the edge of the bed and watched as Priscilla and Larry Myers got it on. According to Valerie, Rufner changed his mind when he observed that Priscilla was enjoying the experiment. "He apparently got jealous and poured a drink on her," Valerie said. This ended the fun and started a fight, but Valerie Marazzi recalled that the group remained friends. Priscilla denied any part in such salacious behavior.

Three weeks after the Winnebago trip Priscilla confronted Cullen about her missing jewelry and stormed off to file divorce papers.

In late August, several weeks after Cullen moved his things into a motel, T-man brought "some cutoffs, a couple of T-shirts, and some jeans" to 4200 Mockingbird and began spending the night. By September he was living full time at the mansion. That same month Sandy Guthrie Myers and a woman friend also moved in with Priscilla and Dee Davis. A few days later, Larry "Squint" Myers joined the group in residence at 4200 Mockingbird. Still others added themselves to the protracted live-in party. From time to time the residents at the mansion were said to include Dee's boyfriend and musician Delbert McClinton and his wife, Donna Sue. McClinton, a well-traveled writer and singer who got his education in the dives along the Jacksboro Highway, was regarded as a genuine star in his field. He was the singer that other singing stars came to hear, a pioneer in progressive country music but more than that an esoteric innovator of rhythm and blues. "He's the best white rhythm 'n' blues man anywhere," a black artist exclaimed. McClinton's hit single,

"Wake Up, Baby," was used as a theme on the local black radio station, KNOK.

From all accounts Priscilla was a magnanimous hostess. Though several of the guests who later testified against Priscilla told of fights and broken furniture and acts of blatant indiscretion, Priscilla must have gone out of her way to provide a pleasant environment. She paid legal fees for Sandy Myers and for Rufner and gave T-man, who wasn't working regularly, gifts of clothes, jewelry, and boots. She threw a surprise birthday party for Sandy Myers, which was attended by more than one hundred, including David Jackson and some of T-man's motorcycle companions. Sandy said that there was cocaine, pot, and pills "all over the house." Rufner slept in the master bedroom with Priscilla, while Sandy occupied Andrea's room—when Andrea came for weekends, she shared Dee's room. Most of the guests had moved on by January 1975 (Larry Myers had moved to the state prison at Huntsville), but Rufner stayed until May and Sandy Myers until July. From time to time Dee Davis's friends Valerie Marazzi and Bev Bass also visited the mansion, as did Priscilla's longtime friends Larry and Carmen Thomas and David and Judy McCrory, who had returned by now from Boston. There were times, too, when W. T. Rufner's dog was in residence at the mansion.

Though he was a lovable fellow, there were moments when T-man's behavior was more than Priscilla bargained for. Rufner and Skipper Nitschke got in a fight and broke a valuable statue. Another time Rufner got zonked on Percodan, a powerful painkiller that Priscilla had been taking since her skiing accident, took out his knife, and ripped the stuffings out of one of the teddy bears that Priscilla kept on her bed. That same night, while the McCrorys were visiting, T-man pushed his way into her bedroom while Priscilla was relaxing in her sunken tub. Not finding the conversation to his liking, he crowned her with a potted plant. Rufner recalled later that Priscilla screamed for him to "take your goddamn junk and get out of here," but then she

70

had told him that on several occasions. It was T-man's impression that she was habitually overwrought. "Talk's cheap," he said. "Pussy and whiskey cost money." Several days later Priscilla allowed him to return, though with not as many clothes as before. Another time Priscilla asked her friend Pat Burleson, a karate expert, to evict Rufner. All in all, Rufner's life with Priscilla was not dull. "There were mornings when it was total harmony," he said, "and mornings when it was total hell."

Priscilla remembered it as "a time of great loneliness in my life. I might have fallen for a number of people. It just happened to be T." Priscilla remarked that Rufner was never "physical" in her presence. Of course they had lovers' quarrels. Friends told of the incident when T-man ripped open her silver fox bed covering after a quarrel over which TV program to watch. There was another altercation in which Rufner is supposed to have taken out his knife and cut off Priscilla's bra and panties. But the one that broke it off for keeps was when Rufner wrecked Priscilla's Lincoln Continental.

This happened in May of 1975. Rufner had already moved out of the mansion, but he continued to date Priscilla. Rufner probably didn't know it, but Priscilla already had plans to replace him. A few months earlier she had met a six-foot-nine former TCU basketball player named Stan Farr. Known around town as "the gentle giant," Farr was pleasant and noncombative, the type who was careful to mind his language and open doors for ladies. Priscilla had enjoyed her sabbatical away from Forth Worth society, but now she missed it, missed her old friends and trips to Colonial and River Crest and wearing furs and jewelry. One thing that made Stan Farr so attractive was his enormous presence. At six-nine he more than filled an average door, and in boots and cowboy hat he dwarfed Priscilla the way a St. Bernard would dwarf a toy poodle. Priscilla could well imagine walking through Colonial on Stan Farr's massive arm. She could picture the looks of envy. Anyway, Farr was much on her mind when Priscilla went out for the last time with W. T. Rufner.

The argument started as Rufner, Priscilla, and Rufner's friend Virgil Davenport were driving to the Old San Francisco Saloon. T-man, who had been washing down Percodan with Scotch and beer, was already thoroughly ripped, and he launched into a harangue about Priscilla's new friends. Actually, they were *old* friends, though Priscilla hadn't seen much of them in recent months. When Priscilla stopped her Lincoln Continental in the parking lot in front of the saloon, T-man announced that he had changed his mind about going in. They argued for a few more seconds, at which time Rufner threw the car into reverse and stomped on the gas. "When I did that, she hit the brakes," he recalled. "I believe we snapped the drive shaft." Priscilla rushed inside, leaving Rufner and Virgil Davenport with the damaged automobile. Shortly, Priscilla reappeared with Larry Thomas and his brother, Jerry Thomas, and several other friends.. They had words with Rufner; then T-man and Davenport left in a cab. Rufner directed the cab to 4200 Mockingbird. He no longer had a key to the mansion, so he rang the bell. Andrea opened the door and admitted Rufner and his friend. Rufner was helping himself to a drink when Priscilla arrived with Larry and Carmen Thomas, Jerry Thomas, and others.

There are several versions of what happened next. Rufner said that he tried to apologize to Larry Thomas for wrecking Priscilla's car but Thomas told him, "The best thing for you to do is go home and sober up." Instead, Rufner went to the kitchen and mixed another drink. This time *Jerry* Thomas, former Golden Gloves heavyweight champion of Texas, told him to leave. "You're in this lady's house and she wants you out," Thomas said.

"Basically, I was about ready to leave," Rufner said. "But when Jerry Thomas said he was gonna throw me out, I told him which way hell was."

Jerry Thomas recalled that Rufner said something about going for his gun. When T-man reached for his hip pocket, Thomas floored him. T-man struggled to his feet and Thomas floored him again. "At one point," Thomas said, "he nearly bit the end of my finger off."

After a few more blows, T-man decided it was time to go home. The party that began nine months earlier was definitely over.

In a few weeks Priscilla had a new bed partner, Stan Farr.

Meanwhile, there was also a new love in the life of Cullen Davis. A month or so after he moved out of the mansion, Cullen began dating Karen Master, a twenty-six-year-old divorcée and the mother of two handicapped children. Within a year he had moved into Karen Master's home in the Edgecliff section about six miles south of the mansion.

At first Karen Master seemed an unlikely choice as the new woman in Cullen's life. She was attractive but certainly not striking, and her manner was so mild and unobtrusive that she suggested one of those housewives you see in why-can't-I-make-good-coffee commercials. A high school dropout at age fifteen, she had moved through a series of mundane jobs, selling shoes at Thom McAn, working part time in a boutique, working nights at Stripling's Department Store. Later she returned to night school at Fort Worth Technical High School. The highlight of her life was being elected Miss Flame of 1965 by the Fort Worth Volunteer Fire Fighters Association. She recalled with nostalgia being invited to cut the ribbon for the opening of the new Carpenters Union Building. As one Arlington Heights socialite put it, "Stick a wad of chewing gum in her mouth and she'd definitely pass for a carhop."

But in the months after she met Cullen Davis, Karen began to look like a new woman. Her mousey blonde hair was coiffured and dyed platinum. She had silicone breast implants. Her plain pipe-rack wardrobe was replaced with originals from Neiman Marcus and with gifts of furs and jewelry. It was the old "Pygmalion" pattern. Some thought that Karen was trying to look like Priscilla: the differences between Priscilla and Karen were more a matter of style than appearance. An Arlington Heights socialite told of her mild amusement when Karen interrupted a small cocktail gathering at the Rangoon Racquet Club and inquired meekly if Cullen planned to be home for dinner. "We were talking business when she came in. She had her hair in curlers and had left her two kids in the car outside," the socialite said. "Cullen was very understanding. He asked if she'd like to join us." It was difficult to imagine Priscilla cooking dinner, much less rushing into the RRC with her hair in curlers and asking if Cullen would care to join her at home. No one could picture Priscilla scrubbing a skillet or operating a vacuum cleaner, just as no once could imagine Karen wearing a RICH BITCH necklace. The platinum hair and silicone breasts went with Priscilla, but Karen wore the trappings like a uniform.

Karen Master seemed more like Cullen's first wife, Sandra. There was even a confusing likeness of names. Sandra's maiden name was Masters and her younger sister was named Karen. The similar names—Karen Master and Karen Masters—had some people believing that Cullen was living with his ex-sister-in-law. There was another similarity, less apparent but more instructive: like both of Cullen's former wives, Karen Master possessed an inner strength, an ability to meet adversity and grow through endurance.

Her mother, the former Dorothy Anderson, and her father, Ray Hudson, separated shortly after Karen's birth, and when her mother married Earl York, Karen was adopted by her grandparents. Curiously, at the time of Karen's birth her mother worked at Mid-Continent and had experienced the tyranny of Stinky Davis. A proud woman, Dorothy Anderson York had become interested in genealogy and traced her family back to the farmers and clergy who helped settle Cumberland, Virginia, in the mid-1700s. Mrs. York's great-great-grandfather, George Slocum, had owned property in or around Fort Worth in 1868. Mrs. York didn't know who owned it now. "We're just ordinary people, the kind of people who make America great," Dorothy Anderson York said. Karen, too, was proud of her heritage and pointed out that "my family has generations of strong women."

A few days after her eighteenth birthday, Karen married Walter Master. They had two children, Walter Adrian Master III, nicknamed Trey, and Chesley Joseph Master, born three years later and named for a distant relative that Karen's mother had uncovered in her tireless search of old courthouse records. Both were normal, healthy boys, but in 1971, when Trey was four, and Chesley was six months, Walter and Karen Master and their two boys were driving home from Sunday services at the Assembly of God Church when a drunk driver hit them head-on. Karen was almost killed—she suffered a fractured skull, a fractured jaw that caused facial paralysis, a burst eardrum, and an arm broken in three places. It was five weeks later when doctors decided that Karen was well enough to be told that both of her children had suffered permanent brain damage. Even then doctors had no concept of the extent of the damage.

In the weeks that followed, it was determined that Chesley was epileptic, hyperactive, and profoundly deaf. Trey had brain surgery on ten different occasions and was forced to wear a special device called a shunt to remove accumulated fluids from his brain. Still later, it was learned that because of the extensive surgery, Trey was partially blind. Less than eighteen months after the accident, Karen and Walter Master were divorced. At age twenty-four Karen Master was unemployed and the mother of two permanently disabled children. Karen found a part-time job as a Kelly Girl, but the bulk of her support came from her father, Ray Hudson. Later, she audited some courses at TCU in deaf education and special education. Though people who knew her marveled at Karen's tenacity and endurance, she seemed painfully withdrawn. Her only social contacts were with the workers in the special education clinic and the people who treated her children. In late September of 1974 a nurse to a Fort Worth brain surgeon insisted that Karen accept a blind date with a man named Cullen Davis.

"I'd heard my mother tell stories about working for Mr. Davis at Mid-Continent, but I didn't make the connection," Karen said. "I almost didn't accept the date.

75

I was worried about my kids. My friend who arranged the date said, 'Don't worry about it. He's got two kids too. He'll understand.' It was on our second date that Cullen did something that touched me a great deal. He suggested we take his two boys and my two boys on an outing. I hadn't dated much since the divorce, and of course none of my dates had offered to take the kids along."

After several dates Karen still hadn't connected Cullen Davis with the Mid-Continent empire where her mother worked for ten years. She understood that Cullen and his bother owned "a little parts company." Karen had once worked at the children's planetarium, but she had no idea that Cullen's mother had paid for it. One day Karen happened to mention that she had a date with a man named Cullen Davis. Dorothy York asked Karen if he had anything to do with Mid-Continent, and Karen said she thought he had an office in the Mid-Continent Building. "Well, it just had to be one of Mr. Davis's sons," Mrs. York said. "I remembered that when I was pregnant with Karen, Ken Jr. worked that summer in the mail room. Then I remembered that Ken had a younger brother named Cullen. I had some photographs of him taken years ago at a company picnic. I told Karen, 'Honey, you better sit down. I've got something to tell you.'"

Like many ex-employees of Mid-Continent, Dorothy York recalled the old man as a benevolent dictator. In some ways her ten years at Mid-Continent had been the best times in her life, and nothing could have pleased her more than to learn her daughter was dating one of Kenneth Davis's boys. The first time Dorothy York met Cullen, she called him "Mr. Davis." Cullen smiled and said, "That was my father's name. My name is Cullen."

By the fall of 1975 Cullen was like a member of the family. He had moved into Karen's modest home in Edgecliff and become a father figure to her two children. Cullen's two sons, Cullen Jr., who was now twelve, and Brian, who was nine, were frequent visitors. Chesley was enrolled in a class for the multiply handicapped at Tarrant County Regional School for the Deaf. With Cullen's encouragement, Karen began working with the parent/professional section of the Texas Association of the Deaf. She recalled that "Cullen was just wonderful to all of us. He was always clipping out magazine articles about the handicapped or looking into new methods of treatment." Cullen encouraged the entire family to learn to ski, even Chesley and Trey, who received special instructions from a college student majoring in deaf education. Trey learned to dance and became an acolyte in the Trinity Episcopal Church. Naturally, Cullen assumed financial responsibility for Karen and her children. He gave Karen between $3,000 and $5,000 a month for household expenses and bought her tens of thousands of dollars' worth of jewelry and furs.

As Cullen settled into his new life with Karen, he seemed to relax, to become more stable than he had been in months. "Karen had a calming effect on him," Hershel Payne observed. "The harmonious family routine obviously agreed with him." Karen replaced Priscilla as hostess of the Sunday Cowboys football games, and the couple usually dined on Sunday night with Hershel Payne, Roy Rimmer, and their group of weekend companions, but Cullen obviously enjoyed his home life more than he had in years. "He would come home around 6:30 or 7:00 and I'd have dinner waiting," Karen said. "We'd have a quiet family dinner and watch television. Sometimes we went to a movie. Cullen is a great movie buff. We saw every movie in town, except the X-rated ones. Contrary to all those stories, he doesn't enjoy X-rated shows." Although the divorce suit was moving more slowly than Cullen anticipated, he seemed content to wait. He never doubted that he was the rightful owner of the mansion, or that the court would eventually see it his way. Karen said, "I never thought much about the mansion. Of course, we could use the extra room, but I only wanted it because that's what Cullen wanted."

Karen didn't fully realize how much Cullen wanted the mansion. But Priscilla did. The mansion was her leverage. According to one source, Priscilla originally demanded a settlement of $300,000, but Cullen stalled, and as the bitterness of the long legal battle increased, so did Priscilla's demands. Billy Wright Parker, a Fort Worth socialite, claimed that while she was seated near Priscilla at the Rangoon Racquet Club, she overheard Cullen's estranged wife vow that she would get the house and $3 million. Billy Parker recalled, "I predicted right then that either he would kill her or she would kill him."

No doubt Billy Parker was joking when she made her prediction, and yet she had more than a nodding acquaintance with murder among Fort Worth's rich. In the mid-1960s her brother-in-law, J. Lloyd Parker, an heir to the oil-rich Parker estate, was convicted of murdering his father. With the assistance of some high-priced legal talent, Parker was committed to Rusk State Hospital for psychiatric treatment. Almost ten years after the murder Parker had yet to serve a day in prison.

Fort Worth was just Stan Farr's kind of town. From the first day he walked across the campus of Texas Christian University he could feel the sweet vibrations. There were no strangers at TCU. The first week in September was called "Howdy Week." The men greeted him with the obligatory "Howdy" and inquired, "How's the weather up there?" Coeds sized him up as though he were 240 pounds of sausage in a display case. Down the hall from his room in the athletic wing he could hear the laughter as a group of jocks tumbled the soft drink machine down the stairs. Someone had thought to install a special seven-foot bed in his room, and as he lay back, his boots almost touching the footboard, he must have been thinking that he had arrived at the Promised

Land. Like it said on the bumper stickers: *"Fort Worth, Ah Luv Yew!"*

The more Fort Worth changed, the more it stayed the same. It was still a bawdy town bent to accommodate, a town on the make, a town that smelled of old oil and tobacco juice and after-shave lotion and pool chalk, of abandoned stockyards and packing plants that smoldered long after the fire was out, a town on the edge of a vanishing frontier where people still met socially at the rodeo and the stakes were always high enough to make it interesting, a town where the social climate was so frosty and the structure so inbred and inhibited that upward mobility was merely a delicious diversion. A football player friend of Farr's explained, "You don't ask a Fort Worth girl if she gives head, you just ask how good."

Downtown was simultaneously crumbling and rebuilding. The old Westbrook Hotel, where many an oil swindle set the tone for its times, was boarded up for good, and the quality jewelry stores on Main had become topless bars. The once great department stores like Leonard's, Stripling's, and Monning's sat fading and flaking like hags cadging coins on the sidewalk. In the shadows of what had been the marvelous wonderland of consumer gluttony known as Leonard Brothers, the Tandy Corporation was erecting an enormous new world headquarters. Charles Tandy epitomized the nouveau riche: he was the Marvin Leonard of a new generation. Mr. Marvin, as the department store mogul was called, pioneered the bargain-basement approach to retailing, but he was remembered for much more than that. Mr. Marvin brought the first escalator to Fort Worth and the first subway train—the subway connected with a massive free parking lot near the river and ran nonstop to the Leonard's complex, where a consumer could purchase anything from a big game hunting rifle to a tractor to a tank of guppies. Leonard had also given the city Colonial Country Club. A fanatical golfer and close pal of Ben Hogan, he had personally built Colonial after a power play with the board of directors at River Crest. Leonard wanted River Crest

79

to install *bent grass* greens on its golf course—bent grass being the rage among serious golfers at the time—and when the board of directors refused, Leonard purchased some river bottom land next to the old Davis farm and designed his own country club and golf course. Colonial became one of the great golf courses in the country. Because of its exceptional design (and Ben Hogan's influence), Colonial was host for the 1941 U.S. Open, the first time in history that the nation's most prestigious golf tournament had been played west of the Mississippi. Now Leonard was gone, and Charles Tandy, who parlayed some handicraft shops and an electronics firm into a multinational chain of Radio Shacks, had replaced him with the traditional flourish. The new Tandy Center, located where Leonard's farm and auto supply division once reigned, was a miniature version of New York's World Trade Center, twin nineteen-story towers designed with an electronic facade that after dark spelled out messages visible all over Fort Worth—GO RODEO! or SUPPORT GOLF! or FROG FEVER! or, more frequently, TANDY CENTER.

When Fort Worth society drew up its list of all-time great parties, it always included Charles Tandy's fiftieth birthday celebration. Newlyweds Cullen and Priscilla Davis were among the guests. One of the hostesses recalled: "We had a lot of bunny girls and we ordered just hundreds of champagne glasses from Pier 1. Then we drank out of them and smashed them in the fireplace." The party didn't break up until dawn.

TCU athletic teams were known as the Fighting Horn Frogs. In the late 1930s when Sammy Baugh and Davey O'Brien were quarterbacking, and again in the late 1950s when Jim Swink was running wild and Bob Lilly was anchoring the defense, the Horn Frogs captured national attention, but in recent years the only signs of life were the fast-stepping downtown businessmen with their "Frog Fever" buttons. Yet no one lost faith; TCU was where the good old boys went, where very night was Honky-tonk Saturday Night. TCU students wore Levi's and tight T-shirts years before they were a national fad. It was a campus where men were still judged on how much beer they could drink and how loud they could fart. At TCU, quantity more than quality attracted attention and Stan Farr had quantity to spare.

Like many oversized boys, Farr developed late. His older sister, Lynda Arnold, who later became one of Priscilla's friends, explained: "Stan shot up like a bean pole his first year in high school in Texarkana. At first it embarrassed him. He got into basketball almost in self-defense. People would come up to him and say, 'Hey, boy, you oughta be playing ball,' so he decided to do it."

Stan's father, Lynn Farr, Sr., had played football at East Texas State and worked as a bit player in Hollywood westerns back in the forties, but his movie career didn't work out, so he returned to Texas and got into the construction business. An older brother, Lynn Jr., was Texas Golden Gloves heavyweight champion in 1965; he went to the nationals, where Jerry Quarry broke his jaw with the first punch. There had been that star-crossed pattern in the lives of the Farr family. After an uneventful basketball career at TCU, most of it spent watching from the bench, Stan operated a variety of businesses—a pizza house, a swank supper club, a topless hamburger joint. They all went bad. He moved to Kansas City and worked for a brewery. He married for the second time (his first was a brief marriage in high school), then returned to Clifton, Texas, sixty miles south of Fort Worth, to join his father and younger brother Paul in the construction business. In the early 1970s Paul was killed in a car wreck. The business just seemed to fall apart after Paul was killed.

Like a nearsighted moth attracted to the only flame it had ever seen, Stan Farr returned now to Fort Worth, where an ex-jock, even one who failed to distinguish himself, was something special. It wasn't his reputation that made him an attraction; it was his size and easygoing, overgrown bear cub manner. "His size was his birthright, something he had been forced to learn to live with," said Billy Gammon, an Austin insurance agent who roomed with Farr at TCU. A beer distributor who liked his looks hired Farr to hang around bars,

81

buying drinks and pitching the product. By now most of the Jacksboro Highway dives had fallen into ruin; now the action was the new and fashionable bars near TCU and along Camp Bowie Boulevard. In a sense Hell's Half Acre had moved uptown, or more accurately, to Arlington Heights. In the course of a day's work, Farr visited the Rangoon Racquet Club, the Old San Francisco, the Sea Hag, the Round Up Inn on the rodeo grounds, Colonial, Western Hills, Green Oaks, the Carriage House, the Merrimac, anywhere the swingers were likely to gather. His job was to create goodwill and he was good at it. On several occasions in the early 1970s he ran across Cullen and Priscilla Davis, but the relationship was only a nodding acquaintance.

Farr tired of buying beer and playing shuffleboard and watching the afternoon crowd in its relentless pursuit of sexual adventure. The dream of owning his own quick-profit business was never far from his mind. The hot venture of the moment was constructing cheap apartment complexes and selling them before the walls began to crack. When a Dallas promoter approached him with a proposition, Farr borrowed all his credit allowed and signed on, but the business folded before they could put up the first "For Rent" sign and Farr was flat broke again. Farr claimed the Dallas promoter stiffed him, but the banks that he had borrowed from demonstrated no sympathy and several lawsuits were forthcoming. Billy Gammon said: "It was typical of Stan's luck that he got into the quickie apartment game ten months after the fire went out." Lynda Arnold added: "My brother was the all-time nice guy, but he was amazingly gullible. Right up to the end, people he trusted were still doing a number on him."

In the winter of 1975, as he was struggling to pay off his debts, Stan met Priscilla. The attraction was mutual and instant.

"Stan always had an eye for the rich ladies," Billy Gammon recalled. "He always had one full-time mama, and invariably she was well heeled. Subconsciously, he seemed attracted to the tough types, the ones who would give him hell. One sorority girl in particular—they checked into a motel and as soon as Stan disappeared into the bathroom, she split with his car. The next day he was with her again, just like nothing happened. He wanted to be big time. He wanted the appearance as much as the security."

Eighteen months later, when Billy Gammon read about the murders in the mansion, a grotesque scenario played through his mind, an imagined horror movie of how the end had come. Gammon remembered Stan and the game of King of the Mountain they had played in college. Though basically the gentlest of men, Farr was proud of his strength and frequently showed off by lifting Gammon like a barbell and pressing him to the ceiling. One day Billy bought a gun. The next time Stan came for him, Billy jokingly threatened to fill him full of holes. Stan *loved* it. He'd squat until his head was about even with Billy's and beg forgiveness. Then, according to the way their game developed, Billy would pretend to shoot him anyway. Stan would act out a marvelous dying scene, gasping and spinning around and finally collapsing in the kitchen with a freshly opened beer in his hand.

"The story in the paper said that the killer dragged Stan from the foot of the stairs to the kitchen," Billy said. "Maybe he did, but that's very hard to imagine. I kept seeing Stan saying, 'This isn't really happening,' all the while staggering toward the kitchen in some other man's house, looking for a beer. The last picture I saw was them loading him into the meat wagon. All you could see were those size sixteens sticking out under the blanket. I thought, yeah, that would be the way it ended. It could have been some tumbledown shack on White Settlement Road, but that's how it had to end."

The beginning of the end came in the winter of 1975, at the rodeo. Priscilla and W. T. Rufner had had one of their arguments, and she was alone when she ran into Farr at the Round Up Inn. Farr was also in the process of being divorced from the wife he had married in Kansas City and had recently moved to Arlington to live with his sister. Lynda was precisely the kind of sister Stan would adore, big and outgoing, the ex-wife of a Fort Worth disc jockey, a thinking woman who always had some pots boiling. Lynda Arnold operated her own thriving business, the Fun Factory, an organization that specialized in pepping up conventions and tired company picnics. A few months after the meeting at the rodeo, Stan Farr and Priscilla Davis started dating fairly regularly. Lynda Arnold noticed that little by little Stan's clothes were disappearing from her house.

By summer Stan Farr had moved into Cullen Davis's mansion and was contemplating some serious changes in his life. He decided to grow a beard and exchanged his suits and sport coats for cosmic cowboy wear. The cosmic cowboy fad had swept across Texas some five or six years earlier, but, characteristically, Stan was slow to see its potential. It wasn't difficult to trace the movement. For years young Texans had been regarded as plowboys and calf ropers, country clods with no more sophistication or culture than a sack of rattlesnakes. Their self-image was lamented in the honky-tonk music of lost loves and lives dimmed by too much beer and wine. Then in the late 1960s it changed—not the music, but the musicians. The musicians decided it was the other way around—the words still spoke of the reckless ways of the cowboys who took their love where they found it and rode on, but the sound was new. The sound was poetry. Writers like Billy Joe Shaver, Jerry Jeff Walker, and especially Willie Nelson spoke with feeling and imagery, and in complex meters, defining for the first time the culture of Texas. It was chicken-fried steak and Charlie Dunn boots and Honky-tonk Saturday Night: cowboys didn't *cry* in their beer, they *laughed*.

When Willie Nelson sang that he had to get drunk and he sure did dread it, many young Texans knew the feeling and interpreted it not as tragedy but as fate. Pride replaced heartbreak and self-pity. Songs such as "If the Phone Don't Ring, You'll Know It's Me" celebrated the frontier virtue of self-reliance that several generations of Texans had forgotten. Maybe one in a hundred had ever ridden a horse, much less a bull, but *rodeo* became the metaphor for the stylish life.

Boots, jeans, faded work shirts, leather vests, and cowboy hats—accented, of course, with plenty of turquoise jewelry and rattlesnake skin—was the wardrobe of the cosmic cowboy. Pickup trucks replaced sports cars as status symbols. Enormous barnlike honky-tonks such as Panther Hall in Fort Worth, Armadillo World Headquarters in Austin, and Gilley's in Houston were contemporary versions of the classic cowtown dance hall—Gilly's even installed a piston-driven mechanical bull where for fifty cents cosmic cowboys (or cowgirls) could demonstrate disdain for bruised groins and broken bones. If Nashville was the home of country music, Austin, Texas, was the home of something better—Willie and Jerry Jeff and the so-called *outlaw* musicians thrived in the free-wheeling atmosphere.

By 1975 the cosmic cowboy industry had spread across the country. That could mean only one thing—that the fad had peaked and would soon be replaced by something else—but Stan Farr didn't see it that way. Not long after he moved in with Priscilla, Farr invested in a new business venture, a pseudo-western discotheque called the Rhinestone Cowboy, located on Camp Bowie Boulevard on the spot formerly occupied by the Sea Hag. It wasn't clear where Farr got the money—he already owed numerous debts, including $11,113 to the Fort Worth National Bank. Priscilla denied that she was his source of new revenue. Priscilla did withdraw a large amount of cash, almost $4,000, from the Ridglea State Bank in the summer of 1975, but no one ever established that this money went to Farr. Some of Farr's close friends had doubts that he had *invested* in the new cowboy bar; though Farr spoke of himself as a partner, the title was perhaps gratuitous. Waitresses and bartenders at the Rhinestone Cowboy had heard Farr speak of "my investment," but they took this to mean Priscilla Davis: *she* was his investment.

Unlike the clandestine affair with W. T. Rufner, Priscilla made no secret of her love affair with Farr. By the summer of 1975 Cullen knew that Farr was living in the mansion, as did many others in Arlington Heights. Priscilla went out of her way to show off her new lover.

They were seen regularly in the night spots and country clubs, the six-foot-nine jock in his boots and beaver hide buffalo-hunter's hat and the five-foot-three "rich bitch" in her flimsy blouses and hip huggers. As though Farr were not sufficiently conspicuous, Priscilla bought him a silver and turquoise genuine bear claw necklace that would have looked like a logging chain on anyone else. Priscilla affected the style of the cosmic cowgirl, frequently going barefoot and wearing nothing but a skimpy halter and very brief Levi's cutoffs. In any crowd they were certain to stand out. Priscilla said: "Being married to a celebrity like Cullen, I naturally attracted a lot of attention. But being with Stan took the limelight off of me, which I enjoyed. Stan and I had an agreement that when we went into a place we wouldn't separate. Otherwise the men would attack me and the girls would attack him."

Inevitably, Cullen and Karen would have to cross paths with Stan and Priscilla. It happened for the first time at the Old San Francisco Saloon. It was like a scene out of a western. When the cowboy band took a break, Cullen walked over to their table, stared at Priscilla, and said, "What's a nice girl like you doing in a place like this?" There was a tense moment, then he turned to Farr. "Bob Lilly is looking for you," Cullen quipped with his customary straight face. Cullen was obviously stretching for a smile—Bob Lilly, the Dallas Cowboys' all-pro defensive tackle, was probably five inches shorter than Stan Farr. But the tension quickly melted. Cullen introduced Karen, then they went separate ways. Over the following months the two couples met on several occasions, and the mood was usually amiable.

After the months of madness with W. T. Rufner and the live-ins, it was ironic that only now tongues wagged about the goings-on at the mansion. Because of his connection with the Rhinestone Cowboy, Farr became friendly with a number of musicians such as David Allen Coe, B. J. Thomas, and Rusty Wier, and the mansion became a haven for pickers, groupies, and night prowlers. In the minds of many that had to mean drugs and free sex. Even before Cullen moved out, there had been rumors of nude swimming parties in the mansion's cavernous indoor pool, and now that the mansion had become an after-hours hangout the rumors intensified. A full-time groupie who followed whatever band was in town said, "I was up there [at the mansion] two or three times, and it was nothing. The only person I saw with their clothes off was me, and I was too ripped to remember." Priscilla denied that there was ever any dope in the mansion, but she remembered the groupie. She remembered specifically that the girl stripped and tried to entice Stan Farr into a bedroom. "I told her to leave and not come back," Priscilla said. "I knew about all those wild stories. Stan and I decided to quit inviting musicians over. I remember being backstage at Willie's picnic watching all those awful groupies. I resented them. I resented people thinking I was one. Those musicians all had beautiful wives; how could they go for those awful things? They couldn't be any good in bed. I'd look at those awful groupies gooned out on Quaas and think, 'Well, I guess that's about as close as they'll ever come to being somebody.' Me, I don't need it. After you've been with the president of the United States and his daughters, you're not gonna be turned on by a few musicians."

It seems likely that Priscilla was beginning to feel her age. It was harder now to recover from a party. Her health was none too good. The ankle that she had broken in the 1973 skiing accident continued to trouble her, and she was developing an ulcer. Fibroid cysts appeared on her breasts, necessitating surgery. By the summer of 1975 she had become dependent on the painkilling drug Percodan. A socialite remarked: "You can tell from the way she dresses that she's trying to look younger. Priscilla is not pretty, just flashy." A Fort Worth advertising executive said: "She reminds me of a woman who has spent too much time around a bowling alley. Scrape away all that paint and she looks like any other dirty-leg." In the spring of 1976, Priscilla made another large cash withdrawal from the Ridglea State Band, this one for $2,500. This time there no mystery where the money went—it went for a "mini face lift."

Stan Farr was five years younger than Priscilla, and they were telling years—the difference between a man of thirty and a woman of thirty-five. This was no doubt one reason Priscilla enjoyed the company of those much younger, particularly Bev Bass, who was in Dee's 1976 AHHS graduating class. Bev and Dee had been friends since the seventh grade and frequently spent the night together, and after Cullen moved out, Bev spent a good deal of time at the mansion even when Dee was away. The daughter of two professional educators, Bev Bass was an exceptionally pretty girl with honey-blonde hair and hazel eyes. She was a good student and athlete—she ran the hurdles on her high school track team. Bev seemed to enjoy the company of older women. Before she started dating Gus (Bubba) Gavrel, Jr., she was a close friend of Gavrel's mother. "We'd go shopping a lot, or have lunch," Bass recalled. "I went over to the Gavrel house a lot for dinner." So while Bev and Dee Davis remained close friends, it seemed natural that Bev and Priscilla would become friends and confidantes. When Bev Bass learned that she was pregnant in the summer of 1975, the first person she told was Dee and the second was Priscilla, who arranged for a secret abortion. A part of that unexplained money Priscilla withdrew from the bank went to pay the abortion clinic.

In her role as confidante and surrogate mother, Priscilla was fulfilling her self-image—*good old Mother Davis*. Many of Priscilla's private conversations with Bass concerned Dee Davis. Dee was definitely a problem. A marginal student, she had frequent disciplinary problems at school, and when Priscilla tried to correct her, the result was a shouting match between mother and daughter. Priscilla was relieved when Dee began dating Brent Cruz, a popular boy from a good Arlington Heights family, but Dee had other friends who were less exemplary and it was this group that concerned Priscilla. Andrea, too, was a problem, though of a different nature. Since the girl's unfortunate encounter with Cullen, Priscilla seemed unable to reach Andrea. In this respect, Bev Bass became a surrogate mother to Priscilla's youngest. Andrea would sometimes talk for hours with Bev, telling her things she discussed with no one else. Andrea expressed her special feeling for Bev by making her a bracelet with charms that spelled "I Love You 2." Bev helped Andrea with her lessons, combed her hair, picked out her clothes, and took her to favorite places—mostly pet shops. Bass recalled, "Andrea would look at the animals in cages and wish she could let them all out. She was the sweetest, most innocent, beautiful child you've ever seen. She really didn't like to be around people as much as she liked to be around animals." In the dirty torrent of charges and countercharges that followed, Andrea Wilborn would be the forgotten person. One of the low points of the murder trial was when lawyers for the defense tried to establish that Andrea kept a small marijuana plant in her room at the mansion.

In late 1975 Arlington Heights was like any other upper-middle-class suburb in America—the kids were richer, wilder, and, seemingly, freer. Martin Bernard, who graduated from AHHS in the late sixties, recalled: "We were superfast in Heights. When other kids in Texas were first getting wild to go crazy, we were *there*. It was the peer pressure, handed down from year to year. We'd try anything, just for the pure hell of trying it. Drugs, booze, any trip to blow your mind—one guy I knew used to mainline *vodka* for chrissake! The great sport was stealing used tires and speeding down the West Freeway, pushing them off the back of a pickup into the oncoming traffic. To hell with formals. This is weird, but the only formals I remember were funerals. *Funerals!* Murders, suicides, car wrecks. Someone was always buying it."

A few days after the murders at the mansion, as Brent Cruz and Dee Davis were driving home from a party, Cruz's car hit a culvert. He was killed instantly. Perhaps because of the sensational headlines surrounding the murders, details of the fatal accident were covered up by police in the Fort Worth suburb of Azle. Glenn Guzzo, a reporter for the *Star-Telegram,* said:

"We heard a lot of wild rumors. We even heard there were bullet holes in the car. The police wouldn't allow reporters to look at the wrecked car. They kept it covered with canvas."

⚬ • ⚬

As the summer of 1976 approached, Fort Worth society played out its ritual of debutante functions, charity balls, golf tournaments, graduations, and class reunions.

All over the state there was a cry for law and order. Jerry Jeff Walker was singing "Getting By on Getting High," and dope dealers were killing each other off with a vengeance that reminded people of Chicago in the 1920s. In Austin alone there were half a dozen unsolved gangland killings involving young middle- and upper-middle-class drug traffickers. The body of William Rawland, Jr., son of the publisher of the *Cleburne Times-Review*, was found in an empty house: the killers had castrated young Rawland, then, for good measure, chopped his penis into five pieces and arranged them neatly on the edge of the bathtub. That same week assassins shot another Austin dope dealer five times and hacked off his wife's head with a machete. The bodies of a young Fort Worth couple, both TCU students, were discovered shot and cremated in the charred ruins of their pickup.

In response to the cry for law and order, Fort Worth's new police chief stationed squad cars in front of the Camp Bowie Boulevard honky-tonks with instructions to stop anyone who looked halfway stoned. District Attorney Tim Curry let it be understood that laws prohibiting gambling paraphernalia would be strictly enforced. Applause turned to dismay when Curry's men raided the annual Fort Worth Opera Association's fund-raising gala, seizing crap tables, roulette wheels, and bejeweled patrons of the arts. Tarrant County sheriff's deputies broke up a crap game that Stan Farr and Horace Copeland had been floating at an area boat club. Copeland, a Fort Worth character who dabbled in drugs, gambling, and other enterprises, had become acquainted with Farr at the Rhinestone Cowboy, where Horace's ex-girlfriend Polly Ware worked. In July, Copeland opened his own cosmic cowboy joint, the Eyes of Texas, formerly known as the Beef and Boogie Club. In August of 1977, a few weeks before the start of the Cullen Davis murder trial, Copeland was shot to death when he broke into a Fort Worth apartment armed with a .32-caliber pistol. Police found $700 in a container of pills on Copeland's body. No one was ever charged with the killing.

In May the cream of Fort Worth society gathered as usual for the golf tournament at Colonial. The Terrace Room was the exclusive province of the Super Saints, those who had purchased a minimum of $1,500 in tournament tickets; as usual it was packed with gossip mongers, revelers, makeout artists, and wool inspectors. *Wool* was the local euphemism for the pubic region. The tournament director was known affectionately as Ol' Wool. It was a time of year when normal rules of conduct were suspended. A Fort Worth doctor caught in the act of leering at a nifty young Heights girl sporting a tight T-shirt that said SPOILED explained cheerfully: "It's OK. I have a clearance from my wife to leer at anything above a 36-B cup."

Cullen Davis, who was still remembered for his private screening of *Deep Throat* at a previous golf tournament, seemed more subdued this year. Again Cullen would cross paths with Stan Farr, and this time his attitude was decidedly icy. Everyone was talking about the pending divorce case. By now it had been on the docket almost two years, and the strain on all parties was evident.

Despite her jangled nerves and burning ulcer, Priscilla was dead set on observing the social mandates of the season. Dee and Bev Bass were graduating, and Priscilla invited all 440 members of the AHHS graduating class to party on the lawn of the mansion. It was a gala in the finest tradition. There were hot-air balloons, a live band called Cahoots, dozens of kegs of beer, and the not-unexpected haze of marijuana smoke. Bev Bass was there with her new boyfriend Bubba Gavrel. Bubba, a young man of considerable size and strength, was a few years older than Bev. By Heights standards the Gavrels were not especially wealthy. Gus Gavrel, Sr., a tough, blunt-spoken man with the Old World bearing of his Greek ancestry, owned the California Leather Cleaners on Camp Bowie. It was a small but thriving business, and Gavrel delighted in giving his sons the things he hadn't been able to afford in his own youth. Bubba had never been much of a student. He had dropped out of AHHS a few years earlier and now worked full time in his father's leather-cleaning shop, but he drove a new Blazer, owned his own bass boat, and accumulated guns. New cars and guns were definite status symbols among the young people of Arlington Heights.

Cullen and Karen were planning a trip to Venezuela, but the thing that most occupied Cullen's mind was his twenty-fifth high school class reunion. Cullen arranged a series of dinner dates with some old classmates, and his mood varied from ebullient to hostile to egomaniacal. Three times he telephoned the wife of a former classmate, who coincidentally used to be Bill Davis's girlfriend, reminding her not to forget to bring the old high school yearbook.

Cullen's classmate Tommy Thompson, whose book *Blood and Money* chronicled the inner workings of murder and high society in Houston, was the main speaker at the class reunion. They talked about those who had made it and those who had failed and those who had died along the way. They gave out the usual cornball awards to the fattest, the baldest, the grayest. Cullen accepted the "playboy" award and thanked them "on behalf of my ex-wife, my present wife, and my girlfriend." Later, as Cullen and his group dined at the Carriage House, Cullen seemed obsessed with the high school yearbook.

The woman who had brought the yearbook remembered: "Karen was very excited about the trip to Venezuela. It was her first trip abroad, and she was showing off her passport and talking about *our* Learjet and how wonderful it all was. For some reason Cullen became very abrasive. Karen started crying and ran out to the car. Cullen seemed mesmerized by the yearbook. We tried to change the subject, then he got off on talking about Ronnie Blankenship."

Blankenship was an Arlington Heights graduate who had achieved considerable notoriety in 1964 when he was accused of murdering a young divorcée and then burning down her house in an attempt to destroy the body. He was acquitted after a sensational trial. Hardly anyone at the table remembered Ronnie Blankenship or cared to discuss his misfortune, but Cullen seemed fascinated with the story and talked about it all through dinner.

The following night they had dinner at the Merrimac where Cullen told dirty jokes in Spanish and talked about oil depletion. In fifteen years, he predicted, oil would be completely depleted; for that reason, he rambled on, he had just added an eightieth company to his conglomerate. This was not the Cullen Davis his classmates remembered. No one had ever heard him tell a dirty joke or talk about business. But what happened next was even more surprising. One member of the party recalled: "Right in the middle of his story he turned to some stranger at the next table and said, 'I heard that. How would you like to step outside?' I couldn't believe my ears."

Cullen insisted on ordering the wine. The scene that followed put a full damper on the reunion. A friend at the table recalled: "We were all joking, saying how about a nice bottle of Thunderbird, Cullen. But when this young waiter came over, Cullen ordered what he called his *private stock*. It was some name with about seventeen syllables. He repeated it twice, but the poor guy couldn't understand what he was saying. Finally Cullen shouted, 'Goddamn it, do I have to write it for you?' He ordered the maitre d' over to our table and dressed him down and said he didn't ever want to find less than eight bottles of his private stock on hand."

At the Rhinestone Cowboy things were going according to pattern, which is to say poorly. Cash shortages amounting to about $200 a week were discovered, and majority owner Ronnie Bradshaw suspected Stan Farr. Bradshaw complained the Farr was spending too much time in the back room with Horace Copeland and others and sometimes disappeared for no apparent reason during the afternoon. Copeland had caused a scene with his ex-girlfriend Polly Ware and she was suing him, claiming Farr as her principal witness. Farr started carrying a pistol under the seat of his Thunderbird.

With the divorce trial less than three weeks away, Priscilla was half off the wall. Debbie Patton, daughter of an independent oilman and a regular at the Rhinestone in the summer of 1976, said that Priscilla was drinking a lot and talking yellow pills. According to Debbie Patton, Priscilla had started carrying a pistol in her purse. Sandy Guthrie Myers, the confessed dope dealer Priscilla had befriended, reappeared on the scene and told stories about the strained relationship between Priscilla and Farr. "She felt he may have taken some things that belonged to her," Sandy Myers said. "She wanted to get rid of him. She told me she couldn't figure out how to, but she wanted to get rid of him." Becky Burns, a bartender at the Rhinestone, recalled with some amusement an encounter in which Priscilla called Farr "a dumb son of a bitch," then pulled off his hat and jumped on it. Others believed it was Farr who was growing tired of Priscilla. He no longer referred to her as "my investment," and when he used the term "rich bitch," the accent was decidedly on the second word. Priscilla didn't know it, but Farr was secretly consorting with a sexy nineteen-year-old TCU coed named Kimberly Lewis. That's where he had been spending his afternoons.

In mid-July, Farr was "terminated" from his position at the Rhinestone Cowboy. Priscilla seemed relieved. She wanted him to run for political office—she thought county commissioner would be a good place to start—

but Stan had other ideas. He was already talking to a group of investors about buying Panther Hall, Fort Worth's honky-tonk of honky-tonks.

On July 28, Priscilla went to the office of Dr. Thomas Simons, the surgeon who had removed the cysts from her breasts. She complained of new lumps on her left breast and of flare-ups from her ulcer, but there was a more pressing matter she wanted Simons to consider. The divorce trial was now two days away, and she wanted Simons to write a letter to Judge Eidson stating that she was in no physical condition to endure the ordeal of a trial. In Simons's waiting room Priscilla had a chance meeting with Sandy Myers. According to Myers, Priscilla seemed terribly distraught. "Something heavy is coming down," Priscilla supposedly whispered. Priscilla didn't elaborate, but Myers had enough experience with drugs to recognize rampant paranoia. So did Dr. Simons. He had been prescribing Percodan, Valium, and other drugs for Priscilla for some months. In his judgment the pills were being dispensed in safe quantities, yet Priscilla demonstrated the symptoms of an addict—irrational fears, dark, unexplained forces, a world crashing around her. Simons didn't know that Priscilla was juggling doctors and pharmacists to obtain many more Percodan than were reflected in his records. There was no physical reason she couldn't face the divorce trial, but her emotional state was another matter. The following day Simons drafted a letter to Judge Eidson stating that the patient was "in no emotional condition" to appear in court.

On Friday, July 30, the letter was read into evidence, to the astonishment and dismay of Cullen Davis and his attorneys. Cullen's lawyers argued that another delay would cause serious financial consequences, not only to their client but to Kendavis Industries and parties of unnamed creditors. Eidson was unsympathetic. The judge noted that Kendavis Industries' profits for the previous year were $57 million, *after* taxes. Cullen Davis didn't strike him as a man on the verge of financial disaster. The judge announced that he would rule on

Priscilla's request for another delay the following Monday, August 2.

Monday afternoon, as Cullen, Ken Jr., and Walter Strittmatter were meeting at corporate headquarters, word of Judge Eidson's decision arrived by messenger. The judge had granted the delay; worse, he had increased support payments from $3,500 to $5,000 a month and ordered Cullen to cough up another $52,000 for maintenance of the mansion and attorneys' fees. Ken Davis, who was already upset by the latest turn of events in their legal battle with the younger brother, was furious and made no effort to conceal it. But Cullen seemed to take the news in stride.

Earlier that day Cullen had lunch with his adopted daughter, Dee Davis. They talked about the fact that she would soon enroll at Texas Tech, and about Andrea, who had been in Houston visiting her grandmother. Jack Wilborn had planned to drive to Houston over the weekend and bring Andrea home, but there had been a change of plans. Dee told Cullen that she had gone to Houston instead and that Andrea was spending the night at the mansion. Dee had promised to work out a budget for the coming semester, but typically it had slipped her mind. Cullen seemed irritated when Dee shrugged and said she had no idea how much it would cost to keep her in college. Dee recalled: "He told me to go home and stay there until I had worked out a budget. I said OK. I knew that's what he wanted to hear."

Dee had not the slightest intention of staying home that night. It was one of those strings of hellishly hot summer days when Arlington Heights kids sleep till noon, devote an hour or less to suntan maintenance, take a dip, take a nap, and reappear in their finery just after sunset. From Dee's point of view, lunch with Cullen had already spoiled her day.

Bev Bass slept till noon, dressed, and drove to the mansion in her 1972 Skylark. She planned to shop for her father's birthday gift, and Andrea was going along. When Bass arrived at the mansion, Dee and Brent Cruz were listening to the stereo and Priscilla was propped up on her giant bed, watching three TV programs at once and talking on the telephone. As usual, Andrea hadn't dressed or combed her hair. Bass selected a brown tube top and skirt for Andrea, brushed the kinks out of the girl's long silky brown hair, and hurried her to the car. At a department store on Camp Bowie, Bass bought a golf shirt for her father's birthday. She also priced waterbeds; her own had developed a leak. They visited two pet shops. Andrea fell in love with a pygmy goat, but Bass pointed out several sound reasons why a goat wouldn't be happy at 4200 Mockingbird, where Priscilla already had an impressive collection of stray dogs. Bev and Andrea cruised Arlington Heights for a while, stopping to visit several friends, then circled by California Leather Cleaners to see what plans Bubba Gavrel had made for the evening. Bubba told Bev that they were having dinner with friends. He'd pick her up around 6:00 P.M. Bass told him to pick her up at the mansion. She kept several changes of clothes at Dee's house and didn't feel like going home.

Bev and Dee made plans for later in the evening. After dinner they would all meet at Brent Cruz's house, where Dee promised to gift-wrap the golf shirt and accompany Bev while she delivered it to her father. Since Bass's waterbed was in bad shape, it was agreed she would spend the night at the mansion.

Despite the good news from Judge Eidson, Priscilla was feeling rotten. Everywhere she turned there was turmoil. Dee was bitching about not having enough spending money, and Andrea had trashed the kitchen attempting to bake a cake, which she never got around to finishing; Priscilla found a bowl of abortive goo stashed in the freezer. Then there was Stan Farr. Since that unpleasant business with the Rhinestone Cowboy, he seemed preoccupied and petulant. Farr no longer felt comfortable in the mansion. Priscilla reminded him that the divorce was sure to be final in another four months. She had to stick it out that long. "In a few months we can get married and build our own place," she told him. Farr didn't reply. Friday had been Priscilla's thirty-fifth birthday, but she hadn't felt like celebrating. But now it was Larry Thomas's birthday and Judy McCrory's wedding anniversary, so she reluctantly agreed to a small celebration that night. She already regretted it. Judy and David McCrory were having marital problems, and Priscilla felt it was foolish to be celebrating a marriage that was about to end. Next to Cullen, David McCrory had become Priscilla's least favorite person. She hated his big mouth, hated his constant yammering about this or that big deal, hated the theatrics and the way McCrory had of making an obvious failure appear to be part of his grand plan for success. Priscilla had a word for David McCrory. He was a *nerd*.

Cullen's activities on the afternoon of August 2 were predictable, up to a point. After the meeting with Ken Jr. and Strittmatter, Cullen went to his own office and worked until after 5:00 P.M. At 5:30 P.M. Cullen walked to the garage where his blue and white Cadillac was parked, but instead of the Cadillac he drove away in a company pickup truck. Thirty minutes later, according to a security guard at Mid-Continent, Cullen returned to his office and stayed until 7:50 P.M. Whatever his plans, they didn't include dinner at home. Several hours earlier Cullen's secretary telephoned Karen Master and told her Cullen would be home late. Cullen claimed later that he left his office at 7:50 P.M., had dinner alone, and went to a movie. But there was no one to support the story. The only person who claimed to have seen Cullen from the time he left the Mid-Continent Building until after midnight were the three witnesses to the shootings.

Around 9:00 P.M. Priscilla and Stan Farr left the mansion to meet their friends. Priscilla kissed Andrea and activated the security system as they walked out the door. As Priscilla anticipated, dinner was a disaster. McCrory prattled on about his newest get-rich scheme, a karate school that his friend Pat Burleson had let him manage. Stan hardly spoke. After dinner they stopped by the Rangoon Racquet Club, where things weren't much better. Bubba Gavrel and Bev Bass were at the RRC when Priscilla's party arrived, and Priscilla motioned for Bass to join them. Bass recalled: "Priscilla leaned over and whispered to me that she'd gotten what she wanted in court that day. I told her I was gonna spend the night with Dee, and she said, 'Good. I'll tell you about it later.' " Even though it was only a little after 11:00 P.M., Farr kept looking at his watch and yawning.

Andrea was alone in the mansion at least as late as 10:30 P.M. That's the time when she talked on the telephone to Stan's sister, Lynda Arnold, and to Lynda's fourteen-year-old daughter, Dana. The only person who knows what happened next is the killer. Sometime after 10:30 P.M. the killer entered the mansion, either with a key or with Andrea's consent. Someone deactivated the security system. As police reconstructed it later, the killer took Andrea to the basement, stood facing her, then shot her just below the left breast with a .38 Smith & Wesson. The killer must have been only a little taller than Andrea. The girl was five foot seven, but the bullet, which entered her chest and exited with no deviation two inches to the left of the midline of her back, dropped two inches in its flight. The killer stood no more than six feet away when he fired the shot. Since there was no sign of a struggle, it was speculated that Andrea knew and trusted the person who took her to the basement. Only the killer knew if she screamed or pleaded for her life or even recognized danger. Her body was discovered in one of the large closets in the basement. She was on her back in a pool of blood; the brown tube top that Bev Bass had selected was stained from the breast down, the skirt hiked up to her waist. There was blood on her arms and on the top of her head, suggesting that she fell face down but that the killer turned her body over to make certain she was dead. Her eyes were open, expressionless and permanently frozen as though death had come instantly. Traces of blood found at the top of the basement stairs augmented speculation that the killer handled the body.

He was hiding in the laundry room just to the right of the mansion's main entrance when Priscilla and Stan Farr returned home about midnight.

Priscilla was not alarmed when she noticed that the security system had been deactivated. This was the sort of carelessness she expected from both Dee and Andrea. Priscilla knew that Dee was expecting Bev Bass; as it turned out, Dee spent the night at Brent Cruz's house, but Priscilla had no way of knowing this at the time. Andrea was especially careless about admitting visitors. Priscilla remembered the time she'd opened the door for W. T. Rufner and his friend. It would never occur to Andrea that anyone who rang the front bell was anything less than friendly. As Stan Farr started up the stairs to the master bedroom, Priscilla walked through the kitchen, turning off lights. This is when she noticed that someone had left on the light at the top of the basement stairs. When Priscilla got close to the door at the top of the stairs, she saw what appeared to be a bloody palm print on the door facing. She called out to Stan Farr, who couldn't hear her, then started toward the stairs leading to the master bedroom.

In statements to the police and later in court Priscilla described what happened next: "Cullen stepped out from the direction of the laundry room. He was dressed all in black. His hands were inside a black plastic bag and he had on a shoulder-length curly black wig, the kind colored people wear. I remember thinking *how ridiculous*. He said, 'Hi,' . . . and then he shot me. I felt the blood and the big hole in my chest. I screamed to Stan, 'I've been shot! Cullen shot me! Stan, go back!' But I could hear Stan coming downstairs. I was lying on the floor but I could see Stan at the bottom of the stairs . . . he had pushed the door shut and was holding it from the inside and Cullen was, you know, pushing from the outside. Cullen fired through the door and I could hear Stan . . . he said something like *Uh!* and I knew he'd been shot. Then Cullen pushed the door open. Stan grabbed him and they wrestled around and then Cullen jerked back and fired again. Stan turned and fell and was kind of, you know, looking at me. He was kind of on his side with his chin up. Cullen stood at Stan's feet and shot him two more times. Stan made a gasping sound, sort of a gurgle. Then Stan just kind of laid his head down—he closed his eyes and laid his head down and died. . . ."

By all reasoning Priscilla should have been dead: she had been shot from almost exactly the same position and in nearly the same part of her chest as Andrea, but the bullet miraculously missed her main artery. The killer must have thought she was dead or dying, because he paid no attention. Instead, he took Farr by the feet and began dragging his body down the hallway, leaving a wide trail of blood all the way to the kitchen . . . toward the basement where Andrea's body lay.

Priscilla testified: "That's when I decided to try for the back door and I unlocked it, you know, and he heard me unlock the door and I ran out, you know, onto the patio part . . . and he came after me and, anyway, I tripped and fell down."

The man in black caught up with her in the patio courtyard, near the marble statue of Aphrodite. He grabbed her arm and started pulling her back inside. "I was pleading with him," Priscilla said. "I was saying, 'Cullen, I love you. I didn't . . . I have never loved anybody else. Please, let's talk. Please, Cullen . . . you're hurting me." The killer relaxed his grip but continued to pull her toward the house, saying very softly, "Come on, come on." Priscilla asked the question for which there was no answer: "Why are you doing this?" She could see the gun muzzle sticking through the plastic bag: the wig kept slipping, and the killer used the gun hand to push it back in place.

Many times, as she recalled the story, Priscilla saw it in slow motion, like a dream with a plot never changed.

"I remember things," she said. "I couldn't understand why he wouldn't shoot me again. I was thinking at the same time—what is he holding onto that *wig* for? You know. No matter what is going on, you are still thinking. I guess it's somewhere in my mind too. What's so important about holding onto that wig? He thinks he is hiding from somebody. Then he got me to the back door and . . . now that's when I don't know why he turned loose of me."

101

It's only speculation, but the killer must have believed that Priscilla was too badly wounded to escape. His priority seemed to be dragging Stan Farr's body to the basement. Perhaps he intended to return for Priscilla and take her to the basement too, take her to the bodies of Andrea and Farr, and then, his revenge complete, finish Priscilla with the one remaining bullet in his .38. But the killer failed to reckon with Priscilla's tenacity, her well-honed survival instinct. As soon as the killer had resumed dragging Farr's body, she literally dove into the bushes behind the marble statues. She could hear him coming after her, then she heard something else. She heard voices from the driveway. She hadn't heard the Blazer—her ears were still ringing from the gunshots—but now she heard a man and a woman. It was Gavrel and Bev Bass, but Priscilla didn't consider that at the time. Her first thought was *It's Dee! She's come home! He'll kill her too!* Later Priscilla realized that in those unbelievable seconds she had allowed herself to think the unthinkable. It wasn't until the following day that they told her Andrea was dead, but somehow she already knew.

Priscilla's testimony continued: "I ran . . . I remember thinking I was going to try to run to Jim Morgan. He owns those condominiums next to the property . . . then I decided I had better not try to go that far, so I decided to cut across to one of the houses. It was like, you know, a dream . . . or a movie. You know, every time I have seen any movies and seen these stupid women fall down, I just . . . well, I thought about it and I fell flat on my face.

"I heard a shot. Screaming. More shots, just a bunch. But I kept going. Then I fell again, and I scratched my head up here and my knee and everything. Anyway, I got up and thought . . . I was really thinking maybe I should walk, that I would last longer. Then I thought, no, Priscilla, just run and stay calm. Don't panic, Priscilla. Stay calm. You know, I was trying to keep from . . . not going into any form of shock. I was trying to breathe through my diaphragm. I was really going through all of this. Just holding my skirt real tight [up

102

around her chest] to keep from bleeding so much. My heart was pounding and it was pumping more blood. That's really what I was trying to keep in my mind more than anything."

The next thing she recalled was banging on the door of a neighbor's home, screaming and banging and finally ringing the doorbell. This was the home of Mr. and Mrs. Clifford Jones, and the thoughts that they must have registered at that moment were never expressed. They could hear a woman's voice screaming, "My name is Priscilla Davis. I live in the big house in the middle of the field off Hulen. I am very wounded. Cullen is up there killing my children. He is killing everyone!" Clifford Jones and his wife had never heard of Priscilla Davis, nor were they about to open the door, but they called out to the woman that they had telephoned for an ambulance and for the police. They still refused to open the door until police arrived.

In sworn statements and court testimony Bubba Gavrel and Bev Bass supported Priscilla's story.

Gavrel, who at five foot ten was about five inches taller than Bass, was first to see trouble. As Gavrel closed the door of his Blazer, he could see something Bass couldn't—over the courtyard wall, he could see a man and woman in some sort of struggle. The woman was blonde, but in the dim light he identified the man only by his voice. The woman was pleading, "I love you! I've always loved you!" and the man was saying, "Come on, come on." Bass recalled that as she stepped down from the Blazer, she heard a woman's scream from inside the house, then a noise like a gunshot or something breaking. It occurred to her that someone was having a fight, but she said nothing to Bubba.

Like Priscilla, the killer probably hadn't heard the young couple arrive; the echo of screams and gunshots must have been ringing in his ears too. The killer disappeared into the house—this was the moment when Priscilla dived into the shrubs. A moment later the man reappeared. He no longer wore the wig. His head was bowed, and his hands were concealed in a shiny black bag. Gavrel recalled saying, "What's going on? Where

103

is everybody?" Bass said that the man was stealing something from the mansion, but before this could sink in, Gavrel saw the man at the courtyard gate and heard him say, "They are right this way. Follow me." Gavrel still didn't recognize the figure, only that it was a man dressed in black. The man led the couple along the front of the garage and around the corner, along the walkway toward the breakfast room door, the mansion's main entrance. The lights over the garage flickered from a short in the wiring; Gavrel still couldn't see much, but he followed close behind the man, and Bass walked just behind Gavrel. When the man was a few feet from the well-lighted breakfast room door, Bass suddenly recognized him.

"Bubba!" she called out. "That's Cullen!"

In one movement the man turned around and shot Gavrel in the stomach. "It felt like a horse kicking me," Gavrel said. He fell backward. For a moment the killer stood directly over the husky young man, pointing the gun at the victim's head. By now the .38 was empty; it's not clear whether the killer knew this as he stood over Gavrel.

Bass said: "Then Cullen looked at me. I was scared he was gonna shoot me, so I started running." She ran back along the pathway, hurdling a low retaining wall, zigzagging down the hill and the rough driveway toward the Hulen Street gate. Somewhere in there she lost one of her Dr. Scholl's sandals, but she kept running and zigzagging, expecting that at any moment the pursuing man would fire. She could see the man over her shoulder, and she called out, "Cullen, please don't shoot me! It's Bev!" She called this out eight or nine times. When she was almost to Hulen, Bass looked around again and the man was no longer pursuing her. She flagged down a passing motorist and jumped into his car.

While the killer was chasing Bass, Gavrel was looking for help. But he was paralyzed from the waist down; there was no feeling at all in his legs. Using his thick arms for support, Gavrel dragged himself to the breakfast room door. It was locked. Through the glass panels he could see the wide trail of blood along the hallway where the killer had dragged Stan Farr's body. Bubba took off a shoe and tried to break the glass. Realizing he needed something heavier, Gavrel dragged himself back along the pathway and tried to pry loose a stone. When he heard the killer returning, Gavrel curled up and played dead. He heard the man run by, then saw him at the door. When the gunman discovered that the door was locked, he reloaded his pistol and fired three times, shattering the glass panel. He kicked out the remaining glass and disappeared inside the house. A few minutes later, Gavrel heard the killer returning. He walked over and looked at Bubba's motionless body and said, "Oh, my God!" That was the last anyone saw of the man in black.

When Gavrel was sure the man had gone, he dragged himself through the broken glass and into the kitchen. He managed to reach a telephone, but it wasn't working. "I was feeling bad . . . real weak," Gavrel said. "I just leaned my head up against the wall and closed my eyes."

Later, there would be much controversy over exactly what time all this was happening. John Smedley, the second person to see Bev Bass after she escaped from the killer, put the time of their meeting at exactly 12:47 A.M. Smedley was a patrolman for Homeguard Security Company, and he had just checked out the service station at the corner of Hulen and Bellaire, the nearest intersection to the mansion. He was reporting to his dispatcher—that's how he remembered the exact time—when he heard a woman's loud whistle. It was Bev Bass, who had caught a ride with motorist Robert Sawhill. Sawhill had stopped at a Mr. M. Food Store across from where Smedley had parked his patrol Jeep. Sawhill had already telephoned police and then called for an ambulance when Bass spotted the patrol Jeep. She put her fingers in her mouth and let out a whistle that could be heard for several blocks. When Smedley looked up from his radio log, he saw a young woman across the street, whistling and waving her arms. Smedley wheeled his Jeep around and pulled across to the Mr. M Food Store. The young woman ran out to meet him.

"She was very excited . . . out of breath," the private patrolman said. "She said in a loud voice, 'You've got to help me. My boyfriend's been shot and he's dying.' There was a man [Sawhill] there and I told him to call police, but he said he'd already called them. The girl said, 'Be damn sure the police have been called.' I radioed my 314 [call letters] to my dispatcher and asked him to also notify the Fort Worth PD that we had a signal 37 [shooting]."

Bass interrupted Smedley, shouting, "You don't *understand!* There's been a shooting! My boyfriend has been shot and he's dying. I saw him get shot!"

"Where?" Smedley asked, trying to calm the girl.

"At Priscilla's!"

Smedley recognized the name; he'd once worked security at the mansion, and friends of his had attended parties at Priscilla Davis's house.

"The big white house on the hill," Bass continued, words tumbling from her mouth almost quicker than Smedley could unscramble them. "My boyfriend is dying. I saw him get shot. I saw him do it."

"You saw *who* do it?" Smedley asked.

"It was Cullen. Cullen did it!" the girl screamed. "I saw his ugly fucking face. He's trying to kill me too. He chased me all over the place!"

Bass pleaded with the private patrolman to take her back to the mansion, but he told her to wait for the police. Within a few minutes, two Fort Worth police cars pulled into the Mr. M's parking lot. Bass ran to the first patrol car, jumped in, and screamed, "Just go! I'll tell you on the way!" By the time the first patrol car reached the mansion, at least eight people had been told of the shootings, and at least five of them heard Priscilla or Bev Bass name the killer as Cullen Davis. The first report had come from Clifford Jones. Police logged the call at 12:42 A.M. Two minutes later Sawhill made the first of two calls to police headquarters; after that Smedley's dispatcher called. At almost the same time, an ambulance had reached Priscilla. She repeated the story that Cullen was killing everyone, and the ambulance drivers reported the name of the suspect to police en route to the emergency room at John Peter Smith Hospital.

Officers Jimmy Soders and J. A. Perez were patrolling the Tanglewood area in separate squad cars when they were dispatched to the Mr. M Food Store less than a mile from the mansion. The time of the call was 12:45 A.M. Soders recalled that the woman he knew later as Bev Bass leaped into his car, told him her boyfriend had been shot, and directed him to the Hulen Street gate. On the way, Soders asked the girl who shot her boyfriend and she told him, "Cullen Davis did it. I saw him do it. I know him."

Perez and Soders both drew their pistols and ran toward the door that Bass pointed to as the main entrance. Bubba Gavrel was no longer where Bass had seen him fall, and she ran and pushed ahead of the cops. "I grabbed her and made her come back and sit by the wall," Perez said. "She was highly excited. I had to be very stern with her." The two cops led the girl back to the private patrolman, Smedley, who arrived just behind them; they told Smedley to keep her outside.

His pistol cocked and ready, Perez entered through the broken panels and saw Gavrel leaning against the wall, holding a telephone. "Damn thing don't work," Gavrel said. The two cops moved slowly; it seemed likely that the killer might still be inside. Soders followed the trail of blood down the hallway to the kitchen where he discovered Stan Farr's body. Farr was on his stomach, his head turned to the right. His eyes were closed, and dark, matted hair covered part of his face. The broad back of his white cowboy shirt was stained with blood.

By now two more officers had joined the search, and at least two dozen more were on their way to 4200 Mockingbird. Perez, Soders, and two others made a quick search of the twenty-room mansion's main floor. It was Perez who discovered a blood smear on the door leading to the basement. Blood dotted the glass window near the basement entrance. More cops and police dogs were arriving at the mansion as Perez and Sgt. J. D. Tigert moved cautiously down the basement steps. The basement was dark, and Perez beamed his flashlight from side to side. Sergeant Tigert checked the right side of the room, and Perez worked the opposite wall, where several utility closets were located. Perez flashed his light on a door and opened it. The small room was filled with lawn furniture. He moved along the wall to a second door. "I had my flashlight in my left hand, the gun in my right," Perez said. "I pressed against the wall. The door opens out, and I held it open three to four inches and looked in. And I saw some feet . . . laying down, toward the door. I closed the door and motioned for Sergeant Tigert. I shined my light in the little room. Sergeant Tigert had his gun drawn. He went inside.' "

In the beam of Perez's flashlight Sergeant Tigert saw the body of Andrea Wilborn, lying on her back in a dark pool, her eyes open and looking at him. In his dozen years on the police force, Tigert had seen many bodies, but the body of the young girl was something he wasn't prepared for; he was trembling as he backed out of the room. All he could say to Perez was "Find the light switch." Perez had already turned away and was running the beam of his light along the basement wall. Upstairs, they could hear dogs and the movement of many sets of feet.

Upstairs, Soders and others were attempting to question Gavrel, who was so befuddled from shock and loss of blood he couldn't even tell them where he had been shot, much less who fired the bullet. Gavrel kept telling Soders, "Get an ambulance."

Outside, Bev Bass watched the ambulance arrive. More numb than hysterical now, she followed the ambulance attendants to the door, watched as they loaded Gavrel on the stretcher, then followed them back to the ambulance. Paul Goheen, one of the ambulance attendants, also recalled that Gavrel didn't know where he'd been shot or who shot him. "Just get me out of here," Gavrel told the ambulance attendants. "He's going to come back and get me." Who? Hell, Gavrel didn't know *who*. Just get him out of here fast. Goheen would also say that as they loaded Gavrel into the ambulance, the victim handed him two Baggies of what appeared to be marijuana. "Get rid of these," Gavrel supposedly said. Another ambulance arrived, and Bass watched as they carted out the body of Stan Farr. "I wanted to see if they had found Andrea," Bass said. "Then they told me she was dead too. All I said was 'Let's go.'" Apparently Bass said several other things. She told police that Cullen Davis was living at Karen Master's house and gave them the address and telephone number. She also told them that Cullen had a private airplane at Meacham Field. It occurred to her that Cullen might be attempting to escape in his Learjet. Then something *else* occurred to her. "You better get somebody out to Bill [Davis] and Mitzi's house," she said. "He might try to kill them too."

The same thought could have passed through the mind of Bill Davis. When he heard news of the killings a few hours later, he telephoned the sheriff and asked for protection, then herded his family to the attic and sat guarding the attic door with a shotgun until the deputies arrived.

Ken Davis, Jr., had also heard of the murders. Shortly after 4:00 A.M. he telephoned Cullen at Karen Master's home. Cullen told his brother he hadn't heard about the killings and that he'd been home "most of the night." He didn't seem particularly upset.

"What are you going to do about it?" Ken Davis asked.

"Well, I guess I'll go back to bed," Cullen replied.

Karen Master recalled that almost as soon as Cullen hung up from the conversation with his brother, the telephone rang again. It was an officer Ford from the Fort Worth PD, asking to speak to Cullen Davis. Cullen spoke briefly and hung up. Karen telephoned her mother, and while they were talking, the operator cut them off and said the police had an emergency call. It was Officer Ford again. He asked to speak to Cullen again.

Ken Davis telephoned a second time, then Officer Ford called a third time. This time Ford told Karen to "remain on the line."

Karen recalled: "We had both started getting dressed. I held the phone to my ear. Every few minutes Officer Ford would come back on the line and say, 'You still there?' He wouldn't let me hang up until Cullen was completely dressed and outside in the yard."

By now Karen Master's house in Edgecliff was surrounded by police cars. In one of the cars sat David McCrory, who had intercepted cops at the hospital and led them to Master's house. At 4:30 A.M. Cullen walked outside and surrendered. His Cadillac, which had been seen as late as 11:50 P.M. at the garage downtown, was parked in the driveway—the pickup that Cullen had driven from the garage earlier was now parked in another downtown garage. Before police took him downtown, Cullen led them to four pistols stashed in his Cadillac and a fifth handgun inside the house. As it turned out, none of the five guns was the murder weapon.

In the massive investigation that followed, Tarrant County Sheriff Lon Evans recalled a curious connection. In June, less than two months before the murders and at roughly the same time Cullen was attending his high school class reunion, two teenagers playing on the banks of the Trinity at the edge of the Davis estate discovered a Colt .45 automatic equipped with a silencer. The gun didn't appear lost, it appeared *abandoned*. It had been recently cleaned, inside and out, and there was no trace of fingerprints. The sheriff had pretty much dismissed the .45, but now he thought again about it and asked Federal Alcohol, Tobacco and Firearms agents to attempt to trace its ownership. They traced it to Roy Rimmer, Jr., Cullen's best friend.

For most of his thirty-eight years District Attorney Tim Curry had prepared himself for a career in law, but nothing in his background anticipated the case that was dropped in his lap on the morning of August 3. Curry grew up in Arlington Heights. He'd known the Davis family for years, though not well. In the late 1950s when he was attending AHHS, Curry's world orbited around places like River Crest and families like the Davises. Curry was nearer the age of Bill Davis, but he knew Cullen by name and reputation. "Cullen was the kind of guy nobody paid much attention to," Curry said. What one did pay attention to was the family name. Stinky Davis's son . . . accused of murder? Tim Curry wasn't ready for that.

The Tarrant County DA came from an impressive line of lawyers and judges. His great-grandfather had been an appellate judge in Tennessee, and nearly every male in the Curry family had gone into some branch of law. Curry had pressed hard through Baylor Law School, twenty-seven straight months without a break, and he'd been admitted to the bar when he was barely twenty-three. He'd never thought about being a prosecutor. It wasn't his style. "At a very early age," Curry said, "I decided that I wasn't going to work for anybody if I could help it." Besides, for as long as he could remember, the office of prosecutor in Tarrant County had been synonymous with scandal and malfeasance. In the early 1970s when the incumbent DA resigned in the latest storm of controversy, a group of prominent Fort Worth lawyers decided that one of their own, Tom Zachery, should run for the office. Shortly before the special election Zachery backed out. The lawyers turned to Curry and he agreed to run. Curry was elected in

1972, then reelected for a full four-year term in 1974. Cullen Davis made a $250 contribution to Curry's reelection campaign. In the interim, Curry had dropped out of Fort Worth society altogether. Instead of attending the Steeplechase and dances at River Crest, Curry began spending all his free time outdoors, hunting and fishing. On the walls of his office in Tarrant County's turn-of-the-century courthouse hung many trophies—an eight-pound bass, several Sonora javelinas, a near-record mule deer. Curry kept a suit and tie in his washroom for appearances in court, but he normally worked in boots and jeans. Curry was no longer interested in Fort Worth gossip—he was only vaguely aware of Cullen's mansion and the divorce suit—but on the morning of August 3 he had the sinking feeling that he was about to be reintroduced.

From the beginning, the case against Cullen Davis seemed open and shut. Though both Priscilla and Bubba Gavrel remained in intensive care and had been unable to make statements, it seemed likely they would corroborate Bev Bass's story. Meanwhile a team of police and DA's investigators were collecting an impressive amount of physical evidence from the mansion. It all seemed to be there—the motive, the means, the opportunity. It seemed apparent to Curry that Cullen's best defense would be insanity. He recalled the 1966 J. Lloyd Parker murder case in which the heir to the Parker oil fortune was convicted of murdering his father, then sent to Rusk State Hospital for psychiatric treatment. Parker had recently exhausted his appeals and surrendered to authorities, but for ten years he had avoided prison. Curry thought that this sort of example should not be repeated in Fort Worth, and he moved quickly to have Cullen examined by Dallas psychiatrist Dr. John T. Holbrook. Just as quickly, Cullen's lawyers stopped him. Although Cullen had been in jail only a few hours, he had been visited by a number of attorneys including Cecil Munn, Hershel Payne, and Bill Magnussen. Curry had heard that famed Dallas attorney Phil Burleson, one of the defense lawyers in the Jack Ruby murder trial, had agreed to represent Davis.

Curry's next priority after the abortive psychiatric examination was to decide on the charge and recommend bond. That afternoon he gathered with his chief assistants, Joe Shannon, Tolly Wilson, and Marvin Collins, to discuss the case. Collins, the best contitutional lawyer on Curry's staff, brought up the possibility of charging the multimillionaire with capital murder. Under Texas law, a capital crime is a murder committed while in the act of another specified felony—robbery or burglary, for example. Collins noted that Judge Eidson had signed a restraining order almost two years before, barring Davis from "coming on or about the premises at 4200 Mockingbird." Collins argued that Eidson's order could be construed to mean that Cullen Davis committed an act of burglary and therefore an act of capital murder. Curry had serious doubts about the theory. He felt that the law might not be construed this way. Their only recourse was to file the lesser charge of murder, which carried a possible life sentence. Normally in the case of a double homicide, the DA would recommend bail at $40,000.

"That's peanuts to this guy," Joe Shannon said.

"Any bail we set is peanuts to Cullen Davis," Curry reminded him.

On Curry's recommendation, Justice of the Peace W. W. Matthews set bond at $80,000, twice the normal amount. Cullen paid the full amount in cashier's checks and walked out Tuesday afternoon, about sixteen hours after the murders.

When citizens of Fort Worth learned that the accused killer was walking the streets, all hell broke loose. Switchboards at the DA's office, Judge Matthews's office, and the *Star-Telegram* sizzled with calls from irate residents demanding to know who was looking out for justice. Between 8:00 A.M. and 9:00 A.M. Wednesday, the DA's office counted sixteen calls from persons demanding to know why the charge wasn't capital murder and what Curry owed Cullen Davis. Judge Matthews received about twenty-five calls, and the newspaper reported dozens of complaints. The DA met with reporters that afternoon to explain: "There was no

113

preferential treatment from anybody that I'm aware of. I've got three attorneys and four investigators on this, so I don't see how anybody could construe that to be preferential. A lot of people don't realize that a bond isn't to keep somebody in jail. It's to ensure they show up at their hearing." Curry added that if the judge had set the bond at $1 million, "he would have gotten out just as easily."

Judge Matthews put it less elegantly. He explained: "This man [Davis] probably will never hurt anybody again. He was just drunk . . . the police told me he was quite drunk, and they say when he gets drunk, he gets really mad."

The judge never explained how he came about the information that Cullen was drunk on the night of the killings. None of the dozens of cops who saw Cullen in the early morning hours mentioned that he had been drinking.

Joe Shannon, Curry's best criminal prosecutor, took charge of the investigation at the start. A former state legislator with a reputation for dogged conservatism, Shannon had also grown up in Arlington Heights, though he had never socialized with the wealthy families. For the next fifteen months Shannon devoted at least 90 percent of his time to the Cullen Davis case. But on August 3, the morning after the murder, Shannon found it difficult to connect the pieces. All he had to work with at the time was Bev Bass's sworn statement and the statements of the Clifford Joneses and the security officer, Smedley.

"The big problem for the first two days was trying to find out from Priscilla what happened inside the mansion," Shannon said. "Nobody had been able to talk to her. We talked to Gavrel very briefly that night [August 3]. His memory wasn't too strong. He was still pretty doped up after the surgery. He was saying, 'Yeah, I think it was Cullen Davis,' but not unequivocally. I had already talked to Bev Bass so I just assumed Bubba would make the same positive identification, but now I had my doubts."

The only people who had been allowed to visit Priscilla were Judy McCrory, who had relayed simple messages back and forth to investigators, and a priest, who had told Priscilla what she had instinctively known—that Andrea was dead. "There was a ton of evidence at the mansion," Shannon said, "but we couldn't make heads or tails of it. [Detective] Claude Davis's first theory was that Stan Farr had crawled around to the kitchen, leaving that line of blood. I disagreed because the trail of blood was too smooth. We had fingerprints, bullets, shattered glass, shreds of plastic, rivers of blood, and a nine-foot door with a hole in the center, but we were only guessing what happened."

It was a miracle that Priscilla Davis was even alive. The bullet that entered her chest made an unexplained turn to the left, barely missing the aorta, the main artery leading from the heart, as it passed through her body. Bubba Gavrel was hurt more seriously. The bullet had entered the left side of his abdomen, below the ribs, and was lodged near his spine. The bullet severed a vein attached to Gavrel's kidney, and he nearly bled to death before he reached the emergency room. Surgeons had stopped the bleeding but decided to leave the bullet lodged near the spine rather than risk the delicate surgery necessary for its removal.

On August 5, Priscilla was well enough to talk to investigators. Though she was still groggy and tubes were running out of her arms and chest, she told the story graphically, in that same slow-motion, highly detailed manner she would use many times in recalling the nightmare. Now investigators had a story to match the physical evidence. As they combed the mansion's 19,000 square feet, what they found was a perfect match. Every piece of the puzzle fit, just as the three witnesses described it. Crime scene investigators found fragments of the plastic bag at the spot where Priscilla said the man in black was standing when he shot her. More fragments were discovered near the door the gunman fired through to hit Farr, and still more in the basement utility room where Andrea was killed, on the sidewalk where Gavrel was shot, and near the breakfast room door, mixed there with the shattered glass. Everywhere the witnesses said shots were fired, investigators found plastic fragments. The plastic bag was discovered on the second floor near the master bedroom. The killer's final act before escaping had been to run upstairs. Why? The logical theory was that he was looking for Priscilla and understood her enough to realize that in moments of trauma she always retired to her bedroom.

All of the bullets were accounted for. One was in the basement, under Andrea's body. It was theorized that the killer reloaded after killing Andrea. Priscilla was shot once and Farr four times—two bullets were removed from Farr's body, and three more slugs were discovered near the spot where the two shootings took place. One bullet was in Gavrel's spine. Gavrel said that the killer had reloaded before shooting out the glass (these were the shots Priscilla heard as she ran down the hill), and three slugs with traces of glass were recovered in the breakfast room. A total of ten, all in place. An autopsy done on Farr's body corroborated Priscilla's story of his final desperate gasps for breath —one bullet penetrated his larynx, causing him to suffocate on his own vomit. Investigators also discovered part of Farr's bear claw necklace at the foot of the stairway where Priscilla had described the struggle. The pieces fell into place so neatly that investigators didn't look for any other theory.

More than forty fingerprints were lifted from the scene, but the only ones that were identified belonged to the maid and to Det. Claude Davis, who supervised the crime scene investigation. The thing that puzzled investigators was that none of the prints belonged to Cullen Davis. In fact, none of the physical evidence directly connected Cullen Davis to the crimes. With three eyewitnesses, it didn't seem to matter.

If anything worried Tim Curry, it was the lack of a murder weapon. They knew it was a .38 Smith & Wesson, but they didn't have it and, as it developed, never would. Curry knew about the Colt .45 with the silencer found abandoned on the riverbank two months earlier. "That silencer is a first-class job," Curry said. "It's no easy job to build a silencer for a .45. It's got to screw

116

inside. A silencer has only one purpose, to kill someone." Priscilla had reported a burglar at the mansion
about the same time that the .45 was discovered, but
that didn't help Curry's case. Nor did the fact that the
gun had been traced to Cullen's friend Roy Rimmer.
Even before the weapon was traced, Rimmer approached Sheriff Lon Evans. Rimmer told the sheriff
that he'd heard someone found a gun similar to one
stolen in a burglary of his home. Evans showed Rimmer the gun with the illegal silencer, but Rimmer said
he didn't think it was the same gun. Digging through
old reports, investigators discovered that Rimmer reported a burglary of his home in January 1972. Rimmer
reported extensive losses, including seven other weapons, but he failed to report the mysterious .45. Rimmer
explained that he apparently overlooked the .45 in filing
his burglary losses. Later, investigators questioned an
inmate in the state prison about the burglary. "He didn't
deny the burglary of Rimmer's home," Sheriff Evans
said, "but he denied taking the gun." Curry knew that
Roy Rimmer was heavily in debt to Cullen Davis, but
that didn't explain why Rimmer's gun was left on the
bank of the river a few yards from Cullen Davis's property. Rimmer's gun would remain one more mystery
in a crazy quilt of unresolved mysteries.

Cullen apparently didn't know it, but Curry's men
had him under constant surveillance; the DA hoped
that the defendant might lead them to the murder
weapon, and Curry didn't entirely dismiss the thought
that Cullen might run for it. But Cullen resumed his life
as though nothing had happened. He went to the office
every morning, usually had lunch at the Petroleum
Club, shot a little pool, and went home early to Karen's
house. A model citizen, in most respects. Now that the
initial outcry was subsiding, time was in Cullen's favor.
A majority of those in Arlington Heights couldn't bring
themselves to believe he had done it. A majority of
those at the Rangoon Racquet Club were already formulating the theory that Priscilla was trying to frame
him. "If Cullen wanted those people killed, he would
have hired a hit man," an oilman at the RCC pointed

out. Bo Rankin, who had known the Davis family since childhood, added that Cullen wasn't *crazy*. "I believe any man's capable of anything," Rankin said. "But if I were he and wanted to kill my wife, I would have been in Mexico City when it happened." "Or at least headed that way a few minutes later," another regular observed. It was all too improbable. *Impossible.*

Not everyone in Arlington Heights thought it was impossible. Some of the people who knew Cullen best harbored deep fears. "If he did it," a woman friend said, "I don't want to know." A male acquaintance remarked, "I'm not saying Cullen did it, but if he *did* . . . you'd just have to know Cullen Davis to know why he'd want to do it himself."

The drinkers at the Rhinestone Cowboy were too stunned to pass judgment just yet. "I'm still having a hard time believing this," said Ron Bradshaw, who had fired Stan Farr just two weeks earlier. "Stan . . . he would do anything for you." Sandy Pierce, an employee, agreed—Stan Farr didn't have an enemy in the world. "What can I say . . . he was a real nice guy. Everybody who came in here liked him," Ms. Pierce said. "He was a built-in bouncer. He was so big. He wasn't rough. He would just pick up somebody who was giving trouble and carry them out. That's all. Then he'd laugh about it and everybody would keep on having fun."

Bubba Gavrel's family and friends found it equally hard to believe. "If this could happen to Bubba," a friend said, "it could happen to anyone." The Gavrels were relative newcomers to Arlington Heights, having moved up from the Greek community on Hemphill Street. They were described as "pickup trucks and beer people, as opposed to Ford and wine. Coarse, below the salt people . . . but good people." Privately, friends worried that Gus Gavrel, Sr., might "do something crazy," like shoot Cullen Davis. But the revenge Gavrel Sr. had in mind was more conventional—a few weeks after the shootings he filed a $13-million lawsuit against Davis. It was the first of many lawsuits filed in conjunction with the slaughter.

Jack Wilborn's friends were also concerned. No one

had ever seen Wilborn in such a state. No one had ever seen him cry, but in the days just after Andrea's death tears seemed his only relief. Wilborn kept remembering how he was supposed to drive to Houston and bring Andrea home. If only he had done it. For some reason he kept remembering the last time Andrea had gone with him to his office. It was just a few days earlier, but it seemed ages. "I remember she wanted some cookies," he said. "There was a cookie shop near there, but I drove right past. I would buy a carload of cookies if I could do it over. Andrea . . . she was so sweet. She could look at you and you'd melt." Jackie Jr. had been away at camp when Andrea was killed. Wilborn met his son at the airport Tuesday afternoon and in a tearful reunion told him that his sister was dead. For some reason, Wilborn couldn't bring himself to tell Jackie about his mother. Maybe deep inside, Jack Wilborn thought Priscilla got what she deserved, but Andrea . . . *why*? Of all the enigmas and impassioned kinks and whims and dirty tricks and inexplicable crossings, why *Andrea*? There was no answer and perhaps never would be. In the weeks that followed, Jack Wilborn became a born-again Christian. He resigned from the Petroleum Club and swore off cards; he still cried, but he prayed more than he cried. "It was the first time I ever made a commitment to God," he said many months later. "I told God—I'm not bargaining. I'll take what You give me. Then the pain began to vanish. I'm not saying there aren't days. even weeks, when I can hardly function, but I'm able to handle it."

Bev Bass had gone into seclusion. For several days after the killings. her parents kept her at home, and a few weeks later they drove her to Lubbock and enrolled her at Texas Tech. After that, about the only people who ever saw Bass were her parents and the Gavrels. She became more than Bubba's girlfriend; she became his nurse and his strength.

As the investigation continued through the second week of August, Tim Curry began to reconsider Marvin Collins's arguments for capital murder. Collins was a sturdy advocate; not a day went by when Collins didn't

119

collar Curry or one of the assistant DA's with some new case history he'd dug up in support of his theory. The theory was this—Cullen Davis entered a habitation with the intent to commit another felony, *murder*. There was no dispute that it was his own house. But he was under civil injunction to not enter that property. The question was this: *was he in fact the owner?* The law broke the question into three parts. An owner is, number one, the person who has title to the property; or number two, the person who has possession of the property, whether lawfully or otherwise; or number three, the person who has greater right to possession of the property. Number three was the key to this case, Collins believed. Gradually, Curry and Tolly Wilson came to agree. Joe Shannon was the last holdout. Shannon recalled: "My thinking was, it just ain't right. The legal aspects ain't good."

By the third week of August, Collins had finally convinced Shannon that the theory was legally sound, but Shannon was still reluctant to reindict Cullen Davis on charges of capital murder. This time his reasoning was not legal but practical. "First," Shannon said, "I don't think a jury will ever give a guy like this death. But my biggest reluctance is the advantage it gives the defense. First, they would demand an immediate writ hearing to smoke out our evidence. We'd have to show our cards in order to convince a judge to hold him without bond. Then when we did get to trial, a charge of capital murder would allow the defense individual voir dire in questioning jurors. Our best shot is go with straight murder where the defense has to question the jurors as a group."

As Curry listened to Shannon's objections, it occurred to him that there was yet another, overriding argument in favor of *Collins's* position—by charging Davis with a capital crime they could probably hold him without bond. As long as Cullen Davis was in jail, Curry could be sure that the defense would cause no great delay in the trial. A fast resolution would be to everyone's advantage. By now Phil Burleson and one of his associates, Mike Gibson, had taken charge of

Cullen Davis's defense. They had hired an ex-FBI agent to head up their own investigation and gave every indication of spending whatever amount they thought necessary to free their man. Curry heard rumors that Davis was considering hiring famed Houston trial attorney Richard "Racehorse" Haynes. Even if the rumor was false, it was apparent to Curry that Cullen's men intended to play hardball.

Still another assistant DA, Jim Bennett, had come around in support of Collins's theory, and now Curry and his staff stood four against Shannon's one in favor of capital murder. What happened next made the vote academic. On the morning of August 20, one of Curry's investigators reported by radio that Cullen was in his Cadillac headed for Meacham Field where his Learjet was serviced and ready for takeoff.

"Maybe he's just going out to Meacham to have breakfast with the boys," Joe Shannon deadpanned.

"Maybe he's flying to Brazil for the sun," Tolly Wilson speculated.

"Not on my ulcers he ain't!" Curry said. The DA had already received an attachment from the court ordering Davis to appear before the grand jury, and Curry instructed his men to use the attachment and haul the defendant downtown. By 10:00 A.M. Davis was charged with capital murder and was back in jail, where he would remain for the next year.

As anticipated, Phil Burleson and Mike Gibson immediately filed a writ of habeas corpus demanding that the prosecution show cause why the defendant should be held without bond. A bond hearing was convened four days later in the 213th District Court of Judge Tom Cave. After hearing testimony from both sides, Cave would have to decide if a future jury was likely to find Davis guilty and sentence him to death. If so, he would order the defendant held without bond. During the four-day bond hearing, both Priscilla and Bubba Gavrel testified from their wheelchairs. Both positively identified Cullen as the man in black. The prosecution didn't call Bev Bass to testify; perhaps they wanted to save her for the murder trial, although somewhere down the line the defense was almost sure to get her on the witness stand and probe for flaws in her story.

After being forced to reveal his case, Curry was curious to see if the defense would attempt to float an alibi or opt for a defense of insanity. They did neither. Cullen Davis's attorneys intended to keep Curry guessing, as long as they could. Instead, they called Water Strittmatter, chief financial officer of Kendavis Industries, who testified that it was imperative to the success of the company that Davis be free on bond. Strittmatter revealed that Cullen was $14 million in debt. Because of the divorce proceedings and other legal matters, his assets were frozen. Though Davis had money in "in excess of twenty banks," Strittmatter continued, it was there to secure loans and could not be removed. In this exchange with Marvin Collins, Strittmatter established that there was probably no bond the court could set that Cullen Davis couldn't pay out of his pocket.

Q: If Mr. Davis could raise ready cash right now, how much could he raise?
A: I'd have to talk to some banks.
Q: Could you raise $1 million?
A: I'm pretty sure I could.
Q: Could you raise $2 million . . . in a week?
A: Yes, I could.

Collins asked the financial expert to estimate the assets of Kendavis Industries, but Strittmatter turned to Judge Cave and replied that he was under court order not to talk about it. The courtroom broke into laughter for the first time during the tedious hearing; even Cullen Davis permitted himself a grin. The court order Strittmatter made reference to was perfectly timed. Only the previous day the federal court had dismissed Bill Davis's lawsuit because of "a pending out-of-court settlement." At the request of Cullen's lawyers, the judge in this case ordered all previous testimony sealed and all parties silenced. At whatever cost (and however late) the Davis brothers had at last put the lid on the family secrets. Or so it seemed. A rumor quickly circulated that the settlement involved a cash payment of $40 million.

The defense called several other witnesses including Ken Davis, Jr., but the witness who galled Tim Curry was Dr. John Holbrook, the psychiatrist whom Cullen refused to see on advice of his attorneys. It turned out that Holbrook had later examined Cullen on behalf of the defense. Holbrook testified that, in his opinion, Cullen Davis was not going to commit violent crimes against anybody in the foreseeable future.

On August 27, without comment, Judge Tom Cave denied bond.

Several other things were happening in the late summer of 1976. Stan Farr's family filed a $9-million civil suit against Cullen Davis, and Farr's ex-wife, Karen Elizabeth Farr, intervened with a separate suit. Jack Wilborn also filed suit, asking $325,000 for his daughter's "wrongful death." In light of Wilborn's grief this was a surprisingly modest sum, but no amount of money would alter the fact of Andrea's death. While Priscilla was still hospitalized, Dee Davis was injured in the car wreck that killed her boyfriend, Brent Cruz. Ex–FBI agent Joe Myers was snooping around, asking a lot of questions about Priscilla's private life, but he wasn't getting many answers. Myers was soon replaced by Steve Summer, a young attorney associated with Phil Burleson. David McCrory was quite active, flitting around town as though he, too, had become an instant celebrity Several hours after the killings McCrory and Pat Burleson (Phil Burleson's cousin, though the two men had never met) went to the mansion, where several dozen cops were attempting to figure out what had happened McCrory's mission was to recover a valuable ring that Priscilla had left in her purse, but the purse had already been gathered up as evidence.

Trial lawyers all over Texas were shocked when they heard that Judge Tom Cave had ordered Davis held without bond. One of the legislators who sponsored the new capital murder law said: "That wasn't the purpose of the law. They're talking about a damn civil injunction from a divorce court. We never meant that to be interpreted as burglary." But Cave had interpreted it that way, and in the months that followed so did the

Texas Court of Criminal Appeals, a U.S. district court, a federal appeals court, and finally, two justices of the Supreme Court of the United States. Marvin Collins's farfetched theory was upheld by every court in the land. The defense hired Watergate lawyer Sam Dash to argue their appeal to the Supreme Court, but Collins's theory prevailed.

One lawyer who wasn't especially surprised when the state appeals court rejected Cullen's efforts to get out on bail was Phil Burleson, the head of Cullen's swelling team of highly paid defense lawyers. Burleson wasn't surprised, but he wasn't worried either. One of the best criminal lawyers in Texas, he knew from experience that cases such as this weren't won or lost in these early skirmishes. Burleson learned his basics moonlighting as a briefing clerk for the Texas Court of Criminal Appeals and later served with distinction as chief of the appellate section under Dallas's notoriously tough DA Henry Wade. Probably no DA in America has sent more men to the executioner than Henry Wade.

The word generally used to describe Phil Burleson was *ruthless*. Burleson called himself tenacious, but whatever the word he didn't deny it. He knew hard times from personal experience. Back in Pennsylvania his family had had considerable wealth, but the bank got it all, and when the Burlesons moved to Texas in 1948, they were poor as doorknobs. Burleson worked his way through school doing odd jobs and surviving on a few hours' sleep when he could get it. On one of the many occasions when he was down and nearly out, he needed legal help. Someone with no insurance had totaled his pickup truck. An old Dallas lawyer took his case, and that's how Phil became interested in the legal profession. Years later, as chairman of the state bar grievance committee, Burleson had to suspend the old lawyer. "It was hard to do," he said. A lot of things in this profession were hard to do. Burleson built his reputation doing hard things. He remembered the day he'd walked in for an interview with Melvin Belli, who was looking for helpers in his defense of Jack Ruby. The famous San Francisco attorney had sized up the tall,

124

silver-haired Texan, admired his expensive, handmade, anteater cowboy boots and his immaculate three-piece suit, then asked a single question: "What do you think?" Burleson answered immediately, "With a lot of hard work and imagination, it's winnable." Belli liked that and invited Burleson to join him in defending one of the most famous killers of the twentieth century the man who killed the man who killed the president. Belli was the superstar, but Burleson helped engineer the famed *climate of hate* defense that took the spotlight off Ruby and put it on the city of Dallas.

Burleson knew that hard work and imagination could win the Cullen Davis case. "Anytime you have what purports to be eyeball witnesses, you have problems . . . until you *interview* those witnesses, put them to the test," Burleson said. "Volumes have been written on the subject. Judge Henry King, who had fewer reversals than any district judge who ever lived, had said that he'd much rather see someone convicted on circumstantial evidence than eyewitness testimony. First, human frailty is inherent in a person's ability to recall some event accurately. Second, you have perjury, intentional or not. You could testify that you saw Gregory Peck on the streets of Dallas, when in fact Gregory Peck was in Los Angeles. You *thought* that was Gregory Peck you saw."

Burleson therefore, was less concerned with the three eyewitnesses than with the physical evidence, or lack of it. He was sure that the state had more physical evidence than it had shown in the bond hearing but he couldn't find out what it was. Fingerprints? Bloody clothes? Traces of hair? Footprints? A gun? Another witness who saw the defendant near the mansion that night?

"There had been nothing in the papers, no speculation at all," Burleson said. "I thought that was strange While Cullen was out on bond, the DA asked us for a copy of his fingerprints, to which they were entitled. We took Cullen down to the police station to be printed, and while we were there, this crime scene officer Jim Slaughter must have thought we were detectives. He blurted out, 'Why do you want all these prints? You got three eyewitnesses.' At that point the real detectives were getting us out of the room fast, and I was beginning to think the prosecution didn't have all that much in the way of physical evidence. They were counting on the eyewitnesses to carry them through."

The eyewitnesses did appear to be a formidable factor, certainly to the public. There had never been a case in Fort Worth exposed to so much publicity. In the glare of daily media accounts, Cullen seemed as good as convicted. Burleson and Mike Gibson anticipated that at some point the publicity would begin to work in their favor—a witness might come forward, for example, to confirm Cullen's alibi—but so far the only news had been bad. The two Dallas lawyers decided their only course was to ride it out. "We were taking our lumps from the press," Gibson recalled. "Cullen especially didn't like it. When he'd read how Priscilla was popping off, he'd naturally want to answer back. We had to keep telling him: 'Cullen, let her try it in the newspapers. We'll try it in front of the jury.' "

Steve Sumner, the lawyer in charge of the investigation, was digging into the private lives of the eyewitnesses and beginning to turn up bits and pieces that could be useful. "We could use some of these things to swing publicity our way," Burleson said, "but we felt our best strategy was to let the prosecution go on posturing and feeling confident." Cullen's lawyers agreed that the pretrial publicity would make it difficult, maybe impossible, to get an acquittal in Fort Worth. They wanted to ask Judge Cave for a change of venue, a motion that the prosecution was likely to resist. But the lawyers' obstacle here wasn't the prosecution or Judge Cave; it was Cullen himself. Cullen wanted to be tried in Fort Worth. Insisted on it. These were his people. Priscilla was the outsider. There was a certain logic in Cullen's contention. Fort Worth was the home of Mid-Continent. Thousands of potential jurors worked for Mid-Continent or one of its subsidiaries, and many thousands more were friends or relatives of Mid-Continent employees.

One lawyer not connected with the case, who believed Cullen guilty, speculated, "If all he'd done was kill Stan Farr and Priscilla, they'd give him a medal." The so-called unwritten law still prevailed in the minds of Texas jurors: that it was permissible for a man to kill his wife and her lover, particularly if the killing took place in the man's own home. Cullen's lawyers were certain that the state would focus its attention on the murder of Andrea Wilborn, but there were many ways to distort this focus.

Cullen's lawyers later filed a motion for change of venue but withdrew it before Judge Cave had an opportunity to make a ruling.

Tom Cave originally set the trial date for October 11, but because of a delay in the bond appeal the trial was soon reset for February 21. Meanwhile, Domestic Relations Court Judge Joe Eidson scheduled final hearings in the divorce case for January 17, though no one except Eidson seriously believed that the divorce would be finalized while the murder case was still pending.

Priscilla was back in the mansion, recovering from her gunshot wound and other medical problems and trying to deal with the complications of her new status as principal witness in Fort Worth's most famous murder case. Mostly, she sat on the double queen-size bed with the silver fox spread and the stuffed animals and yellow-haired rag doll with the pink dress, using the bank of telephone lines to talk to her friends Judy McCrory, Carmen Thomas, and Lynda Arnold. Judy had filed for divorce from David McCrory and frequently spent evenings and weekends at the mansion. Sometimes Priscilla played Scrabble or backgammon with Rich Sauer, the new man in her life. Sauer had played basketball with Farr at TCU. There was always an armed guard downstairs, and the panel of lights on the bedroom wall told Priscilla that all locks were secure. Nevertheless, she kept a loaded .32 under her pillow. The master bedroom was just like before, except now there were dozens of laminated photographs of Stan Farr, the gentle giant, and of Andrea, Dee, and Jackie, and of course of Priscilla herself. Dainty little signs saying things like "Love is being able to let go" were mounted among the photographs.

Priscilla seldom left the bedroom. She had been advised by her divorce attorneys to "stay off the street," and when she did go out, usually late at night and only with her bodyguard and close friends, Priscilla wore the silver-plated .32 strapped to a custom-made holster on her right boot. For the most part, life outside her bedroom had been reduced to a single ritual: every evening as the sun set, Priscilla ventured downstairs and activated the controls that automatically slammed shut the mansion's many drapes, as though shielding out the night was her final measure of security. Friends marveled at her tenacity: how could she stay there in that museumlike chill, surrounded by art treasures and pursued by ghosts of that incredible night? They didn't understand: she had no choice. It was like a fairy tale, only in reverse. Rich little poor girl, a prisoner in her own castle. After all that had happened, the price she had paid, Priscilla was not about to walk out now. The memories sustained Priscilla and strengthened her resolve. When she went downstairs to close the drapes, she passed the door with the pink heart and the words ANDREA'S ROOM. For weeks after Andrea's murder, Priscilla would open the hotel-size refrigerator and discover small concoctions, cookies or half-baked cakes that Andrea had stored for a time that wouldn't come.

Dee came home from Texas Tech and personally supervised Thanksgiving dinner. Jackie Wilborn came to the mansion for the holiday. In some ways, Jackie had taken it harder than Dee. Jackie was only fifteen and had never lived under Cullen Davis's roof; it was difficult for Jackie to understand why Priscilla had not stayed with his father. All this wouldn't have happened. It was a valid question, one Priscilla couldn't touch. Priscilla's seventy-one-year-old mother came for Thanksgiving, and so did a niece and other relatives. What was there to talk about? With the help of a half-dozen TV sets and a blitzkrieg of football, Priscilla survived the family gathering. Her mother was already talking about *Christmas,* for godsakes. Priscilla wanted

128

to ask her: what makes you think there is even going to be Christmas?

Priscilla laughed when she heard that they were dropping her name (but not Cullen's) from the *Fort Worth Social Directory*. She didn't give a damn about that. But she felt the black crones circling. A group of "prominent citizens," including publishing heir Amon Carter, Jr., and power broker Babe Fuqua and some leading bankers, had petitioned to have Cullen released on bond. This was no mere act of charity or friendship; it was good business. They had a sizable stake in the welfare of the man who owed many millions of dollars and still controlled, even from his jail cell, one of the city's great conglomerates. For the first time in memory the subject of prisoners' rights had a majority of advocates at Colonial. The wife of a very rich, very prominent industrialist telephoned Priscilla and asked her to "let Cullen off the hook."

"At first I assumed she was talking about the divorce settlement," Priscilla said. "She pointed out that I had gotten a lot of nice things I never had before. She said how everyone knew Cullen was a weak person, but he wasn't the only person in the world with money. By now I'm catching on what she's talking about. She said, 'Priscilla, I think the best thing for you would be to move out of town and change your name.' I was dumbstruck! All I could think to say was: 'Well, my dear, we all have to answer to God.' "

There were those among the prominently rich who expressed sympathy and seemed to understand the full meaning of the tragedy. June Jenkins, wife of best-selling author Dan Jenkins *(Semi-Tough)*, sent a warm note from their winter home on the island of Kauai. Phyllis Rowan of the Rowan oil luminaries had mentioned "getting in touch with Truman [Capote]," who might be interested in writing Priscilla's story after he finished *Answered Prayers*. But when the hard core of high society talked about Priscilla Davis, as they did almost every day, they spoke of that platinum hussy with the silicone implants and the RICH BITCH necklace. A Fort Worth matron lunching at River Crest Country

Club said: "I'm tired of reading how Cullen and Priscilla were society. Why, the only time Priscilla ever appeared at any real Fort Worth society event was one year at the Steeplechase Ball, and you certainly don't want to talk about that. Everyone would really like to forget it. It was all about as sordid as the mess that came up later [the murders]. Priscilla . . . wore a dress cut down to her waist. I'm sure she didn't have a thing on underneath. She swept in and started dancing with everyone. It was not your usual debutante show." That was the year Cullen lost his cool and scattered everyone's car keys in the mud. The matron assumed that the source of his anger was Priscilla, but others suspected that it was Cullen's own unexpected humiliation that provoked the outburst. He *encouraged* Priscilla to dress that way, both before and after she shocked the Steeplechase Ball.

For whatever reason, because she had a sense of humor or maybe because the mystique was a handy bridge from where she had come from to where she was going. Priscilla didn't labor to correct these impressions. Several months after the murders, she granted an exclusive interview to two Associated Press reporters who, among other things, were curious about the rumor that Cullen had installed a ceiling camera over the bed to film their lovemaking. The interview took place in Priscilla's bedroom in the early hours of the morning, and when the reporters approached the subject of the alleged ceiling camera, Priscilla failed to point out that what the reporters took to be a camera was actually a fancy oscillating light fixture.

The AP men wrote: *A woman of some mystery, a target of high and low rumor, Priscilla swept away all pretenses, smiling wryly as she acknowledged talk about a movie camera focused from the ceiling on her bed below.*

"It doesn't even work," she said.

Again the smile: "I know what I'm doing. I don't need an instant replay. . . ."

To a magazine writer who was allowed to tour the mansion Priscilla revealed a greater insight into her

130

life with Cullen Davis. Standing on the balcony outside the master bedroom, looking at the twinkling skyline of downtown Fort Worth, she shook her head sadly and said: "I guess we both did some things to each other. But this . . . this is what we call *no-takesy-backsy*."

∽ • ∾

In his private cell downtown, where he conducted daily business meetings and had at his disposal a color TV and a bank of telephones, Cullen had reached a major decision. He had decided to add to his team of attorneys Richard "Racehorse" Haynes, the legendary Houston lawyer who had successfully defended plastic surgeon John Hill on charges that he had murdered his Houston socialite wife by poisoning her with French pastry doctored with cultures of human pus and excrement. Cullen had read about Racehorse Haynes in *Blood and Money*, the best-seller written by his AHHS classmate Tommy Thompson.

Even before he was asked to join the defense, Racehorse Haynes was intrigued by the Cullen Davis case. He first heard about the murders a few weeks after they happened, at a Texas Bar Association barbecue in Fort Worth. "I'm a lawyer who is for hire," he said. "I don't take all cases, just those that interest and intrigue me and where, more often than not, I make a fair fee. Besides, it's a Texas case. It starts off in a $6-million house. Television sold a $6-million man; that gets you a little bit interested, right?"

Haynes's own life-style befit his flamboyant reputation—a lavish home in Houston's exclusive River Oaks section, a forty-foot yacht, a Cessna, a $40,000 Porsche Turbo Carrera, a replica of the classic Excalibur motorcar, and enough motorcycles to kill himself eight times

131

over. There wasn't anything in Racehorse Haynes's life that wasn't a challenge, or the fruits of a challenge. He was a skydiver and a motorcycle racer and a champion of the hopeless cause. When he'd had a drop too much Scotch, he'd been known to race his motorcycle through motel lobbies. He once talked his way out of a drunk driving ticket by performing a back flip off the bumper of his Porsche. A man whose ego seemed to be on a permanent collision course with his courage, Haynes was absolutely convinced that with enough time and money he could win any lawsuit anywhere. If Nixon had hired him, Haynes once remarked, the man would still be in office. He could probably get Hitler off on a reduced charge of malicious mischief. He'd defended a motorcycle gang accused of nailing a woman follower to a tree, Houston cops charged with kicking a prisoner to death, the Speaker of the Texas House of Representatives, and the grand dragon of the Ku Klux Klan. The only thing special about Cullen Davis was his enormous wealth, but of course that *was* special; Davis was the richest man ever brought to trial for murder in this country. Haynes liked to envision his own epitaph: "His fees were outrageous, but he did a good job." Though he had attracted national attention in the John Hill murder case, Haynes's reputation remained primarily regional. He wasn't yet mentioned in the same breath with Edward Bennett Williams, F. Lee Bailey, or Percy Foreman.

Early in life Haynes dreamed of being a decathlon athlete. He wanted to do it all, faster, longer, higher, and with more skill and endurance than anyone had done it before. The son of a plasterer who grew up in a tough, blue-collar enclave of north Houston, Haynes was built on the order of a refrigerator. "I grew up to be a midget," he claimed. He didn't remind anyone of a midget Long before he became a famous attorney, Haynes could fill a room with mere presence. People sensed that he was a fierce competitor, that he didn't back down. A nose spread over his face like the blade of a bulldozer testified to the fact that he didn't back away from many fights. As an eighteen-year-old he was

Texas Amateur Athletic Federation welterweight champion and was known as a battering-ram running back at Houston's Reagan High School. The name Racehorse was originally a slur, directed at him by a junior high football coach chiding his habit of running toward the sideline. "What do you think you are," the coach rebuked him in front of his teammates, "a racehorse?" The name stuck, not without Haynes's encouragement. He liked the name, liked the image it connoted—fast, sleek, ready for the distance.

If any man was truly self-made, Racehorse Haynes was self-made. In 1944, a few weeks after graduating from high school, Haynes enlisted in the navy. He was awarded the navy and marine corps medal for saving two lives at Iwo Jima. There had never been a professional man in his family, and Race toyed with the notion of becoming a lawyer. But civilian life wasn't taking him anywhere, and four years after he was discharged from the navy, he joined the army paratroopers with the idea of making a career in the military. It was during this period of duty that he began considering the law again. It came about when a young enlisted man from his company was accused of stealing food from the mess hall. Race knew a little about law—he used to cut class and watch Percy Foreman perform his fire-belching magic—and he was appointed to defend the accused food thief. In those days the Uniform Code of Military Justice didn't provide the accused with a genuine attorney in misdemeanor cases. Nor did it prohibit hearsay evidence. Haynes's client was convicted on the testimony of a witness who told the court what a sergeant told him someone else said. "I checked the book," Haynes recalled. "That was hearsay *twice removed*. I brought this up to the major who was the presiding officer at the court-martial, but he said, naw, it the witness *said* he heard the sergeant say that's what he heard, it's admissible. The kid was selectively prosecuted, then convicted on double hearsay. The inequity of that situation fired me up to the point that I decided to head for law school."

In 1954, Haynes entered law school at the University of Houston, supporting himself with the GI Bill and an assortment of odd jobs that included lifeguarding and hustling pool. He was already married (Race and his wife Naomi have been married twenty-seven years), and Naomi also worked full time. Even in college Racehorse Haynes understood the value of publicity. He was elected student body president after a story circulated around campus that he announced his campaign by parachuting out of an airplane into the campus reflecting pool. It never happened, but it was some years before Haynes got around to setting the record straight. People still swear they saw him jump. Years later people would perpetuate another myth, that Haynes won an acquittal for the motorcycle gang accused of nailing a woman follower to a tree by nailing his own anesthetized hand to the jury box during his closing argument. It became known as the Crucifixion Case (Race claims he took it because it was the first crucifixion case to come along in 2,000 years), and Haynes was no doubt *prepared* to nail himself to the jury box. "I've always regretted that my case was so strong I was able to win without doing that," he says, now that myths are unnecessary to the furtherance of his considerable reputation.

The mythical parachute jump got Haynes his first case. Some University of Houston students charged with violating the state's tough laws against open saloons knew the myth and hired Haynes to defend them. Haynes went first to the law library, then to the medical library where in a few days he made himself an expert on the subject of intoxication. He won the case. It was that expertise on intoxication that set him on his course. Over the next few years he built up his practice by defending hundreds of clients accused of driving while intoxicated. In the early 1960s he won 163 straight DWI cases.

While a large percentage of his law school class became assistant prosecutors or ambulance chasers, or disappeared into some dusty corner of a major law firm, Haynes devoted almost all his attention to the defense of those accused of crimes.

"I never had the stomach to be a prosecutor," he said. "Prosecutors remind me of bullies. I don't like bullies, never have. Look at any indictment. The State of Texas versus Smith. The whole *State of Texas*. Or the United States of America versus Smith. My God!" On the other hand, personal injury cases weren't practical for a young attorney in Houston. They took months, sometimes years, to get on the docket. The client, who was usually injured physically or financially or both, couldn't afford to wait. "They needed money for household expenses, for doctor bills, for X rays, for reports," Haynes said. "Lawyers who took these cases had to support the clients with their own money, which I couldn't afford. If you got to court, you'd go against some large insurance company. They wouldn't send some young, inexperienced lawyer who was your contemporary to court; they'd send some old mossback with thirty years' experience. Even if you won, it would go to appeal. It might be years before you saw any money." But there was something else about criminal law, something that appealed to Haynes's ego and to that unnamed something that some men feel in their guts when they know they've saved a fellow human from what Race calls the Crossbar Hilton. The first felony case he ever tried involved a poor black charged with theft. The fee was $300 and he won an acquittal.

Haynes recalled: "As soon as we heard those words *not guilty*, ol' Jesse was hugging me, his big fat wife was hugging me, his eight kids were hugging me, his relatives were slapping me on the back and saying thanks for saving Jesse and inviting me home to dinner. You don't get that feeling winning money from an insurance company. Then you go down to the bar where all the lawyers hang out. Everyone's saying *good going* and *attaboy!* . . . it's a damned good feeling, you know? I like that."

His mentor, Percy Foreman, first called Haynes's attention to the importance of the voir dire examination, the questioning of potential jurors by attorneys from both sides. Know your jurors, Foreman told Haynes— not just their names, ages, occupations, and religious

135

preferences; know their politics, their economic history, their family history, their medical history, their tolerance for human suffering, their ability to conceptualize beyond the scenario presented by the prosecution; know how they feel about dogs and cats and bald-headed Mexicans and atomic energy. A jury is like a computer, Haynes says: twelve components working together. "The thing has an average IQ of twelve hundred and four hundred years or more of living experience. It's scanning all the time, observing all the time, sworn to pay attention. A formidable machine!" Juries in criminal cases are required to render a unanimous verdict in order to convict. If Haynes picks his jury right, he feels he can convince at least one of the twelve that cobras make honey.

From his early success in defending clients accused of drunk driving, Haynes understood that lawsuits are not won by showboating in the courtroom—they are won by careful attention to detail and by hard scientific analysis. In each case Haynes prepared himself as if he were taking a final exam in criminology—he studied pathology, ballistics, psychology, crime scene investigation techniques, whatever was called for in a particular case. "Many cases have been lost because some chemist bamboozled the defense attorney," he said. In the case of an aircraft mechanic accused of murdering an airline insurance clerk, Haynes made himself an expert on nuclear-activation analysis. The prosecution's case hung literally by a hair recovered from the body of the victim: a scientist for the state analyzed the hair by a process known as nuclear activation and was prepared to tell the jury that the suspect hair could positively be identified as belonging to Haynes's client. "I went to the library and made myself the world's leading authority on nuclear-activation analysis," Haynes recalled. "I convinced the judge that it just didn't fit the legal requirements of that time for scientific evidence. The judge ruled that their scientist's testimony was inadmissible. On the basis of the remaining evidence, the jury voted nine to three for acquittal." He won another case by proving that the impact of an ornamental ball

136

and chain on a human skull was insufficient to cause death. In still another case he snatched victory after interrogating an empty witness chair.

When all else fails, Racehorse Haynes is prepared to win on pure gall. He explained this technique in a talk to an American Bar Association seminar: "Say you sue me because you say my dog bit you. Well, now, this is my defense: my dog doesn't bite. And second, in the alternative, my dog was tied up that night. And third, I don't believe you really got bit. And fourth [here he broke into a sly grin], . . . I don't *have* a dog." Haynes never went into court depending on a single theory or point of law. It was his style, his trademark in fact, to develop a number of simultaneous scenarios, each designed to cast doubt on his client's guilt. When it came time for his final argument, Race picked the one that seemed most likely to work.

A classic case was his defense of two Houston cops accused of violating the civil rights of a black prisoner by kicking him to death. The cops had already been acquitted of murder by a district court in Houston—now they were being tried in federal court on charges they violated the man's *civil rights* by kicking him to death. (The black man was arrested for attempting to "steal" a car that he in fact owned.) For starters, Haynes got the trial moved from Houston to the conservative German-American town of New Braunfels, Texas. "I knew we had that case won when we seated the last bigot on the jury," Race told a reporter later. As he developed his defense, Haynes contended (1) that the beaten prisoner suffered severe internal injuries while trying to escape; (2) that he actually died of an overdose of morphine; (3) that the deep laceration in the victim's liver was a result of sloppy work by the pathologist during the autopsy.

It was late September when Haynes first met Cullen Davis. Tom Cave's ruling denying bail was being appealed, and Davis had been locked up about four weeks. The bond appeal was taking up a lot of time, and they had only two months to prepare for pretrial hearings. It seemed to some courthouse observers that the defense also had a problem of competing egos. After all, Burleson was a star in his own right. For seven weeks he had been in charge of the defense, but now it was Racehorse Haynes who was attracting headlines. Burleson didn't see it as a problem. He'd recommended Haynes. "I'd worked with many topflight lawyers, and we'd never had problems," Burleson said. "Race and I had known each other since the 1960s, when I was in law school in Houston and he was first making a name for himself. Over the next ten years we referred cases to each other and knew each other socially. Having another topflight lawyer on the case was anything but a problem." The only problem, Burleson admitted, was briefing Haynes on all that had happened. "My time was worn thin," he said.

While Haynes, Burleson, and Mike Gibson worked on the legal aspects of the defense, young Steve Sumner worked the streets, gathering fragments of information, pursuing tips and leads, and interviewing potential witnesses. With a staff of five full-time investigators and anywhere from fifteen to twenty part-time investigators, Sumner quietly descended into the netherworld of the Fort Worth drug culture. For the first months his reports were not very encouraging. "We kept getting all kinds of tips and rumors about drugs and sex at the mansion," he said, "but most of them were dead ends. We couldn't find anyone willing to hit the witness stand." The defense lawyers recognized their inherent disadvantage: the state could subpoena anyone it wanted to appear before the secret grand jury, but nobody was required to talk to the defense. "You wouldn't believe the number of con men who approached us willing to say anything for a price," Sumner said. "One guy offered to name the real killer if we'd deposit $6 million in a Swiss bank. His story was that the killings grew out of a dope deal and there was a dope dealer in jail in Colombia who would testify for the right price. This guy lasted about fifeen minutes before I told him to hit the door." Sumner was acutely aware that the district attorney's office would like nothing better than to catch him in the act of bribing a witness. Sumner viewed every source as a potential double agent wired with recording equipment. "Sometimes I would play along to see if they really had information, but I made sure to get two things into every conversation—that we weren't paying any money and that all we wanted was the truth." For every source that Sumner interviewed, he eliminated maybe a dozen.

At first glance, Steve Sumner seemed an unlikely choice for the key cloak-and-dagger role he played in Cullen Davis's defense. In the 1960s he had been a star football and baseball player at Dallas Hillcrest High, but he'd never set any records for academics pretty much abandoning his college education for a career as a professional baseball pitcher. He showed great promise, pitching for the Houston Astros, Chicago Cubs, and Washington Senators, but in 1970 an arm injury forced him to retire suddenly and prematurely It was only after six years of professional baseball that Sumner decided to pursue another career. He picked law, almost at random. By the time he completed law school in 1975 Sumner was an honor student. He had been with Phil Burleson's prestigious law firm only about a year when he was asked to help on the Cullen Davis case.

From the beginning Sumner demonstrated an aptitude for hard work and practical logic. He quickly proved good at gathering evidence and screening witnesses but what impressed Cullen Davis was Sumner's ability to *connect* the bits and pieces. "I came to the conclusion very early that we were making drastic mistakes in our investigation," Sumner recalled. "Things like sending ex-cops out to find out about dope There was no way they could communicate with the young people we needed as sources. I think this is what impressed Cullen. It was Cullen who gave me a much larger role than I might have played otherwise."

The bits and pieces continued to collect, but by early December, less than two weeks before the beginning of pretrial, the defense didn't have a workable scenario. Sumner had an ambulance driver willing to testify that

Bubba Gavrel didn't know who shot him yet was sufficiently lucid to dispose of a marijuana stash before being taken to the hospital. And they knew by now about Bev Bass's abortion, including the fact that Priscilla paid for it and that the two women conspired to use Bass's sister's name on the clinic records. But only Cullen, with his engineer's mind, could connect these facts with the murders.

A few days before the start of pretrial hearings, Sumner asked Cullen if the name William Tasker Rufner rang a bell.

Cullen said it didn't.

"How about Larry Myers? Or Sandy Guthrie?"

"They don't ring a bell," Cullen said. "What does it mean?"

Sumner said he didn't know. At that point they were just names.

By the time Judge Tom Cave convened pretrial hearings on December 20, the defense had filed 102 motions for the court to consider. Among the witnesses called by the defense was Bev Bass. The barrage of questions directed at Bass seemed routine. None of the reporters covering the hearing saw the significance when Haynes asked the witness, "Have you had any operations in the last five years?" Bass replied with a shrug, "I've had my wisdom teeth out, that's about all." Haynes was more than content to let the answer slip through unnoticed. The fact that Bass lied about her September 1975 abortion was not yet for public scrutiny. What mattered to the defense was that Bass's lie was on record. To make sure no enterprising reporter stuck for a morning lead started digging, Haynes already had a headline for them. In the hallway outside Cave's courtroom, Race revealed to reporters the nut of his defense.

Casually, almost as though it were a slip of the tongue, the Houston lawyer said that at the proper time, "we will reveal the name of the true killer."

As the new year approached, the change of venue motion filed in October was still pending. It was a half-hearted motion, a technicality actually, filed in order to meet a court-imposed deadline, but Judge Cave had no way of knowing this. In retrospect, it seems likely that Cave was ready to grant the motion. It went without saying that any Fort Worth judge presiding over the fate of a man of Cullen Davis's stature was, to put it charitably, in a tight spot. The presence of Racehorse Haynes didn't make the job any easier. The judge and the distinguished Houston attorney had already locked horns on a number of pretrial issues, and it was bound to get worse. It was apparent that these squabbles were something more than differences in interpreting the law —the two men simply didn't like each other. Haynes hadn't yet formulated the simultaneous scenarios he would spool out to the jury, but Cave wasn't about to allow the attorney to float any red herrings in his court of law When the defense formally withdrew its change-of-venue motion, Cave didn't look happy.

By the time jury selection began on February 20, Cullen Davis had been in jail six months Though he had a private cell, Cullen hadn't exactly been alone. Jailhouse records revealed that during the months of November December and January, Davis received 399 visits to his cell. Sheriff Lon Evans denied that Karen Master had been allowed to visit her boyfriend, but he defended frequent visits by Davis's business associates. "You're talking about a man who owns eighty-three companies." the sheriff said, "not some convict up there. People come in every day with papers for him to sign and blueprints to look at. He's a busy man."

As the holiday season approached, Cullen and Karen mailed Christmas cards as usual. Dee Davis got one. Cullen also faithfully answered his fan mail, which, according to Hershel Payne, was considerable Hershel's own twelve-year-old daughter became one of Cullen's pen pals. When the attorney visited Davis's cell, he carried sealed notes that his daughter had decorated with hearts and flowers and little girl cryptograms like SWAK. Cullen seemed especially pleased with her latest report card and took time to write congratulations. Hershel Payne's daughter was a playmate of Andrea Wilborn's. By a curious coincidence, her name was also Andrea.

Cullen's attorneys were busy too. In an effort to counter the bad publicity—two magazine articles about the case appeared on the eve of the trial—they hired a press agent. Dallas public relations man Pierce Allman's first press release was a denial that he was a "press agent." He preferred to be called "media consultant" or "communications coordinator." Hiring Allman didn't establish a precedent in Texas—Dallas millionaires Herbert and Bunker Hunt also employed a "media consultant" during their successful defense against federal wiretapping charges. With jury selection under way, Allman rented a hotel suite and invited media people to drink and enjoy hors d'oeuvres, courtesy of Cullen Davis. Allman denied that it was a "press party." It was a "briefing session." Whatever it was, it backfired. Media accounts of the party made it sound as though Cullen were trying to buy the press; he was, after all, an accused murderer, not a politician running for office. Almost as quickly as he was hired, Pierce Allman vanished and no more was said about "media consultants."

After eight weeks of jury selection, only eight jurors had been seated. Cave had sequestered the jury, which meant that as soon as a juror was selected, that juror became a prisoner of Tarrant County—sequestered jurors had even less freedom than the defendant, who was at least allowed to confer with associates and talk freely on the telephone. Sequestered juries are a problem under any conditions, but in a case where it might take four months just to fill the jury box, the situation was fraught with danger. On April 13, six weeks to the day after the first juror was seated, the whole thing blew apart. It was revealed that the fuse had been burning since March 7, when the second juror chosen, Elizabeth Panke, requested permission to visit her terminally ill father in Elmhurst, Illinois. Cave granted the request. Though Mrs. Panke was accompanied by a court bailiff, she made several unauthorized telephone calls outside the bailiff's presence. Cave received information that in at least one call she discussed the Cullen Davis case. Mrs. Panke denied this, but it placed Cave in a tenuous position. Since none of the other seven jurors knew about Mrs. Panke's conversation, many attorneys felt that Cave could merely dismiss Mrs. Panke and continue the process of jury selection. But Cave wasn't sure. He announced from the bench that he wanted to study the case law overnight.

The next morning Cave brought with him a copy of the Texas criminal code. To the hushed crowd in the courtroom the judge read a passage that declared a new trial must be granted in felony cases "where a juror has conversed with any person in regard to the case."

Solemn-faced and trembling, Cave said, "It therefore becomes the clear duty of the court to declare a mistrial of this case at this time."

Cave's proclamation hit like a thunderclap. Three weeks of pretrial and eight weeks of jury selection down the rat hole. It seemed to Haynes that Cave had pounced on the opportunity to get rid of the Davis case, and outside the courtroom, Race issued several of his own proclamations. "The net effect is it has denied Cullen Davis the acquittal he is entitled to," Haynes told reporters. What it really proved, he continued, was that the state's case against his client was so pitifully weak they needed more time. Tim Curry replied curtly, "We have been ready, are ready, and will be ready the next time to try this case." At the mansion, Priscilla issued some proclamations of her own. "Their defense is shaky and anything they can do to gain more time, they will do it," she said. Then she added a personal note: "It's postponing my whole life."

At this stage, Tom Cave wasn't waiting for someone to file a motion for change of venue. Cave could do it himself. He had concluded that there was no way the trial could continue in Tarrant County. He was already looking for another city in Texas, preferably one far from his doorstep.

Cullen's attorneys returned to the problem of getting their man free on bond. It was going to be difficult, if not impossible, since two Supreme Court justices had already refused to hear the appeal. They needed new evidence that would force Cave himself to reopen the question of bond.

That's when Steve Sumner found David McCrory, or maybe it was the other way around. Whichever Cullen's old pool-playing buddy from the days of the Pink Elephant met with defense attorneys and told some amazing stories. The following morning the attorneys filed a motion for a new bond hearing and presented a 113-page document contending that a drug dealer named William Tasker Rufner "once threatened to kill everyone" at the mansion. Attached to the thick document was David McCrory's affidavit.

This nine-page document read like pages from the Inquisition indicting Priscilla Davis on a number of morals charges and pointing the finger at one W. T. Rufner. McCrory's scenario began with the trip to Boston. "When Priscilla and W. T. arrived," the affidavit said, "they brought with them some cocaine pills and marijuana. I personally observed Priscilla Davis and W. T. Rufner using cocaine, pills, and marijuana while in Boston." Rufner supposedly told McCrory "that he planned to get Priscilla hooked on drugs so that he could make a 'customer' out of her." McCrory's affidavit recalled more drug incidents and wild parties at the lake a few month later after he moved back to Fort Worth. "In fact Priscilla said to me that she was taking [he daughter] Dee to some parties at the lake and in their home and thought it was funny" that Dee was there.

After Cullen moved from the mansion the affidavit continued Rufner and a number of dope dealers moved in. McCrory named "Larry Myers. Larry's girlfriend by the first name of Sandy, and other people whose names I don't recall at this time." Priscilla supposedly told McCrory that these people were "dealing drugs out of Cullen's house." McCrory recalled parties at the mansion in which "I saw people using drugs heroin, cocaine, and LSD. I personally observed Priscilla Davis snorting cocaine and heroin. . . ." At the same time, the document continued, Priscilla was drinking heavily and taking pills.

Next McCrory described what he believed to be the breaking up of Priscilla's romance with Rufner: "I saw

W. T. Rufner pick up a large plant and throw it in the bathtub. Priscilla Davis then came running out of the bathroom, nude, yelling, 'Get that son of a bitch out of here.' I then walked up to W. T. Rufner and tried to calm him down. At this point, W. T. Rufner pulled a gun, which I believe to be a .357 magnum pistol. He then stuck the gun in my stomach and threatened to kill me. I told W. T. Rufner, 'You don't want to kill me or you would have already pulled the trigger. So why don't you put the gun down.' Rufner then did put the gun down. That same evening, W. T. cut the head off of a teddy bear that Priscilla had bought him and threw the stuffings from the teddy bear around the room. Later, this same evening, I heard W. T. Rufner threaten to kill Priscilla Davis. W. T., at one point, threatened to kill all three of us . . . Priscilla, Judy, and me. I believe that this is the evening that W. T. Rufner and Priscilla Davis split up their relationship."

Presently, the affidavit came to the fatal night of August 2, 1976. McCrory told of having dinner and drinks with Priscilla, Stan Farr, and the others. He recalled that "I had a headache that night and therefore did not have much to drink that evening." He also recalled that Priscilla offered him a Percodan, which he quartered and took, returning the unused three-fourths. He saw Priscilla take several Percodans that evening, the affidavit continued. Priscilla seemed "extremely nervous." McCrory added that "I have . . . never seen her so nervous and tense in my life."

It was approximately 1:30 A.M., McCrory recalled, when Carmen Thomas telephoned with the news that Priscilla had been shot. The McCrorys rushed to the hospital. At some point in the early morning hours McCrory recalled going into Priscilla's hospital room. There was no one else in the room during the conversation that followed.

"At this particular time," the affidavit continued, "I was curious as to what had happened. I was aware of the drug trafficking that had gone on at the house; I knew of Priscilla Davis's drug involvement, and I was thinking that these killings were probably related to some kind of drug deal. I asked Priscilla what had happened and Priscilla's comment was, 'You have to keep your mouth shut.' I said to Priscilla, 'What do you mean?' Priscilla replied, 'For once in your life, if you keep your mouth shut, you will never have to worry about money for the rest of your life . . . I'll have at least ten million dollars when this thing is over with, and you know what kind of power that brings.''

According to the affidavit, David McCrory was a very busy man during the next forty-eight hours. He managed to run across Bev Bass, who supposedly told him, "I don't know who [the killer] was, but out there in the yard [as both women were running for their lives] Priscilla told me it was Cullen." McCrory recalled that the next time he saw Bass, she was in Bubba Gavrel's hospital room and the two of them were rehearsing their story. Bubba allegedly said, ". . . all I saw was a flash; I didn't even see the guy," adding later, "I wouldn't know Cullen Davis if he walked in the room right now; I have only seen Cullen at a distance."

If Racehorse Haynes had hired a team of Hollywood writers he couldn't have come up with a better scenario than the one David McCrory provided. There was one problem McCrory had neglected to *sign* the document. "He didn't sign because there wasn't a notary available when we took his statement in the early morning hours," Haynes said. "The next morning we couldn't find McCrory." Haynes and Burleson decided to take a calculated risk: they presented the unsigned affidavit to Judge Cave, along with the 113-page document requesting a new bond hearing. "I felt this was a way to get in the door with new evidence, even if it wasn't signed," Haynes said. "We went to the judge and said this is what the man told us, even if he didn't sign."

The reason the defense attorney couldn't locate McCrory was because he was in the DA's office, giving yet another affidavit. Item by item, he refuted everything in the defense's affidavit. This one *was* signed. When Judge Cave compared the two documents he was so outraged that he held Haynes and Burleson in contempt of court. If there was any question about Cave ordering a change of venue, this settled it. Cave turned his full attention to finding another city that would be receptive to the Cullen Davis murder trial. Several judges who were contacted replied that they wouldn't touch the case with a stack of law books. Too close to home.

Then Cave thought of Amarillo. The Texas Panhandle city was a hard 350 miles northwest of Fort Worth, and people there were so isolated that they barely considered themselves a part of Texas. After a few telephone calls, it was done. The case was moved to Amarillo, and the new trial date was set for June 27, 1977.

THE RICHEST MAN
EVER TRIED
FOR MURDER

trip was on that day too. He had repeatedly told Priscilla to tell the truth. "If you've done something bad in your life," he had instructed her, "just pony up to it like a little soldier. Just say 'well, I mean it, I guess I

Amarillo was a randy, bull-headed, good-humored cow-town, the kind of town that Fort Worth used to be, back before the time of Cullen Davis and his generation. Fort Worth called itself "the place where the West begins." Amarillo *was* the West, if not the heart, then surely the spirit.

Though Amarillo was the quintessence of the Texas myth with its foundation in cattle, oil, and natural gas, it didn't feel or think like Texas. It was a part of the Great Plains, a semiarid plateau of rich grasses and painted canyons and deep underground wells. Squarely in the middle of the remote Texas Panhandle, hundreds of miles from the great population centers of Dallas, Houston, and San Antonio, Amarillo seemed less like a city than it did the capital of a territory. It was a place alone, geographically if not culturally closer to Oklahoma City, Santa Fe, Topeka, and Denver than to Austin. It was a place where a man still measured his wealth by the land he owned and was in turn measured by his peers on how he used the land. The land was flat, beautiful, and seemingly endless. Despite a few modest skyscrapers, the horizon stretched 360 degrees, and when a blue norther barreled down the Great Plains, you could hear it coming for forty or fifty miles.

Until the Comanches chased them off around 1700, the Panhandle was home for some more or less permanent tribes of Indians who practiced agriculture and constructed stone temples, the ruins of which could still be found near the Arkansas River. The Comanches were magnificent horsemen who roamed hundreds of miles, hunting, trapping, and sometimes raiding frontier settlements for horses and captives which they traded for Mexican whiskey and guns. Except for an occasional reprisal raid such as the one led by Kit Carson, no white man visited this land until the 1870s. That was when the white buffalo hunters defied the army and began to creep south of the Arkansas River. The Comanches retaliated in a bloody episode that became known as the Battle of Adobe Walls. It was the beginning of the end for the Indians. For the next year or so the U.S. Cavalry, which had originally been sent to keep the white hunters out of Comanche territory, pursued and killed Indians almost as recklessly as the hunters slaughtered the buffalo. By the 1880s the Comanches had been driven to the reservation and domestic longhorn cattle had pretty much replaced the buffalo.

Stinky Davis would have felt very much at home among those early ranchers. They were men of rampant enterprise: profiteers, speculators, adventurers, and roughnecks. Land around Amarillo was cheap and therefore the main commodity. The settlers used it like money, bartering it for goods and favors, using it to pay off gambling debts. Railroads were attracted by the state's offer of sixteen free sections, 640 acres each, for every mile of track they laid. Many of the early cattle empires were financed by English and Scottish investment bankers who never saw the land itself but understood return on the dollar. Even the state capitol building in Austin was a monument to nineteenth-century capitalism; a group of Englishmen financed it in return for the entire western edge of the Panhandle, a shoulder of land 45 miles wide and 195 miles long.

Many of the settlers were entrepreneurs from midwestern and northern industrial states who came not to raise cattle but to get in on the action inherent with cheap land. William Bush, whose grandchildren still own the Panhandle Ranch and the famous "Frying Pan" brand, came down from Chicago with instructions to fence the West. Bush's father-in-law, J. F. Glidden, was the first successful mass producer of barbed wire, and Glidden sent Bush and H. B. Sanborn to the Panhandle to market his wares. In those days the land was "checkerboarded"—meaning that every other section was given to the railroads—and the advantages of fences were obvious. It has been estimated that in one ten-year period in the late 1800s, 40 percent of the steel melted in this country became barbed wire. Bush and Sanborn bought 200 square miles of the Panhandle to demonstrate how well Glidden's wire could contain the onerous longhorn. Unfortunately, somewhere along the way, Glidden lost his patent and was soon priced off the market. Bush used his part of the land to found a great cattle empire, but Sanborn decided that the big money was in towns and set about establishing Amarillo. In 1889 the seat of government was located about a mile west of Sanborn's land. What the enterprising Sanborn did was build the Amarillo Hotel and bribe settlers to move around it; in some cases people literally moved their houses to the new township on sleds. The Amarillo Hotel became the town's first institution, a gathering place for anyone who had anything to buy, sell, trade, or gossip about. For years citizens of Amarillo bragged that the hotel on the corner of Polk and Third streets had the strongest whiskey, the loosest women, and the slickest card players for 500 miles. It followed that Amarillo became the seat of Potter County. Today, you don't hear much about Sanborn, but Bush is a revered name in Amarillo.

The Amarillo Hotel was torn down years ago, but the land around it remained much as it always had, checkerboarded with ranches of enormous size and controlled like feudal kingdoms by the heirs of the old cattle barons, most of whom supplement their income with oil or natural gas. No great reserves of oil were ever discovered in the Panhandle, but there was a great amount of natural gas. Amarillo also had helium in enormous abundance. The city advertises itself as "The Helium Capital of the World," though it has been years since there has been much demand for that particular element. Still, an estimated four-fifths of the Western world's helium reserves is stored in a ten-mile-wide natural underground dome located on the old William Bush ranch.

The cattleman remained the aristocrat in Amarillo

society. In its pure, traditional form, ranching became more a hobby than a business enterprise; it might be compared to riding to the hounds. Mother cows still bred and calves were still born on the ranches, but the big business became feedlots, where yearlings were fattened for slaughter. Cowboys scornfully referred to feedlots as "cow hotels." True "range-fed" beef is served only at the tables of the very rich or the very poor. Stanley Marsh 3, who is married to one of William Bush's granddaughters, explained: "Two groups founded Amarillo. The cowmen and the operators . . . the operators being anyone who used the land for any reason other than raising cattle. Of course in later years it was the operators who made the big money. The hardcore cattle raisers had to drill some oil or gas wells to make ends meet. But the love for the land *as* land . . . as opposed to dirt where you can drill a hole . . . is what separates society in Amarillo. It's not how much money you have that counts, it's how much land. The landed gentry rules this town and always has." Stanley and Wendy Marsh, whose 10,000-acre ranch is modest by local standards, serve only range-fed beef at Toad Hall, their sprawling home located on the site and constructed from some of the same stone used in the old Bush ranch house.

Stanley Marsh 3 (never III), one of Amarillo's wealthiest and most eccentric citizens, descended from that class he identifies as the "operators." He traced his ancestry back to Ohio, where his great-great-grandfather, Andrew Jackson Marsh, deserted the Union army, absconded with the maid and the church funds, and moved to Texas, where he learned the trade of water-well digging. He passed this skill down to his son and grandson, and when oil was discovered in the Panhandle around 1917, the original Stanley Marsh was well trained to get in on the action. The word *amarillo* is Spanish for "yellow," and the first Stanley Marsh used to advise, "Drill where the yellow mud is." In the years that followed, the Marsh family branched out into banking, cattle, television, and other ventures. Stanley Marsh 3 proudly listed his occupation as "capitalist." It wasn't until he married Wendy Bush O'Brien, however, that Stanley came to consider himself a cattle baron.

As befitted a man who had bridged the social structure of Amarillo, Stanley Marsh 3 became the town's ranking maverick. A wondrous teddy bear of a man in his late thirties, Stanley wore baggy jeans, sometimes with chaps and boots, and outrageous shirts with part of the tail hanging out. In a city like Dallas or Houston he would have been dismissed as merely another fruitcake, a man with too much money and time on his hands, but in Amarillo, where he controlled the local ABC affiliate TV station and sat on the board of several banks, he was a force to be reckoned with. He became infamous for his stunts. He conducted high-level business meetings with a pet lion at his feet and once showed up at former Gov. John Connally's bribery trial wearing purple chaps and carrying a bucket of genuine Texas cow manure. Other "capitalists" learned to step lightly when dealing with Stanley. A developer with plans to cram ticky-tacky houses on a tract next to Stanley's land woke one morning to discover an enormous billboard a foot away from his property line. It said FUTURE HOME OF THE WORLD'S LARGEST POISONOUS SNAKE FARM. Stanley's office was on the top floor of the tallest building in Amarillo. In fact it was the tallest building between Dallas and Denver, though, as Stanley explained, "everything in Amarillo is the biggest or best between Dallas and Denver." There wasn't much else out there.

Amarillo endured by its own means and style. If an occasional debutante still preferred to travel 400 miles and select her gowns from Neiman Marcus in Dallas, the majority of the fashion-conscious women in Amarillo relied on "trunk shows"—private showings, usually in the home of one of the city's well-to-do matrons, where they examined and ordered from the collections of famous designers. Amarillo was its own center for banking, for law, for medicine, even for the arts. Stanley Marsh 3, Amarillo's leading art connoisseur and patron, commissioned a number of nationally known works.

155

Stanley conceived of art as "a system of unanticipated rewards." He put one of his best-known commissions in a pasture along Route 66 just west of town. As motorists topped the crest, they were astonished to see ten Cadillacs nose down in concrete sheaths, standing at an angle exactly the same as the sides of the Great Pyramid. Other art objects, such as the *World's Largest Phantom Soft Pool Table* and the nationally known *Amarillo Ramp,* were set miles from the nearest road, unanticipated rewards for roving cowhands, passengers in low-flying aircraft, or refugees from long-lost wagon trains.

Amarillo was isolated, self-contained, and conditioned to independent thinking. Buck Ramsey, a local poet and philosopher who had been a working cowboy until he was crippled a few years ago, described Amarillo as "a place where they send their daughters east to be educated and keep their sons at home to learn how to be bastards like their daddies."

Amarillo was the perfect place to try Cullen Davis.

Tim Curry wasn't just trying to boost morale when he extolled the qualities of Amarillo and told his staff, "This is the best place in the country we could try this lawsuit." People here weren't likely to be intimidated by Cullen Davis's wealth, least of all Judge George Dowlen, a longtime prosecutor appointed to the bench less than two years before. Dowlen initially resisted taking the Davis case, but Curry pressed him, using the good offices of a mutual friend, Potter County DA Tom Curtis. Curry would come to rue this decision, but now, in the early summer of 1977, Dowlen and Amarillo seemed the perfect tandem.

A third-generation descendant of the resilient, God-fearing stock that settled the Panhandle, Dowlen had served for a decade as district attorney in adjacent Randall County. He was considered a fair man with a superior legal mind—they called him "the cowboy judge with the Boston brain"—but Dowlen made no bones about his deep-seated conviction that those who violate society's rules must be dealt with in the harshest terms. The prosecution was seeking the death penalty for Cullen Davis, and Dowlen had spoken out a number of times in favor of capital punishment. He had presided over three capital murder cases—a man accused of killing a jeweler in the course of an armed robbery; an ex-Amarillo cop charged with kidnapping and killing the daughter of a former state representative; and a habitual felon accused of blowing away a clerk while in the act of robbing a convenience store. All three had been convicted and sentenced to death.

Dowlen was a political conservative, but he was also a maverick: former Gov. John Connally once got a taste of Dowlen's independence. It was Connally who in 1964 appointed Dowlen to fill out the term of a district attorney who died in office, but later that same year Dowlen opposed Connally at the state Democratic convention. "I was basically a Connally man," he explained, "but in this particular case I thought he was wrong on the issues that affected my district."

Every lawyer in the Panhandle had a favorite George Dowlen story but the one that caught in the throats of many conservatives (and delighted liberals) concerned an incident involving a sixteen-year-old high school honor student charged with making an obscene phone call. During the course of a lovers' quarrel the boy had allegedly told his girlfriend, "Fuck you!" as he slammed down the phone. Dowlen, chief prosecutor at the time, thought it was a ridiculous charge, but a zealous assistant DA insisted on taking the case to trial and community sentiment clearly supported him. Dowlen finally agreed that the assistant could prosecute, but Dowlen reserved for himself the right to make final arguments. His final argument began like this: "May it please the court . . . ladies and gentlemen of the jury,

157

fuck you!" He paused and looked at the jury and said, "Now is that obscene or not?" Unfortunately, the jury thought it was. They found the boy guilty. Only Dowlen's final desperation plea for leniency saved the boy from prison. Nevertheless, Dowlen continued to receive support from the conservative faction. When Dolph Briscoe made his first run for governor in 1968, Dowlen and his father, a longtime county commissioner, were ardent supporters; Briscoe had pioneered the state's system of farm-to-market roads, and one of the first ran through the Dowlens' hometown of Ralph's Switch. In January of 1975 Governor Briscoe returned the favor and appointed George Dowlen to the bench of the 181st District Court in Amarillo.

Although he had been around politics all his life, Dowlen had never proven himself a strong candidate; both his offices, Randall County district attorney and Potter County judge, had come by way of appointment. But like Tarrant County DA Tim Curry, Dowlen would have to run for his office in 1978. The Cullen Davis murder trial would obviously be an issue, especially if Dowlen mishandled it. From his own experiences in Fort Worth, where public sentiment had originally run strong against Davis, Tim Curry reasoned that Dowlen would be more than fair in presiding over the prosecution's case.

Both sides admired something else about Dowlen—his comfortable, down-home sense of humor. If the judge was anything, he was a good old country boy with an aw-shucks smile. He was lanky and rawboned and usually chewing on a toothpick. Jurors felt at ease in his courtroom; lawyers found him pleasant, expedient, and evenhanded. When lawyers became overheated and tempers flared, Dowlen would drawl, "Awwww, why don't you boys approach the bench for a minute," and in a soft voice that the jury couldn't hear he would tell them, say, about the time his coon dog chased a bobcat through the general store at Ralph's Switch. In an emotional, high-stakes trial such as the one facing Cullen Davis, a trial in which the jury would be sequestered for weeks and maybe months while competing

158

batteries of lawyers fired salvo after salvo, *somebody* was going to have to keep a sense of humor. After all this time and money, nobody wanted another mistrial.

While the prosecution spoke in quiet, confident terms of victory, the defense said hardly a word. They were about to make up for lost time, however. Racehorse Haynes had already sent out some local feelers and was in the process of assembling a staff of behind-the-scenes specialists the likes of which Amarillo or few other places had ever seen. Cullen Davis had spent almost a year behind bars, but the long delay was a kind of blessing. "We thought we were ready for trial before," said Steve Sumner, the lawyer in charge of investigation for the defense, "but we've received an incredible amount of new information in the last few weeks." Nobody connected with the defense was making public statements or suggesting what new information they had, but Haynes occasionally leaked a juicy item. Race repeated what he had said in Fort Worth, that they would establish Davis's innocence by providing the name of the true killer. Nobody said it out loud, but the mere fact that they were dealing with Dowlen instead of Judge Tom Cave delighted the defense. The rapport between Cave and Haynes had never been good, but it hit rock bottom when the defense presented David McCrory's nonaffidavit alleging that Priscilla condoned drug deals and free sex in the mansion.

There were those who believed that Racehorse had slyly forced Cave's hand, impelled him to move the case to another city. It was a calculated risk, of course; they might be jumping from the frying pan to the fire. But if the delay did nothing else, it permitted them time to insulate. Haynes was already formulating the basis of his defense—"to show the true color and character of Priscilla Davis." He couldn't be sure yet how George Dowlen would receive this strategy, but he was absolutely certain it would have crashed in Tom Cave's court.

Haynes wasted no time putting Dowlen to the test. On the first day of pretrial the attorney filed a motion to question several key witnesses privately in the judge's chambers. Dowlen wouldn't allow them to question Priscilla in private, but he granted their request for McCrory, despite the prosecution's heated argument that McCrory was a witness "unworthy of belief." First, Haynes presented McCrory with the affidavit that he had signed for the DA and asked him if he'd like an opportunity to make any changes. McCrory made a few minor changes. Then Haynes took out his own affidavit, or nonaffidavit as was the case, and took McCrory over it, line by line. After each incriminating line, Race would pause and say, "Now did you or did you not tell me that?" McCrory pleaded the Fifth Amendment to each question. It wasn't much, but Haynes was sure he now had his foot in the door. He hadn't yet asked Dowlen if McCrory could be called to testify before the jury, but the predicate had been established. Haynes wasn't sure he *wanted* McCrory as a witness, but he wanted to be ready just in case.

With the coming of Racehorse Haynes to Amarillo there came also droves of reporters, cameramen, and artists. This was the part that Dowlen had dreaded, but now that it was actually happening in his own courtroom, the judge resolved to make the best of it. "Haynes is a charming little cuss," Dowlen was forced to admit. The judge knew of his reputation, but it was something else watching the man actually perform. Haynes could talk on his feet like a veteran actor reciting Shakespeare, forming complex motions almost word-perfect and standing ready to back them up with a ton of law. By the second day of pretrial the defense had filed almost 200 motions, asking Dowlen to do everything from sequester the jury (which Dowlen had already decided was necessary) to declare the state's capital murder law unconstitutional. Though it was true that the blood of the prosecutor roared through his veins, Dowlen soon learned why so many people were hooked on Racehorse Haynes. The feisty Houston lawyer had a way of flattering the court and challenging it, all in the same sentence. The judge could see this was going to be a case unlike any he had experienced. He made plans to fortify himself. A lifelong bachelor, Dowlen had always lived with his mother and father, but now he took an apartment in town, next door to Rhett Butler's, where young singles and would-be singles congregated nightly. Like it or not, the judge was about to become a star.

Racehorse Haynes wasn't exactly a household name in Amarillo, but that too was being adjusted. After the boomerang public relations ploy in Fort Worth, the defense opted for subtlety. The mistake had been trying to direct attention to Cullen Davis. Now the plan was to direct it *away* from Davis to Haynes. In a town of 150,000 the best way was word of mouth, and the defense was already looking for people to spread it. In that respect Karen Master's father, Ray Hudson, became an unexpected asset. Hudson had lived in Amarillo for years and had excellent connections with local businessmen and politicians. The defense decided to write Ray Hudson into their budget (his expenses would total $45,000) as a local consultant, though Cullen thought of Hudson more as "a baby-sitter for Karen . . . to keep her on an even keel." Cullen gave his attorneys a free hand with expenses. Haynes also decided that it would be to their advantage to order daily copies of the transcript. It was an almost unprecedented expense at $4.25 a page (dailies could run to 200 to 300 pages), but it would help with cross-examination and would force the state into a battle of bucks. Haynes reasoned correctly that when taxpayers learned what it was costing to try Cullen Davis, sentiment would turn against the prosecution.

The first hot, dry winds of summer were kicking across the plains as Judge Dowlen called a panel of about 150 prospective jurors to his courtroom on June 27. As expected, Dowlen allowed individual voir dire and put no time limit on how long each side could question each member of the jury panel. The judge allowed each side fifteen preemptory challenges or "strikes," a method whereby the lawyers could eliminate a panelist for any or no reason. Dowlen anticipated that the defense would go through its fifteen strikes and ask for more; this was a traditional ploy among defense attorneys, one that sometimes paid dividends on appeal, and Dowlen had already decided that he would grant additional challenges if either side requested them.

The first few panelists questioned were eliminated by Dowlen himself, either because they admitted preconceived opinions about the case or because they didn't believe in capital punishment. There were very few blacks among the 150-member panel, and the few who were there were disqualified on the question of capital punishment. Amarillo lawyers knew from experience that most blacks just didn't care for the death penalty.

After two days of voir dire, the lawyers had their first juror, Marilyn Kay Haessly, a one-time novice nun who now sold cameras at a department store. Marilyn Kay had never served on a jury, nor had she ever been a victim of a crime or known anyone who had. Three days after that, a second juror, James Watkins, was seated and sent to the downtown Executive Inn where the jury was to be sequestered. Watkins was office foreman for the Panhandle Fruit Company, had been married but was now divorced and had no children, and revealed that he had once applied for a job with the Amarillo Police Department. Normally the defense would have used one of its strikes to eliminate a would-be policeman, but this was no normal case. Karl Prah, a native of Munich, Germany, who had lived in Amarillo for ten years and worked as a customer service agent for Braniff Airlines, became juror No. 3; L. B. Pendleton, a telephone company repairman, was No. 4. It had taken almost two weeks to pick just four jurors, and Dowlen decided to limit the time each side could question a prospect to forty-five minutes. The trouble with this, as Dowlen explained later, was that both sides were now taking their full allotted time. An hour and a half for *every* panelist. At best they were questioning only five or six a day.

The defense was deliberately slowing the pace. Time was very much in their favor and likely to become more so. With four jurors already seated, the defense still had ten strikes.

The defense had already commissioned a $30,000 research project to determine what types of people would make the best jurors in Davis's case. A similar study was done in the Patty Hearst case; although the project hadn't spared Miss Hearst, Haynes saw enough similarities in the cases to justify the expense. What they needed, Haynes was certain, was a jury that wouldn't be prejudiced against Davis's great wealth. They needed to find jurors who were open-minded, who could understand the abstract notion of reasonable doubt, and who could tolerate long periods of isolation. Since the state would parade three eyewitnesses before the jury at the beginning of the trial, the defense looked for jurors who could withhold judgment until they had heard all the evidence. Dallas psychiatrist John Holbrook, who organized the project, estimated the survey would give the defense a 5 to 10 percent edge in picking the jury. The report concluded, for example, that office workers would not look kindly on the defendant. Asked to rate a twenty-five-year-old white female secretary as a prospective juror, Holbrook said, "She'd hang him." Haynes had also employed Dr. Margaret Covington, a psychologist trained to study prospective jurors for various traits—pupil dilation, for example, gave evidence of deception.

At least a dozen lawyers were working on various aspects of Cullen Davis's defense, but Racehorse decided they needed at least two more. They needed one well-known Amarillo lawyer present in the courtroom to dispel the image of themselves as a battery of high-priced outsiders come to city-slick the good folks of Potter County. And they needed a second attorney to work behind the scenes, investigating and evaluating the citizens who would be considered for jury duty. This second role was particularly important because Haynes knew that the Tarrant County prosecutors would conduct only a cursory survey, checking names on the jury list against city directories and local law enforcement files, what lawyers called "the normal investigation." The edge here was psychological as well as strategic. Haynes delighted in watching the faces of the prosecuting attorneys when he turned suddenly to a panelist and asked, "Oh, by the way, Mrs. Jones, how's your uncle doing after that hernia operation?" If Racehorse could keep his poker face, this sometimes resulted in the state blowing one of its own strikes on a juror Haynes wouldn't touch with a fire extinguisher.

To screen and investigate the many names on the jury list, the defense hired a well-known local attorney named Hugh Russell. A tall, soft-spoken, intelligent man, Russell knew the territory. He was a close friend of Stanley Marsh 3 and other social, financial, and political leaders. Russell's job was to use his contacts as discreetly as possible and snoop into the private lives of each potential juror. Corporate presidents and their personnel directors were excellent sources of information.

The original jury list handed down several weeks before voir dire contained 640 names. As the saying went, Russell faced a long snake with a short stick. He used a computer and secretaries to put the list in alphabetical order, printed several dozen copies, and distributed them to friends and associates—particularly lawyers and politicians whose business it was to know a large spectrum of the community. Russell was interested not only in hard facts but in impressions, opinions, anything that night enlighten the defense. Other lists were distributed to Cullen Davis's people in Fort Worth who canvassed hundreds and maybe thousands of Kendavis Industries employees to find anyone who might have information about anyone on the list. Amarillo city directories dating back twenty years were perused to determine "patterns of transience"—who had moved or changed jobs and how many times, records of marriage or divorce, births, deaths, signs of upward or downward mobility, any insight into the lives of the people who might judge Cullen Davis. Russell posted a large city map on the wall of his office and placed colored pins at the address of every name on the list. "I wanted to get an idea where the people lived," he explained. "It was my guess that certain areas of town would be more densely represented than others, and that proved correct. Amarillo was a very middle-class place with a small ethnic population. Juries tended to be homogeneous—the odds were that any jury picked would come from similar class backgrounds."

On June 27, when the court reduced its original jury list to 150, Russell updated his file and moved into high gear. Private investigators photographed jurors' homes and made notes on how well each house was maintained, its approximate sales value, the number and type of cars at the residence, signs, bumper stickers, anything that might identify the owner as a member of a fringe group. Neighbors were questioned, as were potential jurors' relatives, doctors, lawyers, barbers, even newspaper boys. Someone checked the district clerk's office several times daily to find out which jurors had claimed exemptions and could be scratched off the list.

"We were looking for the type of juror that the state would normally look for," Russell said. "Good, solid, basically conservative citizens who would have no affinity for Priscilla and might even find her revolting. We wanted to eliminate cranks or people who had some ax to grind. Any scrap of information might be important, might give us the edge on the state. Basically, we wanted the state to start out in the hole."

As each panelist took the witness stand, Haynes, Phil Burleson, and Mike Gibson took a moment to review the dossier. Russell constantly updated files with new information. They were, in effect, buying time. In some cases time was a spectacular factor. Shortly before they were to question a successful businessman, they learned that he had recently beaten his wife to a pulp. "Unpredictable," Phil Burleson decided. Burleson was considering using one of their strikes when new information reached him that the man had also told a friend that he hoped he would be picked on the Cullen Davis jury as he felt a judicious urge to "hang the son of a bitch." Burleson breathed a sigh of relief. If he could phrase his questions just so, the prospect would reveal his prejudice and disqualify himself. Another juror was apparently recovering from a traumatic experience, they learned. On a recent evening he had been invited to a neighbor's house where, to his surprise, he had been requested to have sex with the lady of the house while the gentleman took pictures. "Did he *do* it?" Race asked Hugh Russell, who assured him that's what their source claimed. Their source was the husband, who said he had pictures to prove it. "Sounds like a character flaw to me," Burleson deadpanned to his colleagues. "If the state doesn't see through him, we better strike him ourselves." Still another prospect had recently committed his wife to a mental institution after first forcing her to confess assorted infidelities to the assembled family. Was it possible they were *over-*investigating? At this rate they might use up their strikes before a representative group of Amarillo citizens used up their character flaws.

On the other hand their fat dossiers had coughed up several prospects who seemed tailor-made for the cause. Haynes's job in such cases was to wear a poker face and hope the state didn't strike them, though, oddly enough, the state seemed to be looking for the same types. One of them was Alma Miller, a sixty-four-year-old grandmother who was active in church, Girl Scouts, Parent-Teachers Association, and garden club. If Alma didn't love Cullen Davis, nobody would. And it was a safe bet she wouldn't like what she heard about Priscilla. Alma Miller was the fifth juror chosen. Juror No. 6 was R. C. Hubbard, a navy veteran and grandfather who worked with several Christian youth groups.

The defense also liked Betty Fox Blair. Betty looked tough. She was a fifty-year-old divorcée who had raised two lovely daughters by herself and had an almost perfect attendance record in her job as a typist. Hugh Russell had known Betty Blair for years and vouched for her as "a real solid person." Betty was likely to be open-minded about everything except drugs and free sex. She would make a very good juror. The state agreed, and Betty became Juror No. 7 on July 18.

There were times when the state's logic appeared terribly twisted; they didn't seem to understand that customs and practices that had worked for years didn't necessarily apply to this case. The defense was looking for tough citizens while the state was striking them because they didn't look tough enough.

As the opposing sides began to deplete their strikes, the final stages of the jury selection could amount to who played the best hunch. It was Russell's hunch that one fellow would make a good juror based on the information that the fellow loved to bet on horse races. Betting on horse races is not legal in Texas. The fellow had to drive all the way to New Mexico to indulge his hobby. He was therefore not likely to be sympathetic to the state, though his solid-citizen credentials were otherwise impeccable. The fellow was eventually selected and served with distinction, as did another man who was chosen on the basis of the belief that he was "henpecked" and would enjoy an extended period away from his wife.

By August 2, the anniversary of the slaughter at 4200 Mockingbird, two more panelists had been added —Walter Lee Jones, a radar technician with the Federal Aviation Administration, and Mike Giesler, a sheet-metal fabricator for Bell Helicopter.

The prospect who was the most difficult to evaluate was Freddy Thompson, a real live cowboy who worked on Stanley Marsh's ranch. Though he had had a cup of coffee at several colleges while pursuing a career as an athlete. Freddy was not educated to the ways of the world he might have to judge. Freddy sometimes referred to himself as a "peon," which was easier than explaining why he preferred the company of cows. Though the profession of cowboying was deemed to be the most honorable way that a man could make a living, *cowboys* were regarded as mostly crazy scum. Who else would work seven days a week from dawn until dark for wages that would barely support a family? Cowboys were about as predictable as sandstorms. Like most cowboys. Freddy had experienced an occasional brush with the law. They say he once caught a deputy sheriff trespassing on the Marsh-O'Brien Ranch and felt compelled to disarm the lawman and watch him dance. Then there was the time Freddy and another cowboy turned a blind steer loose in a darkened hippie bar. But nothing serious. Freddy respected the law, and more than that he respected tradition and old-time cowboy morality. He had been married to the same woman for nineteen years and looked on divorce as the ultimate degradation.

Until he arrived in the courtroom, Freddy had never heard of Cullen Davis or the sensational Fort Worth murder case. Only after he had taken his seat with the jury panel did he learn that the case involved the brutal slaying of a twelve-year-old girl. Freddy had a twelve-year-old daughter, and she was one of the great blessings of his life. "A twelve-year-old girl is something special," he told Racehorse Haynes during the voir dire. Asked if he could be a fair and impartial juror, Freddy said he didn't know. Everyone laughed when they asked Freddy his hobby and he replied, "I think it's beer drinking." After that remark, Freddy was fairly certain they'd send him back to the ranch. But it was late in the game. The voir dire was already into its sixth week. Freddy was the 118th prospective juror to be questioned, and both sides were running low on strikes. When it finally dawned on him that this was *real,* that he was about to be locked up with eleven strangers for an ungodly period of time, and that ultimately they would have to decide the fate of a man who could buy a thousand like them out of his back pocket, Freddy tried to walk out the door. The bailiff grabbed him and read him the law. The law *required* that he sit in judgment. For the next 105 days, Freddy Thompson hardly spoke a complete sentence.

On August 9, Gilbert Kennedy, a mailman for twenty-one years and a devout Christian, became No. 11. A week after that Luis Ayala, a thirty-year-old journeyman electrician born in Juarez, Mexico, was seated as the twelfth and final member of the panel. Cullen Davis, who had been jailed without bond for almost exactly a full year, enjoyed his widest smile in a long time. He was well satisfied with the jury, and so, it appeared, was everyone else. Neither side had used its original allotment of strikes. The jury consisted of nine men and three women, ages ranging from twenty-six to sixty-four. Three were Catholic, three Baptist, three Methodist, one Church of Christ, one unaffiliated

Protestant, and one with no religious affiliation. Most of them were working people, men and women who were used to listening and taking orders. "Look at them," a Potter County attorney said. "They're people who've been stomped every way but flat, but they're good people and they'll be fair." Another lawyer observed: "You'll notice that a lot of them are overweight. Overweight people are docile and submissive. They'll hate Priscilla because of her flashy dress and her living with Stan Farr. People in Amarillo don't appreciate that sort of behavior." If they disliked Priscilla, would it follow that they would appreciate Cullen? "Don't matter," the attorney said. "Racehorse won't let it get to that."

Just as Hugh Russell had helped finger what the defense hoped were the right twelve people, another Amarillo attorney, Dee Miller, joined the team for the purpose of helping remind the jurors who were the good guys and who were the bad. Miller was about as good as you could get in Amarillo. All twelve jurors knew him either personally or by reputation. Dee and his twin brother, Oth Miller, headed one of Amarillo's most prestigious law firms, and an older brother, G. William Miller, was known to everyone in the Panhandle as the chairman of the Federal Reserve Board. Not a week went by that the Aamarillo media didn't use some sort of national story quoting G. William Miller on the state of the economy. Dee Miller was a director of the North State Bank, past president of the Amarillo Country Club, and a cog in the local Democratic party. One of his law partners explained: "Dee has a large following in town. If there's anyone in Amarillo he doesn't know personally, he knows someone who does. Dee's greatest talent is knowing how to make friends and keep them." Miller was regarded as an adequate criminal attorney, but his legal reputation was no factor in his selection to the Cullen Davis defense team. He questioned no witnesses, offered no objections, argued no pleadings; his function for the next five months was to be seen sitting at the defense table close to Cullen

Davis. For this Dee Miller collected the largest fee of his career.

In the weeks and months that followed, Dee Miller introduced his out-of-town colleagues to Rotary luncheons, local bar association meetings, college basketball banquets, country club gatherings, any place where local movers and shakers were likely to be assembled. He arranged golf games with leading citizens and made sure that Cullen Davis was properly represented at charitable functions. In time, Amarillo came to look on Racehorse Haynes, Phil Burleson, and the others as part of the community. More than a public relations gesture, it was a method by which the out-of-town lawyers could sample the mood and temperament of the city while calculating the odds. It was conceivable that the verdict in this case could boil down to *them* against *us*. Miller's job was to make certain *us* included Cullen Davis and his lawyers. If the other lawyers executed their plan properly, Priscilla would become the evil personification of *them*. In a reversal of normal trial roles, the defense would be identified with the establishment and the state would come to be viewed as the outsider.

There was one additional order of business to be completed before testimony could begin. Dowlen would have to rule on several hundred motions filed by both sides.

The state knew that Cullen's attorneys had subpoenaed a number of witnesses who were prepared to describe episodes of drugs, sex, and violence at the mansion and asked that the court require defense attorneys to demonstrate relevancy before blurting it out to the jury. "We want to make sure a whole bunch of skunks aren't thrown into the jury box," Assistant District Attorney Joe Shannon told Dowlen. The judge granted this motion and instructed the defense to make no references to drug use, sexual hijinks, or "specific acts of misconduct" other than felony convictions without first taking it up with the court ouside the presence of the jury. Dowlen stopped short of saying such testimony would be inadmissible. He reserved the right to rule on each issue as it came up. He also granted a prosecution motion prohibiting the characterization of Priscilla's friends as "dope fiends, pillheads, traffickers in narcotics, prostitutes," and various other derogatory expressions, unless supported by evidence. "If they don't admit it, we won't call them that." Haynes smiled to the judge. "We'll let somebody else call them that. We do not intend to engage in name calling, but there are prosecution witnesses who have referred to other prosecution witnesses in such terms." The state also asked Dowlen to forbid references to Priscilla's relationship with W. T. Rufner and restrict questions about her conduct at social events. Dowlen hedged on these motions, however. He would have to wait and view them in context.

The defense renewed its request that Cullen Davis be released on bond. Although a dozen district, state, and federal judges had already denied bond, Dowlen promised to hear new evidence and review the motion, even though Judge Tom Cave retained the final voice in all bond matters. Most of the new evidence concerned the testimony of Bubba Gavrel. There was a statement that the prosecution had been required to turn over to the defense in which three Fort Worth police officers who had been at the murder scene said that Gavrel couldn't identify the man who shot him. The defense also produced an affidavit from Tommy Jourden, who occupied the bed next to Gavrel just after the shootings. Jourden was now claiming that he overheard Gavrel tell his father he didn't know who shot him, to which Gus Sr. responded: "Well, it was Cullen who did it. This girl out there [Bev Bass] said to say it was Cullen who shot you and if anyone asks you, you tell them that."

None of the new evidence impressed Joe Shannon. He already knew Gavrel was the weakest of their three eyewitnesses; it was common knowledge that the young man had seen Cullen Davis only on a couple of brief occasions in dark barrooms before the night of the shootings, and of course Gavrel's $13-million lawsuit against Davis reflected poorly on his credentials as a fair and impartial witness. Still, they had two other eyewitnesses who seemed unimpeachable. It seemed inconceivable to Shannon that George Dowlen would overrule two Supreme Court justices and, at this late date, free Cullen Davis. In fact, it was another matter entirely that brought Shannon to Dowlen's chambers late on the evening of Friday, August 19. Shannon was curious what the judge thought of the jury they had just finished picking. Shannon was absolutely stunned when Dowlen told him, "You don't have a capital case, and you haven't picked a capital jury."

Attorneys for the state tried to look self-assured the following morning as Tim Curry made his opening remarks to the jury, but Shannon had the creepy feeling that they had committed an irrevocable blunder somewhere back in the beginning stages of this case. Shannon had felt from the start that their best shot was a straight murder charge. He didn't believe there *was* a jury with convictions strong enough to sentence Davis to death. If Dowlen understood the good people of Amarillo nearly as well as the state had led itself to believe, they were in trouble. By pressing on with their charges of capital murder, the state had already given the defense a definite edge in jury selection. Shannon listened as Tim Curry outlined the case and for the first time supplied the jury with the motive. Curry told the jurors of the divorce court's decision to raise Priscilla's alimony from $3,500 to $5,000 monthly and also pony up another $52,000 in additional expenses. "We expect the evidence to show that the defendant learned of that decision on the afternoon of August 2—the day these murders took place," he said. That night Davis went to the mansion with the intent of killing Priscilla, Curry continued. By the time he had completed his ghastly mission, Andrea Wilborn and Stan Farr were dead, and Priscilla and Gus Gavrel were seriously wounded. Though there was no eyewitness to the murder of Andrea Wilborn, the state intended to prove that she was killed with the same weapon that killed Farr and wounded the others. It all sounds so simple, Shannon thought. A defendant frustrated and angered by the latest round of divorce proceedings, three eye-

172

witnesses, matching bullets: Cullen's attorneys were expected to counter with what lawyers call an "alibi defense," but Shannon doubted that Cullen Davis had an alibi. It had taken Curry less than thirty minutes to outline their case for the jury. Curry still felt they had done the right thing, but Shannon couldn't shake the feeling that the state was in trouble. He knew one thing: *Dowlen* believed they'd picked the wrong jury.

An hour later, Shannon was certain they were in trouble. Dowlen unexpectedly granted the defense's motion for bond. Defense attorneys posted certified checks totaling $1,650,000 in Fort Worth and Amarillo, and Cullen Davis was temporarily a free man. As TV cameramen and reporters clogged the parking lot outside the Potter County Courthouse, Cullen walked to his chauffeured Cadillac, carrying a portable color TV set and wearing a smile wider than a Panhandle sunset. Karen Master walked beside him, smiling and waving to the cameras. Cullen's two sons by his first marriage were en route from Dallas for an emotional reunion. Cullen told reporters that all he wanted to do was "talk to my kids, go eat a seventy-two-ounce steak, visit my employees in Potter County, and sleep in a good bed." By the time testimony began the following Monday, Judge Cave would have revoked the bond and ordered Davis returned to jail. For the moment, however, the man who had everything just wanted to savor freedom and exult in victory. He had been a long time without either.

On Sunday, August 21, as Cullen secluded himself in the Hilton Inn with his family, friends, and attorneys, Priscilla arrived at Amarillo International Airport. The state's star witness was technically on leave from Fort Worth's St. Joseph's Hospital and carried with her a letter from doctors stating that she would probably have to go to Pittsburgh in a few weeks for major surgery to repair nerve damage incurred in the shooting. Priscilla looked pale but determined. She had waited more than a year to tell her story to the jury, and now her time had come.

A few minutes later she too checked into the Hilton Inn. For the first time since their separation in the summer of 1974, Cullen and Priscilla spent the night under the same roof.

∽◦∽

Long before George Dowlen called the court to session on Monday afternoon, all fifty-two seats were taken and people jammed the hallway clear back to the stairs.

"What's she wearing?" asked a shapeless and badly used Panhandle housewife with her cheeks heavily rouged and her hair tinted raven black. The woman had driven more than fifty miles that morning, not realizing that dozens of other housewives would likewise be eaten up with curiosity. These were soap opera addicts, and they did not miss the chance to see the real thing. They filled the courtroom and spilled into the corridors— from which, ironically, they watched the proceedings through a glass panel about the size of a small TV screen.

"Look at her!" another housewife said.

"I can't see. What's she wearing?"

"I can see. I can tell she's guilty just by looking."

Priscilla's guilt or innocence wasn't an issue in the case, of course, but that didn't faze the housewives, the majority of whom were already convinced that the Priscilla Davises of their experience were responsible for the evils of mankind. This seemed strange because at this point they knew nothing at all about Priscilla except the little they'd read and heard two months earlier when she appeared at a pretrial hearing. They didn't remember what she'd testified, but they recalled vividly what she wore—an expensive outfit with frills of virginal white lace and a tiny gold cross dangling between her silicone breasts. The women who swarmed the

174

courtroom instinctively concluded that Priscilla was a woman without shame. They were incensed by the story of an Amarillo newspaper reporter who accidentally encountered Priscilla carrying a Bible and walking down the hallway of the Hilton Inn. "I think that image of Priscilla with the Bible and gold cross hurt the state more than any single thing," Hugh Russell said later, months after the trial ended. "There are a lot of sincerely religious people in Amarillo, and they were turned off by that. A lot of [prospective jurors] mentioned it in voir dire. They saw her as a Bible-toting phony."

What wasn't reported by the Amarillo newsman was that Priscilla was *also* carrying a suitcase—she was caught in the act of changing rooms. Nor was it mentioned that the gold cross was the same one that had been found in her purse just after the shootings of August 2, 1976. None of the cameras and prying eyes could see the agonizing pain that Priscilla continued to endure even as the predators hacked at her: doctors had implanted a catheter in her back to drip medication to raw nerve endings shattered by the passage of the bullet.

The gaggle of spectators had to wait for Priscilla's entrance on Monday, however, because the state called Judge Joe Eidson as its first witness. Eidson's testimony was intended to establish the motive for everything that happened. The state quickly developed the point that on the day of the murders Eidson had given Cullen Davis some bad news, then turned the witness over to Racehorse Haynes for cross-examination.

Haynes walked briskly to the witness stand and read the divorce judge a list of ten names. Eidson said he didn't recognize any of them. Racehorse smiled and said that was a shame because it was a list of ten men and women, many of them known felons, who were living at 4200 Mockingbird while Cullen and Priscilla were in the act of divorce. For the present, however, the name Racehorse wanted to pursue was that of one Stanford Farr. Eidson didn't seem able to place the name, so Haynes cleared it up for him: "The man was living there! She was buying him things such as boots and cars and paying his business expenses. Are these circumstances for which it is necessary to increase alimony?"

Eidson replied that he didn't know about Stan Farr, but if he had: "I might have granted the increase, I might have left it as it was, or I might have terminated it."

"You might have terminated it because there was no statutory authority to support continued alimony for a woman supporting another man?" Haynes asked, holding his hand to his ear as though he anticipated a very soft answer.

"That could have been the grounds," Eidson admitted.

On redirect questioning, Joe Shannon fired back, asking Eidson if he had been told that Davis was living with Karen Master.

Shannon Do you recall any confession [from Davis] that he was using any funds from community property to support Karen Master?

Eidson· No.

Q: Do you recall any confession or representation that he was using any funds from community property to support the children of Karen Master?

A: No.

Eidson did seem to recall that Davis was one of two principal owners in Kendavis Industries International, Inc., the eighty-three-corporate business empire.

Q: Do you recall what the profits of Kendavis Industries were after taxes in 1975?

A: I believe $57 million.

"The number $57 million is one you can recall," Haynes observed.

"Well, I think it's rather impressive," Eidson shot back.

Shannon asked Eidson about the restraining order barring Cullen Davis from 4200 Mockingbird, the one necessary to their contention that Davis was a burglar as soon as he entered the mansion intending to kill his wife.

Shannon: On August 2 and August 3, 1976, did Priscilla Davis have a greater right to possession of the residence at 4200 Mockingbird than the defendant, Thomas Cullen Davis?

Phil Burleson jumped up to object, but Dowlen over-ruled.

Eidson: Yes.

Eidson and Priscilla passed in the hallway as she prepared to take the witness stand, but the judge apparently didn't notice her. He must have been the only one in the courthouse who didn't. The corridor sounded like a chicken yard at feeding time as Priscilla moved through, smiling and nodding.

Joe Shannon had cautioned Priscilla several times about her appearance in court. He had told her, "Wear something like you'd wear to church." Shannon didn't want the state's key witness to appear in pigtails and pinafore, but neither did he want her in the plunging necklines that had become her trademark. Taking Shannon at his word, Priscilla spent $25,000 on a new wardrobe. The outfits that she selected had high necklines, low hems, and an abundance of lace and ribbons. Shannon looked at the new wardrobe and approved. "It wasn't what I'd want my wife to wear," he said, "but I thought it was in good taste." What did surprise Shannon was that in her eleven days on the witness stand, Priscilla never wore the same thing twice.

Racehorse Haynes had anticipated that the state would use Joe Shannon to lead Priscilla through direct examination. She was certain to supply the most dramatic testimony, and of all the prosecutors on Tim Curry's staff Shannon had the best flair for drama. Instead, Tim Curry elected to question Priscilla himself. Racehorse watched with new interest as Curry took her around the course in his easy, low-key, what-next style.

Right away he got her to acknowledge that she and the late Stan Farr had been lovers. In fact, Farr was living with her at the mansion while she was in the process of divorcing Cullen Davis. There was no use sparring about these points because Racehorse Haynes had already developed them when he cross-examined Eidson.

Priscilla began to shake when Curry asked her about her three marriages and children. Before the trial Joe Shannon had repeatedly warned her: "Just tell the truth. Some of the questions are going to be hard, but just pony up to the truth." That's what Priscilla was trying to do, but she had anticipated the next question would be about Andrea, a name that often brought tears to her eyes.

Q: Do you have any other children [besides Dee and Jackie Wilborn?]

A: Yes, sir.

Q: And what was that child's name?

A: Andrea Lee Wilborn.

Q: How old was she?

A: She was twelve.

Curry then led Priscilla through the nightmare of August 2–3. How Andrea was left home alone for the evening while she and Stan went out to dinner to celebrate birthdays and anniversaries of close friends. How Priscilla had locked the back door manually and activated the electronic security system. When they returned about midnight, the door was still locked but she could see by the panel of lights inside that the security system was no longer activated. With Curry leading her gently, Priscilla described finding the bloody handprint. calling out to Farr, and her astonishment when Cullen stepped out of the laundry room, said "Hi," and shot her between the breasts. She told about Cullen's struggle with Farr, and how Cullen stood directly over her lover to squeeze off the last two shots. About trying to escape, about Cullen coming after her and how she pleaded for her life, about Bev Bass and Bubba Gavrel driving up and how she took that opportunity to run—the whole story exactly as she had told it many times before. Curry was pleased; no matter how many times Priscilla told the story, she told it the same way, down to the hand gestures and tears as she recalled a particularly painful moment. She was a damn good witness, Curry thought.

Racehorse Haynes thought Priscilla was a little too

good and objected repeatedly that the witness was expanding her answers outside the scope of the question. During his own questioning Haynes bore in, marveling that Priscilla couldn't seem to recall how many times she had "rehearsed" her testimony with lawyers for the state, and repeatedly referring to "your version" of the murders. Priscilla interrupted him at one point and blurted out: "You keep saying my version. I want to make it clear what I said is what happened."

At the end of the day Cullen lingered in the courtroom and talked with reporters, as he would many times in the days that followed. Priscilla's tears were as phony as the rest of her story, he said, then asked, "You've never seen a person who could turn tears on and off like a water faucet, have you?"

By mid-morning of the third day Curry had completed his direct examination and turned the witness over to Haynes. Racehorse intended to waste no time with amenities. Whatever the jury or the crowd in the courtroom may have thought of Priscilla before, she had been impressive under direct examination. Haynes's whole case was based upon discrediting her as a person and as a witness. In the week that followed he did that and more.

Introducing into evidence photographs of three drinking glasses found at the crime scene, the lawyer spoke of his list of "phantoms" and implied that three glasses proved that Andrea had not been alone at the mansion between 9:00 P.M. and midnight. He questioned Priscilla about the security system and about a burglary that had taken place at the mansion in the months just prior to the killings. He followed with a series of questions designed to show that a number of people might have had keys to the mansion during the months after Davis moved out. Priscilla first claimed that the only people who had keys to the main entrance were herself, Farr, Dee Davis, and two maids. Later, she admitted that a number of live-in guests might have had keys from time to time, but this was before she had the locks changed. This was the opening Racehorse was probing for, and now Priscilla was forced to acknowledge his

179

mysterious list of "phantoms." They included W. T. Rufner, country and western singer Delbert McClinton and his wife Donna, Jan Scurlock, Sandy Guthrie Myers and her husband, Larry Michael Myers, a convicted felon. Priscilla admitted that each had lived in the mansion for periods ranging from several weeks to several months. In the days that followed, this list of phantoms increased, but for now Haynes was content to use only four names to challenge her identification of Cullen Davis as the killer.

Q: Was it [the killer] Horace Copeland?

A: No, it was Cullen Davis.

Q: Was it Robert Downing?

A: Who? . . . No, sir, it was not.

Q: Do you know a Robert Downing?

A: No.

Q: Was it David Hack?

A: No, sir.

Q: Do you know a David Hack?

A: Yes, sir.

Q: When was the last time you saw David Hack before August 2, 1976?

A: I really couldn't tell you.

The jury had heard the name Rufner before, but this was the first mention of David Hack or Robert Downing. As the case developed, their names remained obscure, but Horace Copeland, who had been shot to death in a Fort Worth apartment only a few weeks before, emerged later as a central figure. The defense planned to contend that Copeland and Stan Farr had been partners in a drug deal that went sour shortly before the killings and that Copeland had threatened to kill Farr. But for the moment the phantom that Haynes wanted to implant in the minds of the jurors was the rogue motorcycle racer, W. T. Rufner. The jury had already heard Rufner's name but didn't yet know that Rufner had moved in shortly after Cullen moved out and at roughly the same time as his own drug bust. Now it was time for the jury to take a look at Rufner, and Racehorse had a dramatic visual aid—a photograph he wanted to introduce as evidence.

He had it printed poster-size on paper so thin it was nearly transparent. Casually, Haynes approached the bench. As he unfurled the photograph for the judge's inspection and displayed it so that the fluorescent lights in the courtroom ceiling clearly illuminated it for those in the jury box, all four prosecutors jumped to their feet. "You can see right through it!" Tim Curry protested. "He [Haynes] did it deliberately!" Racehorse protested his innocence, but you could see the smirk on his face. In previous testimony outside the jury's presence Priscilla testified that she didn't recognize the picture, and on this basis Judge Dowlen refused to admit it into evidence. But the damage was done. Everyone in the jury box, in fact everyone on that side of the courtroom, could see that the color blowup was a picture of W. T. Rufner and Priscilla. Priscilla wore a low-cut halter top and hip-hugger slacks, and T-man was buck naked except for a red-and-white candy-striped Christmas stocking covering his genitals. They posed with arms around one another. Dowlen ordered that a piece of cardboard be taped to the back of the photograph before permitting Haynes to continue grilling Priscilla.

Priscilla repeated that she'd never seen the picture before and in fact believed it to be a trick manufactured to embarrass her. Haynes challenged this and asked, "Have you ever seen W. T. Rufner in a social atmosphere when he was running around without his clothes on?"

"I don't recall that I have," Priscilla said.

"You have never seen W. T. Rufner naked as a jaybird with his you-know-what in a sock? You do recognize the man in the photograph as W. T. Rufner?"

"Well," Priscilla said, studying it again, "I recognize the face. I don't recognize the sock."

Haynes turned to the bench and told Dowlen, "I have a difficult time believing anyone could see W. T. Rufner in that attire and not remember it."

"So do I," Priscilla shot back. "That's how I feel about it exactly." The jury snickered.

Later, the defense tried to introduce two other sexually explicit photographs. The pictures were blurred and the subjects had their backs to the camera, but it appeared to be a man and a woman, both naked, cavorting about in the shallow water of a lake. Haynes tried to connect the photographs with a trip that Priscilla, Rufner, and some others took to the Willie Nelson Fourth of July Picnic in 1974, a few weeks before Priscilla and Cullen separated. Again, Dowlen refused to allow the photographs into evidence, but this did not prevent Haynes from pursuing his line of questions designed to show that Priscilla was messing around with Rufner even before the separation.

"It is true, is it not, that you knew W. T. Rufner before you separated from Thomas Cullen Davis?" Haynes asked. Priscilla said it was true. "Isn't it true you started seeing him before you separated?" Priscilla answered that she had seen him a few times.

As Joe Shannon stood to object, he again had that creepy feeling that Priscilla, the strength of their case, the one eyewitness who could connect the bizarre events of August 2–3, could in fact be their weak point. Priscilla had assured the prosecution that her relationship with W. T. Rufner was purely platonic until well after the separation, but now Shannon wasn't so sure. The defense was continuing to harp on the July 4 Winnebago trip to the Willie Nelson Picnic in College Station. If Priscilla had really been just a mother hen chaperoning her daughter Dee and the other teenagers, then how could she explain those naked people cavorting in the photographs? The jury had not yet been allowed to view the pictures, but Shannon knew that Racehorse Haynes had not given up trying. Sooner or later the defense was bound to find a witness who would admit being there and verify the pictures into evidence Sooner or later the defense was bound to question her about the trip with W. T. Rufner to visit the McCrorys in Boston. Sooner or later they would trip her on that one too. He had repeatedly told Priscilla to tell the truth. "If you've done something bad in your life," he had instructed her, "just pony up to it like a little soldier. Just say, well, damn it, I guess I did. People will forgive you for making a mistake, but they won't forgive you for lying." Shannon was less concerned about what the jury might be thinking than he was about what Priscilla's testimony might force from the court. A witness who volunteers false information automatically opens the door for what lawyers call *collateral impeachment*. The defense could attack or impeach a witness on matters relevant to the case, but not on collateral or secondary issues. Unless, of course, the witness lied about some of those irrelevant issues. Priscilla believed that her private life was in no way related to the issue in this case—the murder of Andrea Wilborn—and the prosecution fully agreed. So did Judge Dowlen, up to this point. But the judge had already allowed the defense to stray into an area whose relevancy was suspect: if Priscilla insisted on lying or even leaving false impressions with the jury, the defense would be permitted to dredge up all the sordid details. Up to this point Priscilla had left the impression that she barely knew W. T. Rufner. Because of this, it was entirely possible that the court would allow the defense to demonstrate collaterally just how well she did know him.

It was Priscilla's fourth day on the witness stand when Haynes began to probe her drug habits. Outside the presence of the jury, Haynes announced to the court that Priscilla had used LSD, cocaine, heroin, and marijuana for the past several years and asked permission to question her about the drugs. Prosecutors objected strongly, but Dowlen ruled that the defense could pursue this line of questioning as long as the jury did not hear. Racehorse opened by asking about cocaine. Priscilla replied that she had never used it.

Q: You've never snorted it? Did you ever snort a white powder when you didn't know what it was?

A: I don't do things just because they seem to be fashionable.

Q: Have you ever in your life taken LSD?

A: No, sir.

Q: Have you ever in your life snorted heroin?

A: No.

Q: Used heroin?

A: No.

Q: How about speed?

A: I have tried diet pills.

Q: Have you ever used marijuana?

A: I have tried it—when I was teenager years ago.

Assistant DA Tolly Wilson objected as Haynes began to drift into other topics, declaring that the only purpose of these questions was to get the witness on record "so they can come back tomorrow with the daily copy [transcript] and find some small inconsistency." Haynes replied that it was his intention to provide "independent proof that the fidelity of this witness's answers are questionable."

When the jury had returned to the courtroom, Haynes began questioning Priscilla about her use of the prescription painkiller Percodan, the suggestion being that the drug might have impaired her ability to recall the details of August 2–3. Priscilla told the court that she first took Percodan in 1973 after breaking her ankle skiing, but added that she took the drug only occasionally until after the shooting. Before the shooting, she said, her prescription for Percodan was limited to twelve tablets. Later, as the pain from the bullet wound became unbearable, her personal physician, Dr. Thomas Simon, and the surgeon who operated on her the night of the shooting, Dr. Charles Crenshaw, wrote prescriptions for up to 200 tablets a week.

"Did you have any idea at all that the continued use of Percodan could become habituating?" Haynes asked the witness. Priscilla said she didn't.

Q: No physician ever told you that?

A: I've been told it's possible to become addicted to Excedrin. I've been told it's like anything, including alcohol, that if you overdo it, it can have bad side effects.

Q: Have you been told Percodan is addictive?

A: I've never been told I was addicted, nor am I.

Judge Dowlen called a recess at this point, and the prosecutors huddled with their witness in one of the back rooms. The defense had already subpoenaed prescription records from two Fort Worth pharmacies. Although Priscilla was claiming that she used only small amounts of the powerful painkiller in the months prior to the murders, the records showed that she refilled her prescription every month from September 1975 through July 1976. The prescriptions hadn't been for twelve at a time, as she had said under oath, but for fifty. Not fifty a month, but fifty a week. During the month of July, for example, records showed she got fifty tablets each on the sixth, twelfth, seventeenth, twenty-third, twenty-seventh, and twenty-eighth.

Tim Curry felt that the defense hadn't yet damaged his witness with the questions about the illicit drugs, though it was possible they might be able to impeach her collaterally later. But now Haynes was moving into a dangerous area. The subpoenaed pharmacy records would prove beyond a doubt that Priscilla had received enough Percodan to addict several people.

"Are you addicted to Percodan?" Curry asked in his soft, professional voice. "Just tell me the truth."

Priscilla hesitated, then answered, "I guess I am."

"Then don't lie about it," the district attorney told her.

When Haynes resumed his questioning after the recess, Priscilla was ready to pony up.

Q: And are you saying you were not addicted to the use of Percodan?

A: No, sir. I don't mean to mislead the jury.

Q: You are addicted to Percodan, aren't you?

A: Yes, sir, there's a possibility.

Q: Don't you know it to be a fact?

A: It's highly possible.

Q: How many Percodan were you taking a day?

A: Due to the pain from the gunshot, I was taking far more than 100 a week.

Q: Were you taking more than *200* a week?

A: That may be closer to it. I was having to take four every couple of hours.

Priscilla went on to explain that her doctors had become concerned about her addiction and had her admitted to the hospital in July, even as the jury selection

185

was proceeding in Amarillo. "It got to the point where I couldn't take the pain anymore," she said, looking at the jury now. "I went into the hospital for spasms in my back and had a nerve block."

The court recessed for the day.

～⌀ • ⌀～

Friday, August 26, was the birthdate of Lyndon Johnson, and the court was recessed for the holiday. Nobody talked about LBJ that day, but the entire Panhandle crackled with gossip about the trial. A local TV reporter called it "the biggest thing to ever hit Amarillo." In every bar, restaurant, and department store the major topic was Cullen and Priscilla. Mrs. Lozelle Graham, who had commuted to the trial every day from her home in Lockney, 100 miles from Amarillo, admitted that she had spent most of her time in the hallway just trying to catch a glimpse of Priscilla. "I don't have to be in the courtroom to tell you what I think," Mrs. Graham told *Dallas Morning News* reporter Maryln Schwartz. "I think she's lying and Cullen is innocent." Many of the housewives had no idea who was murdered, but they could recall exactly what Priscilla wore each day. "I can't believe she was wearing a suede outfit in the middle of August," said Mrs. Donna Davis, another highly interested observer. "That's not going to help her, not a bit." The housewives snickered at the young woman who usually accompanied Priscilla to court. The woman was a nurse, but the wags called her "Priscilla's hairdresser." Her bodyguard was sometimes identified as her "hit man." They had all heard about the poster-size picture of "Priscilla and that naked man," and they clustered around a courtroom artist who had sketched it.

186

It seemed as though everyone in Amarillo had a special interest in one or more of the characters assembled for the trial. An eighteen-year-old Amarillo College pre-law student named Bill Bragg showed up in court one day wearing a T-shirt that said, "Sock it to 'em, W. T." Dowlen ordered him escorted out of the courtroom. Bragg's mother, Bonnie Bragg, had become one of Cullen Davis's middle-aged groupies and sometimes brought the Fort Worth millionaire packages of Life Savers. Thomas Preston, Jr., who was also known as Amarillo Slim and had won the World Championship of Poker, accepted an invitation to have lunch with Cullen, who expressed a desire to play some gin rummy in his cell. "I believe I could punish him," Slim admitted to a reporter. Slim did not deny rumors that he had participated in high-stakes poker games with Davis's defense lawyers but observed, "There isn't a one of them that could track an elephant in four feet of high snow." Earlier, when Cullen was temporarily free on $1,650,000 bond, Stanley Marsh had preserved his own reputation as the town nut by calling all the airlines in Amarillo and reserving tickets to Rio de Janeiro in Cullen's name. Even the cowboys on the Marsh-O'Brien Ranch had paused to consider local affairs. The cowboys missed their cohort, Freddy Thompson, and were taking bets on how long it would take him to break out of the Executive Inn where the jurors were sequestered.

Outside the courtroom Priscilla couldn't stop talking about the trial. After two days of grueling cross-examination, she was more determined than ever to get "the truth as I know it" to anyone who would listen. During the Friday recess she told reporters: "I'm not saying I'm Miss Goodie Twoshoes, but their only defense is to destroy my credibility. It is obvious they don't have a case if the only thing they can do is destroy my credibility. To insinuate that I had some big drug orgies is absurd. They are dragging a bunch of dogs. It doesn't matter if I was the biggest hooker, doper, or what have you. It has absolutely nothing to do with what he did. . . . They are trying this like a smutty divorce . . . while in reality it is a murder. A twelve-year-old child

187

was killed. They seem to forget that. I never will. They say the truth died with Andrea. It didn't."

Cullen was talking too. If Priscilla was the wanton hussy that the defense lawyers were claiming, reporters wondered why Cullen married her in the first place. Priscilla changed, Cullen told them. "I knew she was taking a lot of drugs, but only in retrospect did I realize how seriously they had affected her. During the past year of investigation I have discovered that Priscilla has caused my home to make Sodom and Gomorrah look like Petticoat Junction." Earlier in the summer Davis had appeared edgy, haggard, and depressed, but now that the trial was under way, he seemed calm, even jovial, as he quipped with reporters and mingled with the groupies. "Many people have been wondering how I could be so well adjusted after so long in jail," he said at one point. "Possibly the answer can be found in the old saying, 'If rape is inevitable, relax and enjoy it.' "

While those with time on their hands indulged in gossip, the real infighting was taking place in the judge's chambers. One issue concerned an affidavit signed by a Joe L. Crow who claimed to have overheard a telephone conversation in which W. T. Rufner threatened to kill a girlfriend, Carmey Green, unless she agreed to supply him an alibi for the night of August 2, 1976. According to the affidavit, Rufner told Carmey Green, "I'll kill your ass," unless she swore in writing that he was with her on the night of the murders. The affidavit didn't say who Crow was or how he happened to overhear the conversation. Court papers filed by the prosecutors claimed Crow used an illegal wiretap. Also at issue was a defense affidavit signed by Sandy Guthrie Myers, this one to the effect that Rufner had once threatened the lives of both Priscilla and Stan Farr.

Dowlen ruled that testimony regarding alleged threats and violence was immaterial at this point of the trial, but once again he didn't rule out the possibility that it could become relevant later. On these grounds he allowed the defense to probe the stormy relationship between Priscilla and Rufner outside the jury's presence.

Although the prosecution objected repeatedly, Racehorse Haynes bombarded Priscilla with questions about Rufner's alleged penchant for violence.

Q: Do you recall an incident at 4200 Mockingbird when W. T. Rufner was choking you so hard that you thought you were going to die and the only reason he stopped was a cigarette was burning a hole in the bedspread?

A: W. T. was not physically violent with me ever.

Hardly allowing the witness time to catch her breath, Haynes asked her about other incidents—had Rufner once pulled a knife and sliced her dress from waist to hem, had he once cut off her bra and panties, had he once fought over her with Larry Myers? Priscilla denied each allegation. She did recall a time when T-man threw a potted plant at her as she was taking a bath, but she denied Haynes's contention that Rufner had also pulled a pistol. She verified the story about the time he had wrecked the transmission of her Lincoln Continental Mark IV outside the Old San Francisco Saloon and how when she returned home that night with ex-boxer Jerry Thomas, Rufner was waiting inside the mansion.

The following morning Dowlen permitted Haynes to question Priscilla in front of the jury about the incident outside the Old San Francisco Saloon.

Q: Was W. T. Rufner unhappy with you?

A: I guess you could say that.

Q: Was he unhappy about the fact you were dating Stan Farr?

A: I don't know that he was. I was also dating several others.

Q: How did he get into the house?

A: Andrea.

"*Andrea* let him in?" Haynes asked, as though he could hardly believe his ears.

"Yes, sir," Priscilla said evenly. "They were just talking." She went on to explain that she asked Rufner to leave, and when he hesitated, Jerry Thomas "was on him instantly . . . just pulverizing him. I had to break it up."

Q: After that time did Stan Farr tell you W. T. Rufner threatened to kill him?

189

A: No, sir.

Q: Did Stan Farr say he was going to Florida to kill the person who took money from the Rhinestone Cowboy?

A: No, sir.

At the conclusion of the sixth day of testimony, the defense argued in chambers that because of Priscilla's poor health and imminent surgery, they should be allowed to present evidence out of sequence. Specifically, the defense wanted to question Priscilla about Sandy Guthrie Myers's claim that Priscilla knew before the night of the killings that something was about to happen. The problem was, Myers was a witness for the defense and it wasn't yet their turn to call witnesses. Therefore, they wanted permission to call Myers now, while Priscilla was still available in Amarillo. Phil Burleson told the judge this was only fair; because of the surgery the state's key witness might not be available for questioning when it was the defense's turn. Dowlen rejected the motion as improper, but both sides sensed that he too was worried that Priscilla's health might jeopardize the trial somewhere down the way.

"They're trying to bootstrap themselves up. I wouldn't be surprised if the judge doesn't let them do it," Joe Shannon said. "We've asked the judge to require them to connect all this trash. They keep saying: our theory is, it was a drug deal that went sour. Our response is: show us what evidence you have there was in fact a drug deal happening that night. They haven't done that. But the judge is getting antsy. He's antsy about Priscilla being in the hospital and not being able to come back for further cross-examination, so he's giving them a lot of latitude. He's letting them develop a lot of stuff that he wouldn't if Priscilla were hale and hardy. Once they open the door, they begin to bootstrap themselves. They're saying: well, judge, we've already gone into this, so now we need to go into this . . . when in fact they shouldn't have been allowed to go into all that trash in the first place."

Tim Curry agreed: "I thought we came up here to

try a murder case. We've gone so far afield it's ridiculous."

It was at this point in the trial that members of the press became privy to the defense's master plan. Whether inadvertently or on purpose, defense lawyers conveniently left a memo on the table next to exhibits already admitted as evidence. It was no secret that reporters checked the contents of this table during recess. According to the memo, it was the defense's plan to show (1) "Priscilla Davis knew something was about to happen that night"; (2) "Beverly Bass could not see who shot Gavrel"; (3) "The person who did the shooting was, in fact, after Stan Farr and did not intend to shoot Priscilla."

Confronted with the memo, Phil Burleson admitted to reporters that the memo was "substantially correct" and that the defense also planned to prove that there was a conspiracy between at least two people to put the blame on Cullen Davis. Burleson wasn't yet ready to name the two conspirators, but it was apparent that he meant Priscilla and Bev Bass. If the defense had intentionally arranged for reporters to see the memo, the question was *why*. It appeared to some that, even very early on, the defense intended to take the offense. At this point their only shots had been at Priscilla's credibility. The jury might believe that Priscilla was a liar and a tramp, but it was asking a great deal for jurors also to believe she would deliberately conceal the true identity of the person who killed both her lover and her twelve-year-old daughter. The defense's plan appeared to have two edges: it would supply a motive for the murder of Stan Farr (revenge) and Priscilla's cover-up (greed), *and* it would take the focus off the murder of Andrea Wilborn.

Still, leaking this strategy to the press and getting it to the jury weren't the same thing. Or were they? There had been a number of reports that the jurors were receiving unauthorized visitors. There were also rumors about unchaperoned visits from jurors' spouses. If the rumors about conjugal visits were true, God knows what had been said or conjectured. Maybe they had even played Cullen and Priscilla.

When Priscilla had taken the witness stand for the seventh straight day, Racehorse Haynes fired off a barrage of questions designed to establish that both she and Farr suspected trouble in advance of August 2. This was exactly the line of questioning the prosecution feared, and Shannon objected heatedly that it wasn't relevant. Dowlen overruled him and permitted Haynes to proceed.

Q: Do you recall seeing Sandy Myers in the office of Dr. [Thomas] Simons a few days before August 2, 1976?

A: I recall seeing her one time in the waiting room when I had an appointment.

Q: Was it just a few days prior to August 2?

A: I don't recall the date.

Q: When you did see Sandy Myers, did you tell her you wanted to talk to her?

A: No, sir.

Q: Did you tell her "Something heavy is coming down"?

A: No, sir. I did not say that.

Q: You don't remember what was said.

A: I remember what she said to me.

Q: You don't remember what you said?

A: I don't believe I told her anything.

Haynes wanted to pursue this conversation, but the state objected again and this time Dowlen cut Haynes off. Haynes then asked Priscilla about the .357 magnum that Farr carried in his black Thunderbird. Didn't this indicate he feared for his life? Priscilla replied that Farr only carried the pistol when he transported large sums of money for the Rhinestone Cowboy. Racehorse treated the jury to his mystic smile; he wanted them to remember this later when he developed the fact that the pistol was still in Farr's car on the night of the murder, several weeks after he was terminated from his job at the Rhinestone Cowboy.

"Were you present [at the Rhinestone Cowboy] when

192

Stan Farr told Horace Copeland, 'Get the hell out of here'?" he asked quickly. Just as quickly, Priscilla replied: "Stan did not talk that way to anyone. Not in my presence." Earlier in this same cross-examination, Haynes was questioning Priscilla about her ambulance ride to the hospital when he asked abruptly, "You knew at the time, did you not, that Andrea Wilborn was dead?" Priscilla had answered, "No." Race thought now about returning to the question but decided that the implication might do more harm than good. He'd rather not attack her motherhood just yet. He had again insinuated to the jury that Farr had poor relationships with both Rufner and Copeland; that was enough for now.

"We have no more questions for this witness at this time," Haynes announced suddenly at the end of the day.

Priscilla's ordeal was nearly over. That night Tim Curry and his assistants considered their own strategy for the redirect examination. It was becoming obvious that Cullen Davis would never take the witness stand. The prosecution therefore decided that the jury needed to be educated about the man whose fate they would judge, his impulsive spending habits, his fondness for guns, his well-documented temper tantrums. Dowlen wasn't likely to admit testimony concerning isolated episodes of rage, but he would have to entertain questions along these lines if they pertained to the victim, Andrea Wilborn.

The state got an unexpected break the following morning. As Curry was asking questions about Andrea's relationship with Cullen, leading up to the revelation that the girl had been so frightened of Davis that she finally refused to visit the mansion, Priscilla blurted out how Cullen had once kept Andrea awake most of the night working on her math. Before the defense could object, Priscilla told the jury that Cullen had kicked at the girl and called her stupid. Dowlen ordered the attorneys to approach the bench, but even as they argued, Curry knew his side had won a point. Despite objections by the defense, Dowlen now allowed the state to question

Priscilla about the occasion a few months before the separation when Cullen ordered her to telephone Andrea and instruct her to come to the mansion for the weekend.

Priscilla told the jury: "He [Cullen] told me to call Andrea and tell her to get over this weekend. And I told Cullen I wouldn't lie to her. He said, 'Damn it, I said call her and get her over here.'" Again the defense objected. Curry cautioned his witness, "Now don't tell me what Andrea said. That would be hearsay. Just tell me what you said to her."

Priscilla continued: "I said, 'Hi, Andrea. Why don't you come see us sometime. We sure do miss you. . . . Andrea, you know you need to work on your math. Cullen just wants you to work on your math. I wish you would come over.'"

That's when Davis jerked the telephone from her hand. Priscilla then revealed what Cullen had said to Andrea.

"He said, 'Goddamn it, Andrea, I want you over here this weekend.' Then he said, 'I don't give a goddamn what your plans are, I want you over here. . . . All right, goddamn it, you're not welcome over to this . . . house again until you're ready to do exactly what I tell you. And furthermore, you're to return everything I ever gave you. I don't give a goddamn what it is, you are to return it.'"

"After that phone call," Curry asked softly, "did Andrea Wilborn ever return to 4200 Mockingbird while the defendant was living there?"

"No, sir," Priscilla said, tears welling in her eyes, hands and lips trembling.

"How old was she at the time?"

"She was ten."

When Curry questioned her about the guns that Cullen kept around the mansion, Priscilla told about the frequent times she had watched Cullen shoot target practice at the family home at Eagle Mountain Lake. He was a very good shot, she recalled.

Q: How many handguns did he own?

A: I don't know. He had several.

194

Q: Where have you seen them?

A: Under his bed, in the closet, on a shelf in the old house, on a shelf in his dressing area in the new house, on the floorboard on the driver's side of his automobile, and in the trunk of his car.

Priscilla wept as Curry delivered his final volley of questions.

Q: Mrs. Davis, did W. T. Rufner shoot you and Stan Farr on August 2, 1976?

A: No, sir.

Q: Was it Horace Copeland who shot you and Stan that night?

A: No, sir.

Q: Tell the jury, Mrs. Davis, who it was that shot you and Stan that night.

A: It was Cullen Davis, the defendant.

Most of the defense's final assault came while both Priscilla and the jury were out of the courtroom. Haynes argued that he should be allowed to question Priscilla about her divorce litigation with Jack Wilborn, about how she had lured Wilborn into sexual encounters, then screamed rape. It was all a part of her long-established pattern as a "greedy schemer," Haynes told the court; she used sex to skin Jack Wilborn, now she was trying murder on Cullen. Haynes claimed this line of questioning went to the very heart of the matter. "The motive for fabricating a story against Cullen Davis was this woman's personal greed and design to obtain his fortune," Haynes declared. The prosecution argued that testimony from a divorce case that was ten years old was both irrelevant and highly prejudicial. Dowlen agreed, but he made one concession to the defense: he permitted them to ask questions about Priscilla's current divorce suit against Cullen.

Haynes was hell-bent on establishing that Priscilla had signed a prenuptial agreement and damn well knew she signed it; that's why she had to frame Cullen. Priscilla stuck to her claim that the agreement had been obtained by fraud. Haynes claimed the agreement was witnessed and notarized by Cullen's secretary, Fern Frost, two days before the marriage, but Priscilla testified that she had never seen Frost until the very day of the marriage, in the hospital reception room as Stinky Davis lay dying. Haynes launched one final foray. He wanted the jury to believe that the reason Priscilla spent $20,000 a month while she was married to Cullen was to accumulate separate property for the time when she planned to dump him. Priscilla didn't deny spending $20,000 a month, but as to the suggested motive she responded, "I never gave it any thought."

When Haynes questioned her about the Davis family property on Eagle Mountain Lake, Priscilla referred to it as "our lake house."

"That is the editorial *our?*" Haynes inquired, looking down his half-moon glasses at Priscilla.

"Well, it would be kind of foolish to run around saying everything was Cullen's," Priscilla replied in that little girl's don't-be-silly voice she used on such occasions.

"Everything was Cullen's, wasn't it?"

"Not to my way of thinking."

"Yes, ma'am!" Haynes declared, looking hard at Priscilla, who shook her head and returned his glare.

After eleven grueling days on the witness stand Priscilla was excused and allowed to return to Fort Worth. Both sides reserved the right to recall her as a witness, but as it developed, neither side exercised that option. Instead, for the next two months Priscilla remained the trial's major offstage character, maligned almost daily by the defense and defended by other state's witnesses as they corroborated her story of the events of August 2–3.

"I don't think they laid a glove on her story about the murders," Tim Curry said that night as he shucked his cowboy boots and prepared to relax with a few beers. "They came at her with everything they had, but she came through it very well." Certainly the defense had soiled her reputation and would continue to. She had been less than truthful about her relationship with W. T. Rufner and her drug habit, and Curry was reasonably sure that the defense would bring forth witnesses who would swear that Priscilla knew she was

196

signing a premarital document. Priscilla had also denied mentioning her divorce case when she talked to Bev Bass at the Rangoon Racquet Club in the hours just before the killings, but this seemed like small change in a high-stakes murder case. What pleased the district attorney was that the defense hadn't been able to shake her story about the night of the murder.

Although he didn't admit it at the time, even Racehorse Haynes agreed that Priscilla had made a better witness than he anticipated. "I thought it was a stroke of genius the way Tim Curry handled her," Haynes said later. "He brought her to the end in super style. I'd have to give him an A."

As the final spectators crowded out of the courtroom on September 7, sated by nearly two weeks of testimony detailing Priscilla's love affairs, drug addiction, and association with numerous rogues, felons, and phantoms, members of the press clustered around the accused killer, Cullen Davis. In a scene reminiscent of a football locker room after a tough game, there was an almost self-conscious reverence in the questions put to the dapper, cool-mannered defendant. Whatever sins had been laid at Priscilla's doorstep, reporters agreed among themselves that she was very convincing when she identified Cullen as the killer. Nobody who had followed the case believed that Cullen would take the witness stand and deny the accusations, but that seemed to be the only question anyone dared ask.

Cullen answered straight out: "I am not particularly looking forward to getting on the stand, but I wouldn't hesitate to do it for one minute. I am not going to get up and get in a liar's contest. I don't care to get in a liar's contest with someone over such unscrupulous lies. It makes me cringe and disgusted that she says things like I kicked Andrea and called her stupid. She has no one to back that up, and Andrea is not here to confirm it. I am the only one left alive to confirm that that is not true."

That night over cocktails at Rhett Butler's, Judge George Dowlen admitted that it had been the most harrowing two weeks in his career. The judge had originally reckoned that once the jury was selected, the case would take about a month to reach a conclusion; half that estimated time had elapsed and only one major witness had testified. "This is an unusual situation," Dowlen said, stirring his Scotch and water with a celery stick. "Both the state and the defense came here prepared to spend whatever it takes to try the case. No one side can outspend the other. It's not a situation where a big, expensive defense lawyer comes into town and shoots down a young prosecutor. The prosecutors in this case are capable, experienced people. This is what the system is all about. This is what makes it work."

Dowlen ordered an extra ration of celery sticks and shook his head in wonder. "Cullen and Priscilla are the only ones who know the truth," he said. "And one of them is lying. Every once in a while their eyes make contact. And they *know*. Nobody but the two of them. God, it's a strange deal."

~ • ~

Any sensational murder trial is bound to attract its share of adventurers, opportunists, publicity seekers, and garden variety nuts, but they seemed to sprout around this trial like toadstools over a septic tank.

As the trial entered that tedious, protracted stage where the state must prove up its case in the quickest possible time, with a maximum of stately decorum, the fifth-floor hallway outside Judge Dowlen's courtroom resembled a human zoo. Journalists, cameramen, artists, private investigators, bodyguards, and informants jostled with housewives for available space. There was a rumor, helped along by Racehorse Haynes himself, that a Hollywood producer was offering "six figures" for exclusive rights to Cullen's story. A Dallas radio station was giving play to a new country and western song called "Good-bye, Priscilla," and a local printer was working on an order of W. T. Rufner T-shirts featuring a reproduction of the famous poster. A couple of television reporters jokingly planned to film a takeoff on the current series of American Express Card commercials. This one would open on a man in black creeping toward a mansion in the dead of night. As he approached the lights of the entranceway, the man would turn to the camera and say: "Hi there! I'm a wealthy Fort Worth industrialist on my way to kill my family. But a lot of people don't know my name. That's why I carry. . . ."

It was a trial that cut across the grain of society and the consensus of taste. As one investigator put it, "A whole lot of people have a whole lot at stake in this trial." In some ways it was the great leveler—bank presidents as well as dope dealers kept a keen eye on the proceedings and walked a little more carefully because of what was happening in Amarillo. The investigation hadn't stopped but rather intensified as the trial continued. The defense alone had as many as twenty investigators working in various areas, sorting out tips and evaluating information. The district attorney's office kept its own investigators busy and was not above putting the arm on potential witnesses who had unrelated but unresolved problems with the law. Any number of improbable characters came forward to volunteer information. Most of it was bad, but both sides were obligated to check it. There had been a time when the defense thought it could link the murders at 4200 Mockingbird with the unsolved slaying of a wealthy West Texas used-car dealer, but it hadn't proved out. Another story persisted that someone other than the killer had secretly visited the Davis estate that fatal night. Yet another rumor maintained that the murder weapon would surface shortly. "There's at least one person who knows where that gun is," Joe Shannon reasoned. "You don't suppose W. T. Rufner might wake up dead some morning with that gun conveniently sticking from his hip pocket, do you?"

Several of the principals in the case had reported death threats, including Judge Dowlen. On more than one occasion Steve Sumner, the lawyer in charge of investigation for the defense, had found his motel room ransacked. Sandy Myers, the convicted cocaine dealer whom Priscilla had befriended and who was now expected to testify for the defense, had been threatened by telephone calls and by people trying to break down her door while she hid inside her own home.

One day in court, as the lawyers gathered in front of the bench to argue some objection, Dowlen's secretary brought him the morning mail. He opened an envelope and out dropped a spent .38 bullet. "I don't know what to make of it," Dowlen said later. "Is it a threat? Evidence? A joke? You tell me." Dowlen gave the bullet to a member of the Fort Worth crime lab, who examined it and reported that it did not match any of the .38 slugs recovered at the crime scene. But "the judge's bullet," as it came to be called, was another item to baffle the court and confuse the jury.

Something more sensational was delivered to the court in early September. Fort Worth attorney Charles Baldwin contacted Judge Tom Cave and said he had a client who thought she could produce the murder weapon, an R & G Industries .38 pistol once owned by Horace Copeland. Although the jury was ostensibly unaware of this dramatic development, it was front-page news for several days. If Copeland's gun did turn out to be the murder weapon that the prosecution had never been able to locate, the case against Cullen Davis would crumble, but Curry wasn't worried, only annoyed. Ballistics had established that the murder weapon was a Smith & Wesson, not an R & G. Still, the new gun had to be tested, and until the results were conclusive, there was a public shadow over the state's case. Attorney Charles Baldwin didn't help by speculating to the press that there was "a fifty-fifty chance" Copeland's gun would prove out.

In the long run it wasn't the gun but the story that went with it that damaged the state. Baldwin's client who produced the gun was Polly Ware, a former barmaid at the Rhinestone Cowboy. In the summer of 1976, shortly before the killings, Polly Ware claimed that Copeland had beaten her up. Ms. Ware asked for an injunction to prohibit Copeland from bothering her or even entering the Rhinestone Cowboy. Apparently, Stan Farr had witnessed the scuffle. Baldwin told reporters that he had subpoenaed Farr for a hearing scheduled the week of August 3, but Farr refused to testify. "Farr said he was afraid to show up because Horace Copeland had threatened to kill him," Baldwin said. When ballistics experts had examined the R & G .38 and both sides were satisfied it was not the murder weapon, everyone forgot the gun. But the story about Copeland's threat against Stan Farr lingered in the courtroom and shaded the proceedings until the end.

The next major witness for the state would be Bubba Gavrel, but first the prosecution called a series of witnesses to corroborate parts of Priscilla's story.

Mr. and Mrs. Clifford Jones, who owned the home next to the Davis estate, substantiated almost word for word Priscilla's story of how she had beaten on their door that night, bleeding from a hole in her chest and shouting that Cullen was up at the mansion shooting everyone. Ambulance driver Thomas Southall told of picking up a terrified Priscilla at the Joneses' home and later helping remove the bloody corpse of Andrea Wilborn from the mansion. Southall had also heard Priscilla identify Cullen as the killer.

It was toward the end of the third week of testimony when Bubba Gavrel hobbled into the courtroom on crutches and was sworn in. Like the other state's witnesses, Gavrel confirmed key parts of Priscilla's story and filled in details as he had in previous statements. Joe Shannon began by asking Gavrel if he had worn a watch that night—there were some uncomfortable time discrepancies in the various statements, and Shannon wanted the jury to understand that the witnesses were only approximating time to the best of their recollection. Gavrel replied that he didn't have a watch and was therefore guessing at the time.

After telling the jury that he and Bev Bass had talked

with Farr and Priscilla for about forty-five minutes at the Rangoon Racquet Club, Gavrel told about first driving by his parents' house, then heading for 4200 Mockingbird where his date planned to spend the night with Dee Davis. He estimated that it was between 11:25 P.M. and midnight when he parked his Blazer in the guest parking area near the mansion. Shannon asked what happened as Gavrel and Bev Bass stepped into the driveway.

"I heard a woman screaming, 'I love you. I've always loved you.' I looked toward where the screams were coming from." Pointing to the courtyard on the diagram near the witness box, Gavrel said he saw a man pulling a woman by the arm. The man was saying, "Come on. Come on." Gavrel couldn't recognize either, but the man wore dark clothes and the woman was a blonde. As he and Miss Bass began walking along a wall that separated the driveway from the courtyard, Gavrel said the man walked to the courtyard gate. "He was wearing dark clothes and he had a garbage sack," Gavrel said, demonstrating for the jury how the man held the sack in front of his abdomen. "I asked him, 'What are you doing? What's going on?' and he said, 'Let's go in.' " The man in black led the couple in front of the garage to the walkway leading to the mansion's main entrance. The courtroom was dead silent as Shannon asked what happened next.

"That's when he shot me," Gavrel said in a cold monotone. "She [Bass] said, 'Bubba, that's Cullen,' and that's when he turned and shot me."

"At the time he shot you," Shannon asked the witness, "did you have an opportunity to observe him?"

"Yes, sir," Gavrel said. He looked at the defense table and pointed to Cullen Davis.

Gavrel told about being paralyzed from the waist down and crawling to the front door as Cullen chased after Bev Bass, about trying to open the front door and looking through the window at the blood-smeared floor, about playing dead as the man in black returned, and watching as he shot out the windows and disappeared inside the mansion. A few minutes later, Gavrel said, the man came back through the windows and started down the sidewalk. "He looked at me and said something like 'Oh, my God!' " Gavrel told the jury.

As Bubba Gavrel recounted the rest of what he could remember from that bloody night, Phil Burleson's mind was racing ahead. As the defense lawyers had anticipated, there were some inconsistencies between the story Gavrel was telling now and sworn statements he had made on previous occasions. The exact position where he first saw the man dragging the woman, for example. In one statement Gavrel had indicated the sidewalk, and in another, the courtyard. It seemed like a little thing, but Burleson was looking for little things; Gavrel's veracity as a witness in this case was none too good, and it would get worse with each inconsistency that the defense could bring to the jury's attention. By the time most of the state's major witnesses reached Amarillo, they had already given statements to the police, testified at the bond hearing, and given depositions in various civil suits. Once they had undergone direct examination in Amarillo, their version would be on record at least four times. One of Burleson's jobs was to match carefully each of the four versions before beginning the cross-examination. The lawyer had devised a sort of storyboard using index cards and colored markers to indicate points of dispute.

Since court was about to recess for the weekend, Burleson decided to save his loaded questions for Monday morning.

As the fourth week of testimony began, Burleson quickly established several things designed to show that Gavrel was less than a fair and impartial witness. He got Gavrel to acknowledge that his family had filed a $13-million lawsuit against Cullen Davis, and he asked if Gavrel and Bass had drunk and smoked marijuana on the night of August 2. Gavrel said they had a few drinks but denied using grass. Burleson let that hang for a minute while he questioned the witness about inconsistencies in previous statements.

203

Q: Did you ever say he [the man in black] turned to the left?

A: Yes, sir.

Q: But you're telling the jury now that he turned to the right?

A: Yes, sir.

After leading the witness through various inconsistencies, Burleson asked abruptly if Gavrel had ever heard the name Paul Goheen. Gavrel stiffened slightly as he admitted that he had heard Goheen's name. In an affidavit for the defense, Goheen, the ambulance attendant who escorted Gavrel to the hospital, said that Gavrel didn't know who shot him and that en route to the hospital Gavrel gave the attendant two Baggies of marijuana.

Q: During the time you were in the ambulance, you say you don't remember [anything]?

A: I remember the ambulance guy in the back telling the driver to slow down. I told them to go faster.

Q: Anything else?

A: I remember the guy in the back cutting my shirt off.

Q: Do you remember giving the attendant anything?

A: No, sir.

Q: Do you remember giving the attendant two Baggies of marijuana?

A: No, sir.

Q: Do you recall [Fort Worth policeman] J. L. Soders asking who it was that shot you and you saying, "I do not know the man"?

A: No, sir. I don't remember talking to him.

Q: Do you remember telling police the man who shot you was much shorter than you are and about thirty-four years old?

A: No, sir.

Later, Burleson tested Gavrel's memory regarding conversations with his parents in the hospital.

Q: Do you recall your father saying, "Well, that girl out there said it was Cullen Davis so if anyone asks you, you say that's who it was"?

A: No, sir.

Q: Do you remember Tommy Jourden?

A: No, sir. I know what he says and all that but I don't remember him.

Burleson's small points were beginning to make an impression. Gavrel's testimony was beginning to look too neat, his memory too selective. Burleson finished his cross-examination feeling that the jury had its doubts about Gavrel—and in a criminal case, reasonable doubt was all the defense needed. The witness was handed back to the prosecution for redirect examination.

The prosecution spent the next several days trying to establish that Gavrel and Priscilla were both too badly wounded to "conspire" against Cullen Davis. Dr. Michael Heard, the intern on duty the night they brought the two gunshot victims to the emergency room of John Peter Smith Hospital, testified that Gavrel was in shock and had lost four pints of blood, about one-third of his body's capacity, by the time he was carried into the emergency room. Within a matter of minutes he was anesthetized for the three hours of surgery that followed. Under the skillful questioning of Marvin Collins, the doctor described the anesthetics used to "crash" Gavrel. One was an LSD-type drug that sometimes caused patients to hallucinate. After surgery, Gavrel was given Demerol, which, like the pre-op anesthetic, could explain the young man's temporary memory loss.

Dr. Heard's contention that Gavrel was in shock was a clear setback to the defense, and they objected repeatedly, but Dowlen allowed Collins to continue. Backtracking to show that Gavrel's memory loss even before reaching the hospital had a medical explanation, Collins asked the doctor a series of hypothetical questions. Gavrel had testified, for example, that after he crawled into the mansion breakfast room he forced himself to sit up and reach for a telephone.

Q: What will happen if that person were lying down and sits up?

A: It will aggravate the symptoms of shock.

Q: What does that include?

A: Light-headedness . . . dizziness . . . further drop in blood pressure.

Q: How long would it take for this to occur?

A: It could happen within minutes.

Q: Is it possible the patient could be unconscious?

A: The patient could range from clear consciousness to coma.

Q: Do you have an opinion in reasonable medical probability that this person could have his eyes open?

A: Yes.

Q: Do you have an opinion that this person might suffer from any memory loss?

A: He might or might not.

Q: Do you have an opinion that he might have been talking and not remembering what he said?

A: Yes.

Heard went on to explain that after surgery both Gavrel and Priscilla Davis had tubes connected to respirators inserted in their windpipes. They were placed in different rooms. During the three days before her transfer to another hospital, Heard continued, Priscilla Davis made no attempt to walk, and of course Gavrel couldn't walk. The doctor added that the bullet that had lodged in Gavrel's spine remained there to this day.

For the next two days Racehorse Haynes attacked Heard's testimony, but with very little success. Pointing to medical records, Haynes noted sarcastically that there was no mention of Gavrel suffering from shock or memory loss.

Q: If he was in shock, it would be noted [in the records], would it not?

A: Not if somebody was bleeding to death from a gunshot wound. It might not be noted. . . . We don't use the word "shock" in our records because it's an ambiguous term. We record what we see—the blood pressure, the blood loss, exactly what we can measure.

For once Haynes seemed stumped by the medical jargon that is normally one of his best tools. Reduced to scattershooting, the lawyer questioned the young doctor's qualifications and asked him to define several medical terms, but he failed to shake Heard's conclusion that neither patient was in any condition to devise a conspiracy. What was worse from the point of view of the defense, the jury now had expert testimony explaining Gavrel's curious loss of memory.

Racehorse attempted one last gambit, asking Heard why Priscilla was given emergency treatment in June, just before the trial. Even this backfired. The defense had claimed on several occasions that the emergency was a drug overdose, but the doctor explained that the patient was admitted because of severe recurring back pain "secondary to a gunshot wound."

As the trial entered its second month, the prosecution paraded before the jury a number of police and crime scene investigators. The state's strategy at this point was to bolster the testimony already given by Priscilla and Bubba Gavrel and to prepare the jury for their third key witness, Bev Bass. It was time, one DA investigator explained, "to get all the bodies, all the bullets, and all the bloodstains in place."

The leadoff witness for this segment of their case was Officer J. A. Perez, one of the two Fort Worth cops that Bev Bass led back to the scene of the murders. Since the defense had challenged Gavrel's identification of Cullen Davis partly on the contention that the poor lighting conditions would make it impossible to recognize the gunman, Joe Shannon opened by asking Perez if there was enough light outside the mansion that night to read a newspaper.

"Yes, sir," Perez said. "You could read a newspaper or any other book there. There was a lot of light."

There was an eerie silence in the courtroom as Perez described approaching the mansion that supercharged hot August night. Through the broken window Bev Bass spotted Gavrel lying bloody and motionless on the breakfast room floor. "She tried to push past me," Perez said. "I grabbed her. I made her come back and sit behind the wall." Perez and Officer Jimmy Soders drew their sidearms and moved slowly toward the broken window and into the mansion. At this point they thought the killer might still be inside. While Perez looked after Gavrel, Soders followed the broad trail of blood to the kitchen and found the body of Stan Farr. By now several other officers had arrived, and more were on the way. After a quick search of the twenty-room mansion, the officers returned to the kitchen. That's when Perez noticed a blood smear on the facing of the door leading to the basement.

"Right here on the stairway there was a smear of blood that appeared to be a handprint," Perez said as he pointed to the diagram of the mansion interior. There were also dots of blood on the window near the basement entrance.

With his flashlight in one hand and his gun in the other, Perez led Sgt. J. D. Tigert down the steps and into the basement. In the beam of light the officers could see several doors along the basement walls. Moving to his left, Perez opened a door and stepped back quickly. He didn't know what he was expecting, but all he found was some lawn furniture. Very slowly, he moved to the next door and opened it. "I pressed against the wall. The door opens out, and I held it open three to four inches and looked in. And I saw some feet . . . laying down, toward the door. I closed the door and motioned for Sergeant Tigert. . . ."

What Tigert saw was the body of Andrea Wilborn, lying on her back in a pool of her own blood. More blood stained her face and arms. Her eyes were open, but she was clearly dead.

Meanwhile, upstairs there were at least twenty-five Fort Worth cops inside the mansion and possibly that many again outside. By some estimates there were maybe eighty cops at the scene, though nobody seemed to know for sure. This inability to determine just who was at the scene immediately after the murders was particularly handy to the defense. Racehorse Haynes complained: "The same thing that made this a sensational case in the press prevented the cops from doing a good job at the scene. It happened in the big house on the hill, the place everyone had wondered about. Instead of going up there and doing a good professional job, they were running around ogling the place and speculating on the wealth." It was a complaint that the defense hammered at repeatedly as the state continued to question crime scene officers and introduce physical evidence. "The crime scene people didn't do a damn thing," Haynes said at one point. "They didn't check the rug under Stan Farr's body for the presence of other stains . . . they didn't explain the various blood-type stains, such as those on the windows . . . they didn't explain all the fingerprints . . . they didn't even bother to fingerprint Stan Farr's shoes. Here we have a lady claiming someone pulled him by his feet and no-body took fingerprints of his shoes! What they did, they accepted the first version handed down and did just enough investigative work to corroborate that version."

For two days Haynes cross-examined Det. Greg Miller, using sections of the Fort Worth Police Department crime scene manual to suggest that the officers were sloppy in gathering evidence. Haynes grilled Miller about bloodstains that were not scraped for crime lab analysis and areas of the mansion not dusted for finger-prints, about pieces of plastic bag that had been ig-nored and sometimes stepped on as investigators moved about the mansion, about another plastic garbage bag that had never been recovered by investigators but that an ambulance driver had reported seeing outside the mansion grounds, and about the curious discovery of Bev Bass's sandals. One of the sandals had been found along Bass's path of escape, where it might be expected, but the second sandal wasn't immediately located. It was the eventual discovery of this second sandal that Haynes was most interested in pursuing.

"What person was it who delivered the shoe to you?" he asked Detective Miller.

"It wasn't a person," Miller had to admit. "It was a dog."

A *dog?* Racehorse arched one eyebrow at the jury as if to ask *did you hear what I heard?* One of the dogs running loose at the mansion had located the missing sandal and obligingly turned it over to police. Later, Haynes produced a crime scene photograph showing an unescorted dog inside the mansion breakfast room, wandering freely among such evidence as the bloodstained telephone, cigarettes, and a glass. The photograph showed a policeman in the background, looking disinterested in the dog's activities. At the next recess, Haynes told reporters, "No wonder there was a dog carrying shoes around. The police weren't interested. How would you like to be charged with murder and have dogs walking around the crime scene and smoking cigarettes?"

The interlude of the dog was mostly fun and games, but the state wasn't laughing about the general line of questions Haynes fired at their witness. Prosecutors asked to inspect the document Haynes had used in his cross-examination of Miller—pages photocopied from the Fort Worth PD crime manual, which, Haynes claimed, proved that investigators were negligent in gathering evidence. Haynes refused to surrender the document, noting that it had been offered as a defense exhibit but not entered into evidence because of objections by the prosecution. "They can't have their cake and eat it too," Haynes told Dowlen. The cake hit the fan moments later when Joe Shannon accused the defense of *altering* the police document by "Xeroxing out" a section of the manual that says search officers may use discretion at a crime scene rather than relying on the manual as a rigid set of rules. Shannon charged that Haynes's cross-examination "left the unfair impression that this officer has not followed the manual when, in fact, they have deleted that part which shows this witness acted properly."

Haynes came out of his chair like a man shot from a cannon, calling Shannon's comment "a gross and scurrilous accusation." The defense attorney demanded that the judge instruct the jury to disregard Shannon's remarks, but Dowlen refused, pointing out that the defense had been instructed not to read from the document in the first place. When the jury had been excused for the day, Phil Burleson made a formal motion for mistrial. The judge denied it, to the great relief of both sides.

For the next several days the state introduced a wide variety of physical evidence, much of it bloody and gruesome and all of it designed to reinforce testimony already on the record. This evidence included:

• The nine-foot door with the bullet hole through which Stan Farr took the first of four shots.

• Morgue photos of the bodies of Stan Farr and Andrea Wilborn. There were four views of Farr, each displaying a different gunshot wound. There was one of Andrea Wilborn's naked chest, showing a gunshot wound just below one breast.

• The blood-soaked, striped tube top Andrea had worn the night of her murder.

• Stan Farr's bloodied shirt.

• A dozen blood samples and photos of bloodstains taken from the basement utility room where Andrea's body was discovered and from the entrance leading to the basement.

• Bloodstains removed from the breakfast room area where Priscilla and Farr were shot, from the hallway along which Farr's body had been dragged, and from the patio walkway Priscilla had described in her first escape attempt.

• Bev Bass's sandals and purse.

• Two bullets, one found on the stairway where Farr was first shot and the second outside a glass door which could have been penetrated by bullets that Gavrel said Cullen Davis fired to regain entry into the mansion. Earlier in the trial, the state had produced five more bullets, one discovered under the body of Andrea Wilborn and four from the breakfast room. Two more bullets recovered from the body of Stan Farr would be produced when the state called Fort Worth crime lab director Frank Shiller to testify. The remaining bullet was lodged near Gavrel's spine. The ten bullets fit the state's scenario exactly. The gunman had executed Andrea Wilborn, then reloaded as he waited. That was one. The second bullet wounded Priscilla. Bullets three, four, five, and six killed Farr. The seventh bullet wounded Gavrel. This also explained why the killer

211

had chased but not shot Bev Bass. He would have been out of bullets. Gavrel testified that the gunman reloaded before firing three shots through the window and entering the mansion.

• Fragments of the garbage bag found in the breakfast room, on the stairs where Farr was shot, and in the basement utility room. The plastic bag itself, which was found upstairs in the master bedroom, had already been introduced, as had other fragments.

• Synthetic fibers from a wig found on the plastic bag.

Det. Gary Nichols, Greg Miller's partner, had been called to identify most of the physical evidence. In cross-examination, Phil Burleson zoomed in on the three drinking glasses found in the kitchen, the ones that were supposed to prove that Andrea Wilborn wasn't alone between the hours of 9:00 P.M. and midnight. Burleson asked whether any liquid had been discovered in one of the glasses. Nichols replied that it had, but it wasn't tested.

Q: Were you not trained to preserve liquids from a crime scene as a member of the crime scene search team?

A: We're trained to use our own discretion.

Q: Well, what did you do with the contents of the glass? Did you throw it away? Did you drink it?

A: I poured it down the sink.

In rapid-fire questioning, Burleson asked Nichols if he had taken footprints in the area around the house, or vacuum samples from carpeting and upholstery, or fingerprints from Farr's shoes, and finally if he had found any "plastic bags with a white powdery substance in them in the home."

In each case, Nichols answered that he had not.

Farr's stained shirt and Andrea's bloody tube top and the other pieces of evidence were placed on a table near the jury box where they remained throughout the trial. As each new item of evidence was introduced, it was added to the gory collection. It was like watching someone dress a stage.

As the Cullen Davis trial moved from summer into autumn, the Panhandle wind shifted to the north, kicking up dust devils on the plains and releasing trapped layers of heat from the broken sidewalks of downtown Amarillo. The year seemed to begin here with autumn. There was a new punch in the air. The trial still dominated conversations, but now there were other topics to consider—livestock prices, winter wheat, football. Shoppers who patronized the fading downtown stores paused to examine new fall fashions. But from time to time the spell was broken, and people would stop and stare as two bailiffs herded a pitifully isolated group of nine men and three women between the Executive Inn and the courthouse. The Cullen Davis jurors had the loneliest job in town. *They* were the prisoners.

At one point testimony was interrupted while one of the jurors, L. B. Pendleton, made an emergency trip to the dentist. The dentist reported that Pendleton had an impacted wisdom tooth. There were two choices: the dentist could operate immediately, in which case the trial would be delayed for at least a week, or he could prescribe a painkiller. Dowlen instructed the dentist to give the painkiller. It turned out to be *Percodan*. Dowlen quickly countermanded the prescription and ordered that the juror be given codeine instead. There was some good-natured laughter around the courthouse. God knows what was said in the jury room. It must have seemed like the judge was saying that the drug Percodan was too heavy even for a large man like Pendleton. Then how were they to believe it would affect a woman half his size?

From his cell at the top of the courthouse, Cullen looked down at the elms reflecting a brilliant yellow in

213

the lowering fire of daylight. Once again the Fort Worth millionaire was unable to use his box seats at Texas Stadium, but he watched his favorite NFL team on TV, and there was plenty of football talk in the hallways and offices. Cullen's friend Roy Rimmer made certain the seats did not go unused or unappreciated. As jail life went, things weren't all that bad for Cullen Davis. The jail was so overcrowded that many prisoners slept on the floor, but Cullen enjoyed a private double-bunk cell. He had his color TV—his favorite program was "The Fugitive." Cullen said he liked it because "you know he's innocent, but the cops can't catch him." Cullen joked with reporters about the jailers "taking away our peanut butter privileges," but most of his meals were catered. The only luxury really out of reach was freedom. Cullen was always freshly groomed and immaculate in his expensive business suits, very much the corporate president, collected and in control. Most evenings at 6:00 P.M. a deputy brought a fresh change of clothes and drove Cullen to see his chiropractor. There was a popular image of Cullen as a man alone, abandoned to the cold-steel world of jailers, lawyers, and hard rules, but that was not the case at all. Karen Master was always close by, as were Cullen's corporate subordinates, crisp, efficient men trained to stay out of sight and ahead of the game. A vice-president of Mid-Continent visited him every other day, bringing corporate news and papers to sign.

In many ways Cullen had never enjoyed so much attention, so much popularity. The Menopause Brigade, as one bailiff called the housewives and groupies, fawned over him like loving aunties, resolving to do anything they could to see that he stayed comfortable. They scolded Deputy Sheriff Al Cross for not seeing to it that his bed linens were changed properly. They brought him cookies and pies and flocked around him at every opportunity. They brought their children and grandchildren to meet him and—for some strange and convoluted reason—had him autograph their copies of *Blood and Money,* the best-seller about the famous John Hill murder case in Houston, a case in which a commoner husband was accused of scheming to murder his fabulously wealthy wife. One had him autograph her neck brace, and another offered to iron his shorts and socks.

Why did they do it? They didn't merely acquit the man that three eyewitnesses had placed at the scene of a brutal murder—they *adored* him. It was as if he were someone to whom they were beholden, someone born to royalty, whose very birthright, courage, and fortitude set him above the struggling masses. In some inexplicable way, Cullen promised meaning to their own lives. "The Cinderella's Sisters Syndrome," you might call it. Why did the Prince pick *her*? And where did Priscilla Lee Childers Wilborn Davis get off acting high and mighty? He had given her everything, and what had she given him? Betrayal!

During each recess Cullen moved freely among his admirers, shaking hands, posing for pictures, exchanging pleasantries, talking football or finance. Cullen's people (as they were eponymously called) had installed a telephone in the judge's outer office, and it was common to see the defendant making corporate decisions on long distance. The housewives loved this aura of power and the plain-spoken, almost boyish manner that went with it.

Not all the groupies were shapeless and middle-aged. There was a nifty, dark-haired young morsel who enjoyed getting Cullen in the corner and discussing sociology. And there was a stream of young beauties, most of them escorted from Dallas or Fort Worth by Cullen's subordinates, who frequently decorated the seats behind the defendant. They shared catered luncheons with Cullen and Karen and at night visited the better clubs around town, the Hilton Inn or Rhett Butler's or other places frequented by the movers and shakers of Amarillo. One particularly striking young woman was Rhonda Sellers, a Dallas Cowboys cheerleader and the former Miss Metroplex of Dallas–Fort Worth. Rhonda was the daughter of one of Karen Master's best friends. Cullen had sponsored Rhonda in the Miss Texas Pageant. Members of the jury probably didn't know her name, but they would not forget her face. *She* was for Cullen Davis. It seemed unthinkable that this lovely, openly wholesome young woman would support Davis if he were a cold-blooded killer.

On September 22, 1977, Cullen celebrated his forty-fourth birthday, his second straight birthday in jail. Karen surprised him with a new painting. It was done by one of the courtroom artists in the style of the highly publicized painting of Cullen and Priscilla that hung in the mansion, only this one portrayed Cullen and Karen with all their children spaced around them like satellites. Cullen's first wife, Sandra, who had been in virtual seclusion since the murders, flew to Amarillo for the occasion with their sons, Cullen Jr., fourteen, and Brian, eleven. Though Cullen no doubt knew about this "surprise" in advance, there had to be a lump in his throat as his two boys came bursting into the courtroom, hugging him and crying and saying how much they missed their daddy. As reporters gathered close, Cullen Jr. was heard to sob, "Daddy, I just want to be with you alone." It was hard to say what Cullen was thinking; he wasn't much for expressing emotions. Maybe he was thinking about his own daddy.

Some cynical members of the press speculated that ol' Race had planned this birthday display as another means to gain sympathy for his client. Even if the jurors didn't see it, they were bound to hear about it. But when reporters went looking for Haynes the following day, he sidetracked them with a father-son story of his own. Haynes had informed the court that he was taking Friday afternoon and all day Saturday off; they could either adjourn or go ahead without him as they pleased. Race had promised his oldest son, Blake, a sixteen-year-old starting linebacker for the Houston Kincaid High School team, that he would attend the annual Father-Son Night football game, whatever the cost. Two years ago, a friend died unexpectedly and Race stood in for him at the annual game. "He was a neighbor and a damn close friend," Race recalled. "He didn't drink or smoke. He trained religiously, running three miles a day. Then one day he fell over dead in a massive heart attack. He was forty-three. His son was a star fullback on the team, and when the Father-Son game came up, the son asked me to stand in for him as a father. It's an important day for the boy and an important day for the dad. My friend missed his time, and I decided I wasn't going to miss mine." It was a pledge he made to himself.

As he hurried to catch the afternoon plane to Houston, Haynes had to feel that the trial was going well. If, as he claimed, he couldn't yet read the jury, he could certainly decipher the mood of the community. Those who weren't pro-Cullen were at least anti-Priscilla. A month after Priscilla's testimony, people still spoke of her in tones normally reserved for vermin. Judge Dowlen's own secretary seemed unable to bring herself to speak Priscilla's name, referring to her as *that woman,* and had joked that she might write her own book about the case and call it *Silicone and Sex.* That's how *she* saw the issues. Things looked better by the day. With luck, they would all be home by Thanksgiving. Cullen had already made Thanksgiving reservations at a Colorado ski lodge. It made Racehorse happy to see his client happy. But Race was a natural worrier, and for reasons he couldn't explain he was worried now.

In the next couple of weeks, several things happened that dampened the defense's enthusiasm and reflected poorly on the client. There had already been talk about lax security, but the rumbling got louder when a convicted murderer on his way to the state prison at Huntsville was left unguarded in the hallway while a deputy sheriff looked in on Cullen Davis. Upstairs in the jail, while Cullen continued to occupy a private cell and watch his private TV, an eighteen-year-old prisoner in a cell with eight others was viciously gang-raped.

The defense was naturally concerned about security—in a case this sensational there was a possibility that some crazy could walk into the courtroom and, before anyone saw what was happening, blow away Cullen Davis—but now there were grumblings about other types of security. It was not uncommon to see

Cullen, a man charged with capital murder, walking unguarded along the hallway. One day, accompanied only by an attorney, the defendant who could not qualify for bail walked out of the courtroom and took an elevator to the ground floor. He didn't try to escape, but he could have. On another occasion, a deputy left Cullen alone in the jail booking office. When the telephone rang, Cullen looked around, saw no one, then answered it himself. No other prisoner would have tried that, but Cullen knew he wasn't just any other prisoner.

The ripper came the first week in October when Cullen was observed chatting privately with the mother of juror Marilyn Kay Haessly. Miss Haessly had been sequestered since June 29, but like the others she had been permitted telephone calls and visits by her family. These visits were supposed to be monitored by bailiffs, but that didn't turn out to be the case. Now it came out that married jurors were being allowed *conjugal visits,* unsupervised naturally, originally without Judge Dowlen's knowledge but later with his permission. The judge reasoned that the jurors were already under enough hardships and that denying them normal sexual recreation bordered on a cruelty he was not prepared to dispense. Of course, there was the possibility that husbands and wives could make love without speaking of Cullen and Priscilla, but, as someone pointed out, what else was there to talk about?

Tim Curry was livid. The prosecution heard rumors of conjugal visits, but nobody could confirm them. The judge kept rolling his eyes and turning away. In the quick revelations of early October, there was nothing for the state to do but proceed with its case. "The conjugal visits were the worst thing that happened to us," Curry said later. "If it had been the other way around, it would have been sure grounds for reversal. But what can you do? The state doesn't have a right of appeal. When you leave the state without that lever, then the judge can do anything he wants to." Curry no longer seemed enchanted with Amarillo or George Dowlen.

After the incident with Marilyn Kay Haessly's mother, Dowlen announced that new security guidelines would be forthcoming. "And," he added, "they will be followed." Even as courthouse observers were discussing shutting the barn door after the horses are into the next county, yet another revelation reached the public. The Tarrant County auditor sent a query to Amarillo asking *who is going to pay the jury's liquor bill?* Until then it had been assumed that members of the jury took nothing stronger with their meals than Dr Pepper.

When it came time for Bev Bass to take the witness stand and tell her story, Phil Burleson was ready. Though Bass portended to be the state's strongest witness, the tall, silver-haired Dallas lawyer saw any number of holes in her story. At the heart of it all was the *curious relationship* between Bass and Priscilla Davis. Burleson didn't for a minute believe that it was a mother and friend-of-daughter thing, as the state contended. Nor could he swallow the older sister–younger sister relationship. No, it was something more. No one ever used the term *bisexual* in the courtroom, and no one introduced any actual proof of bisexual conduct, but the defense's many innuendoes and repeated allegations of their *special relationship* planted the idea in the minds of many.

Later, Burleson explained his personal theory like this: "Priscilla knew who the killer was and struck a deal. Bev's mind was on Cullen that night—she and Priscilla had talked about the divorce at the Rangoon that night. Remember, Priscilla's involvement [in the divorce trial] that Friday was not *lightly* done. She had gone to a great deal of trouble to convince a doctor to write a false report. She had spent time posturing, so that the following Monday, when they got a report on the judge's ruling, she wanted to tell someone. Bev says she was going out there that night to spend the night with Dee. Hell, she knew Dee was shacked up with her boyfriend. Bev wanted to know exactly what had happened in court that day. I really think they got together . . . somehow that night they got together and decided to name Cullen as the killer. Maybe they knew the real killer, or maybe they didn't, but they decided to put it on Cullen."

As the pretty teenager with the honey-blonde hair took the witness stand and began telling her story, no one listened more intently than Phil Burleson.

Bass told of driving her own car to the mansion earlier on the crucial day of August 2. As she recalled, it was about noon when she arrived at 4200 Mockingbird. Andrea had just returned from vacation Bible school in Houston the previous day, and Bev had made plans to take the girl shopping. The image of Andrea as an innocent child, trusting and dependent on the judgment of older friends and family, was reinforced by Bev Bass's recollection of how she'd helped Andrea pick out a blouse and get dressed. Tim Curry felt that it was vital that the jury get some sort of *feeling* about Andrea, that they picture her as a soft, artistic, sensitive girl enchanted by the simple beauty of life and so delicate that she could train her bird and cat to coexist. As things stood, all they knew about the girl was that she was twelve and dead. In her civil depositions, Bass had touchingly described that afternoon with Andrea, how the girl had talked about the Bible school and how Andrea had lingered for a long time at a pet shop, not to buy anything but just to talk to the animals. But, of course, the defense had studied the same deposition, and when Bass got to the part about the pet shop, Haynes successfully argued that the testimony was not relevant and so the jury never heard it. It was somewhere around 4:00 P.M. when Bass and Andrea returned to 4200 Mockingbird. Priscilla, Dee, and Dee's boyfriend were there. They talked for an hour or more; then Bubba Gavrel arrived.

At the very beginning of Bev Bass's testimony, Tim Curry established that the young woman had known the Davis family for seven years and was therefore not likely to be mistaken in her identification. The district attorney asked about the several stops that Bass and Gavrel had made earlier on the evening of August 2, about the accidental encounter with Farr and Priscilla at the Rangoon Racquet Club, leading her skillfully to the murder scene. Bass recalled that they left the club about 11:30 P.M., twenty minutes or so after Farr and Priscilla. Like Gavrel, she was not wearing a watch and could only approximate the times. She told of arriving at the mansion and, as she climbed from Gavrel's Blazer, hearing what sounded like a scream "coming from the house."

Bass supported Gavrel's version almost point by point. In the courtyard she could see the man in black, and her first thought was that they had stumbled on a burglar breaking into the mansion.

"And what if anything did Bubba Gavrel say to the man?" the district attorney asked.

"He said: 'Hey, what's going on? Where is everybody?'"

The man told Gavrel, "They are right this way. Follow me." Bass said that Gavrel followed the man and she walked a few steps behind Gavrel, past the garage and down the walkway toward the door leading to the breakfast room, the main entrance to the mansion.

Q: At the time you got to the [well-lighted] area how close were you to the man?

A: Well, Bubba was about three feet behind him, and I was right behind Bubba.

Q: Did you ever recognize the man in black?

A: Yes, sir, as he was turning the corner.

Q: At the time he turned the corner did you say anything?

A: Yes, sir. I said, "Bubba, that's Cullen!" He turned around and shot. Bubba screamed, and he stumbled and fell in front of me.

Q: Well, what did the defendant do?

A: He leaned over Bubba with his hands out.

Q: When he leaned over, how close was he to [Bubba]?

A: About two feet. I screamed, and he [Cullen] just stood up and looked right at me. I turned and ran . . . and he followed me.

Q: How long did you stand there face to face with him?

A: A few seconds.

Q: Did you say anything?

A: I said, "Cullen, please don't shoot me! It's Bev!" I just kept screaming, "Cullen, please don't shoot me! It's Bev!"

Bass testified that she hurdled a small retaining wall and ran in the direction of Hulen Street, zigzagging between the grass and the gravel driveway, thinking that at any second the man would fire at her. "I kept turning around and watching him." she said, her voice unsteady and her hands trembling as she looked across the courtroom at Cullen Davis. "I saw the garbage bag in his hand, and I knew he had a gun in it. I couldn't tell if he was shooting at me because my ears were ringing . . . and I kept screaming, 'Cullen, please don't shoot me, it's Bev!' When I got about three-fourths of the way [to Hulen Street] . . . I turned around and he was there. I couldn't tell if he was standing or running. He kept raising the sack . . . I was afraid he was going to shoot me, so I kept running back and forth on the road and over the grass. And then I looked back again and he was gone. He just disappeared."

At this point the jury was excused while Curry questioned Bass about statements made to motorist Robert Sawhill, who picked her up on Hulen, and later to security guard John Smedley and the two police officers who arrived shortly. The district attorney was attempting to establish that the young woman was still under the emotional impact of the shooting and that therefore her testimony should be admissible under the hearsay guidelines.

Although all the prosecutors felt that Bass had told her story well, Curry knew that on at least one point they had problems. According to Bass, she had identified Cullen Davis as the killer to the first four people she encountered—Robert Sawhill, the motorist who first picked her up on Hulen; security guard John Smedley; and the two cops. But in the weeks of investigation following the killings, the state hadn't made much of an effort to locate Sawhill—Bass hadn't been able to remember the name of the motorist who picked her up on Hulen, and Sawhill didn't immediately come forward. To Curry's embarrassment, it was a newspaper ad placed by the defense that finally located Sawhill, and now the man who should have been able to corroborate part of Bass's story was a witness for the other side.

Later in cross-examination, the defense would ask Bass about "the newspaper article" in which she first learned the name of Robert Sawhill. Dowlen wouldn't allow her to answer that question, but Curry knew that the defense would eventually call Sawhill and that his story wouldn't support all the things Bass recalled telling him that night. That was a bridge they would have to cross when they reached it. Right now Curry had only two more questions for his witness. First, he solicited testimony that after their accidental meeting at the Rangoon Racquet Club, Bass didn't see Priscilla Davis again "for three or four days."

Curry had one final question for Bass, and the DA knew it was going to be a shocker. His face was grim as he walked back to the table and took something from an envelope, then whirled and shoved it in front of her. "Can you identify who this is?" Curry asked bluntly. Tears seeped into Bass's eyes as she looked at the frozen-in-death body of Andrea Wilborn lying on the floor of the utility room. "It's . . . Andrea . . ." Bass said. Then she broke down completely and was led sobbing from the courtroom. After a thirty-minute recess, Dowlen announced that the witness was in no condition to continue and adjourned for the day. It was a cruel but necessary ploy for the prosecution; Curry wanted the jury to dwell at least overnight on Bev Bass's story before the defense began attacking her.

The unexpected recess also gave the defense a chance to review the inconsistencies in Bass's various statements. By the following morning Racehorse Haynes was snorting fire and brimstone as he hurled questions at the young witness. To everyone's surprise, Bass maintained herself fairly well. At times she came across as a spoiled rich girl and at other times as a silly teenager, but the

223

defense was never able to shake her on the one key point—that she recognized Cullen Davis as the gunman in black.

Instead, Haynes concentrated on showing that Bev Bass was something less than an innocent, wide-eyed teenager accidentally caught up in a murderous web and just trying to tell the truth as best she could recall. In early testimony the district attorney had asked what Stan Farr was drinking that night at the Rangoon Racquet Club. Bass had once said that Farr drank bourbon, but now she couldn't remember. Wasn't it *Chivas?* the prosecutor inquired, to which Bass answered rather naively, "What's Chivas?" Curry told her it was the brand name of a Scotch. then hurried on to the next question. But now it was Haynes's turn, and he called her attention to that same question.

Q: Miss Bass, you are acquainted with alcohol, are you not?

A: What do you mean?

Q: You weren't trying to suggest to the jury that you are so naive that you thought Chivas was *bourbon,* were you?

A: I'm sorry, I didn't know what it was.

Haynes asked several questions about "your personal problem" and "your special relationship with Priscilla Lee Davis," then he directed her attention to the gathering at Brent Cruz's apartment an hour or so before the meeting at the Rangoon Racquet Club. Tempering his cutting edge with a fatherly smile, Race wanted to know who was there "in that little room." He was especially interested in Brent Cruz's thirteen-year-old sister. "Was she there all the time or just part of the time?" the lawyer wanted to know. And what were they doing "in that little back room?" Now Bass was on the verge of tears. It wasn't so much what Haynes said, it was the way he said it.

"I don't understand what you're trying to do," she said, her voice trembling badly.

"The truth is," Haynes said, leaning in close to the witness, "the group of you were all alone in that little back room, were you not?"

A: I don't remember.

Q: You didn't have any sort of mood modifier while you were back there in that little room, did you?

A: No, sir.

Q: And you didn't see Gus James Gavrel put anything in his undershorts, did you—a green vegetable substance in a plastic bag?

A: No, sir.

For the next hour or more Haynes led the witness over an almost minute-by-minute account of her activities before and after the murders, pressing her for exact times and places, who did what and went where. The lawyer had a large blackboard carted into the courtroom, and as Bass attempted to answer each question, Haynes listed the answers chronologically in chalk letters easily visible from the jury box. Every time the witness answered, "I don't remember," Haynes wrote I.D.R. on the blackboard. In short order, there was an impressive list of I.D.R.'s for the jury to consider, a list that would remain visible throughout the remainder of the trial. Just as the prosecution had dressed the set with the bloody clothes of Stan Farr and Andrea Wilborn, Haynes had his own props and his own method of dressing the stage.

Referring to Bev Bass's deposition taken in October 1976, about two months after the murders, Haynes grilled her about her conversation with Robert Sawhill.

Q: So, on October 16, 1976, you didn't say that you told the man [Sawhill] that Cullen Davis had shot your boyfriend, did you?

A: No. It was my first deposition, and they didn't ask me things in as great detail.

Q: You were trying to be truthful, weren't you, ma'am?

A: Yes.

Q: Well, the fact is you don't really remember what you told the man in the car, do you? You either said it was Cullen Davis or the man who owns the big house on the top of the hill, didn't you?

A: I don't remember which.

Q: And now you remember. Your memory has improved, has it?

A: I just now calmed down where I can sit down and remember it.

Haynes produced yet another statement, the one that Bass made to Det. C. R. Davis in the early morning hours of August 3. Passing close to the jury box to make certain he had everyone's attention, Haynes read a passage in which Bass stated: "While we were walking on the walkway, I heard loud noises coming from inside the house. I heard a woman scream. I think I heard one shot. A man was walking in front of me and Bubba. . . ."

Haynes looked over the rim of his half-moon glasses as he phrased his next question.

Q: Is it your testimony now that the man in black was *not* walking with you and Bubba at the time you heard the shot?

A: Yes, sir.

Q: So what you said in the statement of August 3 is not true?

A: It's out of sequence. Will you not let me explain it?

Q: You want to say that when [Det. C. R.] Davis typed it up, he typed it out of sequence?

A: If you're asking me if I'm lying, the answer is "No, sir." But you're making it very difficult for me to answer.

Q: You say you heard a noise that *sounded* like a gunshot?

A: I'm not sure what kind of noise it was.

However inconsequential the questions, Bass became increasingly frustrated, and Haynes appeared increasingly suspicious of her flawed memory. At one point she said, "I have an explanation if you'll just let . . ."

"I'm *sure* you do," Haynes said, taking off his glasses and walking away from the witness stand as if to say that he had heard all the lies he could stomach for one day. "I'm *positive* you do." Several members of the jury smiled and exchanged glances. But Racehorse wasn't done yet. He continued to question her about the noise she claimed to have heard.

Q: Are you saying that the noise was comparable to the sound of gunfire?

A: What does comparable mean?

This time several jurors laughed out loud. It was Racehorse Haynes at his best. Suddenly, without warning, Haynes slammed a briefcase on the table. You could hear the noise at the opposite end of the hall.

"Comparable," Haynes said, treating the witness now to his condescending smile. "Did that sound like a gunshot?"

Bass didn't answer, but the look on her face said it did.

In its efforts to impeach Bev and tar her with the same brush already used on Priscilla Davis, the defense was counting heavily on Bass herself. They were certain that somewhere along the way she would either lie or leave a false impression with the jury, and that would open the door for collateral demonstrations, just as it had with Priscilla.

Earlier in the cross-examination, Haynes had probed Bass's relationship with Priscilla.

Q: The relationship between you and Priscilla Lee Davis was a personal relationship, was it not?

A: I don't understand.

Q: She was more to you than just Dee's mother. You and she discussed your own personal situations, did you not?

A: A few times, yes, sir.

Q: When you had this problem of a personal nature in August of 1975, you went to Priscilla Lee Davis, did you not?

A: Yes, sir.

Q: In reaching a resolution to this problem, you used the name Priscilla Lee Davis, did you not?

A: I don't remember.

That was the opening Haynes sought. He now produced a document to refresh her memory and had Bass identify both her own handwriting and the name of Priscilla Lee Davis. When he was satisfied that Bass fully recognized the document, Race resumed questioning.

Q: So Priscilla Lee Davis accompanied you to the place where you solved your problem?

A: Yes, sir.

Q: And she extended financial assistance to you, didn't she?

A: She loaned me some money.

Q: And how old were you at the time?

A: Sixteen.

Although Dowlen had ruled that the defense could not actually use the word *abortion,* he permitted questions concerning previous statements. "Just enough rope to hang her," one lawyer observed. It now developed that Bev Bass had tied the noose herself almost a year earlier in a deposition taken in December 1976.

Haynes waited until Bass's fourth and final day to spring the trap. Using records subpoenaed from Pregnancy Control, Inc., he began by asking about a "consultation" she had had with a doctor in August 1975. Bass didn't remember it.

Q: Do you recall when you were giving testimony in December 1976 you were asked if your health was good and you indicated it was good and had always been good?

A: Yes, sir.

Haynes adjusted his glasses on his nose and read from the deposition.

Q: Question. "Have you had any operations in the last five years?" And your answer was, "I've had my wisdom teeth out, that's about all."

A: Yes, sir.

Q: Now that answer you gave in December was not truthful, was it?

A: No, sir. It was something I wanted to forget about, and I had forgotten it.

Before Haynes could ask his next question, Bev Bass started crying. In a voice choked with tears she asked Dowlen, "Could I please take a break?" Dowlen called a recess, and the prosecution hustled Bass to a back room. Curry told her the same thing he had told Priscilla: just tell the truth. Curry felt that the defense had pretty much fired all its shots by now. Bass had

228

been smeared by her association with "the Queen Bee" (as Haynes was now referring to Priscilla), but her basic story hadn't been challenged. When Bass had stopped crying, she returned to the witness stand resolved to make the best of it. Haynes tempered his tone accordingly.

Q: You had consulted with a medical person back in August 1975, hadn't you?

A: Yes, sir.

Q: So when you said no, you had just forgotten about the consultation, isn't that right?

Bass didn't immediately reply. She seemed again on the verge of tears as Haynes rephrased his question.

Q: The truth of it is, you hadn't forgotten about that incident. You had just decided that it wouldn't be discovered.

A: No, sir.

Q: You had used your sister's name in seeking a resolution to your problem, hadn't you?

A: Yes, sir.

Q: So your *sister's* name now appears on that record, isn't that right?

A: Yes, sir.

Q: And after Priscilla Lee Davis testified [at the same hearing], she told you about this line of questioning and that she had lied, didn't she?

A: No, sir.

Q: And you were prepared to forget about that incident again until yesterday when you found out those records had been subpoenaed, weren't you?

A: No, sir, Mr. Haynes. I told you, I tried to block that from my memory and I had.

Bev Bass was about to break down again, but that was all right. Haynes had finished with her.

As members of the defense gathered at their suite of rented apartments for the nightly strategy session, Racehorse allowed that what he'd like right now was a bottle of Cognac and a readable scientific study detailing therapeutic coefficients of one man opposed to one bottle. Race believed that scientific analysis was a good thing, but damned if he hadn't had too much of a good thing. Some months ago he had read that alcohol rotted away the brain's beta cells, thus destroying the indulgent drinker's memory bank. He had sworn to himself that he would give up the devil's tonic for the duration of the trial, and except for one single occasion no one had seen him touch a drop. The occasion was a party the previous Saturday night at Stanley Marsh's ranch house, Toad Hall. Stanley had called it a "cast party" and invited everyone connected with the trial, including Cullen Davis, who, of course, had been otherwise detained. The party was a smashing success. Race was observed clinging to the neck of a bottle of Cognac, playing Willie Nelson songs on a guitar, and at one point remarking that there was no end to his genius as a criminal defense attorney. "I dream of the day," Race told reporters, "when I am cross-examining a witness and my questions are so probing and brilliant that the poor bastard blurts out that *he,* not my defendant, committed the foul murder. Then he will pitch forward into my arms, dead of a massive heart attack." After lecturing several writers on the evils of drink and its proclivity for rotting the old memory bank, Race observed, "The trouble is, when you give up the juice, you start remembering what it was you started drinking to forget."

By now there had been thirty-five days of testimony, not counting weekends and holidays and other recesses, thirty-five days of steady shelling by the best witnesses the state had in its arsenal. Race decided that though he deserved a drink, he didn't need one. He was high enough on his own accomplishments. He was certain they had shot down two out of three eyewitnesses, or would just as soon as they started calling their own witnesses. Bev Bass he wasn't sure about. If she hadn't already soiled herself in the eyes of the jury, it was probably too late. The district attorney was out there now telling the press what a solid witness Bev Bass had made. It pained Haynes to admit it, but it was entirely possible the DA was correct. Bass's testimony had obviously not supported the defense's conspiratorial theory.

But Haynes was not about to abandon his theory of

BLOOD WILL TELL

The mansion. *(UPI Photo)*

Priscilla and the Wayne Ingram portrait of her and Cullen.

Cullen.
(Wide World Photos)

Andrea.

Stan and Priscilla at
Willie Nelson Picnic.
(Jim Higgins)

Stan and Priscilla at
Colonial Country Club.
(Gene Gordon)

Looking into the breakfast room. *(Gene Gordon)*

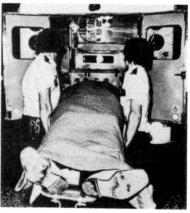

Stan. *(Gene Gordon)*

Cullen arrested for murder. *(Gene Gordon)*

District Attorney Tim Curry.
(UPI Photo)

Phil Burleson, Cullen, and Racehorse Haynes in Amarillo. *(UPI Photo)*

W. T. Rufner. *(David Bowser)*

Acquittal: Karen and Cullen leaving the courthouse in Amarillo. *(UPI Photo)*

Racehorse celebrating at Rhett Butler's. *(David Bowser)*

Racehorse and Cullen at Rhett Butler's. *(David Bowser)*

The murder-for-hire bond hearing: Judge Arthur Tipps and David McCrory. *(Sketch by Harold Maples, Fort Worth Star-Telegram; Wide World Photos)*

Joe Eidson. *(Wide World Photos)*

conspiracy. Conspiracy wasn't something he had to prove, only a seed for the jury to warm over when they finally wrestled with the question of *reasonable doubt*. Haynes knew from experience that the jury could believe that Bass was telling the truth and *still* believe that she conspired to blame Cullen. If Bass left one indelible impression with the jurors, it was her loyalty to Priscilla, coupled with an open hostility toward Cullen. This was the impression Haynes wanted the jury to take with them when it came time to deliberate the verdict.

As the prosecution questioned security guard John Smedley the next morning, Haynes, Burleson, and Mike Gibson were looking ahead to another trouble spot. As expected, Smedley supported Bass's story all the way. The most damaging part was Dowlen's ruling that Smedley could repeat for the jury what Bass told him in the passion of the moment. She told him: "It was Cullen. Cullen did it. I saw his ugly fucking face. He's trying to kill me too. He chased me all over the place." After Dowlen's ruling, there was very little the defense could do to challenge Smedley.

What worried the defense was the state's next witness, Fort Worth PD fingerprint expert Jim Slaughter. The prosecution had admitted from the start that none of the fingerprints taken from 4200 Mockingbird matched those of Cullen Davis, but nobody said anything about *palm* prints. The defense received a report that the state was preparing a bombshell—that a bloody palm print taken from the door facing at the entrance to the basement could definitely be identified. The defense's own expert had examined the palm print, but he hadn't been able to "rap it" (match it) with any of the known prints. From what the prosecution was saying, it appeared that they had made a positive identification. Joe Shannon was saying, "We think it is significant." Asked by reporters if he could shed light on the mysterious palm print, Racehorse said, "You can damn sure bet it's not Cullen Davis's, and you can make book on that." But even as he said it, Race realized he might be whistling in the dark.

Cullen Davis's annoying tendency to appear arrogant

231

and shoot from the hip any time there were reporters present didn't help matters. As reporters examined photographs of the mysterious print, Cullen quipped, "Well, there it is. That about wraps it up, doesn't it?" Cullen was only joking, but it didn't look that way when it appeared in print.

Haynes spent the better part of the following morning trying to disqualify Jim Slaughter as an "expert" on the identification of palm prints, but Dowlen refused to go along.

"We were puckered up pretty tight when they started questioning Slaughter," Phil Burleson admitted. "Even if he said it might be Cullen's print, we were in trouble." And then, just as suddenly as it surfaced, the mystery of the palm print was explained.

Q: And do you have an opinion as to who the print belongs to?

A: Yes, sir.

Q: And what is that opinion?

A: Aurelia Cooper.

As usual Cullen Davis sat there without expression, but Burleson let out a slow breath and adjusted his tie. Aurelia Cooper was the housekeeper at 4200 Mockingbird. What had been billed as a "bloody palm print" was actually a latent print lifted from the blood smear on the door. The print could have been there for days before the murder. Marvin Collins explained later: "The only reason we brought it up was that it had been mentioned to the jury earlier, and we felt we had to explain it. I didn't really think the defense would get all that uptight about it, but when they did, we decided to play it for all we could."

The state had reached the homestretch, and soon it would be time for the defense to present its case. The final two prosecution witnesses would be Dr. Feliks Gwozdz, the Tarrant County medical examiner who did the autopsies on the bodies of Stan Farr and Andrea Wilborn, and Frank Shiller, director of the Fort Worth crime lab, who had been assigned the very important task of explaining the physical evidence. In the final analysis Shiller's job was to prove the state's circumstantial case—namely, that the bullet that killed Andrea Wilborn was fired from the same gun that killed Stan Farr.

Racehorse had looked forward to matching wits with Dr. Gwozdz, though he was aware of the risks. They talked about expert witnesses; none was more expert than the Tarrant County medical examiner, and few were as ingratiating in the eyes of a jury. A native of Poland and a survivor of the infamous Nazi death camp at Dachau, Gwozdz (rhymes with *quotes*) was a jolly, pink-faced man of infinite patience and wit, the kind of man women jurors wanted to take home in their purses and men jurors wanted to shake hands with. Gwozdz was not a man to be rattled, or trifled with. Haynes was sure of this; he was *counting* on it, in fact. For some days now Haynes had been mulling over a theory that Andrea Wilborn was killed somewhere other than the basement utility room. If Gwozdz was as good as his reputation, he might be able to confirm this, thus punching a large hole in the prosecution's version of how things had happened that night. "I felt like it was a critical spot in the trial," Haynes said.

There was a detectable queasiness in the courtroom as Gwozdz told about examining the bodies of the two victims. The girl, he said, had two wounds—an entrance wound in the right chest and an exit wound in the left back, two inches below and three inches to the left of the entrance wound. The bullet penetrated Andrea's aorta, the doctor said, producing shock and massive bleeding, probably causing death in a very short time.

When it was the defense's time to cross-examine, Racehorse went straight to what he considered the critical part. Looking at Gwozdz's own report, he asked why there was no mention of a urine specimen from the body of Andrea Wilborn. The doctor answered that the girl's bladder had collapsed, and there was no urine to examine.

Exactly! "Isn't it true, doctor," Racehorse asked, "that people who die traumatically have an involuntary emptying or voiding of the bladder?"

Gwozdz acknowledged that this was usually the case. Race thanked him.

"And is it not also true that within *moments* of voiding, the bladder begins to fill up again?"

Gwozdz made several remarks about bladders and their strange workings, but he never got around to answering Haynes's question. Racehorse repeated the question several times, still with no results. No one in the courtroom, least of all the jury, understood this line of questioning, and Haynes was finally forced to drop it. He explained later: "I'd been through this sort of testimony with doctors before and I *knew* that it was true . . . that as soon as a bladder is empty, it begins almost at once to fill up again. Andrea's bladder was empty. Yet there was no trace of urine in the utility room. No one mentioned the smell of urine on her panties, or on the floor. Urine has a very distinctive odor that any trained crime scene investigator would have to notice. Involuntary bladder function at the scene of a homicide is not at all unusual. Crime scene investigators see it all the time. But it was *not* there. That suggests just one thing—that she was killed somewhere else. The empty bladder proved that she had an involuntary bladder function within a minute or a minute and a half of the killing; otherwise the bladder would have filled up at least a little. But for some reason I never could get Gwozdz to acknowledge it." Haynes considered calling in his own expert, but he sensed that the jury was becoming impatient and decided that on this he had reached the point of diminishing returns. All he could really hope to prove was that Andrea wasn't killed in the place that the prosecution contended and that the cops had once more botched the investigation. Besides, Haynes had bigger things on the line. What would later become known as the "Ordeal of Frank Shiller" was about to begin.

Shiller, an intelligent, articulate, soft-spoken man who directed the Fort Worth crime lab, was to be the final and in many ways the most important witness for the state. In his opening remarks to the jury almost two months earlier, Tim Curry had acknowledged that the state's case was circumstantial but promised that testimony would be presented proving that the gunman who killed Stan Farr also killed Andrea Wilborn. It sounded easy. But even as Shiller was being sworn in, the jury looked across the courtroom at a preview of the ordeal to come—Racehorse Haynes, a splendid figure in his three-piece suit and handmade cowboy boots, sat puffing on his pipe as he examined *each tiny piece of evidence with a magnifying glass*. It was probably an illusion, but to those who had watched the magnificent lawyer for many days now it even appeared that he had bleached his temples for the occasion. Like any great courtroom lawyer, Racehorse was part detective, part actor. It was impossible for the jury to know where the one role ended and the other began. Haynes himself probably didn't know.

Point by point and item by item, Shiller's testimony substantiated the testimony of the three eyewitnesses concerning how and where the massacre of August 2 took place. As each bullet was labeled and offered into evidence, Shiller told where the bullet was found and in what condition. Some of the bullets were too badly damaged to make accurate comparisons, Shiller told the jury, but the bullet removed from Farr's body matched a bullet found on the breakfast room floor. This bullet in turn matched the bullet that killed Andrea Wilborn. And all three of these bullets matched the bullet found behind the stairway door. There was no doubt at all that this was precise and accurate, Shiller said. The crime lab director was about to tell the jury that no fewer than three experts hired by the defense had examined these same bullets and reached the same conclusion when Haynes's objection cut him short. By now Shiller had been on the witness stand for two and one-half tedious, excruciatingly slow days.

On Monday, October 17, as the trial entered its ninth week, Haynes went to work on Shiller. First, he muddied the water by bringing up "the judge's bullet," that mysterious projectile that had arrived by mail weeks before. From there he went on to establish the hypothesis that any ten bullets fired from the same gun would each show "dissimilarities" because of the residue each would leave in the gun barrel. No one had ever produced the murder weapon, he reminded the jury, but several other guns had appeared. In addition to the Horace Copeland gun, still another .38 now known as the September 15 gun had come into the hands of the court. ("Some nut from Wichita Falls sent it in," one of the prosecutors explained.) This gun, too, was a red herring, but Haynes used it effectively. Shiller had test-fired the September 15 gun, and now Haynes solicited his admission that even though Shiller *knew* that the test bullets were all fired from the same gun, he couldn't prove it by ballistics examination.

"Their whole strategy at this point is to delay," Marvin Collins observed during a recess. "We're trying like hell to keep the issue in focus, and they're trying just as hard to get it out of focus. The longer it drags on, the easier it is for the jury to lose sight of what really happened."

During one barrage of questions the defense discovered the titillating bit of information that for a short time just after the killings the clothes of the victims along with other evidence had been stored in an unlocked cabinet at the Fort Worth police station. Maybe this didn't seem important to some people, but "locker thirteen," as it soon came to be called, fascinated Racehorse Haynes. He asked Shiller repeated questions, referring to "the celebrated locker thirteen." Tolly Wilson objected angrily to Haynes's use of the word *celebrated,* and Haynes demurred. Thereafter, he referred to the "unique and unlocked locker number thirteen."

As the trial dragged into its forty-third day, half the seats in the courtroom were empty. One juror dozed for minutes at a time, and the others seemed less than interested in the proceedings. Several jurors had picked out familiar faces in the audience and frequently made eye contact, sharing some amusing, unspoken observation at the expense of whoever was speaking for the record. Marilyn Kay Haessly, who was known among courtroom regulars as "the nun," had taken to smoking cigars in the jury box; after twenty-four weeks of being locked up, who could say what went on in her mind. The jurors must have felt the way children feel when adults attempt to talk over their heads. It was like the whole outside world spoke nothing but euphemisms. They didn't say *abortion,* they spoke only of "personal problems." Cocaine became that "white powdery substance," and marijuana was that "green leafy substance." Freddy Thompson, the cowboy, seldom spoke, but he broke them all up one night when he looked at the sprig of parsley on his dinner plate and cried out, "My God, there's a green leafy substance in my food!" But comic relief was in short supply. There had been several heated arguments among jurors, and if someone didn't get on with the trial, there would be many more.

Nevertheless, the ordeal of Frank Shiller continued. The tempers of the lawyers weren't much better than the jurors', though the lawyers at least pretended to know what was being said. After a grueling session in which Haynes questioned Shiller about his opinion that Andrea Wilborn had been shot point-blank from a distance of less than five feet, reporters asked the lawyer *why!* Why was he going *on and on* like this?

Haynes replied, "I'm only showing that they tailored the distance to fit their own configurations."

When Tolly Wilson heard this, he exploded: "I'll tell you what it shows. It bloody well shows the killer knew who he was shooting. It bloody well shows it was intentional. And it bloody well indicates that the son of a bitch was looking a twelve-year-old girl square in the eye when he shot her!"

By the seventh and final day of Shiller's ordeal, even the groupies had left. Haynes asked a last series of questions of Shiller, this time about the filaments of the wig and how they were recovered from the scene. When Haynes was done, Tim Curry got to his feet and almost offhandedly said, "May it please the court, the state wishes to call no more witnesses at this time."

It did please the court; it pleased damn near everyone. A kind of collective sigh of relief went through the courtroom, though Cullen seemed not so much relieved as defiant. You could see the old Texas Aggie spirit boiling over. They had made it a little rough, but now it was his turn. In the judge's chambers Dowlen had given his own estimate of where things stood. "I'd say we're tied at halftime," Dowlen cracked, "but the Dallas Cowboys haven't had the ball yet." Gathering up a fresh change of clothes for his nightly visit to the chiropractor, Cullen found himself surrounded by reporters as he walked to the waiting deputy's car. But Deputy Al Cross walked beside him, a constant reminder that no matter how much money he had and how defiant he felt, he was still a prisoner. For that he had Judge Tom Cave to thank, and Cullen's anger suddenly got the better of him.

"You want something for the record?" Cullen exploded. "OK, quote this. Tom Cave is a chickenshit. Make that a chickenshit son of a bitch. Make that a motherfucking, chickenshit son of a bitch. A motherfucking, cocksucking, chickenshit son of a bitch. And put a little in front of it. Got it? I want to see that quoted in all the papers tomorrow."

"What did he say?" one of the groupies asked.

"Nothing," someone said. "That's just the way Aggies say good night."

❧ • ❧

There was a full house as Racehorse Haynes delivered his opening remarks for the defense. The housewives in the hallway jostled one another to get a glimpse of the famous Houston attorney, and W. T. Rufner moved among them, trying to hawk autographed T-shirts for $100 a copy. They were being modeled by a trained chimpanzee named Racehorse. The picture on the T-shirts was not the same one that the defense had blown up to poster size; Rufner denied any knowledge of the

238

famous photograph, backing up Priscilla's claim that the whole thing was a trick engineered by Cullen's people. But the similarity was unmistakable. In this one, T-man posed alone, naked except for the Christmas stocking covering his genitals. Below the picture were the words "Sock it to 'em, W. T." T-man realized that at $100 a pop he wasn't likely to sell many T-shirts, but as he told a Dallas television crew, "I'm here for the exposure."

The packed house included a newspaper editor and several out-of-town lawyers who had flown to Amarillo just to watch Haynes in action as he outlined for the jury the case that the defense planned to present.

He started with the motive, which the state had contended was Judge Eidson's ruling ordering the defendant to increase alimony payments. The defense planned to demonstrate that what the state claimed was motive was in fact the very antithesis of motive. "We will prove that Priscilla Lee Davis knew of the prenuptial agreement," Haynes said. "That she knew she couldn't get into his separate property—the family estate. The lack of motive is this—Cullen Davis was *saving* money. It is true that the court ordered him to pay $5,000 a month, but she was spending *$20,000* a month before [the separation]."

Haynes promised the jury that "we will bring in Robert Sawhill to show that Miss Bass took liberty with the truth. And we will show the relationship between Priscilla Davis and Beverly Bass. We will show that Priscilla Davis stood to profit if Cullen Davis was found guilty. We will show that Bubba Gavrel stood to profit and that he in fact said, 'I don't know who shot me.'" Haynes pointed out that the state had conveniently neglected to call Officer Jimmy Soders, one of several witnesses who claimed to have heard this denial. The state argued that Gavrel was in shock at the time, Haynes said, but the defense would show that he had enough presence of mind at the scene to ask an ambulance attendant to dispose of his stash of marijuana.

"We will show you a different picture of Stan Farr," Haynes said. In the weeks before his murder, Farr carried a pistol. He had failed in business, and there were a number of judgments against him. "The type of people with whom Stan Farr was doing business," Haynes continued, "were not the type to resort to the courts to collect debts." Farr had, or claimed to have, more than $100,000 at the time of his murder, Haynes said, and Horace Copeland knew this. The defense would show that Copeland was a man worthy of Farr's fear. Regarding W. T. Rufner, the purpose of his testimony would not be to disparage the character of Priscilla. "In that regard," he said, looking up from his notes, "I think Priscilla Lee Davis stands on her own." Instead, the purpose of his testimony would be to establish that for a period of time he had a key to the Davis mansion, as did a number of other people of questionable character.

Finally, the defense would show that Stan Farr was the target of the assailants. Haynes used the plural, indicating that he believed more than one assailant was involved. He repeated his contention that the assailants were "persons who do not resort to the courts to collect money owed." Andrea Wilborn, Haynes concluded, was "an accidental victim." Priscilla herself was not the primary target, nor was Bubba Gavrel, who happened to stumble onto the massacre.

Haynes added one final, intriguing footnote: "Maybe at the conclusion of the defense's case there will be some development that will surprise you . . . some development that at this juncture is not foreseen."

This final note about future unforeseen developments caused much speculation in the media, and perhaps some second-guessing among prosecutors, but all it really reflected was the defense team's faith in its own ongoing investigation. Steve Sumner was beginning to connect the hundreds of bits and pieces of miscellaneous information his investigators had collected. In recent weeks it had occurred to Sumner that they were dealing with several groups of informants who didn't intersect—there were Cullen's friends, Priscilla's friends, and then a whole new group that didn't fit into either category. This new group, or "second world" as members of the defense began calling it, ran the scale of

Fort Worth society, from dope pushers and petty criminals to some of the city's wealthiest, most prominent citizens. On a typical day, Sumner might have lunch at the Petroleum Club, conduct a secret afternoon interview in the back office of a warehouse, then have dinner with still another source at the Colonial Country Club. Although Sumner hadn't been able to weave his collection of information into a single scenario, he impressed the other defense attorneys with his "second world" theory. It went a long way toward explaining how the estranged wife of one of Fort Worth's leading citizens could bounce from high society to low society without batting an eyelash. Priscilla was an odd one, Sumner said. He'd never met her, yet he maintained that he knew her better than anyone he'd ever met. "She's a two-worlder," he told the others. "Two or more." Certainly W. T. Rufner and Horace Copeland came from another world than the one Cullen Davis appeared to inhabit. *Appeared* was the key word; appearances were everything now. Though the defense had planted the seed in the minds of jurors that any number of other-worlders could have committed the murders, it would be necessary now to focus on a single theory. Rufner wasn't working out. He'd dropped out of the mansion scene some eighteen months before the killings; pointing to him as the killer was too farfetched. He might be a buffoon capable of hawking autographed T-shirts in the hallway, but he was not a convincing candidate as a killer. Horace Copeland seemed much more believable. For one thing, he had been around both Stan Farr and Priscilla just prior to the murders. For another, he was dead. The defense wasn't obligated to produce the killer, of course; all they had to do was create reasonable doubt of Cullen's guilt. The cornerstone of their defense rested in making the jury believe that Stan Farr was indeed the primary target, because, they contended, Cullen Davis had no reason to kill Farr. After all, Sumner pointed out, Farr had been living at the mansion for about fifteen months before the killings, and Cullen knew it. Several witnesses, including Jerry Thomas and Karen Master, were prepared to testify

241

that Cullen and Farr had met socially on several occasions and the mood was always amiable.

As the lawyers reviewed their case and arranged their order of witnesses, Sumner pointed out the probability that they'd just scratched the surface in their search for other-worlders. Horace Copeland could be a mere pawn. It could go much deeper. Copeland's own death might be a related factor. In recent days Sumner had attempted to track down a potential dynamite witness. It was still a long shot, but in another week or two they might find someone who could shatter the state's case in a single stroke. In the meantime, they had a number of more conventional witnesses lined up to demonstrate that the state had done only enough investigation and called only enough witnesses to support its prejudged conclusions.

As Haynes had promised, the defense opened its case the next morning by attacking what the state contended to be the "motive." Defense Exhibit No. 1 was the alleged prenuptial document. Mrs. Fern Frost, who was identified as Cullen's girl Friday at the time of his marriage to Priscilla, testified that on the evening of August 27, 1968, she took the document to the Green Oaks for Cullen and Priscilla to sign. She was certain that Cullen read the document before signing. Cullen never signed anything without first reading it carefully. Typically, Cullen caught a typing strikeover, *t* as she recalled, and brought it to her attention. Frost couldn't swear that Priscilla *read* the agreement, only that she "turned the pages." The following morning, Frost said, Priscilla called her and asked if Cullen's first wife had signed a similar document. "I told her that I didn't know, and if I did, I couldn't discuss it," she told the jury. During cross-examination the state probed at inconsistencies in the secretary's testimony. Was she saying that she prepared the document on the same day it was signed? In early statements she had said it was prepared "two weeks" and even "eight months" before. The prosecution also claimed that the date was typed on a different typewriter than the body of the document.

Still on the subject of the prenuptial agreement, the defense called Beth Auldridge, a former Chamber of Commerce representative who had invited Cullen and Priscilla to host the Miss Teenage America Pageant in 1968. She testified that during a luncheon Priscilla told her that she signed the agreement because "Cullen's family thought I was after his money. I signed it to assure them I wasn't."

Cecil Munn, the Fort Worth attorney whose law firm had represented the Davis empire for some years, testified that he was at a meeting at Mid-Continent with Cullen and Ken Davis on August 2 when Cullen received the news that Judge Eidson had not ruled favorably in their case. Cullen's reaction was "matter-of-fact," Munn recalled. "He exhibited no unusual emotion. There was no hatred or inflammatory emotion in evidence at the time." Munn pointed out to the jury that despite the fact Cullen owed $11 million in community debts, "he was in an enviable position as far as personal wealth was concerned." The increased payments, Munn added, were "minimal to the amount of money involved." While it was true that the court order tied up Cullen Davis's corporate funds and other investments, making it necessary to seek a separate court ruling on each business transaction, Munn told the court that "this was an inconvenience but no great obstacle." Besides, Judge Eidson's ruling was only temporary. The end to the long divorce litigation "was in sight," Munn concluded, inferring that rather than being upset by this small setback, Cullen Davis was in fact looking forward to his future freedom.

During cross-examination Tolly Wilson attempted to portray Cullen Davis as a callous, unprincipled man interested not in his family but only in holding on to his substantial fortune. Dowlen ruled that there could be no mention of the bitter litigation with his brother, Bill Davis, but permitted the state to ask limited questions about documents filed in that suit. Papers from that suit contended that Cullen's personal debts were $16 million, not $11 million. Corporate debts in a single company, according to Bill Davis, ran to $46 million. Bill

243

Davis further contended that Cullen used corporation funds to back other loans, thereby "recklessly increasing the indebtedness of the corporation to sums in excess of $150 million." The way Tolly Wilson interpreted it, Cullen's financial problems were something more than "minimal." The court records jolly well proved that Priscilla had him by the sore place; Wilson questioned Munn at length about the August 2 meeting with Cullen and Ken Davis, pointing out to the jury that Bill Davis was specifically *not* invited. Munn testified that before the meeting, Cullen had lunch with his adopted daughter, Dee Davis.

"Did Cullen Davis tell you [at the meeting] that Andrea was back in town?" Wilson asked the witness.

Munn said he didn't recall.

"And when he heard the results [of Judge Eidson's ruling] there was no reaction?"

Munn answered that he couldn't recall any reaction from either Cullen *or* Ken Davis. Certainly Cullen demonstrated "no hatred," Munn repeated.

"Would you describe killing a child's cat in front of that child an act of hatred?" Wilson asked before anyone could stop him. Racehorse Haynes bolted out of his chair like his pants were on fire, angrily objecting to the question. Dowlen called all the attorneys to the bench for a cooling-off period. There was no doubt in Tolly Wilson's mind that the question was out of order. But he didn't regret it. It would very likely be the only time in the trial that Cullen Davis would be accused of any misdeed prior to the murders.

For the next several days the defense focused its attack on Bubba Gavrel. Doris Costello, a clerk in the emergency room at John Peter Smith Hospital on the night of the shootings, testified that Gavrel was "conscious" when they brought him in and was sufficiently lucid to give his name, address, and telephone number and to sign a consent form. The state countered by asking Costello if Gavrel had seen Priscilla Davis that night. Costello said that he hadn't to her knowledge.

Ambulance attendant Paul Goheen testified next, telling the jury that when he first entered the mansion,

Gavrel was seated on the floor, holding a telephone. When the ambulance attendant asked the victim where he had been shot, Gavrel answered, "I don't know. Get me out of here." When Goheen asked *who* shot him, Gavrel gave the same answer: "I don't know. Just get me out of here." Moments later, as Goheen was attempting to remove the victim's trousers in the back of the ambulance, Goheen testified that Gavrel produced two Baggies of marijuana and said, "Get rid of this." Goheen said he threw the Baggies out of the ambulance window. Bev Bass was "cussing . . . she was very excited," Goheen continued. "Her eyes looked glassy . . . consistent with using drugs." Goheen told the jury that he no longer drove an ambulance—he was now a policeman in a Fort Worth suburb.

There was a hollow ring to parts of Goheen's story, but prosecutors failed to point this out to the jury. Even as attendants loaded Gavrel into the ambulance, it must have been apparent that some sort of major criminal activity had taken place. Didn't Goheen know that marijuana was illegal? Didn't he realize it was evidence? Then why did he throw it out the window? *How* did he throw it out the window? Did the rear of the ambulance have roll-down windows? Which window did he use to dispose of the marijuana? These were all legitimate questions, but the prosecution didn't ask them.

Prosecutors had to be embarrassed when the defense called its next witness—Fort Worth police officer Jimmy Soders. The reason that the state had neglected to call this key witness became apparent when Soders admitted that Gavrel told him, "I don't know the man" when asked who did the shooting. The state won the point back in cross-examination. When Soders asked Bev Bass who shot her boyfriend, she replied: "Cullen Davis did it. I saw him do it. I know him."

The big gun in the defense's assault on Gavrel was Tommy Jourden, who shared an intensive-care cubicle with Gavrel after the shootings. Even before Jourden took the stand, it became apparent that the big gun might backfire.

Jourden was a calculated risk. There were aspects of

Jourden's life that might cause him to appear less than worthy to a jury—he had been unemployed for more than a year, had applied for welfare on the grounds that a back injury made him totally disabled, and had more than a passing acquaintance with personal injury suits—he had been involved in three, one of which was still pending. However unfair the judgment might have been, Jourden *appeared* to be a hustler. Racehorse Haynes was confident, however, that these matters could be kept from the jury. Weighed against what Jourden claimed to have overheard, it was a risk they had to take.

Jourden testified that on August 3, the day after the murders, Gavrel's father visited the intensive-care cubicle. According to Jourden, the conversation between father and son went like this:

Gus Sr.: Do you know who shot you?

Gus Jr.: No, sir, I don't. It all happened so quick and it was dark and I didn't see who it was.

Gus Sr.: It was Cullen that done it. A girl out there [Bev Bass] said it was, so if anybody asks you, you say it was Cullen. Someone is going to pay for doing this.

After Gus Sr. left, Jourden continued, he engaged Bubba in a conversation in which the victim again denied knowing the gunman. Jourden said that he then told Gavrel: "You know, if this rich man shot you, you're going to be a rich man yourself. You can file suit on him."

Jourden quoted Gavrel as replying: "I guess you're right. I hadn't thought of that."

Cross-examination brought out the curious fact that Jourden had waited four months before reporting the hospital conversation. The witness denied the prosecution's claim that he finally came forward "for the purpose of bettering yourself [financially]." Jourden, who appeared to consider himself a good witness, didn't appear shocked at the question.

When Jourden had completed his testimony, both sides claimed that he had helped their case. This was in keeping with the defense's strategy, part of which was to implant in the minds of the jurors that the state had

246

called only the witnesses who fit their concept of what happened. Burleson, for one, believed that the state was in danger of becoming complacent; that they had lived with their concept so long they failed to notice its inherent flaws, or appreciate the new flaws that the defense was preparing to explore. "They think we're scattershooting," Burleson said. Burleson was positive that if they kept scattershooting long enough, they were bound to hit some nerves.

One of their next witnesses, Robert Sawhill, was a case in point. Since Sawhill was the first person Bev Bass encountered as she fled for her life, why had the state not called him? It might be assumed that Sawhill would contradict part of Bev Bass's testimony, and this was true. Bass claimed that as she jumped into Sawhill's car, she identified the gunman as either Cullen Davis or "the owner of the big house on the hill." Now it was Sawhill's turn to deny it. The only time Davis's name was mentioned, Sawhill testified, was when the girl told him, "You know there's a divorce case going on up at the Davis estate." But as Burleson continued to question Sawhill, something else emerged, something that was not obvious in the beginning but would grow much larger in the minds of the jurors as the case progressed. There had already been some confusion about the exact times that everything happened, but Sawhill was very sure that when he telephoned the police that night it was 12:20 A.M. He remembered that when he and some business associates left the Ramada Inn, someone pointed out that it was uncivilized to close the bar at midnight. Sawhill remembered looking at the clock in the lobby and then at his own watch—it was exactly 12:05. The distance from the Ramada Inn to the place on Hulen where he first saw Bev Bass was precisely 9.5 miles—he had checked it later to be certain—and taking into consideration one detour on Interstate 20, driving at his normal speed, it would have taken him thirteen minutes. He estimated that another two minutes elapsed from the time he picked up Bass until he called the police. Therefore, he called the police at exactly 12:20. According to police records, this was twenty-two minutes before they received Sawhill's call (and at least twenty minutes before Priscilla was beating on the door of a neighbor's house, screaming for them to call the police). The conflict of times became more apparent when it was recalled that security guard John Smedley, who arrived just as Sawhill was calling the police, placed the time at 12:47. Records kept by Smedley's dispatcher confirmed this.

The next witness for the defense supplied yet another mystery to the time and events of that night. John Brutsche, general manager of a moving and storage firm, told the jury that as he and his wife drove along Hulen and passed the mansion that night, they saw a large, expensive, late-model car turning slowly into the driveway of the Davis estate. He couldn't tell the color of the car, only that it was a single color (unlike Cullen's white-on-blue Cadillac which was supposedly parked in a downtown garage). Brutsche guessed that the time was 10:50 P.M. He based his guess on the fact that as he and his wife left the parking lot of a downtown church, they looked at the clock at the top of the Continental Bank Building and observed that it was 10:33. He remembered that they had promised the baby-sitter to be home before 11:00 P.M. and stopped at a convenience store to get some change. So it had to be around 10:50 when he passed the Davis mansion. This would have been at least an hour before Stan Farr and Priscilla arrived. As Racehorse excused the witness, he walked by the jury box with that *who do you suppose was in that car?* expression, scratching his head and rolling his eyes.

The mystery of the large, expensive, late-model car intensified when the defense's next witness told of driving past the Davis estate at 12:35 and observing "a large blue car" peeling out of the mansion drive in a cloud of dust. Brad Gandy, a college freshman, recalled that he had been watching TV that night at the home of his girlfriend, Julia Hall. The ABC-TV movie that night was *Days of Wine and Roses,* and Gandy recalled that at exactly midnight his girlfriend's mother yelled from upstairs that it was time for him to leave. "I know it was midnight," he said, "because we both looked at the grandfather's clock above the fireplace. At 12:15 Mrs. Hall yelled again that it was time for me to leave." Gandy estimated that he and his girlfriend stood outside beside his new yellow Firebird for ten to fifteen minutes; then he started home. Roughly five minutes later he turned onto Hulen, and that's when he saw the car spinning out of the mansion drive. "It left a cloud of dust clear across Hulen," he recalled. "I had to roll up my windows it was so thick." A few seconds later he heard sirens and saw two police cars "racing side by side" in the direction of the mansion. Gandy had originally told his story to the district attorney, but nobody seemed interested. In fact, the DA's office had given Gandy's statement to the defense, as required by law. But the jury didn't understand this; it must have seemed to the jury that here was another case of the state picking only the witnesses who went along with the prosecutorial concept.

In his cross-examination, Joe Shannon got Gandy to admit that "time sure flies when you're having fun." Now that Gandy thought about it again, the television movie must have been *over* before Julia walked him to his car. "And I guess you're really not too sure how long you and Julia stood out there kissing good night?" Shannon asked, grinning to show the young man he understood how things went. "In fact, wasn't it *12:50* when *Days of Wine and Roses* was over?" Now that Gandy thought about it, maybe it was 12:50. Shannon knew damn well it was. He had checked. Shannon was dead certain that any car racing out of the Hulen Street exit after 12:50 would have had to run over several cops first.

Nevertheless, the defense had made its point. There was considerable doubt now about what time things took place. There was a gap of twenty to fifty-seven minutes, an insignificant amount of time measured against all that had happened but enough time to allow for a conspiracy. The large car (or cars) seen entering and leaving the mansion grounds needed some clarification, and the defense called its next witness to estab-

249

lish that Cullen Davis was driving his pickup on the night of the killings. Jack Smith, night cashier of the parking garage in the Continental National Bank Building where Cullen parked both his pickup and his white-on-blue Cadillac, testified that Davis had left the garage at 5:30 P.M. on August 2, driving the pickup truck. Jake Smith could say for a fact that Cullen's Cadillac was still in its parking place at midnight when he got off duty. "I could see it from my booth," Smith said positively. "Mr. Davis's car stayed right there!" To support his memory, the night cashier produced his log from the night of August 2—a list of the license numbers of all the cars still at the garage when Smith checked out at midnight. "Yep, there it is right there," Jake said, pointing to the list. Smith added that he didn't see Cullen or the pickup again that night.

"Hell, what does that prove?" Joe Shannon said during the recess. "Does anyone believe that Cullen Davis didn't have access to another large, expensive car?" During cross-examination, the prosecution used the garage records to trace the comings and goings of Cullen's two vehicles in the days just prior to the murders. On the evening of July 29, Jake Smith recalled, Cullen parked the pickup behind the Cadillac, removed something from the Cadillac trunk and placed it in the pickup, then left in the pickup. The following night, July 30, the pickup was in its parking place when Smith made his check at 11:15 P.M., but it was gone the following morning when the day cashier made a new check. Since this was a weekend and the garage didn't keep logs on weekends, there was no way to show how many times the two vehicles entered and left on Saturday afternoon or Sunday. Smith had already told about Cullen leaving in his pickup on Monday, August 2. On the morning of August 3, the pickup was parked in *another* garage across the street, and the Cadillac was parked in the driveway of Karen Master's house. What did it all mean? Only that sometime after midnight, Cullen or someone returned the pickup and took the Cadillac.

It was Halloween Eve when Haynes, Burleson, and the other attorneys met and decided the time had come to present Cullen Davis's albi—Karen Master. Karen would testify that in the early morning hours of August 3, she woke up at 12:40 and saw Cullen asleep beside her. She had gone to bed around 9:00 or 9:30 P.M. and couldn't say what time he came home, but she was sure he was there at 12:40 A.M. She remembered looking at the digital clock on the nightstand. As with some of the other witnesses, the defense knew it ran a calculated risk by putting Karen Master on the witness stand. She would have to admit to the jury that Cullen had lived at her house from September 1975 until the morning of August 3 when he was arrested. Having made much hay of the fact that Priscilla was shacking up, it might be embarrassing to shed some light on *Cullen's* private love life. It was difficult to explain why many of the same people who thought Priscilla so shameless for bedding down with assorted characters saw nothing wrong with Cullen shacking up with Karen, unless it was the fact that Karen was ten years younger than Priscilla and not nearly as independent. Who could tell, in ten years she might *be* Priscilla. People talked a lot about the money that Priscilla spent on clothes, but nobody thought it curious that Karen was always the model of fashion in suede and leather and fine furs. They envied her, but there was nothing malicious in their envy. A man might perceive Priscilla as a threat, but not Karen. Something else bothered the defense attorneys—when Karen had testified before the grand jury and again at the bond hearing shortly after the killings, she said nothing about waking up at 12:40 A.M. Though Haynes hadn't yet joined the defense team at the time Karen appeared at the two hearings, he had an explanation for her failure to supply an alibi that might have spared her live-in lover many months in a jail cell. "Back then 12:40 didn't do us any good," he said. "They were playing games with the times then. We knew that grand juries ask loose, sloppy questions and play fast and free with numbers—'When did you kill your grandma and do you drive a 1948 Ford?' That's the sort of thing grand juries ask. It was only after we nailed them down on times that Karen's testimony had any meaning."

To those who had endured two months of jury selection and more than two months of testimony, Karen Master was an object of fascination, possibly because it was so difficult to assess her role in these bizarre happenings. Karen was a mature and no doubt courageous woman who had cared for her two handicapped children with a minimum of complaint, but in many ways she seemed painfully dependent on those around her. She was pretty in the way that a doll is pretty, with bright sunflower eyes and a smile as innocent as fresh paint. Because she was a potential witness, Karen wasn't allowed in the courtroom, and yet she always seemed to be there—chatting in the hallway and in the judge's waiting room with secretaries, reporters, friends, looking after things, caring for her children, preparing elaborate lunches that she would share with Cullen and his people, always waiting for something. Day after day, *waiting,* her composure and her faith seemingly unshaken. Karen's very presence in Amarillo gave force to a twisted logic in defense of the man she loved. The wife of a local attorney, who specialized in education for the handicapped and had worked with Karen's younger son, said, "I *know* Cullen didn't do it because I know Karen Master. She is a wonderful mother. A woman like that wouldn't live with a killer."

At night when they returned Cullen to his cell, Karen Master and her constant companion, Kathy Sellers, could be seen, sometimes at the Hilton Inn bar with Karen's father, Ray Hudson, sometimes with members of the press, dancing at the Caravan Club, or sipping pink icy drinks at Rhett Butler's. Karen seemed to enjoy dressing up and being in the company of men; perhaps the reason for this was that men enjoyed *her* and went out of their way to see that she was protected.

As she took the witness stand and began to tell her story, Karen was almost a caricature of sweetness and composure. Hands folded in her lap, she listened attentively to each question that Racehorse Haynes asked, then turned in exaggerated slow motion and smiled to the jury as she answered. One cynic of the press declared that she had obviously been rehearsed for this once-in-

252

a-lifetime role, to which someone replied: "By who? Walt Disney?"

With Haynes feeding her the questions, Karen described the events of August 2–3 as she recalled them. It was a normal morning, she said. Cullen left for his office around 7:30 or 8:00 A.M., driving his Cadillac. She took her two children to school and spent the remainder of the morning and part of the afternoon at a new beauty shop she'd heard about. Late in the afternoon she took the children to a snow-cone stand. Somewhere around 5:00 P.M. Cullen's secretary called and told her he would be late, which wasn't unusual; Cullen often came home after Karen and the children were asleep. Her friend Sherry Jones telephoned around 6:30 P.M., inviting Karen and Cullen to dinner. Karen recalled telling her friend: "No, it's already prepared. It's in the oven. He's going to be late for dinner." Sherry Jones called again about 8:30 P.M. Karen didn't remember what they talked about. (One of the many rumors that circulated was that Sherry Jones called a third time, around 11:30 P.M., at which time Karen told her she was worried about Cullen and wanted to go look for him. But Karen denied this.) Somewhere around 9:00 or 9:30 P.M., Karen continued, she took a sleeping pill and went to bed. This was earlier than her normal bedtime, but Karen remembered feeling tired.

"And what is the next thing you recall?" Haynes asked.

"I awoke very briefly at 12:40. I raised up and looked at the digital clock. Cullen was in bed. He appeared to be asleep. He was wearing just his shorts and was half uncovered. I went back to sleep."

The next thing she knew, Karen told the jury, it was about 4:00 or 4:15 (she apparently didn't look at the clock), and the telephone was ringing. She walked around to the other side of the bed and answered. It was Ken Davis, wanting to talk to his younger brother. She recalled that the conversation between the brothers was brief, no more than three minutes. She heard Cullen say, "Oh, no! My God! Really? Who was shot?"

Q: And what did you do next?

A: I got up. I walked to Cullen's side of the bed. He was awake, laying down. . . .

At that point the testimony was abruptly interrupted by the wailing of sirens in the street below the Potter County Courthouse. The county's civil defense alert had somehow been triggered by accident, and while custodians rushed to silence it, Karen sat smiling at the jurors, most of whom were smiling back. This break in dramatic tension came as a relief for most of those in the courtroom, but Karen didn't seem to mind one way or another. She looked at Cullen and said something about dinner. When the sirens had been shut down, she continued: "I sat down on the bed. We looked at each other. The phone rang again immediately. I picked it up. It was a male voice. Officer Ford of the police department. He asked to speak to Mr. Davis."

Just to clear the air, Racehorse then asked, "Has and does Cullen Davis assist you financially?" Karen turned to the jury as she answered yes. In conclusion Racehorse asked, "Are you in love with him?" And again Karen turned in slow motion, smiled at the jury, and said, "Yes."

Joe Shannon opened his cross-examination by inquiring why Karen Master kept turning and smiling at the jury. Karen turned to the jury, paused, smiled, and said: "I have not had an opportunity to look at the jury until now. I think they are very interesting people, don't you?" Shannon was immediately sorry that he had asked, and he moved on to other questions about her activities both before and after the killings, leading her to August 12, 1976, the day she appeared before the Tarrant County grand jury. Yes, Karen remembered the day. Shannon opened a copy of the grand jury transcript as he considered his next question; theoretically, in fact legally, Karen Master should not have disclosed to the defense *anything* said in the grand jury room, but Shannon was fairly certain she had. He didn't intend to make an issue of it. It was much more important that the jury concentrate on the questions he was about to ask. Approaching the witness with the transcript in his hands, Shannon said: "And do you remember being asked the question: 'Between midnight and 4:00 A.M. what is the first thing you remember?' And do you remember answering: 'I do not remember the time. The phone rang and both of us woke up'?"

Karen pursed her lips as though trying to think hard, then shook her head; she didn't remember the exact question and answer. Without waiting for a reply, Shannon asked if she recalled telling Det. C. R. Davis, "The first thing I knew, the phone was ringing." Karen answered with an emphatic "No!" Well, Shannon said, holding up another document, she certainly didn't tell Detective Davis that she woke up at 12:40 and saw Cullen in bed.

Q: Did you tell Sherry Jones on the morning of August 3, "He took off his clothes and lay down on the bed and went to sleep"?

A: No, not in those exact words.

Q: Did you tell Sherry Jones, "I thought he came home between 12:30 and 1:00"?

A: Not that I recall.

Q: Were you less precise with Sherry than you are with this jury now?

A: That is correct.

Very early in the trial Dowlen ruled that it would be improper for the jury to know that the defendant had been denied bail; therefore the state was not allowed to mention the bond hearing nine days after the murder. It was therefore incumbent on the prosecutor to ask his questions gingerly, referring only to "your previous testimony." Shannon went about his business in a clear, professional manner, establishing that on at least three occasions when authorities had asked about that night, Karen had not once mentioned waking up and seeing Cullen in bed at 12:40. She had told her friends Rosemary Mabe and Sherry Jones about 12:40; wasn't it curious that on three occasions when she had opportunities to clear Cullen's name—she had not *once* mentioned the alibi?

Shannon turned her attention now to the night of August 4, to a conversation she had with Cullen Davis outside Schick Hospital in Fort Worth. Shannon was curious about the nature of this conversation.

Q: Did you tell the grand jury that you had to satisfy yourself what time Cullen got home?

A: No.

Q (reading from the grand jury transcript): "Well, of course Cullen prefaced our conversation with the fact that his attorneys advised him not to discuss the case. But I asked him to satisfy in my own mind what time he got home, and he said a little before 11:00."

Karen didn't answer, but neither did she appear shattered by the apparent contradiction.

Q: Wasn't the reason that you had to satisfy your own mind that you didn't wake up until 4:00 when the *phone rang?*

A: That is not correct.

Q: In that conversation outside Schick Hospital, didn't Cullen tell you that he had worked at the office, then gone to the chiropractor, then back to the office to work another two or three hours? Then he went to eat? Then he came home. He got home a little before 11:00.

A: Yes, I told the grand jury that.

Q: But now you deny it?

A: I was confused.

Q: When was the first time you told any lawyer for Cullen Davis that he was home with you at 12:40?

A: About the same time I talked to the grand jury. I can't recall exactly.

Shannon wanted to ask her forbidden questions about the bond hearing, but he knew that violating court orders could blow their whole case. As it turned out, he didn't have to; Karen did it herself. Apparently confused by his repeated references to a "prior court hearing," she finally blurted out, "Are you referring to the bond hearing?"

The words were hardly out of her mouth before Haynes was on his feet requesting permission to approach the bench. By now it was late afternoon. The jury looked tired. Shannon had time for one more question before Dowlen recessed for the weekend. His question was, "Isn't it a fact that you didn't take the stand and testify even though your attorneys knew you had this information?"

"That's true," Karen acknowledged.

But *why?*

"It didn't seem relevant," she replied.

On Monday morning, October 31, Shannon again directed Karen Master's attention to her testimony before the grand jury, nine days after the shooting. Again, Karen answered that it didn't seem relevant to tell the grand jury about waking up at 12:40. Besides, she said, "the grand jury did not ask me that."

Shannon proceeded to quote from the grand jury transcript.

Shannon: Question: "Now between the hours of 12:00 midnight and 4:00 A.M., *when* is the first thing you remember and what time was it?" Answer: "I do not remember the time. The phone rang and both of us were asleep."

Karen: I understood the question to mean in effect, "When is the first thing you remember hearing?"

Shannon continued to grill Karen Master about her testimony before the grand jury, and Karen continued to insist that she had told the truth.

Karen: At that time 12:40 didn't prove guilt or innocence either way. It had no relevance. It didn't seem significant.

Q: And you told the grand jury the whole truth?

A: Yes, I told the whole truth.

Q: And you didn't know on August 12 the time of the murders?

A: No, sir.

Q: And that's the very reason, is it not, why you didn't tell the grand jury about that man, Thomas Cullen Davis, lying in bed with you . . . because you didn't *know* what time it was supposed to be!

A: No, that's not true.

And why, Shannon demanded to know, hadn't she apprised Det. C. R. Davis of this piece of pertinent information?

A: I found out later that C. R. Davis had been hired

257

by Priscilla Davis to do personal work for her. I didn't think it was appropriate [to tell him].

Shannon pointed out for the jury that Karen was also misinformed on this point. Priscilla hired several off-duty policemen as bodyguards, but C. R. Davis wasn't one of them.

There was one final segment to Cullen's alibi. The defense called James Mabe, a business and social acquaintance, who testified that on the night of the murders Cullen called his home and discussed a trip to Mexico that Mabe and his wife Rosemary had planned with Cullen and Karen. Mabe recalled that the phone call came at 12:15 A.M. The witness could not say for certain that Cullen telephoned from Karen Master's home, only that that's where Cullen said he was calling from. As Joe Shannon pointed out later, the call to Mabe was not only suspiciously "convenient," it sounded downright phony. Mabe said that Cullen called to ask about travel visas for the trip. Cullen Davis would have qualified as an expert on travel visas; he must have known that all the documentation needed to enter Mexico was a passport, a birth certificate, or even a Texas voter registration certificate. So why would he be calling Mabe after midnight *except* to create an alibi? Shannon's cross-examination of Karen Master and James Mabe didn't totally destroy the alibi, but it shot it through with large holes.

Cullen later supplied his own version of the alibi to members of the media, contradicting Karen's story that he told her he arrived home "a little before 11:00." Cullen told reporters that on the evening of August 2 he worked late, ate alone, went to a movie, and arrived home at 12:15 A.M.

As the trial recessed for the weekend, Racehorse Haynes was trying to fight off a head cold. Saturday night he took a few slugs of Cognac and fell asleep watching TV. He woke Sunday morning in a cold sweat, kicking at the covers and trying desperately to escape voices pounding his head. They were saying: *Let's kill all the people!* It was some seconds before he realized the voices were coming from the TV set. "It was a program about terrorists," he said, "but, my God, it sounded real!" They were all jumpy as a cat in a room of rocking chairs. Spies had been photographed taking pictures of spies. One of their investigators turned out to be a double agent. Someone planted drugs in Steve Sumner's motel room. Sumner was sure they were all being followed. Still, Sumner thought they were getting somewhere. A few weeks earlier Sumner violated one of his own rules and agreed to a secret meeting with a person regarded as "untouchable" because of his connections with the enemy camp and the information that he was capable of violence. The man wanted Sumner to meet him at midnight in the parking lot of the Botanic Gardens near Forest Park. "Come alone," the man told Sumner.

With considerable trepidation, Sumner kept the midnight rendezvous. The informant made two conditions —no lights and no notes. As Sumner listened, he began to believe that the informant could provide useful information, maybe even proof. But there was a catch: the man wanted money. Sumner wrote him off as another con man, but in the last several days some of the information gained that night had checked out.

"He could be the dynamite witness we've been looking for," Sumner told the other defense attorneys. In fact, they code-named him Mr. Dynamite. They weren't yet ready to put Mr. Dynamite on the witness stand. They weren't even sure they could put him on the witness stand. Mr. Dynamite fit the category of phantom— no job, no address, no telephone number, just a character in the shadows, a man perpetually between bus stations.

The attorneys decided that Sumner should interview Mr. Dynamite again, but when Sumner relayed instructions to his men in the field, word came back that Mr. Dynamite had vanished without a trace.

It was early November when the first swirling snow blew down the Great Plains, snarling traffic at Amarillo Airport and at times obliterating highways. Lawyers, reporters, and witnesses attempting to reach Amarillo had to deplane at Lubbock and travel the final 100 miles by bus. It was a spectacular and frightening experience: when the wind blew, as it did almost constantly, it was impossible to distinguish the highways from the endless track of white swirling powder. Under the best conditions the Potter County Courthouse could charitably be described as cozy, but now that winter was approaching, the narrow hallways and dim offices resembled a refugee camp.

Something else was stirring, something that at first seemed unrelated to the Cullen Davis trial but in the months to come would reveal itself as a by-product, if not an outgrowth, of Amarillo's obsession with the defendant. It developed into a full-fledged local scandal nicknamed Pottergate, but when it first sparked in early November, the only effect it had on George Dowlen's fifth-floor courtroom was to triple the confusion. It started with a court of inquiry into accounting and inventory procedures in county offices. Sheriff T. L. Baker, who would later be charged with pampering Cullen Davis and failing to provide security, was subpoenaed, along with some of his top deputies. The same week three of Baker's most trusted men submitted their resignations. Since this was obviously the tip of an iceberg, Baker and his chief deputies declined to testify, citing their Fifth Amendment rights against self-incrimination. On another front, county commissioner Bob Hicks was arrested on charges of felony theft, after construction workers told the court of inquiry that Hicks was illegally profiting from his use of county building funds. Newly appointed county judge Hugh Russell, who had been so instrumental in helping Cullen's lawyers pick the jury, pushed the murder trial off the front page briefly by announcing that if Bob Hicks had made money from work on county buildings, Russell's office would "go after the money." Potter County DA Tom Curtis was meanwhile investigating Baker for neglecting security at the Cullen Davis trial. Old-timers in Amarillo said that the county was merely going through one of its periodic bloodlettings, a local ritual in which politicians sacrifice other politicians to the glory of their own self-interests. To many, the mammon of this ritualistic purge was Cullen Davis; they contended that the publicity and the enormous amount of money being squandered on the trial had divided the town in a way that it hadn't felt since the days of the pioneer land rush. Nobody knew it in the beginning, but Judge Dowlen himself would be swept up in the torrent of anger, frustrations, and political vendettas called Pottergate.

In the sanctity of his thirtieth-floor office, Stanley Marsh 3 reveled in the daily reports from both Pottergate and the murder trial. Marsh was a close friend of both Hugh Russell and Tom Curtis, and every day at noon Stanley invited various politicians, writers, and artists to share his daily "picnic" lunch and gab about the scandal. Stories about the lack of security surrounding the trial naturally gave birth to a scheme to snatch Cullen, crate him in cedar, and ship him to South America, where, under more graceful circumstances, he would no doubt reward the picnickers handsomely.

Stanley would stand at the window looking down at the Cullen Hilton where his Fort Worth peer had spent so many unhappy days. He'd put his thumbs in the back pockets of his baggy jeans and ask, "What's Cullen really like?"

"I don't think anybody knows," someone said.

"Do you think he did it?"

"I don't think the jury thinks he did."

"My sister-in-law doesn't believe he did it," Stanley

261

mused. "She doesn't believe wealthy husbands shoot their wives."

Stanley removed his thick glasses and cleaned them on the tail of his shirt, and you could tell he wanted to do something. Cullen probably expected it; the more Stanley thought about it, the more he was *certain* Cullen expected some action on his part. Second-generation rich share a feeling that they are not bound by normal rules of society, and so it was with T. Cullen Davis and Stanley Marsh 3. Among the Fort Worth establishment Cullen was celebrated for his temper tantrums, his taste for ostentatious extravagances, his high tolerance for pornography. On the walls of Cullen's office in Fort Worth hung paintings by nineteenth-century European masters. Stanley's tastes were more earthy. When asked what art was, Stanley would point proudly to the back-yard of Toad Hall where the giant letters A-R-T were erected. The most prominent painting in his office was a giant circus poster. His current art project involved tattooing dogs. The idea was a carry-over from an ear-lier tattoo job done on his 400-pound pet pig, Minnesota Fats. Long before the cast of the Cullen Davis trial hit town, Stanley and Minnesota Fats whiled away the eve-nings at Toad Hall watching marvelous Panhandle sun-sets and sharing bottles of Mateus wine.

Like his Fort Worth peer, Stanley too had known recent tragedy—it happened on Easter morning when Fats, his judgment muddled by too much Mateus, ODed on chocolate Easter eggs and went to that big sty in the sky. Stanley had his old pig pal stuffed, and now Fats reposed on the floor of Stanley's office like a giant footstool. During business hours you could usually find one of Stanley's five children pretending that the stuffed pig was a hobbyhorse. Stanley loved children and found it very difficult to believe that any man could murder a twelve-year-old girl. That sort of viciousness was completely foreign to Stanley, whose style of re-taliation was always gloved in a prank. "Stanley prac-tices what Camus called 'lyrical inhumanity,' " said Buck Ramsey, the crippled cowboy who grew up with Stanley and remained his close friend even though their natural worlds were light-years apart. "Stanley can be cruel, like telephoning some politician convicted of stealing county funds in the middle of the night and asking about a loan. But he keeps it on a lyrical level."

So it was that on a cold, rainy November night Stanley hatched a plan to leave his own mark on the Cullen Davis trial. Overnight, Stanley's famous phantom soft pool table disappeared from its isolated ranch pasture and reappeared on the roof of a building across from the Cullen Hilton. This gave birth to a strange rumor that Stanley was in cahoots with Racehorse Haynes and together they were sending secret messages to Cullen in his jail cell. When a local newspaper columnist called and asked if the rumor was true, Stanley agreed to it immediately. This quote from Stanley appeared the following day: "Since Cullen's cell faces east [the soft pool table was west of the jailhouse], he loosens the bars from his cell, escapes, climbing to the courthouse roof from where he can see the soft pool table, reads the message, and then secretly returns to his cell. . . ."

A few days later, when Stanley made one of his rare visits to the courthouse, Cullen asked to meet him. "We talked about *skinny-dipping*," Stanley said. "I'd heard all those stories about Cullen's naked swimming parties at the mansion, and I asked Cullen what he knew about skinny-dipping. He said he knew practically everything about it. After all, the man is a graduate engineer from Texas A & M. He went into great technical detail about how to arrange the lights for maximum privacy. At first I thought he was joking, but I decided he was very serious. I don't think Cullen ever jokes about technical problems."

Stanley promised Cullen that at the conclusion of the trial he would host a party at Toad Hall. "I just hope you can make it," Stanley told Davis.

In the vortex of all this collateral weirdness, W. T. Rufner returned to Amarillo.

To set the stage for Rufner's appearance before the jury, the defense first called Jerry Thomas to describe the fight that he and Rufner had at the mansion in May of 1975. Thomas testified that he hit Rufner only after

T-man appeared to be reaching in his pocket for "a knife or a gun." Next, a Fort Worth pharmacist told the jury that in the weeks just prior to the murders Priscilla ordered hundreds of Percodan and Percoset (a similar painkiller) from the Summit Park Pharmacy. In the six weeks before the killings, pharmacist Daryl Spence said Priscilla filled prescriptions for 450 Percodan. Another pharmacist, Ollie Chote, who worked for Whitten Pharmacy, showed that Priscilla had juggled doctors and pharmacies to obtain still more painkillers. In the four weeks prior to August 2, she had filled a prescription for 250 Percodan at Whitten Pharmacy— this in addition to the 450 pills she got from Summit Park Pharmacy.

Dr. Thomas Simons, who along with the surgeon who had operated on Priscilla prescribed most of the painkillers, testified that in addition to Priscilla he had also treated Stan Farr, W. T. Rufner, and Sandy Guthrie Myers. The doctor kept no independent records to show how many Percodan he had prescribed for Priscilla, but he recalled that the prescriptions began in July 1975. The period that most interested the defense, however, was July 28–30, 1976. The defense contended that on July 29 Sandy Myers ran into Priscilla in Dr. Simons's waiting room. This is when Priscilla supposedly told Sandy Myers, "Something heavy is coming down." On the morning of July 30, a few hours before the scheduled divorce trial, Priscilla visited Dr. Simons's office to pick up a letter that he had prepared stating a medical justification for again delaying the divorce proceedings. "She told me she was in no condition to appear in court," Dr. Simons testified. "After examining her, I agreed."

"But isn't it a fact that you agreed to write the letter even before she came to your office?" Racehorse Haynes asked the doctor.

"Yes, based on her emotional state at the time," Dr. Simons admitted.

On the morning that he was to begin testifying, W. T. Rufner woke in his Amarillo motel room pursued by dark visions and surrounded by unsold T-shirts. Though he had reduced the price from $100 to $10, T-man had many more T-shirts than customers, and though the promised interrogation by Racehorse Haynes seemed sure to punch up his business, there were other, more serious problems to consider. Not the least of these was the fact he was still on probation from his drug bust of March 1974. T-man knew that some of the questions he would be asked might not sit well with his probation officer, particularly since Haynes was likely to concentrate on the months *after* he was placed on probation. T-man had never seen the inside of a prison, but he knew that he might if Haynes established that he violated the terms of his probation. On advice of his attorney, Rufner decided to take the Fifth Amendment on any incriminating questions. To settle his nerves, T-man downed a handful of Valium with a few slugs of Scotch. He looked around the cluttered room for his pocket knife, then remembered that a deputy had taken it away from him the previous day as he sat in the judge's reception room peeling an apple. Damned if he wouldn't rather be somewhere else.

Haynes opened by asking Rufner's occupation. "I'm a union electrician," T-man responded. "I also work on motorcycles. I'm also in the T-shirt business." Several jurors smiled when he admitted that T-shirts were "a relatively new enterprise." Apparently some of the jurors had already got word.

Q: Are you in love with Priscilla Lee Davis?

A: I'm in love with a lot of women. Some of them I haven't even met.

More smiles from the jury.

Haynes had never met Rufner until that morning, but he wasn't surprised at the answers. He anticipated that T-man would milk the jury for a few laughs. Haynes was content to guide the witness through the ups and downs of his tempestuous relationship with Priscilla, particularly the parts about feuding, fighting, fornicating, and getting stoned. In a way, Rufner's candor worked for the defense. In her own testimony Priscilla had portrayed the Boston episode as an accidental meeting and had described Rufner as "obnoxious," but that wasn't how T-man remembered it.

Q: While in Boston, Massachusetts, were you paired up together?

A: I don't know what you mean by paired up. We weren't tied up together.

Q: You weren't tied up. Did you keep close quarters, though?

A: I had a place to sleep. She had a place to sleep.

Q: There was not mutuality? You didn't share the same couch, so to speak?

A: Yes, we shared.

It was hardly necessary for Haynes to point out to the jury that the sharing of a couch in Boston took place at least four months before Cullen and Priscilla separated. T-man declined to answer questions about narcotics at his three-day birthday celebration in June or the July 4 Winnebago trip to College Station, but again it was apparent that Priscilla and Rufner continued to frolic behind Cullen's back. Haynes wanted the jury to share his understanding of the Winnebago trip, the cast of characters assembled by Priscilla, the Queen Bee, how she had not only allowed but encouraged her daughter Dee and other teenage girls to travel in the company of men twice their age, men who had records of drug arrests and no qualms whatsoever about soliciting sexual favors from available nymphets.

Shortly after Priscilla filed for divorce on July 30, 1974, W. T. acknowledged that "we fell in love." By early September he was spending the night at 4200 Mockingbird.

"You moved in, did you not?" Haynes asked.

"I had some of my clothes there," Rufner admitted. "Several pairs of cutoffs, a few T-shirts, a pair of jeans." Rufner added that "I've always had more than one lady in my life." But in September he started dating Priscilla "exclusively." Within a week or two, Rufner continued, he had stashed most of his wardrobe at 4200 Mockingbird—"four or five shirts, six or seven pairs of jeans, two pair of shoes, my shaving kit." Haynes established that Dee Davis continued to live at the mansion, and in short order Sandy Myers, Larry Myers, and a number of others took up more or less permanent residence.

Haynes grilled the witness about other house guests and incidents in the fall of 1974. Wasn't it true that Rufner's friends Danny McDaniels and David Jackson were there on the occasion of his birthday when Priscilla opened the safe in the master bedroom and gave W. T. "a plastic bag with a white powdery substance"? T-man took the Fifth Amendment. What about the time that W. T. whipped out his knife and cut off Priscilla's dress, bra, and panties? W. T. took the Fifth again. Did W. T. recall slicing up Priscilla's silver fox bedspread after an argument over which TV program to watch? Or the fight with Skipper Nitschke when the expensive statue was broken, or the time he ripped the head off the teddy bear, or the time when he surprised Priscilla in the bathtub and crowned her with a flower pot?

Q: How did the flower pot get in the tub?

A: I honestly can't say. I don't remember if I was sitting on the side of the tub and knocked it over or what.

Haynes directed the witness's attention to another evening at the home of Larry Myers when the cast consisted of Rufner, Priscilla, Myers, and the teenage Valerie Marazzi. They were all in bed together, were they not, when Rufner took offense at something and poured a glass of Scotch over Myers's head? T-man admitted that the four of them were "in the bedroom," and as for the incident with the glass of Scotch, it was hard to remember. "I did that [poured Scotch over Myers's head] on more than one occasion," he explained.

The defense attorney went on to establish that Rufner usually had a key to the mansion and that he was familiar with the security system and knew the locations of both the upstairs and downstairs safes. In fact, Haynes continued, hadn't Rufner boasted about his knowledge of the security system and even given several friends, including Danny McDaniels, a tour of the basement where the elaborate panel of electronic instruments was located? Rufner admitted that "out of professional curiosity" he once showed McDaniels and others the basement wiring. Haynes asked if Rufner knew a man named Horace Copeland and if he once demonstrated the security system for Copeland. The witness answered that he didn't know Copeland "much" and had no recollection of showing him how the security worked.

Haynes questioned Rufner about other out-of-town trips in the company of Priscilla. How about the trip to the motorcycle races in Ontario, California? Yes, T-man recalled it. And the trip to Waco, and the trip to Houston. He recalled those too. And hadn't they also made a trip to Oklahoma City?

"If I'm not mistaken," Rufner said, nodding his head.

"How could you be *mistaken* about going to *Oklahoma City* with *Priscilla Lee Davis?!*" Haynes demanded to know. If Rufner was playing for the jury, Haynes felt he could do no less. It pleased him that the jury seemed amused by his last observation.

Calling Rufner's attention to yet another altercation with Priscilla, Haynes asked, "Didn't she tell you at that time to take your junk and get out?"

T-man smiled as he told the jury, "She told me that more than once."

"And so you took your several pairs of cutoffs and jeans and moved out. But you returned, did you not?"

"Not with as many clothes," Rufner replied.

Haynes established that this pattern of feuding and making up continued until the incident of May 1975, when Rufner wrecked Priscilla's car in front of the Old San Francisco Saloon and later got creamed by Jerry Thomas. Wasn't this the last straw, so to speak? Yes, Rufner remembered it well. Particularly the fight with Jerry Thomas.

"I possibly took a swing at him," Rufner recalled.

Q: Did you possibly reach for your pocket?

A: Very possibly.

Q: You made a hip pocket reach?

A: I think he misunderstood. I may have reached back to swing. He must have hit me, because I hit him, then he hit me a couple of times. He said, "I'm gonna hurt you if you don't get the hell out of here."

268

Q: Did he get his little finger between your teeth? Did you bite him?

A: I don't know. I wanted him off me.

Q: Did you make any reprisal-type statement then?

A: No, sir. I just told him, "You're a hell of a man. Maybe I'll buy you a drink next time I see you."

Q: And shortly after that you took your several pairs of cutoffs and jeans and moved out for good?

A: It didn't feel like home to me anymore. I felt more comfortable with my mother and my dog.

By now the jury must have had a degree of sympathy for W. T. Rufner. He was a rogue, but a rogue with charm. Several jurors smiled when T-man summed up how it was, living with Priscilla: "There were mornings when it was total harmony. There were mornings when it was total hell." Rufner didn't come across as a killer. On the contrary, it must have appeared to the jury that he was the one usually in danger of getting killed. The defense had failed to prove that Rufner had any kind of relationship with Stan Farr or Horace Copeland; in fact, Rufner had pretty much dropped out of the scene by the time Farr moved in. The only unanswered question was why in the weeks just after the murders he had moved with such determination to establish an alibi, cajoling and perhaps threatening Carmey Green to sign a statement swearing he was with her on the evening of August 2.

Haynes made one last attempt to introduce into evidence the photograph of Priscilla and W. T. "with his business in a sock." Rufner denied any knowledge of the photograph. But he admitted that in the interim between Priscilla's testimony and his own appearance in Amarillo, he had talked to Priscilla and the subject of the photograph had been discussed.

Q: Did Priscilla Lee Davis offer you money to say you'd never seen this photograph before?

A: Priscilla Lee Davis has never offered me anything.

"Now wait a minute," Haynes said, cutting his eyes to the jury, "I'm only talking about this *picture!*"

At this point Dowlen cleared his throat (in lieu of using a gavel, which he abhorred) and asked the at-

269

torneys to please approach the bench. Dowlen had ruled repeatedly that the photograph was inadmissible and was disturbed by this latest violation of the rules. The earlier question about Danny McDaniels observing Priscilla removing a bag of "white powdery substance" from the safe also went beyond the limit of the rules. Since Haynes seemed determined to pursue the subject of drugs, Dowlen took this opportunity to excuse the jury.

With the jury safely removed, Haynes returned to Danny McDaniels and the white powdery substance.

Q: You know what cocaine is, do you not?

A: I know what the substance is. I've read articles about it.

Q: You've done more than read articles about it, you've possessed it, haven't you?

The prosecution quickly objected, but Dowlen allowed Haynes to continue.

Q: Did you keep any narcotics in the safe at 4200 Mockingbird?

A: No, sir.

Q: Was narcotics ever kept in the safe at 4200 Mockingbird when you were there?

A: I cannot say for sure. I did not have the combination to the safe.

Q: Did you ever see any narcotics . . . cocaine, heroin, amyl nitrate, anything we might call narcotics . . . on the premises at 4200 Mockingbird?

By now T-man was sweating freely. He clasped his hands together to keep from shaking. Not even the overload of Valium he had taken for breakfast helped any longer. "I take the Fifth Amendment, your honor," Rufner told the judge. For the remainder of the day Race fired off questions about drug use at 4200 Mockingbird, and Rufner invoked his constitutional rights against self-incrimination.

When his first day on the witness stand ended, T-man and two reporters rushed straight for the bar at his motel and ran up a $96 tab, which Rufner insisted on charging to Cullen. The day hadn't been a total wipeout, he said after his third drink. He'd sold five T-shirts, and one of Cullen's groupies had told him he reminded her of Kris

Kristofferson. One of the waitresses said she would like to buy an autographed T-shirt, and T-man grinned and told her to follow him to his room. "Like they say in the Willie Nelson song," Rufner told the waitress as he escorted her to the elevator, "sometimes it's heaven, sometimes it's hell, and sometimes I don't even know."

While W. T. Rufner was unwinding and sampling the pleasures of Amarillo, Joe Shannon was jogging down a dusty road behind the Holiday Inn, contemplating his cross-examination. Shannon had decided that the trial was a perfect time to lose weight. By dieting and jogging four or five miles each night, the assistant DA had lost thirty pounds. Shannon was now in charge of the prosecution. Tim Curry had gone back to Fort Worth to supervise prosecution of a multimillion-dollar fencing operation and generally sort through the backlog of cases that had accumulated during the Cullen Davis trial. But he was leaving Cullen's case in the hands of his three top assistants, Shannon, Tolly Wilson, and Marvin Collins.

For all their setbacks, Shannon still felt their case was going well. Rufner's testimony had done a fair amount of damage, but nothing like the prosecution expected. Some of the damage could be repaired in cross-examination. Shannon couldn't do much about the lies Priscilla told regarding her sexual adventures with Rufner, but he could clear up the part about Carmey Green and the alibi that Rufner had worked so quickly to obtain. In fact, Shannon saw an opportunity to make a point of his own in the cross-examination of Rufner.

T-man appeared considerably more composed when Shannon began his questioning the following day.

Q: Were you afraid for your life in late 1976 and early 1977?

A: Yes, sir.

Q: And were you afraid that one of these days you would wake up dead with a certain pistol in your pocket?

A: Yes, sir.

Q: Had you heard there was money on the street and

there were people who would assist in making you a patsy in this double homicide?

A: Yes, sir.

Q: Did you hear this once or more than once?

A: More than once.

Q: Did you ever hear that the defense was planning to pin this whole deal on you?

A: Many times.

Q: And was that your concern when you went to Carmey Green?

A: Yes, sir.

Q: Did you hear that it would be easier for the defense if both of you [Rufner and Green] were eliminated?

A: Yes, sir.

Q: Did you communicate this to Ms. Green?

A: I did.

Q: Did you hear that the plan of the defense was to try to lay this whole thing on a dead man?

A: I did.

Q: And did you hear that dead men tell no tales?

A: I know that to be a fact.

Shannon knew that the defense would continue pointing the finger at Horace Copeland, but the point that he wanted the jury to keep in mind was this: *dead men tell no tales.* Rufner's alibi was at least as good as Cullen's, and Copeland couldn't defend himself. That night as he jogged along the road behind the Hilton Inn, Shannon had another thought. "Their case really boils down to ABC," he told investigator Rodney Hinson. *"Anybody But Cullen."*

The defense had squeezed all they could from Rufner, but Haynes wanted to leave the jury with one final reminder of how the Queen Bee operated. He called ex-teenagers Becky Ferguson and Valerie Marazzi. Valerie, who was seventeen at the time, described the free use of drugs and open sex aboard the Winnebago. Then Racehorse asked her about an evening at Larry Myers's house when Myers, Rufner, Priscilla, and Valerie were all naked in Myers's bed. Valerie spoke of the incident as though she were recalling the senior prom.

"At the start, W. T. was with Priscilla and I was with Larry," she told the jury.

Haynes: All right. And was there sexual activities when the first pairings off were . . .

Valerie: No.

Q: So, did W. T. have some comment to say, some observation, with reference to who ought to be with whom?

A: Yes.

Q: And as a consequence of his comment or observation, who got together with whom?

A: Larry and Priscilla got together.

Q: And what did you and Mr. W. T. Rufner do?

A: Nothing.

Q: And where did you all do this nothing?

A: Sitting on the side of the bed.

Q: And where was Priscilla and Larry Myers?

A: In the bed.

Q: And what did they do? Did they do nothing or did they do something?

A: They did something.

Q: Did they have sexual intercourse?

A: Yes, sir, they did.

Q: And as a consequence of that situation . . . what did W. T. Rufner do?

A: He apparently got jealous and poured a drink on her.

Q: Was she still in *criminis particeps*?

Valerie gave him a blank look, so Race reworded his question.

Q: Were they still *doing it*?

A: Yes, sir, they were.

Q: All right. Did pouring the drink on Priscilla make her stop?

A: Yes, it did, real quick.

For the next several days the defense called a series of witnesses to establish that Priscilla had been less than truthful in her testimony about Stan Farr and that Horace Copeland had a motive for killing Farr. Dowlen had postponed ruling on the admissibility of Sandy Guthrie Myers's testimony about the accidental meeting

273

with Priscilla in the doctor's office, but now the judge viewed it in a new light. Since this part of Sandy Myers's testimony was offered as impeachment of Priscilla's earlier denial, Dowlen let the jury hear Myers's version of the conversation two days before the murders.

Myers said that Priscilla started the conversation by inquiring how Larry Myers was doing in the state prison. "Then she became very intense and said, 'Something heavy is coming down,' " Myers recalled. "I asked if it had to do with the divorce and she said no, but she couldn't discuss it with me at the doctor's office." At this point Dowlen excused the jury, taking the sting out of the remainder of Sandy Myers's recollections. Earlier, when Haynes had asked Rufner if he ever threatened Priscilla or Stan Farr, T-man replied angrily, "That's a lie!" But Sandy Myers recalled a morning in March 1975 when she and Rufner were in the kitchen of the mansion and Rufner appeared badly upset by the prospect of being replaced by Stan Farr. According to Myers, Rufner told her, "I'll get that tall son of a bitch and I'll get that cunt." Myers also remembered running into Rufner at Dr. Simons's office a few weeks after the murder, at which time Rufner supposedly told her: "They aren't gonna stick me with this one. The threats I made about Priscilla and Stan, I've got a good alibi."

In support of their contention that Priscilla was extremely nervous and apparently expecting trouble before August 2, the defense called Sylvia Meek, a private investigator, who told the jury that Priscilla apparently had a "premonition" of impending danger because she tried to hire Meek as a bodyguard on July 5. Debbie Patton, a friend of the family, testified that on July 31 Priscilla "seemed very worried . . . upset . . . nervous." Debbie Patton was a regular patron at the Rhinestone Cowboy in the spring and summer of 1976, and she told of seeing Stan Farr and Horace Copeland talking "in the back room" of the bar on more than one occasion. About that same time, Debbie Patton continued, she opened Priscilla's purse to borrow her lipstick and saw a silver-plated pistol.

Becky Burns, a Fort Worth barmaid, told of walking

into the kitchen of the Rhinestone Cowboy and observing Farr and Copeland snorting cocaine with country music star David Allan Coe. Burns testified that on several occasions she saw Farr and Copeland with large sums of money. She knew that the two men had a "gambling activity" at the Pelican Bay Yacht Club in the spring of 1976.

"Did you know that in addition to his other activities, Horace Copeland engaged in trafficking narcotics?" Haynes asked Becky Burns.

"Well, I knew he was dealing in narcotics," she answered. She also claimed that Farr and Copeland had made several out-of-town trips together, including one to Mexico. Miss Burns admitted that she was acquainted with drugs; in fact, she was currently under felony indictment for obtaining drugs with a forged prescription. The fact that she was testifying against the wishes of the same prosecutors who would try her own case made Burns a very reluctant witness, as defense lawyer Mike Gibson would shortly point out.

Gibson: Are you afraid of what will happen to you as a result of giving testimony?

Burns: Yes, I am.

In cross-examination, Tolly Wilson asked Burns, "What are you afraid of?" She told the prosecutor: "I just don't like it. I don't want to get involved. I didn't want to come up here. I certainly don't want to antagonize the district attorney's office." Burns said that a number of people had advised her against testifying, including an investigator from the Tarrant County DA's office, a Fort Worth policeman, her attorney, and her mother, who was a secretary in the radio patrol division of the Fort Worth Police Department.

The defense then called another former Rhinestone Cowboy waitress, Polly Ware, Horace Copeland's one-time girlfriend, who had caused much confusion early in the trial when she called her attorney, Charles Baldwin, and said she thought she could produce the murder weapon—Copeland's R & G Industries .38 pistol. The gun hadn't checked out, but it had created sensational headlines, as had Baldwin's comments to the press that

275

Farr feared Copeland was planning to kill him. Until Ware took the witness stand, the jury knew nothing of these allegations.

Polly Ware told the jury that she lived with Copeland from October 1975 until January 1976. A month or so after they broke up, Ware said, she learned that Copeland was married. In July 1976, there was an incident in the Rhinestone Cowboy in which Copeland grabbed her and roughed her up. That's when she asked attorney Baldwin to seek a civil injunction against her former lover.

Baldwin, who followed Ware to the witness stand, told the jury that he subpoenaed Farr as a witness in the legal proceedings, but Farr refused to testify because he feared reprisals from Copeland. Baldwin testified that Farr told him: "You don't know Horace. If he won't do it, they will." *They* apparently referred to Copeland's friends and associates.

By now the defense had clearly established a relationship between Farr and Copeland, contradicting Priscilla's contention that the two men were only casual acquaintances. Priscilla had told the jury that Horace Copeland never visited the mansion, but the defense called another witness, former TCU football player Randy Garmen, who said he accompanied Copeland and Copeland's son, Rick, to a party at 4200 Mockingbird. Garmen didn't remember any drugs, but at one point in the party he saw "Horace and Priscilla Davis go in this small room and close the door." It must have appeared to the jury that Farr and Copeland had *something* cooking—there was the trip to Mexico, the white powdery substance that several witnesses saw them put in their noses, and the large sums of money that Becky Burns recalled. Other witnesses had testified that Priscilla thought Farr was stealing from the mansion. On more than one occasion Farr had referred to Priscilla as "my meal ticket" and "my investment." Then, too, there were stories about money missing from the till at the Rhinestone Cowboy.

Ronnie Bradshaw, co-owner of the Rhinestone Cowboy, took the stand to support much of the previous testimony. He testified that Horace Copeland was a regular at the club and that Farr was fired about two weeks before the murders and after cash shortages were discovered. He also recalled Copeland's troubles with Polly Ware. It was about that time, Bradshaw told the jury, that Farr asked him to return a gun that Bradshaw had locked in his desk drawer. "He told me he needed the gun back because he was scared of Horace Copeland," the club co-owner said. "He told me, 'Ronnie, I've got to have the gun back. I've been subpoenaed to testify in the Horace-Polly thing.' He said he didn't think Horace would get him, but he might have somebody else do it."

The prosecution scored an unexpected point in cross-examination when Bradshaw admitted that Farr had also expressed fear that "he would have some trouble with Cullen Davis." Whatever Farr's reasons for wanting the gun, he never had a chance to use it. The gun was found under the seat of his Thunderbird after the murders.

To nail down their theory that Stan Farr was the primary target, the defense had one more witness—Farr's sexy nineteen-year-old secret lover. If Kimberly Lewis's appearance in Amarillo came as a surprise to the prosecution, imagine Priscilla's reaction when news reached Fort Worth. The ex-TUC coed with the long, light brown hair and cover girl face told the jury that she and Farr were keeping secret rendezvous from March 1976 until the day of his murder. They would usually meet at the housing project that had become Farr's latest venture. Lewis testified that in the week before the killings Stan carried a gun in his car. "He said he needed it because people were after him," she said. When Kimberly Lewis last spoke to Farr a few hours before the shooting, "he sounded very nervous."

Haynes and Burleson felt that their case had about reached the point of diminishing returns. Unless their investigators could track down the potential witness they had code-named Mr. Dynamite, the defense had shed about all the light on the subject that the jury could tolerate. The trial was in its eleventh week. The jurors had sat through sixty days of testimony. It had been more than four months since the judge had sealed off the fourth floor of the Executive Inn, and even though the jurors continued to receive limited family and conjugal visits, it was apparent that the twelve people chosen to decide Cullen Davis's fate were approaching the breaking point.

"Their social life is down to about zero," said deputy Al Cross, who by now was referring to his own wife as The Widow Cross. "There's not a whole lot of conversation among the jurors anymore." Bailiff Wylie Alexander had a more earthy appraisal: "They're just like seagulls. All they do is eat, squawk, and shit." An Amarillo psychologist pointed out that even prison inmates have some choice of companions. Haynes had read studies about people forced to endure long periods of isolation with no selected social interaction; they tend to go bats. They lose the capacity to concentrate, and petty grievances tend to magnify and distort. Without normal sexual and social outlets, emotional tension was bound to erupt into personality clashes among the jurors. Studies of such cases proved that people "tend to make decisions out of desperation." The one thing nobody wanted at this point was a divided jury.

Since his order six weeks earlier tightening security, Dowlen had occasionally relented and allowed this particular jury special considerations. Breaks were more frequent, and whenever possible Dowlen tried to hold sessions to no more than five hours a day. Jurors had been permitted to eat their meals in restaurants other than the Executive Inn Surf Room, and on several occasions bailiffs had been authorized to escort the jurors to movies, providing all twelve could agree on a single movie. So far all they had seen was *Star Wars* and *One-on-One*. A pool table, Ping-Pong table, and exercise equipment had been provided for the prisoners of the fourth floor. Jurors were not allowed to make or receive telephone calls, or to listen to the radio, but they could watch previously screened television programs in the presence of bailiffs. Even the TV movies were sometimes vetoed; the jurors weren't allowed to watch the story of the Sam Sheppard murder case, for example. Dowlen encouraged jurors to use free time reading censored articles from *Reader's Digest,* playing cards and darts, and pursuing hobbies. Karl Prah had started sketching designs on Plexiglas. R. C. Hubbard was restoring and refinishing old firearms. Walter Lee Jones, a radar technician with the FAA, was studying new electronics techniques. Marilyn Haessly, the ex-nun, worked with pastels. Freddy Thompson, the cowboy, played his guitar and lamented his fate in life.

Dowlen had bent the rules and permitted the jurors to vote in the November general election. The irony wouldn't be apparent for a number of months, but one issue approved by voters in that election was a constitutional amendment specifying that a judge may hold a defendant without bond for up to sixty days if there is "substantial evidence" the defendant committed a new crime while free on bail.

The session's first major blizzard was roaring down from the north that second week in November when the defense team gathered in its apartment compound for a final review of strategy. Steve Sumner, who had been on the road again, had nothing encouraging to report. Sumner had at least fifty new witnesses on his string, but their tales of drug dealing and back-alley intrigue added very little to what the jury had already heard. The investigators still hadn't cornered Mr. Dynamite. Worse yet, of the hundreds of people that Sumner and his detectives had interviewed, there wasn't a single witness who remembered seeing Cullen Davis on the night of August 2. It appeared that Karen Master would be the only witness who could establish an alibi for the defendant. In another two weeks it would be Thanksgiving, and all the lawyers agreed on one thing: they didn't want the jurors celebrating Thanksgiving locked away from their families.

The way Haynes saw it, there were only two more witnesses necessary to the completion of their case. Racehorse wanted the jury to hear testimony from Katherine Brooks, Horace Copeland's former business partner, who would tell about Copeland's comings and goings on the night of the murder. And he wanted to call to the witness stand a nationally known drug expert to reinforce their "two-worlder" theory. If Sumner hadn't uncovered a bombshell witness by then, the defense would rest its case. Both sides would still have an opportunity to call rebuttal witnesses. If the state wanted to hold the jury all the way through Christmas, let the state assume the risk of a jury mutiny.

But Sumner called their attention to one final item on the night's agenda—the disturbing and recurring story that on the night of August 2 someone else had visited the Davis estate. For several weeks they had heard the rumor that a would-be burglar about to enter the mansion was frightened off by the unexpected appearance of a car or a person. Sumner had relegated the rumor to his nut file, but it wouldn't stay down. "It's coming now from four different sources," Sumner told the others. Now they had a *name,* along with a sketchy report—it seemed that a Fort Worth nurseryman who had been pressing Priscilla for an overdue bill had secretly visited the estate on the night of the murders. The way Sumner heard it, the nurseryman, Uewayne Polk, had ridden his motorcycle down the hike and bike trail that ran along the Trinity River bottom adjacent to the estate. He parked his bike and crossed the river on foot, then crept across the mansion grounds. His intention was to take back some of his plants. The mysterious nurseryman was about to enter an unlocked door beside the swimming pool when he was frightened off by something or someone. "Unbelievable!" Burleson said. "But I don't see how we can ignore it." Burleson was certain that the prosecution had also heard the story. A Fort Worth attorney who had been contacted by Uewayne Polk believed that the story had also been leaked to a Fort Worth newspaperman. "Get on the phone to that lawyer," Haynes told Sumner. "Tell him to get Mr. Uewayne Polk up here. Get him here tonight!"

Later, Burleson described what happened that night: "Steve and Mike and Race and I stayed up most of the night talking to Polk. We pounded on him, asking questions about every aspect of the case. There was no way we were going to put a bombshell witness on the stand at that stage of the game if there was any chance he would blow up in our face. Even after questioning him all night, we still didn't know whether to believe him. We told him to go back to Fort Worth while we checked out his story."

Haynes asked Sumner for an opinion. Was Polk's story logical?

"I don't know," Sumner admitted. "It doesn't fit with any of our other information. I think we've got to consider this as separate and apart from the rest of our defense."

Burleson decided to fly to Fort Worth and check Polk's story himself. To the lawyer's surprise, it seemed to check. Burleson even walked down to the river bottom to determine for himself if it was possible for a person to cross on foot. "The water was only two or three inches deep when I checked it," Burleson said. "I called the Corps of Engineers. Their records showed that it would have been about that shallow on the night of August 2."

Burleson collected other evidence—a photograph of Polk's motorbike and a copy of a business receipt the nurseryman had presented to Priscilla—then hurried back to Amarillo to confer with the other lawyers. Burleson still felt that Polk's story was unbelievable, but he recognized an even greater risk. What if they refused to

281

call Polk to the stand? What if the *state* called him? And what if Polk suddenly changed his story and remembered that the man he saw creeping up to the mansion that night was Cullen Davis? Either way, Burleson was sure that the story would break in the *Fort Worth Star-Telegram* in the next day or two.

"If we're going to call him," Burleson said, "we better do it fast."

The next morning as Uewayne Polk and his attorney met with lawyers behind the closed doors of Judge Dowlen's chambers, rumors of a "bombshell" witness spread through the courthouse. From time to time reporters caught a glimpse of the mysterious, neatly dressed bearded man and his attorney being quickly escorted along the hallway, but nobody could predict the testimony that would follow. "Is this your dynamite witness?" someone asked Sumner. "All I can tell you," Sumner said, "is hold on to your seat." Even reporters for the *Fort Worth Star-Telegram,* whose paper had agreed to hold the story for another day, had very little warning of what was about to happen.

Behind the closed doors of Dowlen's chambers, Haynes made a formal request: "Since we don't have a grand jury like the prosecution does, can we put him under oath in here?" Dowlen agreed that it was better to air Polk's testimony in secrecy, and Haynes proceeded to question the witness under oath.

"It was probably the most traumatic moment of the trial," Haynes said later. "Polk described the fellow he saw that night at the mansion, and it didn't sound like Cullen, but we didn't have a good picture of Cullen to show him. We decided to call Cullen into the judge's chambers. He wouldn't say anything . . . he'd just walk in, do a front, a left, and a right profile, then leave. That's what happened. Then I asked [Polk] the question: 'Well, is that the man you saw or not?' Just as I asked the question, my blood went cold. What if this was a trap set up by the prosecution? What if the SOB said *yes!*"

Polk played with a button on his vest, then answered firmly: "No."

There wasn't a vacant seat in the courtroom, or a square foot of unoccupied space in the hallway, as Uewayne Polk poured out his bizarre story to the jury. At a glance the thirty-three-year-old witness could have passed for a dance instructor or maybe a high school art teacher, but he began by explaining that he was a landscaper and part owner of the Wedgewood Nursery in Fort Worth. In the spring of 1975, Priscilla Davis called him to 4200 Mockingbird and asked him to draw up preliminary designs for both interior and exterior work on the mansion. Polk told the jury that he completed the designs but didn't hear again from Priscilla until May of 1976. She was planning a party and needed the work done as quickly as possible. Polk did the work on schedule and on June 7 presented her with a bill for $677, which she failed to pay. Polk said that he returned to the mansion in late June but again failed to collect his money. In July he tried two more times, both without results. Priscilla claimed that she lost the bill. Polk told her he would return with a new one.

Polk testified that he again appeared at 4200 Mockingbird on Monday, August 2, bill in hand. He remembered it was about midday when the maid let him in. Priscilla didn't come downstairs but agreed to talk to him on the telephone.

"At this point I got pretty mad," Polk said. "I could have talked to her by phone from the nursery. Priscilla said she was going to see Cullen in court that day. She told me, 'I'll see if Cullen wants to pay for it.' I looked around. There were plants dead all over the place. It looked like they hadn't been watered in days. Plants were in the wrong place . . . plants that needed sun were in the shade and vice versa."

On Priscilla's instruction, Polk said, he tacked the new bill to the bulletin board above the kitchen telephone. He walked down the hallway and turned left to the area of the indoor swimming pool, thinking of his next move. He decided that he would come back that night and take the plants that rightly belonged to him. Through a panel of glass he could see the two maids working in the kitchen. They had their backs to him. Polk unlocked the sliding glass doors separating the pool from the mansion lawn. Having supplied himself an entrance, he walked back toward the kitchen and departed by way of the breakfast room door.

Polk told the jury that it was about 7:00 P.M. when he arrived at his home near Eagle Mountain Lake. He ate dinner with his wife and read the evening paper. Around 9:00 P.M. he filled his trail bike with gas, loaded it in his truck, and drove to where the Loop 280 Bridge crosses the Trinity River, a spot about two miles from the Davis mansion. Wearing jeans and a dark shirt and carrying a burlap bag, Polk followed the trail as far as the Hulen Street Bridge. There he hid his bike in the brush, removed his shoes, and crossed the shallow stream heading in the direction of the mansion.

"I had my tow sack with me," he continued, explaining that he intended to use the bag to repossess his plants and shrubs. "I sat down under a tree to dry my feet and put my shoes on. I looked at my digital watch. It was 11:11. I remember thinking this was my lucky night."

While he was drying his feet and putting on his shoes, Polk saw a man with a sack over his shoulder walking toward the Hulen Street Bridge. "I thought he was a hobo," Polk told the jury. "It's close to the tracks, and a lot of hoboes hang around down there."

Polk testified that the man walked toward him. When he was about eight feet from where Polk sat, the man squatted, took out a cigarette lighter, and lighted a cigarette. That's when Polk got a good look at the man. He was five-eight to five-ten, chunky, and had very big eyes. "I could see white all around the pupils," Polk recalled. This man had no beard but wore his curly hair short. His face was round and his cheekbones were high. When the man finished his cigarette, Polk continued, "he headed toward the Davis mansion. The same direction I was headed."

For a few minutes Polk lost the man in the darkness, but as the nurseryman was approaching the northwest corner of the mansion, the corner nearest the pool area, he again caught sight of the man. "He was squatting down on his knees," Polk told the jury. "He put something on his head and walked toward the front of the house. I ran back [to some hedges] where it was dark. Then I saw a figure *inside* the pool area. I froze behind a palm. It was the same man I'd seen by the river."

At this point Racehorse Haynes asked his bombshell question: "Was the man you saw Cullen Davis?"

"He was definitely not Cullen Davis," said Polk, looking at the defendant.

"And what did you do then?"

"I ran back toward the river. I got back on my bike and went home."

Haynes asked Polk why he had waited more than a year to tell this strange and disturbing story.

"Out of fear," said Uewayne Polk. "Fear for my business. Fear of the man who really did it. Fear of Priscilla Davis's friends. I had built up a really good clientele. I couldn't see dragging it down."

"Because of your activities that night?" Haynes asked.

"Of course."

Even before Dowlen could call a recess, reporters bolted for the door, scattering the groupies in a mad dash for the few telephones. It was like a scene out of *Front Page*. "I never thought I'd find myself fighting over a telephone," said Dallas free-lancer Tom Stephenson, "but there I was pushing and shoving and threatening anybody in my way." Those who were not burdened by deadlines stood numbly in the hallway, shaking their heads and trying to digest the implications of what they had just heard. One of the first things that came to mind was the obvious contradiction over the security system: if Polk had unlocked the sliding door as he testified, Priscilla would have noticed the light on the security panel as she and Stan Farr left that night. Then there was the apparent impossibility of Polk attempting to carry away all those plants in a burlap bag. During the recess several new facts about the mystery witness emerged. "He told his lawyers he didn't want to talk to the state," Marvin Collins said. The state had known about Polk for at least a week and had also checked his story. "It's an insult to the intelligence of the jury," Tolly Wilson claimed. The state's investigation had revealed something else about Uewayne Polk's past—in January 1969 he had pleaded guilty to armed robbery and been sentenced to ten years' probation.

Joe Shannon used fewer than ten minutes to cross-examine Polk.

"How much have you been paid to come up here and tell that cock-and-bull story?" the outraged assistant district attorney demanded to know.

"Not a red penny," Polk replied.

"You just came here as a fair, good-hearted citizen?"

"I was worried about a man losing his life."

"And so you waited sixteen months to tell your story."

"I wanted to forget it."

"I have no more questions for *this* witness," said Shannon, taking his seat at the prosecution's table.

It had been weeks since anyone in Amarillo had talked to Priscilla, but at the lunch break several reporters telephoned her from Stanley Marsh's office. She had just heard Polk's testimony on the noon news and was enraged. "He's a lying goddamn motherfucker!" Priscilla said. "Did anybody ask him *how* he planned to repossess all those plants? They were all inside. There are ten or twelve plants around my bathtub . . . a little plant by the guest bath downstairs . . . three ming trees in the hallway. Maybe one by the pool. Isn't it just perfect that all these people are coming forward with their stories? Karen . . . James Mabe . . . after all these months they're coming forward. And that story about Stan skimming money at the Rhinestone Cowboy. Stan got fired because he knew who really was skimming."

After Uewayne Polk, the defense's final two witnesses were, to say the least, anticlimactic.

Katherine Brooks, who was in partnership with Horace Copeland in a bar called The Eyes of Texas, told the jury that on August 2 Copeland arrived at the club about 6:00 P.M. "He went directly to the office

286

and locked the door," she said. "He stayed in the office about an hour. Then about 7:00 P.M. he came out and left. I didn't see him again that night." Brooks testified that when she again saw Copeland the following night, "he wouldn't talk" about the murders at the Davis mansion. In cross-examination the prosecution established that Katherine Brooks and Horace Copeland had dissolved their partnership in October 1976, eight months before Copeland was killed. "It was not a friendly breakup," the witness admitted. At the time of Copeland's death she was suing him, alleging that Copeland put his name on a deed of land belonging to her and used it to borrow $45,000 from a bank. The defense had one final question: what kind of car was Copeland driving on August 2, 1976? "A 1975 silver Cadillac," she replied.

On Friday afternoon, November 11, twelve weeks after the first witness appeared in Amarillo, the defense called to the stand Dr. Robert Miller, a nationally recognized expert on dangerous drugs. A professor at the University of Minnesota, the pharmacologist was currently studying the use of opiates for the United Nations. At considerable expense, the defense had brought him to Amarillo to detail the evils associated with the habitual use of the opiate-based drug Percodan. Perhaps because they sensed that their own ordeal was nearing its end, the jury seemed especially attentive as Dr. Miller described the devastating effects of the drug on a person's memory as well as that person's ability to perceive reality. When mixed with alcohol, Miller told the jury, the drug had a "potentiating effect."

"In other words," Racehorse Haynes prodded the witness, "you have a situation where one plus one equals three."

A: That is substantially correct.

Q: Would that person [who mixed Percodan with alcohol] actually believe that a fictitious episode was true?

A: Yes. But it depends upon the individual. Some are more prone to do it than others.

As Haynes hoped he would, Dr. Miller then intro-

287

duced the term *two-worlder* to the jury, describing those people as "the Dr. Jekyll and Mr. Hyde, so to speak, of the drug dependency field. They live in one world where they are relatively honorable members of society, and they live in another world where their behavior patterns are drastically different."

Could such a person be a socialite and yet associate with "criminal elements"? Haynes wondered. "Could you have a Mrs. Jekyll and Mrs. Hyde?"

"I would agree to that," Miller said.

"I have no more questions," Haynes said.

On Monday morning, the prosecution called Uewayne Polk's estranged wife as a rebuttal witness.

Answering questions directed to her by Tolly Wilson, Paige Polk immediately defused the bombshell. It was true that Uewayne Polk made a mysterious, late night visit to the Davis mansion, she told the jury, but it wasn't the night of August 2.

"A few days before the murders, Uewayne told me he had been to the mansion that night but had not taken anything," Paige Polk testified. "He said he drove the truck in and took the dirt bike out of the truck and drove it to the riverbed . . . then went on foot through the trees toward the pool area of the house. He was outside and was considering messing with the glass, and then a few cars came up the driveway, so he left."

Even if the date had been correct, it would have been impossible for Polk to look at his digital watch to determine the time as 11:11 P.M., she added. Polk's watch hadn't worked for several months, not since Polk fell out of a boat and into the water. Finally Paige Polk said that she spoke to her husband by telephone the previous Wednesday, just before he left for Amarillo. A divorce court judge had ordered Polk to pay his wife $75 a week, but he was "about $350 behind." Paige Polk said that she asked him about the money.

Q: What did he tell you?

A: That he was going to Amarillo, and as soon as he got back, he would pay me.

At this point the state requested a recess. For several hours the prosecutors met behind closed doors, apparently trying to decide on their next witness. Shannon joked to reporters that the time had come to "call our atomic bomb witness."

He went on to explain: "We have a swimming pool attendant who claims Priscilla didn't pay him. On the night of August 2, he showed up with a pail to empty the pool, and that's when he saw Cullen Davis, wearing a name tag and carrying a bazooka."

While the prosecution was reviewing final strategy, Steve Sumner was eating a packaged sandwich on the courthouse steps. The recent storm had passed, and now it was a warm, Indian summer day, the kind that reminded Sumner of baseball. The young lawyer felt very good about the case, particularly his own part in heading the investigation. He had finally located the elusive Mr. Dynamite. "I didn't have him ready to hit the witness stand," Sumner said, "but it was starting to look good. I figured the state would need another three or four days for their rebuttal witnesses—I was certain they would call Priscilla back. We'd come at her with a ton, and they'd just let it lay. There was no question in my mind they'd call Priscilla back to town."

As Sumner was finishing his lunch, Rod Hinson, one of the investigators for the Tarrant County DA's office, came rushing down the courthouse steps.

"What's your hurry?" Sumner said.

"Haven't you heard?" Hinson grinned. "We just rested our case."

Sumner took the courthouse steps four at a time, almost running down a groupie as he sprinted to the fifth floor where Haynes and the other defense lawyers were holding a secret caucus. "I think everyone was as surprised as I was," Sumner said later. "It was a horrible judgment on their part." Sumner brought the other attorneys up to date on the possibility of Mr. Dynamite and the other potential witnesses. Burleson just shook his head. It was no time for heroics.

An hour later, Racehorse Haynes stood up, looked at Cullen, then at the jury, then at the judge, and announced, "At this time, the defense rests."

Shannon had guessed some weeks ago that the defense would not put Cullen on the witness stand, but Tolly Wilson and Marvin Collins were stunned. "I can't believe a defendant would come to West Texas and not get on the witness stand himself," Collins said. "If you're gonna try to float an alibi," Wilson remarked, "you sure as hell better take the witness stand." Racehorse Haynes claimed later that it was one of the hardest decisions of his career, but the consensus among defense lawyers was that "Cullen is very poor witness material. He doesn't emote. It's doubtful he could look sincere and honest." A skeptic might argue that Cullen didn't *have* an alibi, but perhaps he didn't need one. Of the entire cast of characters who had appeared with their sordid tales of duplicity and foul deeds, the only one who remained a total stranger to the jury was Cullen Davis.

As the lawyers closed themselves off in Dowlen's chambers to begin drawing up the charge that would be read to the jury on Wednesday, someone asked Cullen what he was thinking.

Cullen replied that he was thinking about going skiing. In fact, he had already made reservations for the Thanksgiving weekend.

On Wednesday, November 16, as the attorneys prepared to deliver their final arguments, Judge George Dowlen read his charge to the jury. In a rare somber mood, Dowlen warned the audience against any outbursts or demonstrations of emotions. Extra security measures had been taken. Armed investigators from the Tarrant County DA's office were stationed around the packed courtroom, and extra deputies patrolled the hallways. Roy Rimmer, Jr., Cullen's main man, also had a bodyguard standing by, correctly anticipating that things would move very fast from this point. Rimmer and a delegation of Cullen's people, including his brother Ken, sat in a section reserved for the defendant. Across the aisle in a section set aside for friends of the prosecution sat Jack Wilborn, father of the murdered girl, his deeply tanned face twisted with grief.

In charging the jury, it was necessary for Dowlen to explain the complicated statute of capital murder by

which this case was being prosecuted—in order to find
the defendant guilty of capital murder, the jury had to
agree that he had first violated the state law against
burglary. If the jury did not not find the defendant guilty
of capital murder, it would then consider the lesser
charge of murder. But the key phrase in Dowlen's
charge was "reasonable and moral certainty." In order
to return a verdict of guilty, the jury would have to
reach a reasonable and moral certainty that the defendant committed the crime, to the exclusion of all
other possibilities. In other words, if any one of the
twelve had a *reasonable doubt,* it was that juror's duty
to bring in a verdict of not guilty.

Dowlen had allowed each side three and a half hours
for closing arguments. By law, the state would both begin and end the arguments, but each side was permitted
to allocate its time according to its own wishes.

Tolly Wilson opened for the state, reviewing in detail that bloody night at the mansion and pointing to
Cullen Davis as the man in black who came there with
the premeditated intention of "killing the source of all
his troubles [Priscilla] and anyone else who got in his
way." First, it was necessary to kill Andrea Wilborn.
His second bullet was reserved for Priscilla, Wilson told
the jury. Cullen assumed Priscilla was dead or dying
when he dragged Stan Farr's body to the kitchen, but
Priscilla was able to run into the courtyard. Cullen
caught her, but the unexpected appearance of Bubba
Gavrel and Bev Bass diverted his attention, and she
was able to escape. "If Bubba Gavrel and Bev Bass
hadn't arrived when they did," Wilson continued, "we'd
have three unsolved murders . . . three bodies in the
basement and a bushy-haired stranger driving off." After
apparently killing Gavrel and chasing Bass until it was
obvious he couldn't catch her, Cullen then returned to
look for Priscilla. Discovering the door locked, he reloaded and shot out the window and raced to the place
he was certain she would be hiding—the master bedroom. Unable to find Priscilla and realizing that the
police would soon be alerted, he dropped the plastic

bag used to conceal his fingerprints and made his own escape.

As for the defense's claim of a conspiracy, Wilson said, the contention that two women running in opposite directions, one seriously wounded and the other frightened for her life . . . "the very idea is so far beyond human experience as to be ridiculous." The defense had made a great fuss about discrepancies in time, Wilson pointed out, but the main discrepancy was in the testimony of Robert Sawhill. Wilson had an explanation for this. "Sawhill was wrong," he said. Sawhill had *also* testified that while Bev Bass was seated in his car, she took out a cigarette and lighter, and yet "her cigarettes and lighter were found back at 4200 Mockingbird." Regarding the alibi, Karen Master had destroyed her own credibility by not telling it to the grand jury. And the testimony of Uewayne Polk was hardly worth rebutting. "Can you believe that he intended to put all those plants in the tow sack, get on his motorbike, and go back home?" Wilson asked the jury. *"But* . . . if just one of you twelve believes Uewayne Polk . . . if you have a *reasonable doubt* . . . then Polk did his job."

The defense selected Mike Gibson to lead off. Gibson pointed out that the state had called twenty-three witnesses and the defense had called forty-four, and the sum of the testimony "showed you the true color and character of Priscilla Davis." Just look at Priscilla Davis, Gibson challenged the jury: "All those young people around her . . . massive amounts of Percodan . . . illegal drugs. Priscilla claimed her relationship with W. T. Rufner was platonic, but W. T. called it love. And why was W. T. trying so hard to get an alibi?" Because he had a good idea who really did the killings, Gibson contended. He connected three pieces of seemingly unrelated testimony for the jury's consideration: (1) the allegation that shortly before the murders Stan Farr was flashing a large roll of money; (2) the testimony that two of Rufner's pals, Danny McDaniels and David Jackson, once watched Priscilla open the upstairs safe and take out a bag of cocaine; (3) and the fact that the killer had left the plastic garbage bag upstairs where the safe was located. "David Jackson or someone who did the killing was going for that safe upstairs," Gibson claimed. He again reminded the jury of the many dope dealers and convicted felons who lived at the mansion with Priscilla. "The flow of substances through that house and through that lady was *phenomenal*," Gibson said, shaking his head at the mere thought.

Sandwiched between the arguments of Gibson and Racehorse Haynes, Phil Burleson's closing statements had a practical, matter-of-fact, almost cutthroat quality. He reminded the jury that neither Bev Bass nor Bubba Gavrel knew who killed Stan Farr, only what happened to them—"that someone was up there they thought was Cullen Davis." As for Priscilla, it hardly seemed reasonable that she could remember anything with all that Percodan and alcohol churning in her head. "How many times have you heard the words 'I don't remember' from their witnesses?" he asked. "From *their* witnesses, but not from ours." Burleson added that "the absence of rebuttal witnesses by the state proves that our witnesses were truthful. We brought you the real facts." Priscilla had told the jury that when she first heard Bev Bass's voice in the driveway that night, she thought it was Dee. Burleson pounced on this. "Why didn't she call out, 'Dee, run!' if she thought Bev Bass was Dee?" Burleson wondered. "Either she lied, or she was totally unconcerned for the safety of her own daughter. Here is a woman so selfish—so concerned with her own self—she will do anything." Burleson reviewed the lies that Priscilla had told on the witness stand, then posed this key question: "If she wanted you to believe this one thing [that Cullen did it], why didn't she tell you the truth about everything?"

Now it was Racehorse's turn and no circus-tent evangelist ever approached his subject with more righteous indignation.

"They brought you the very best case they could," Race opened, thumbs in his vest, "and it fell woefully short." Haynes told the jury that he had no doubt the state would accuse him of "endeavoring to assassinate the character of their witnesses." It was an accusation, he would have the jury believe, that cut to the quick. "I only wish [Bubba Gavrel] could see the light," Race said. "I do feel sorry for the Bubba Gavrels of this world . . . [but] I can understand why he got into it; there were others behind Gus Gavrel, Jr." Race paused to allow the brimstone to heat properly. "But I do *not* forgive him for lying, nor should you. Because when you raise your hand to God, things like parents or peer group pressure mean nothing at all. No, the person I hold hostility against is Priscilla Lee Davis, that corruptor of young people, the Machiavellian influence behind this whole thing."

Haynes put Priscilla aside for the moment to assail the investigative job done by the Fort Worth police. "Isn't it odd, isn't it curious, don't you wonder . . . *why* there was no picture of the bullet in the basement—if in fact [the bullet] was in the basement?" Why didn't the prosecution call a single supervisory officer to testify? Why didn't they call Det. C. R. Davis, who was in charge of the case? "You will remember what happened when *we* called Officer Soders. And why didn't they call Soders? These are questions only the learned counsel for the state can answer?" Haynes reviewed a long list of apparent foul-ups on the part of the investigators; about the only thing he could find for approval was the fact they found none of his client's fingerprints at the murder scene.

A man of evangelical zeal, Racehorse saved his best for last. *Everything* . . . every bit and piece of the state's case . . . "is predicated on the testimony of Priscilla Lee Davis, who is not worthy." Race could hardly find words to describe Priscilla, but the ones that came to mind were "the Queen Bee" . . . "the Dr. Jekyll and Mrs. Hyde . . . "the other-worlder" . . . "the lady in the lah-dee-dah pinafore" who rubbed elbows with socialites and hobnobbed with known criminals. It was difficult to keep from smiling when Haynes told the jury in a soft, wondering voice, *"I didn't understand Priscilla Lee Davis until Dr. Miller explained her."* Pounding his fist on the railing of the jury box, Haynes said, "Dr. Jekyll became Mrs. Hyde . . . using that big house to bring in those people . . those scalawags and thugs . . . skuddies, rogues . . . brigands . . . Sandy Myers . . . Larry Myers until he went to prison . . . all those people that Priscilla Lee Davis in her other life associated with. Don't you wonder . . . why would a grown woman permit her own daughter to associate with those people? Because she was in that other world!"

As Joe Shannon sat listening to Haynes's final remarks, he could also hear the occasional wails and sobs from the back of the room. Without looking around, he knew that Jack Wilborn was breaking apart inside. Days and sometimes weeks had passed without a single mention of Andrea Wilborn, whose tragic ending was the whole reason they were here. The jury had no real feeling of Andrea as the warm, sensitive, unobtrusive child who had become the almost accidental victim of wanton violence and illegal skulduggery. Because of legal restrictions, the jury had heard none of the bond hearing testimony about Cullen's previous acts of violence, the threats, the beatings, the broken bones, the mutilated kitten. Shannon wondered if the jury could look through Cullen's cool, poised, high-born demeanor and recognize a man capable of murdering a twelve-year-old girl. The state had considered calling Jack Wilborn as a rebuttal witness. Wilborn was prepared to tell the jury that Andrea was terrified of Cullen Davis.

It was too late now for second-guessing. The defense seemed shocked that the prosecution hadn't called Priscilla back to Amarillo, but Shannon dismissed that thought with a firm conviction. "All Priscilla could have done is get up and deny all the things those skuddies and rogues said about her," Shannon reasoned. "All that would do is give Haynes another chance to ask her the things he wished he'd asked in the first place." The prosecution had thought about calling an expert on computer records to pin down the exact times of the phone calls to the police. Like the defense, they had concluded that if the jury had to spend Thanksgiving at the Executive Inn, they had rather not be responsible. They'd even thought about calling Ken Davis to detail the telephone conversation with Cullen just after the killings. When Ken Davis told Cullen about the murders at the mansion and asked what he intended to do, Cullen replied, "Go back to sleep." There were several problems with Ken Davis. One, he was recovering from open-heart surgery. But more dangerous to Shannon's way of thinking was the potential of backfire from a witness obviously sympathetic to the defense. "You gotta be damn careful when you handle a snake," Shannon said. "If you don't hold it by the head just right, the son of a bitch will bite you." Haynes had come hard with his second-worlder theory, but he had also timed it just right; there wasn't time for the state to rebut it with its own expert. All the second-worlder theory really did was grind Priscilla a little deeper into the dirt, or so Shannon believed. No, it was too late for second-guessing. The prosecution would stand by its case. Regardless of the lies, Shannon felt they had two things going for their case. First, there was a great deal of physical evidence to support the stories of the three eyewitnesses. They were solidly in line with the physical evidence. Then there were the statements made by Priscilla and Bev Bass in those crazy moments just after the shootings—what lawyers call *resgestae* statements. *Excited utterances,* Shannon called them. If the prosecution had done its job, the jury would believe that when the two women ran from the estate telling everyone that *Cullen did it,* they spoke only the passionate truth of new believers. It didn't seem reasonable to Shannon that Priscilla and Bass had a motive, much less time, to construct elaborate lies.

As Shannon took the floor and began to address a courtroom that was deathly silent except for the periodic wails of Jack Wilborn, he knew one thing for sure—this was it. This was the last dance.

Shannon took a photograph from the evidence table, but he held it against his chest so that nobody could see. He started on a low note, talking for a while about the physical evidence and sometimes the lack of it. "What difference does it make that we don't have a photograph of the bullet in the basement?" he asked the jury. The jury followed Shannon with one eye as he began talking about Uewayne Polk . . . "a self-confessed would-be burglar who just happens to beat burglar No. 1 to the mansion . . . just happens to note that it is not T. Cullen Davis. I'm surprised burglar No. 1 didn't wear a name tag that said W. T. Rufner."

Wasn't it curious, Shannon asked the jury, that Haynes failed to ask Uewayne Polk if the man he saw was *Horace Copeland?*

Glancing at his famous adversary at the defense table, Shannon reminded the jury that "a good defense lawyer is a master of illusion. Illusion No. 1—W. T. Rufner. He's a free spirit, but does that make him a killer? No, it just makes him a patsy. Illusion No. 2—Horace Copeland. Copeland and Stan Farr were in fact friends. As a copout they call Bradshaw to testify that Farr was *afraid* of Copeland. You may also recall that Bradshaw told you Farr was afraid of *Cullen Davis.* This illusion is climaxed by the fact that dead men tell no tales. Illusion No. 3—there is no evidence that Farr owed Copeland any money, as the defense promised to show in their opening remarks. Not one shred of evidence to show any peculiar relationship between Bev Bass and Priscilla Davis. You must know by now that Priscilla paid for Bev Bass's abortion. Let's get it out in the open . . . *abortion,* that's what everyone has been talking about. I'm sure you've figured that out. Was that the motive for Bev Bass to lie, because she owed Priscilla a favor? Illusion No. 4—Uewayne Polk."

As Shannon approached the jury box still clutching the photograph to his chest, he reminded the jury of Polk's testimony, the part in which the witness told of tacking his bill of $677 to the kitchen bulletin board on the afternoon of August 2.

"I would like you to look at this picture labeled Defense Exhibit No. 10 and tell me if you see a bill tacked to that bulletin board," Shannon said, matter-of-factly, as he placed the photograph on the railing of the jury box. Shannon surely had to resist the temptation of a broad smile. The photograph of the kitchen bulletin board taken only hours after the murders had been one of a number of pictures introduced by the defense very early in the trial. Nobody seemed to remember why. But the picture was as clear as the implication: there was no nursery bill on the bulletin board. Several jurors exchanged knowing glances as the picture was passed around.

"If we were here trying the murder of Stan Farr," Shannon continued, "this case wouldn't be circumstantial. The only circumstantial evidence is that the same gunman who pumped four shots in Stan Farr also shot Andrea Wilborn. If you believe that T. Cullen Davis killed Stan Farr, you have to believe that he shot Andrea."

Shannon reminded the jurors of the sequence of witnesses. "Thirty percent of this lawsuit has been devoted to trying a divorce case," he estimated. "Another 50 percent has been Priscilla's association with those skuddies that Mr. Haynes told you about. The remaining 20 percent has tried to answer the question who killed Andrea Wilborn. It really doesn't matter what you think of Priscilla. What in the world did Andrea Wilborn have to do with any of this business?"

The defense had claimed that Priscilla was gooned out on Percodan, but the prosecutor reminded the jury that Priscilla didn't start heavy doses of the drug until *after* the murders. "Do you remember the question [to Dr. Miller]: 'If a person takes six Percodan a day and has a few drinks, would she be out of her mind?' Dr. Miller's answer: 'Absolutely not!' They twisted it to make you think she was taking thirty-five Percodan a day before the shooting. Maybe they were saying that she has taken so many since then that she can't remember what happened. And yet she told exactly the same story just a few days after the shooting. They haven't made one single dent in her story of what happened on August 2."

It was important to keep in mind, Shannon continued, that the gunman reacted and shot Gavrel only after Bev Bass said, "That's Cullen!" Shannon posed this question: "Would Horace Copeland have reacted to this or just kept on walking? [The gunman] was luring them into the house, but he turned and fired at the mention of the name Cullen Davis."

In an evangelical tone every bit as righteous as that employed by his adversary, Shannon also reminded the jury that the defense had even attempted to smear Andrea Wilborn by suggesting that she had "a little bitty marijuana plant behind the door of her room."

Shannon turned and looked straight at Cullen Davis. "What you've seen in this court," he said, "is an attempt to run over everyone that gets in this man's way. Just like on August 2 . . . People were in his way and he *fixed their twats*—that's exactly what he did. . . . Their whole defense has been ABC—*Anybody But Cullen!*"

Shannon could see Dowlen glancing nervously at the clock: time was up. He had already reviewed the physical evidence, so Shannon went straight to what he considered the heart of their case—the *resgestate* statements of the two women witnesses. They were terrified and running in opposite directions, he repeated, and yet they told the same story. *Cullen did it.* "When people are excited and shook up," Shannon told the jury, "they tell the truth. That's why it is admissible as evidence."

The prosecutor avoided looking at Jack Wilborn as he reached once more for the color photograph of Andrea Wilborn's body. By now everyone in the courtroom knew that the man weeping was Andrea's father. Shannon directed the jury's attention to the blood on the top of the dead girl's head. "How does a person shot in the chest get blood on her head?" he asked. "I'll tell you how. She fell on her stomach in a pool of her own blood. The killer turned her over to make sure she was dead. That's how he got blood on him and at the top of the stairs."

There was one final mystery that Shannon wanted to clarify for his audience. The lingering question throughout had been this: if Cullen came to kill Priscilla, why hadn't he finished the job immediately? First shot doesn't do it, try again.

"I'll tell you," Shannon said softly. "He had one

more way of hurting her. He wanted to drag Priscilla down to that basement and show her Andrea's body. That would be it—the final hurt."

Shannon allowed himself a dramatic pause, then concluded: "Power! Greed! He was going to have it his way. And that's what he did that night. The judge. The jury. The executioner."

Shannon thanked the jury for its time and patience, then took his seat. He had given a magnificent performance and he knew it. So did everyone in the courtroom, including Racehorse and the defense lawyers. Perhaps because he had the last word, Shannon had made a profound impact on the jury. Mike Gibson admitted later, "When we got back to our apartment that night, we were all a little down." Dee Miller, the Amarillo member of the defense team, put it more bluntly. "Joe Shannon scared hell out of me," Miller said. It was almost 7:00 P.M. The November sun had long since dropped below the horizon. The jurors didn't feel like getting straight to the business at hand. It was unanimously agreed that the best thing was to start fresh in the morning. The only thing the jury felt like voting on was where to have dinner.

On Thursday, November 17, at 9:20 A.M., the nine men and three women chosen to determine Cullen Davis's fate began their deliberations by electing Gilbert Kennedy, a forty-nine-year-old mail carrier, as foreman. Courtroom regulars had speculated that either Kennedy or Walter Jones, the radar technician, would be selected to head the jury. Kennedy, a deeply religious man (his wife said later that the hardest strain on her husband was not being able to attend church), had been the eleventh juror chosen, which meant that he had been sequestered for 101 days. Marilyn Kay Haessly had been locked up since June 29, 143 days. For whatever it was worth, they would all go in the record book: this jury had been sequestered longer than any other jury in Texas history, and Haessly had been sequestered the longest of all. After all that time nobody expected the jury to rush its verdict, but it was generally assumed that each of the twelve had already come to some conclusion. A rumor floated around the bar at Rhett Butler's the night before that the jury stood ten to two for acquittal: the source of the rumor was one of Cullen's people.

As the jury pondered his fate, Cullen sat quietly with his attorneys at the front of the courtroom. Ken Davis, Karen Master, Ray Hudson, Roy Rimmer, and other friends and relatives waited on a front row bench. People who had anything to say said it in whispers. Now and then one of the groupies would appear and say something in Cullen's ear and pat him on the back, but if the defendant had any advance notice of how the jury was thinking, he didn't show it.

In the hallway the middle-aged housewives were arguing among themselves, not about the outcome but about whether Cullen looked more like Cliff Robertson or the actor who played the surgeon in "As the World Turns." Of the courtroom regulars who had not taken a personal interest in the defendant, Gladys Post, an elderly nurse and widow of an Amarillo oilman, summed up the prevailing mood. "I think they're all guilty as hell," Gladys said. "But I don't think Cullen did it." Nobody seemed particularly interested in the Pottergate scandal that was raging two floors below. Even as jury foreman Kennedy passed around the first ballots, Sheriff T. L. Baker and his top deputy were being indicted. Baker was accused of using his office to seek embarrassing information about the special counsel for court of inquiry and also of participating with county commissioner Bob Hicks in the theft of a county-owned air compressor. Capt. Don Smith was charged with the sexual abuse of a jail prisoner. Later, Baker was acquitted and charges against Smith were dropped, but Hicks was found guilty and put on probation.

Over the next three hours the jurors sent several notes to Dowlen, requesting various things. The first message inquired about the height of the bullet hole in the door through which Stan Farr took the first slug. "Let 'em take a good look," Dowlen said and ordered bailiffs to cart the heavy nine-foot wooden door to the jury room. Another note indicated that some of the jurors were confused about a discrepancy in Bev Bass's testimony—on the witness stand Bass had told the jury that she heard screams and a shot from inside the mansion within seconds after arriving with Gavrel, but in a statement given to Fort Worth police four hours after the murders she told of hearing the screams and a shot while she and Gavrel followed Cullen Davis along the sidewalk. On hearing the contents of this note, Cullen smiled and whispered something to Phil Burleson, whose diligence had uncovered this confusion.

Shortly after 1:00 P.M. Dowlen summoned all the attorneys to the bench and said in a somber tone: "I have a note from the jury. They want to visit the scene of the crime."

Fulfilling this request would be, to say the least, a staggering logistical problem. Haynes nearly bit the stem off his favorite pipe.

"Awww, you guys, I'm only kidding." Dowlen smiled after a proper pause. Then he read them the true contents of the message. It said, "We want eight Cokes and four Dr Peppers." Dowlen was certain the jury was close to a verdict. Someone had asked the judge at Rhett Butler's the previous night what he thought would happen the next day. Dowlen crooked his mouth and stirred his Scotch with a celery stick and made an offhand prediction. "Awww, I'd guess the jury will come back around 2:30 with a not guilty." Those attorneys who had suggested at the very beginning that Dowlen had a keen sense of the mood and temperament of Amarillo were on solid ground.

At 2:32 P.M., as the court reporter was searching for additional testimony requested by the jury, Dowlen appeared unexpectedly from chambers in his robe and announced, "Ladies and gentlemen, the jury has reached a verdict." As spectators hurried for their seats, Dowlen again warned against any demonstrations. At 2:38 P.M. the jurors filed into the courtroom for the last time. Dowlen ordered Cullen Davis to stand. Though Cullen had said many times that he had not the slightest doubt he would be acquitted, the pallor of fifteen months in jail seemed to settle over him like a hood.

Then Dowlen read the verdict: "We, the jury, find the defendant, Thomas Cullen Davis, not guilty."

Despite Dowlen's warning, the courtroom erupted in applause and cries of victory. For the next several minutes almost everyone was hugging and kissing. Cullen embraced Sumner and Haynes at the same time. He told each of the lawyers, "Thank you. Thank you very much." Karen Master was crying, and Haynes was trying to keep from it. Sumner recalled later the reaction of Phil Burleson. "It was so in character," Sumner said. "I remember we were all hugging and congratulating each other. I looked over at Phil. He wrote *N.G.*, then the time, then closed his book."

Joe Shannon, thirty-five pounds lighter than when he had arrived in Amarillo, stood to one side, counting the change in his pants' pocket. When someone asked him what he was thinking, Shannon permitted himself a thin smile and replied: "I was thinking that I had exactly eghteen cents in my pocket. Life's a funny old duck, ain't it?" Months later, when the dust of Amarillo had settled, Shannon would make another observation, a remark that must have been extremely difficult for a card-carrying political conservative. "I never thought I would say this," the prosecutor admitted, "but it seems we do have two systems of justice in the country. One for the rich and one for the poor."

Reporters pushed through the mob in an attempt to question Cullen, but deputy Al Cross, his pistol drawn and ready, hurried the freed man to the jail downstairs where he would be formally released. Those reporters who did not face an immediate deadline rushed three blocks to the Executive Inn where the jurors were already packing and being reunited with their families. All except Freddy Thompson. The split second that Dowlen told the jury they were dismissed, Freddy literally leaped out of the jury box and disappeared.

Every single juror who agreed to be interviewed used two phrases from Dowlen's charge to explain how they resolved many months of legal haggling in such short order. The phrases were "moral certainty" and "reasonable doubt." "I'm not sure we all thought he was innocent," said Karl Prah, the Braniff agent. "But there was room for reasonable doubt, and that's what we were told to find." Prah and others made it absolutely clear that the source of their doubt was the mouth of Priscilla Davis. "I didn't believe her," Prah said. Juror James Watkins agreed: "Some of the things she said I didn't believe. I think maybe she didn't lie to us, but she didn't tell us enough of the truth." Toying with a beer at the Surf Room bar, Mike Giesler wondered if the verdict would have been the same if Priscilla had openly confessed that she was addicted to Percodan, that she slept around as it pleased her, and that she selected a procession of unsavory bed partners and house guests. "They pretty well had her pegged," Giesler continued. In his twenty-eight years, Giesler said, he'd had experiences with women like that. On the prosecutor's master list of jurors there was this notation beside Giesler's name: "been divorced, bitter as to way treated . . . wife had somebody else's baby, took as his own. Felt 'used' when found out later. . . ."

"I don't think Priscilla's as bad as ol' Racehorse made her out to be," said Walter Jones, "but I think most of the jury felt she had lied to them about a number of things, so they couldn't take her word about anything."

Jury foreman Gilbert Kennedy told reporters, "I don't think the defense did all that much to shake her story about the shootings, but there were so many things she denied about herself that were later brought out. We didn't give much credibility to her testimony as a whole."

Curiously, the rumor that circulated the previous night that the jury stood ten to two for acquittal was totally accurate. On the first ballot Kennedy and Jones voted guilty. Jones told *Fort Worth Star-Telegram* reporter Glenn Guzzo that he couldn't swallow the defense's theory of conspiracy. He initially voted guilty because the independent accounts of Priscilla and Bev Bass were almost identical. "I couldn't find any way to let them get their stories together," Jones said. When Jones marked his first ballot, he thought he might be the only juror voting guilty. Even at ten to two, Jones admitted he felt overwhelmed. "When ten people jump up and say, 'Not guilty,' you wonder if there was something you didn't see. If it had been closer, we might still be there." Neither Kennedy nor Jones put stock in the defense's contention that Stan Farr was the killer's real target. Their reasonable doubt was not predicated on their belief that Horace Copeland or someone else committed the crimes. They changed their votes based on discrepancies in times and on the entrance and exit of the large, expensive car (or cars) that two witnesses saw at the mansion about the time of the murders.

None of the jurors believed Uewayne Polk's strange tale, and most of them had grave doubts about the credibility of Tommy Jourden and Karen Master. All of the jurors looked on Bubba Gavrel as an innocent victim who didn't know who shot him, and all of them seemed to believe Bev Bass. And yet, by some convoluted logic, they refused to accept Bass's identification of Cullen Davis *because* it matched Priscilla's story.

As *Star-Telegram* reporter Guzzo discovered a few days later, the juror who exercised the most influence on the deliberations was Karl Prah. In those long nights of isolation, Prah had dwelled on Racehorse Haynes's suggestion that eyewitnesses can be badly mistaken without really lying, and he had formulated his own theory to explain how two women running in opposite directions at the same time could compare stories. Prah labeled his theory "coincidental conspiracy."

In a specal section of the *Fort Worth Star-Telegram* devoted entirely to the Cullen Davis affair, Guzzo wrote: "Prah's theory of 'coincidental conspiracy' seemed rather simple to him; he was surprised no one else had thought of it. And it explained how Priscilla and Miss Bass could get their stories together without implicating Miss Bass in a plot to frame Cullen Davis.

"Prah recalled that Priscilla said her flight across the field after she had been shot was a long one. While she ran, she heard a shot, then screams and a series of shots. The time span between the first shot (at Gavrel) and the series of shots (which Gavrel saw fired through

305

the glass) could have been a minute or several minutes, but either way it was a long time to be running. The suggestion was that Priscilla could hear the very loud noises in that dead night air no matter how far away from the mansion she got. If she heard the screams (of Miss Bass) then she also may have heard the words the voice was shouting, over and over again: 'Cullen, please don't shoot me, it's Bev.' Eight or nine times Miss Bass said she had repeated her desperate plea to the killer she thought was the man she had come to know well over the past five years."

The more Prah thought about it, the more certain he became Bev Bass's cries sparked the coincidental conspiracy. "That's where Priscilla could have gotten Cullen's name, even if she knew it was somebody else who did it," Prah suggested. Why would Priscilla conceal the identity of the person who had just murdered her daughter and her lover? Prah had that figured too. "At that time Priscilla did not know her daughter was dead," Prah told Guzzo. "When she fled, it was convenient to blame Cullen, so she could be safe from the real killer if the shootings were drug related. Once she found out Andrea was dead, it was too late to backtrack."

When defense attorney Steve Sumner heard Prah's theory he observed, "God, that's so bizarre we wouldn't have dared try it on a jury!"

Minutes after the reading of the verdict some of the jurors congregated in the Surf Room bar where Ray Hudson, Karen Master's father, was buying drinks. At Hudson's invitation four of them were chauffeured across town to Rhett Butler's, where Cullen's victory party was commencing. On Roy Rimmer's instructions, Cullen's people had taken over Amarillo's favorite watering hole for a celebration that Texans would talk about for months, not always favorably. At first the party was limited to Cullen's people and the attorneys, but gradually five jurors, three bailiffs, a few select groupies, at least a dozen reporters, and even Judge George Dowlen himself would be a part of the party. Partly because of the hysteria called Pottergate, Dowlen

would come under considerable heat over his attendance at the celebration. It was a bad rap, and the
judge would eventually be given a "clean bill of health"
after appearing before the State Commission on Judicial
Conduct in Austin.

The judge had spent almost all his evenings for the
past four or five months at Rhett Butler's. The demands
of the trial had been especially hard on Dowlen—among
other things, his girlfriend had broken off their relationship—and so on this particular night Dowlen did what
he did every night: went straight to Rhett Butler's and
started ordering Scotch and celery sticks. He didn't join
the party, *the party joined him.* "I guess what I should
of done is got up and leave when Cullen and his people
came in," Dowlen said later, "but, damn it, I didn't
have anywhere to go."

As the party grew, it resembled the dressing room
of a Super Bowl winner. Flashbulbs popped, people
hugged and kissed and laughed and cried and flashed
victory signs, and normally intelligent newspaper people
milled about like teenyboppers at Graceland. Dee Miller, who hadn't questioned a witness, drank a toast to
the largest fee of his career; and Racehorse, whose own
fee was rumored to be astronomical, proposed a toast
to all the money spent on photographs of investigators
taking photographs of investigators. Jurors James Watkins, Mike Giesler, and Betty Fox Blair seemed to enjoy
the adoration and talked freely with reporters. One
drunk reporter kept patting the jurors on the ass and
telling them, "You guys are the true heroes in all this,"
and the jurors appeared to believe it. Deciding the fate
of a man as rich and powerful as Cullen Davis was no
small act. On the other hand, *convicting* a man so rich
and powerful seemed as unthinkable now as it ever did.
Most of the jurors would have to agree with Stanley
Marsh's sister-in-law: "Rich men don't kill their wives."
Juror Betty Blair agreed. "It seems like if someone that
rich wanted it done, he'd hire somebody," Betty Blair
said.

You could see Racehorse glowing like a long-smol-
dering forest fire. The illustrious Houston attorney was

well into his cups and having abstained for so long was in no mood to stop now. Race was the Vince Lombardi of trial lawyers: he hated to lose, but God, did he *love* to win. Considering the publicity and the fee and the test of endurance, this would be his biggest. Now it was over. Race was persuaded to sing a couple of verses of his favorite Willie Nelson song. Then Race and Cullen moved into the glare of TV lights and did the kind of slap-palms-bump-asses number you would expect from two rookies who had just combined on the winning touchdown. An Amarillo television man had pushed through the crowd to Haynes. They were doing the nightly news *live* from Rhett Butler's, and they wondered if Race would mind making a statement. The attorney ordered another drink and said he wouldn't mind at all. Race took himself downstairs, thrust his chin toward the camera, and made a statement that he probably regretted the next morning.

In a strident evangelical crescendo, the famous lawyer told the television audience about Priscilla Lee Davis. "She is the dregs," he said. "She's probably shooting up right now. She is the most shameless, brazen hussy in all humanity. She is a charlatan, a harlot, and a liar. She is a snake, unworthy of belief under oath. She is a dope fiend and an habitué of dope. She is the most sordid human being in the United States, in fact the world. Someone ought to put up a barbed-wire fence around her and keep her there."

At 4200 Mockingbird the mansion was overlit, as it was almost every night, bright and silent as a ghost ship motionless on the horizon. Lynda Arnold, Stan's sister, was there, and so were a few other close friends, but Priscilla wasn't receiving. James McDaniels, a chauffeur and bodyguard, told inquiring reporters that Priscilla was "in a state of shock" and in no condition to make statements to the press. Lynda Arnold was openly enraged by the verdict in Amarillo. "I hope all the money it took to buy all the lies gives those people a lot of joy," she said bitterly. "I hope all the people who lied can live with it." Later, Priscilla talked to two reporters who called from Amarillo. "I know the truth. I know he did it," she said. "But he can't hurt me anymore. Now he'll have to answer to God. That's one he can't buy." There was a long silence, then Priscilla added: "It looks like everyone won today except me. Cullen has his freedom, Racehorse has his million dollars, you guys have your stories, your books, and your movies. The cost has been tremendous. Just remember one thing: it cost me a child I loved very much. That's the part that nobody wants to talk about."

For the first time in almost sixteen months Cullen Davis went to bed that night a free man. Technically, he still faced murder charges in the death of Stan Farr and charges of attempted murder in the shootings of Priscilla and Gavrel—he would remain under bond totaling more than $1 million—but the chances he would be tried on the remaining charges were poor. He was still front-page news across Texas, but now the stories had a fluffy, gossipy society slant, as witnessed by this opening paragraph the following day on the front page of the *Amarillo Daily News*:

"He sat there, slowly sipping his wine. After thinking for several seconds, the defendant in the longest murder trial in Texas history said the trial would not prevent him from resuming his life."

As their first act in the return to normality, Cullen and Karen hosted a small luncheon on Friday for the jurors and selected members of the media. Cullen appeared urbane and slightly arrogant, telling reporters that his reaction to the verdict was, "I guess I showed those guys." One positive aspect of the ordeal, Cullen said, was that he had increased his understanding of criminal law. "I was always under the impression that a person could get bonded out of jail when charged with a crime," he said. "I learned that's not always the case." Karen appeared sweet and deeply grateful as she described her own reaction: "Thank God the truth has finally surfaced." Someone asked Cullen if he knew the identity of the true killer, and Cullen replied "probably." But he had no intention of supplying that name, either to the press or to the prosecutors. "I'm not going to do the DA's work for them," he said. "Let them find out who it is." Cullen and his entourage had started talking about who should play Cullen in the movie version of the story—Cullen favored Al Pacino—when AP writer Mike Cochran asked out of the blue, "By the way, Cullen, what movie *did* you see on the night of August 2?" The urbanity and arrogance fell away, and there was a long, chilling silence. Then he answered, "That will have to wait for the next trial."

On Saturday night, two days after the verdict, Stanley Marsh 3 came through with his promised party at Toad Hall. He invited the whole cast, including Cullen and Karen. Cullen appeared less jubilant than he had at the victory luncheon. Too long had he been a martyr; now he conducted himself with the quiet, relaxed dignity of a hero. There were people at the party who had never seen Cullen wear anything except a business suit, but tonight, he came casual in an Ultrasuede shirt, slacks, and loafers. It was like chatting with one of the boys, as Cullen joked about his ordeal and predicted that Priscilla would end up working in an all-night doughnut stand in Waco. Stanley Marsh 3 was fairly licking his chops as he zoomed his attention to his guest. "It's always nice to have an ex-accused murderer at Toad Hall," Stanley said, and Cullen shook hands and said he was glad to be there. Cullen didn't seem particularly interested in discussing art, even though Stanley directed his attention to the backyard where the large letters A-R-T were silhouetted against a harvest moon, and he showed very little interest in the pair of Chinese hairless dogs that Stanley had caused to be tattooed with wings and flames. Stanley asked Cullen about Priscilla. If she was such a hussy and harlot, why had Cullen married her? When someone asked Stanley later about this conversation, the Amarillo millionaire explained: "Cullen told me she changed for the better after they were married. But when Fort Worth society refused to accept her, she went back to her old ways. Well, I told him, a tiger can't be expected to change her spots. Cullen corrected me. He pointed out that tigers have stripes."

A reporter wondered what Stanley thought of Cullen now.

"Let me put it this way," Stanley said. "I don't think Minnesota Fats would have enjoyed drinking with Cullen."

"Can I quote you on that?"

"I insist," Stanley said. "Fats was just a pig, but he had standards. Blood will tell, I always say."

The final remnants of the circus pulled out of Amarillo the morning after Stanley's party. There were a lot of sad farewells, as there are at the finish of any ordeal. There was television footage of Cullen and Karen shaking hands as they boarded his Learjet. Cullen said they would spend Thanksgiving skiing in Colorado, but for now he planned to be back at his desk at Mid-Continent on Monday morning. Racehorse Haynes had already departed for Boston, where he was scheduled to make a speech. Members of the press returned home to resume their customary fare of car wrecks and honky-tonk stabbings, all except Evan Moore, who resigned his job at the *Fort Worth Star-Telegram* to become a cowboy in the small Panhandle community of Happy, Texas. Judge Dowlen had patched things up with his girlfriend and was ready to work on his badly neglected docket. Amarillo began forgetting Cullen Davis. When bankers, lawyers, and politicians met at Stanley's office for the daily picnics, someone always said, "Don't tell me any more Cullen Davis stories." There was plenty of Pottergate scandal to occupy the conversation, and if anyone got bored with that, Stanley would be delighted to tell them about his plans to have 500 acres of wheat mowed into the shape of a giant hand—the *Great American Farmhand,* he would call it.

Two weeks after the trial Stanley still hadn't located his missing cowboy, juror Freddy Thompson. Then one night in December, at 3:22 A.M., Freddy appeared in Stanley's bedroom and shook him by the toe.

"He had crawled in through the doggy door," Stanley said. "He was covered with frozen mud and had a glass of whiskey in his hand. He wanted to know if I thought he'd done the right thing in acquitting Cullen. He was

311

apparently taking some ribbing from the other cowboys. I told him I didn't know. I thought Cullen probably did it, but I also thought the state didn't prove its case. I told him that if I had been on the jury, I'd probably have voted the same way. That's all he wanted to hear. He went home."

The following morning Freddy was back at work with the rest of Amarillo.

THE OPERA
AIN'T OVER TILL
THE FAT LADY
SINGS

By Learjet it is less than four hundred miles from Amarillo to the ski slopes of Aspen, Colorado, but it seemed light-years to Karen Master. After nearly fifteen months of confinement the man she loved was free. Cullen was thinner, and his temples were flecked with gray that hadn't been there in August of 1976, but both of them had withstood the bitterness of those months and Karen believed they were stronger for it. It was a time for quiet reflection; Karen left her sons, Trey and Chesley, in Fort Worth to visit their father while she and Cullen took their long-awaited vacation. Until now, Karen hadn't dared plan for the future. But the future had come. Final hearings on Cullen and Priscilla's divorce were set for January, at which time Karen planned to become Mrs. Cullen Da is. There was so much to do. Cullen was certain he would win custody of the mansion. Karen admitted to Kathy Sellers, her constant companion in Amarillo, that the responsibility of the mansion was frightening, but that's what Cullen wanted and she could adjust. Karen was soon to be named president of the parent/professional section of the Texas Association of the Deaf. With Cullen underwriting part of the cost, her job was to help publicize the Miss Deaf Texas Pageant. She'd thought, too, of enrolling in a creative writing course. Maybe it would help her put her feelings into words.

As they flew to Aspen with a small group of friends, accompanied by Amarillo TV newsman Ben Boyett, Karen prepared herself to forget. As soon as they arrived, she had second thoughts. It hadn't occurred to her during the long daily routine of Amarillo, but in this new place, surrounded by new and strange faces, Karen realized that she and Cullen were celebrities. It wasn't an unpleasant sensation. Strangers approached Cullen for autographs and took snapshots of Karen. "Here I was in my goggles and ski attire, my hair an absolute mess," she said. "But people were very complimentary. They'd tell me how much better looking I was than those awful newspaper pictures." Cullen's appetite for the outdoors seemed insatiable. He made reservations at Aspen or other ski resorts for every weekend and holiday through the winter season. Even this wasn't enough. Already an accomplished skier, Cullen wanted more: he wanted to ski on virgin snow, on snow no one else had ever attempted. He rented a helicopter and had himself ferried to the top of an otherwise inaccessible glacier in Montana. This was a bit much for Karen. She planned to watch from some secure place while Cullen made his long, lonely descent. She'd had enough thrills for several lifetimes. "I'm just so very glad it's over," she said.

But it wasn't over. The bitterness, the accusations, the headlines—there had been a brief respite, but nothing had changed.

Within minutes after their Learjet landed at Fort Worth's Meacham Field, Karen learned that her ex-husband had been doing more than just baby-sitting for the children—he'd won temporary custody of them. A temporary restraining order issued by a divorce court judge while they were in Aspen prohibited Karen from taking her sons "around or near Cullen Davis." The order was signed by Joe Eidson, the domestic relations judge who had caused Cullen so much discomfort.

Karen was stunned. It had seemed to her that Walter Master wasn't much interested in his sons; now, suddenly he was lobbing shells. In his petition filed with Judge Eidson, Master claimed that his ex-wife was using the boys as a "status symbol"—the petition didn't spell out how custody of two handicapped children qualified as *status*—and charged that Karen was an unfit mother who acted in ways detrimental to the children's "physical health, moral development, and psychological and emotional security." A primary witness against Mrs. Master, the petition continued, would be her former

316

psychiatrist, Dr. W. Bryan Liston. Liston was supposedly prepared to testify that Karen Master "does not have the ability to have a mother instinct toward her children, nor can she control her own emotions and cannot face the realities of life." Walter Master's petition asked for permanent custody of the boys, permanent use of the house at 4 Arthur Drive in Edgecliff—and *child support* from Karen Master.

Karen eventually won the battle with her ex-husband, but for the next two weeks the Cullen Davis affair was back in the headlines. Karen's attorney claimed that Eidson did not have jurisdiction in the custody fight because the original divorce decree had been issued by another domestic relations judge, Eva Barnes. The case was returned to Judge Barnes's court. After enduring yet one more hearing, Karen regained custody of her children. On December 7, almost as soon as Cullen, Karen, and the children returned to 4 Arthur Drive, an extortion letter arrived. The author claimed to be a professional killer hired by unnamed parties to assassinate Cullen but offered to spare his life and reveal the names of the parties who had negotiated the contract in return for $10,000. The letter was signed D.M.R. Two FBI agents visited Cullen and Karen and ordered a tracing device attached to the telephone at 4 Arthur Drive, but the extortionist was never caught, and after a few weeks the investigation was dropped. This time Karen harbored fewer illusions that the affair was over and done.

District Attorney Tim Curry had a problem that was both legal and political—what to do about the three cases still pending against Cullen Davis. Popular sentiment in Fort Worth had shifted in Davis's favor. This was an election year, and the DA was certain that any further attempt to prosecute Cullen would have serious, if not fatal, consequences for his own political future. Leaving aside the moral question, the cost of the Amarillo trial was astronomical. Bills were still coming in. A single item—meal and hotel expenses for the DA's staff—easily exceeded Tarrant County's entire 1977 budget of $50,000 for *all* change of venue expenses.

Then there had been the cost of daily transcripts, an expense seldom encountered. The complete transcript contained 13,110 pages—at $4.25 a page that came to $55,717. The county hadn't yet received all the bills for the jury's hotel and meal expenses, but the figure already exceeded $65,000. There were dozens of lesser expenses—$8 a day for Cullen's room and board in the Potter County jail, salaries and fringe benefits for Potter County bailiffs and deputies, shipping and airline expenses, car rentals, long-distance calls, office supplies, not to mention such miscellaneous items as the $114 tab for theater tickets for jurors and bailiffs and $222 for visits to the beauty parlor by female jurors. Tarrant County auditor Jack Benson had in some cases refused to reimburse Potter County—the jurors' $7,000 liquor tab, for example, and the $25,000 in "overtime premiums" due to deputies and bailiffs. Counting the $14,126 for jury selection in Fort Worth, before the trial was even moved to Amarillo, the total tab would exceed $300,000. This didn't include what the auditor called "extracurricular costs," namely, the salaries of Curry and the seven members of his staff assigned to the case. The Cullen Davis murder trial had not only been the longest and most sensational in Texas history; it had also been the most costly.

Even if Curry was willing to hit the taxpapers with another Cullen Davis murder trial, there were legal obstacles that might make it impossible. Texas law prohibits a wife from testifying against her husband unless he is being tried for assaulting her or a minor child. While Priscilla was permitted to testify in the murder trial of Andrea Wilborn, she wouldn't be allowed to testify in the murder trial of Stan Farr, even though she was the only eyewitness. A divorce would free her from this restriction. There was yet another reason to put the decision on hold until after the divorce trial. Many attorneys, including Marvin Collins, believed that the legal doctrine of *collateral estoppel* prohibited further criminal action against Cullen Davis. Collateral estoppel was roughly the same as double jeopardy— Marvin Collins interpreted it to mean that once a fact has been determined by a final judgment—a jury—the issue cannot be litigated again between the same parties. The doctrine grew out of a case in Missouri in which a man was accused of robbing a tableful of poker players. After the man was acquitted of robbing Player No. 1, prosecutors tried him for the robbery of Player No. 2. This time they got a conviction, but the Supreme Court overturned it. In the years since that decision, the Supreme Court had overturned a number of cases involving multiple victims and double jeopardy. "Since the Supreme Court is construing the double jeopardy issue so radically in other areas," Marvin Collins noted, "it portends a similar construction in the collateral estoppel area." Curry wasn't convinced. He intended to keep his options, at least until the conclusion of the divorce trial. The divorce trial could bring out new evidence.

Indeed, Priscilla's attorneys predicted that the divorce would produce startling testimony. "It will be a whole new ball game," said Jerry Loftin, who, with his partner, Ronald Aultman, had been on the case three and a half years by now. "I can't go into the evidence, but there will be highly significant testimony which prosecutors could not bring out during the Amarillo trial. We will be operating under new rules of evidence. They will let us present testimony which was not admissible in the murder trial. And we will be able to call Cullen Davis to the stand." The basic issue before Judge Eidson was the distribution of property, but Priscilla's lawyers claimed that the judge could "properly consider the causes of the divorce and the relative earning powers of the couple in making a fair division of property." It was their belief that the judge could compensate Priscilla for her mental anguish resulting from Andrea's death, if the judge concluded Cullen was responsible. "And we believe he will," Loftin said. Cullen's attorneys maintained their contention that the prenuptial agreement limited the amount Priscilla could claim, but Loftin held to the position that the agreement was an act of trickery, and therefore not binding.

The exact date of the trial remained an open question. It was mid-February before Eidson got around to firming it up. He set the date at April 17, 1978.

Cullen's attorneys reacted to this newest postponement by filing a carefully worded motion asking that Eidson be disqualified from presiding over the divorce battle. Grounds for the motion were that Eidson had testified in the Amarillo murder trial. "We do not for a minute imply that there was any impropriety in Judge Eidson's testifying," the motion said. "Indeed he was subpoenaed and had no choice. But the considerations which dictate against a judge's hearing a case about which he has been talking publicly are equally strong whether his public comments are voluntary or involuntary." The motion contained nothing but high-blown praise for Cullen's longtime nemesis. Attorneys who know Judge Eidson, the motion continued, "have respect and personal fondness for him, [and] we believe he could rise above those conflicts and maintain the dignity of the bench—if any man could. But we question whether any man can. Judges are men, not saints."

Priscilla's attorneys launched an immediate counterattack, and they minced no words. Loftin and Aultman accused their adversaries of taking the position that "we don't have this judge in our pocket, so let's shop elsewhere." According to their document, the real issue was this: "Can one man control the judges of the State of Texas? Can one man manipulate the courts of the State of Texas, or do we follow the laws of the State of Texas and the Judicial Canons of Ethics?"

It was Eidson's strong opinion that he had violated no code of conduct or ethical standards, and therefore there was no reason he shouldn't continue to preside over the divorce suit. But he decided to place the matter in the hands of an administrative judge, Louis Holland. The following day Holland overruled the motion filed by Cullen's attorneys, and Eidson remained on the case. Four days later Eidson decided to postpone the divorce again, this time from April 17 to an unspecified date in May. Eidson gave no reason for the new delay.

For some time Cullen Davis had considered bringing in his heavy artillery. Almost as soon as Eidson issued his latest delay, Cullen hired Racehorse Haynes to join Cecil Munn and the other lawyers who had been working on his divorce suit. A new batch of motions was immediately filed. Four days later Eidson confirmed Haynes as one of Cullen's lawyers and ruled on the various motions. The judge refused Cullen's request to reduce support payments from $5,000 to $3,500, but he ruled that Davis was no longer financially responsible for paying the off-duty policemen who had been guarding Priscilla and the mansion. The judge also released Cullen from his obligation of paying $1,500 a month for Priscilla's private nurses. Cullen was allowed to sell 59,000 shares of Great Western Drilling Company stock, 29,916 shares of First United Bancorporation, and 4,620 shares of Texas American Bancshares. Funds obtained from the stock sales could be used "for payment of indebtedness and current expenses," Eidson ruled, but they could not be used (without specific permission from the court) to pay off bills from Phil Burleson's law firm. The judge also authorized Cullen and his attorneys to visit the mansion, for the purposes of inspection and inventory.

Eidson's order closed on a curious, contradictory note. First, it set the new divorce trial date for May 15 and said that the judge would not postpone it again "except in the event of extreme and unforeseeable emergencies." But further down in the order, the terminology shifted from trial to *jury* trial. If Priscilla's lawyers were not prepared for a jury trial by May 15, the order concluded, then Eidson "would entertain a motion for a reasonable postponement."

This time it was Priscilla who was incensed by Eidson's rulings. The order cutting off payments for her nurses and bodyguards seemed intolerable. Priscilla anticipated that the judge would *increase* her support payments. Instead, Eidson had imposed on her a new financial burden. "I'm not about to stay here without a bodyguard," she said angrily. "Does anyone seriously think Cullen won't try it again? I know him—I was married to him for six years—he won't give up trying to kill us all." Priscilla already found it impossible to live on $5,000 a month; now she would have the added expense of the guards who maintained a twenty-four-hour vigil at the mansion's main entrance. She'd have to do without the nurses. This was no mere case of poor-mouthing—Priscilla was in bad shape, financially, physically, and emotionally. She had been hospitalized for several weeks in February. Surgeons planned to perform a delicate operation to repair nerve endings damaged by the gunshot wound but at the last minute changed their minds and settled for another relatively simple nerve block. The pain not only persisted, it was worse. Priscilla had lost considerable weight—her tight dresses hung on her like raincoats—and it had been weeks since she'd had her hair done properly. Dark circles rimmed her eyes. "I suddenly feel old," she said. She looked old. She could still do her magic with enough cosmetics, but they didn't hide the pain, the fear, or the indignation. Although the court forced Cullen to cough up nearly $4,000 for her current medical expenses, Priscilla was strapped. The mansion's monthly electric bill alone was $1,500. The country club bills averaged $500. Dee was always wanting something. Priscilla had been forced to borrow a considerable sum of money from a bank, using her jewelry and a $23,000 Ching Dynasty jade carving as collateral. The jade and the jewelry (including a 16.31-carat platinum-and-diamond bracelet) were still in hock, and the money was almost gone.

Priscilla's ability to withstand shock was impaired by other events, real and imagined. Society page items about Karen Master sent Priscilla into a rage. On the subject of Karen Master, Priscilla was totally irrational. On the one hand she ranted that Cullen was paying all of Karen's bills, and on other occasions she remarked, "I know for a *fact* that the hairdresser at Neiman Marcus won't let Karen charge a thing without a written note from Cullen." When Priscilla read in *Texas Monthly* magazine a description of Karen as Cullen's "attractive girlfriend," she telephoned the writer. "How can you say that she's attractive?" Priscilla said. "Take away the false eyelashes, the boob job, the

hair, and the fake fingernails . . . she's Miss Mouse."
Vanity and envy were two of Priscilla's least attractive
traits, and in the aftermath of her defeat and humiliation in Amarillo they nearly consumed her.

Even her old friends were falling off, one by one.
Lynda Arnold, Stan's sister, was busy with a new enterprise, a party ranch located near Justin, Texas, frequented by travel agents and conventioneers. The self-
proclaimed "party queen of Texas" seldom had time to
visit the mansion. Larry and Jerry Thomas had a fist
fight and were suing each other. Priscilla's old friend
Judy McCrory had at last got rid of David and married
a lawyer named Steve Brown. Priscilla and Steve Brown
didn't care for each other either, and so Judy didn't
come around much anymore. The world was going
crazy. Judy worked for Larry Thomas, who was suing
Jerry Thomas, who was being defended by Steve Brown.
David McCrory was back in town, hanging out at joints
like the Sylvania Bar and Billiards, shooting off his
mouth about how he was almost a star witness in
Amarillo. For some inexplicable reason, Cullen hired
David McCrory to work for one of his recently acquired companies, Jet Air Corporation. Where was it
leading? When would it stop?

About the only constants in Priscilla's life were Rich
Sauer and the bodyguards she now hired with the
financial assistance of Bill Davis. One night in March,
Priscilla slipped her .32 into her boot holster and took
a sentimental trip to Panther Hall, the place that Stan
Farr was trying to buy the night he was killed. Her
bodyguard, a Fort Worth homicide detective with a
tough reputation, chauffeured Priscilla, Sauer, and a
writer friend to the hall. Willie Nelson was playing,
and one of Willie's own bodyguards met Priscilla's party
at the rear entrance and ushered them upstairs to a private booth where Willie's entourage watched, secure
from the masses. It was the first time in weeks that
Priscilla had been out, and she was enjoying it. It was
one of the few places where she felt like a celebrity—
here among the "outlaws" of progressive country music.
Later Priscilla and her party stopped for drinks at the

White Elephant—not the famous Hell's Half Acre saloon, which had been closed for years, but a replica on the north side near the stockyards. For a few hours Priscilla was like her old self, bubbling with life, laughing, forgetting.

A few days after that, Cullen, his attorneys, and a photographer came to the mansion to photograph and examine the place. Cullen ordered pictures of the carpets, furniture, drapes, paintings, art objects, anything subject to wear and abuse. Attorney Cecil Munn told reporters that it was a crying shame the way Priscilla had let the mansion deteriorate. Priscilla was certain that one thing Cullen would insist on inspecting was his prize gold-and-jade chess set. Priscilla left word with the maid that the chess set was locked in the upstairs safe. Then she loaded the chess set and some other valuables in the trunk of her Lincoln Continental and drove around, crying and cursing. When Cullen opened the safe, staring at him were photographs of Andrea Wilborn and Stan Farr.

What amazed and delighted Cullen's acquaintances was how little wear and tear he showed for his long ordeal. "It was almost as if Amarillo never happened," Hershel Payne observed. Cullen was a little more reserved, but only a little, and only for a short time. On the contrary, he appeared stronger, more resolved and in touch with himself. Weekends on the ski slopes returned his color, and home cooking fleshed out the hollow spots in his face. He arrived early at his office, had lunch and shot some pool at the Petroleum Club, worked until 5 P.M., had a few drinks at the Merrimac with Roy Rimmer, Hershel Payne, Buddy Doyle, and a few others, then turned in for the night. He was congenial and took special pains to repay those who had befriended him during his ordeal. It wasn't so much that he repaid them with money, though he did that too; he repaid them with dinners, small gifts, special considerations. James Mabe, whose testimony had helped establish Cullen's alibi in Amarillo, was in the process of a divorce, and Cullen tried to help the couple with a reconciliation. It didn't work, but Cullen tried. Later, it was reported that Cullen awarded Mabe's office supply firm with a contract from Kendavis Industries. Rosemary Mabe married Jerry Brown, who used to live with Dana Campbell, who was Cullen's longtime woman friend. The same crazy world that was driving Priscilla up the wall didn't unbalance Cullen. For all his incredible ordeal, Cullen Davis appeared to be the sanest man in Fort Worth.

Slowly, a step at a time, Cullen reemerged in Fort Worth society. During his long confinement his name had been dropped from the *Fort Worth Social Directory*. This was an oversight, according to Mrs. Catherine Lipscomb, who publishes the *Directory*. As Mrs. Lipscomb explained to *Dallas Morning News* staff writer Maryln Schwartz: "We remember his mother so well that Cullen wasn't dropped from the *Directory* even after the trial and the publicity. But in order to stay, one has to answer a questionnaire before each new book is completed. Cullen didn't answer the last questionnaire." Throughout the winter and spring Cullen remained a news item in the Dallas–Fort Worth Metroplex, but now the items were mostly flattering. The *Star-Telegram* ran a large photograph of Cullen and Karen at the Steeplechase Ball and again when they attended Charles Tandy's sixtieth birthday party. Tandy's sixtieth birthday was one of the highlights of the social season in Fort Worth, upstaging the rodeo and Colonial. Tandy made his grand entrance in a sultan's outfit, riding an elephant.

D Magazine listed Cullen Davis among "People to Watch in 1978," citing him for directing "the restoration of the downtown Continental Life Building while still ensconced in the Amarillo jail" and adding that "now that he's free, Fort Worth expects to see a lot of action."

There was yet more evidence that 1978 was the year of Cullen Davis—one of Roy Rimmer's deals was paying off. Rimmer had talked Cullen into investing more than $7 million in business schemes that had never panned out, and there had been no reason to suspect the Willcoxson Ranch Property deal would be any

325

different. It started like the others, with a nearly bankrupt corporation in need of an immediate financial transfusion. The details are complex, but in essence Cullen bought Willcoxson, which owned uranium leases in New Mexico. By 1978 Cullen's total investment had been $650,000, and he hadn't yet recovered a penny. But in the spring of 1978, Hershel Payne negotiated the sale of the claims for nearly $8.5 million. Of course not all that went to Cullen. Payne owned 6.5 percent, and the Willcoxson heirs owned another 12.5 percent. Rimmer's part of the action amounted to 25 percent, though this would presumably be forfeited to repay the money he owed Cullen.

The sale of the Willcoxson claim was strategically timed as part of the divorce settlement. Since all this took place after the marriage, it couldn't possibly be covered by a prenuptial agreement. Cullen's attorneys conceded that this was community property. But there was a string attached. If Priscilla claimed a share of community assets, it could be argued that she also inherited a share of the community liabilities, including Cullen's heavy losses in deals with Roy Rimmer.

Some observers saw the Willcoxson sale as an attempt to sweeten the pot and perhaps reach an out-of-court settlement. It was assumed that Cullen would be willing to part with a few million just to avoid additional publicity. It was also assumed that Priscilla would call off her hounds for a cash settlement of, say, $4 million, plus $1 million for attorneys' fees. "Four million is better than a poke in the eye," a regular at the Rangoon Racquet Club concluded. Both assumptions failed to reckon with the bitterness of the contesting parties. The tentative offer of $4 million was roughly $96 million shy of the figure that Priscilla was now demanding.

On March 27 attorneys for both sides requested that the divorce suit be postponed until summer. Eidson granted the request. Cullen's attorneys requested a trial by jury, which Eidson also granted. Texas is the only state that permits jury trials in a divorce case where child custody is not an issue. Although jury findings on property settlement and other key issues are not binding on the judge, most domestic relations judges tend to heed the jury's advice. No one had forgotten how Racehorse Haynes cast his spell over the jury in Amarillo, but Cullen Davis was planning yet another big gun for his arsenal. He already had plans to hire attorney Donn Fullenweider, partner to Racehorse Haynes and a specialist in family law. Fullenweider had the same reputation in divorce trials that Race did in criminal trials. He was considered the best in Texas—and by extension, one of the best in the country.

Eidson set the trial date for August 14.

∽ • ∽

Cullen and Priscilla were the headliners, but they didn't have a monopoly on the bitterness.

Two years after the shootings Bubba Gavrel still walked on crutches, a bullet lodged in his spine and a pair of dead legs dragging behind. He'd lost forty pounds; in that respect he'd never looked better. Months of physical therapy had tightened and thickened his arms and shoulders, and muscles rippled down his torso. From shoulders to waist, Bubba looked like a weight-lifter; from the waist down he could have passed for a scarecrow. The real tragedy, though, was in his mind; maybe half a man was better than no man at all, but Bubba hadn't learned to accept it. Occasionally his dad and brothers took him fishing or to baseball games. Mostly he just sat around the house. His $13-million lawsuit against Cullen Davis was now set for trial on November 6, and this is what sustained him.

Bev Bass was physically sound, but her emotional state ranged from poor to awful. She suffered periodic depression—not just days of depression, sometimes weeks when it seemed almost impossible to get out of

327

bed. "I feel like I'm at least forty," she told reporter Glenn Guzzo a few months after her twentieth birthday. There was no way she could forget that night, nor forgive Cullen Davis. "He's ruined my life," she said. "He's ruined Bubba's life. Bubba was always so big and strong. Now I have to do everything for him. It's like they've taken away his manhood."

Jack Wilborn, who once felt like he was "dying of a broken heart," suffered a heart attack in May, then two more in June. He'd undergone open-heart surgery, and his life was touch and go. He blamed overwork and fatigue but conceded that "it's probably a combination of things." Wilborn's lawsuit against Cullen Davis was still pending. He didn't think about it much anymore. No jury verdict could change what had happened.

Even Racehorse was paying a price. Though his brilliant victory in Amarillo added to his fortune and ensured his fame—he was *now* being mentioned in the company of Percy Foreman, F. Lee Bailey, and Edward Bennett Williams—there were certain drawbacks. It was harder to pick a jury for example. Everyone had heard of him. They all knew his reputation. This helped his ego, but it didn't help his clients' cases. Nor did it help his concentration: he wasn't quite as hungry as before. A case in point was the Sylvia Meek murder trial in August, two weeks before the scheduled start of the Cullen Davis divorce trial. Sylvia Meek was one of the defense witnesses in Amarillo; she was the private investigator who testified that not long before the murders Priscilla tried to hire her as a bodyguard, indicating that Priscilla therefore knew something was about to happen. Meek was accused of shooting a business associate to death in a dispute over a polygraph machine, and now it was Racehorse's job to defend her. Almost every potential juror questioned had heard of Racehorse Haynes. Several potential jurors disqualified themselves, claiming they were prejudiced against Haynes, and Race thanked them for their candor. But the flattery was disconcerting. At one point in the voir dire Race asked a potential juror if he believed in *community property*. My God! he thought as soon as he'd asked the question. *Wrong trial!* "Community property? I can't believe I said that," he told the juror, embarrassed at his own blunder. "Oh, well, tell me how you feel about it anyway." Sylvia Meek was convicted. Racehorse was beaten by a young Tarrant County prosecutor, Jerry Buckner. The state's case was strong, but Racehorse had to wonder if he was slipping.

As the countdown for the divorce trial continued, Eidson issued another ruling that provoked Cullen Davis and no doubt made Racehorse Haynes uncomfortable. He made public a 251-page deposition in which Priscilla's lawyers asked Cullen nearly 2,000 questions, covering such subjects as the vast assets of Kendavis Industries, Cullen's physical outbursts, his sex life, his gifts to and financial support of Karen Master, and the amount of money Cullen had spent on lawyers. Much of this had already appeared in other public records, but the part about attorneys' fees had only been speculated about. It had been rumored, for example, that Racehorse Haynes received somewhere between $750,000 and $1.5 million for his part in the murder trial. Race refused to comment on such talk, though he made it clear that his fees were substantial. William Randolph Hearst approached him about defending Patty, Haynes admitted, but decided inste d on F. Lee Bailey, whose fee was considerably lower. Now, unexpectedly, Eidson allowed Cullen's deposition into the public record, and among other things Cullen revealed that Haynes's fee was far less than had been speculated—$250,000 in fact. Though still a staggering fee by most standards, it took some of the edge off Race's mystique.

The total tab for Cullen's acquittal came to about $3 million—ten times what it cost Tarrant County. The deposition revealed that Cullen paid Phil Burleson's law firm $1.25 million and still owed it another $300,000 to $400,000. This figure included monies paid to Mike Gibson and Steve Sumner, but it didn't include the cost of hiring all those investigators, nor did it include expenses. A number of other attorneys were involved in Cullen's defense, including Bill Magnussen of Fort Worth, state Sen. Bill Meier of Euless, former Watergate investigating committee counsel Samuel Dash, University of California professor Caleb Foote, and Amarillo attorneys Hugh Russell and Dee Miller. Their fees were not mentioned. If anything, the figure of $3 million seemed conservative.

On the surface, at least, none of the 2,000 questions directed at Cullen Davis seemed to harm his case. Racehorse Haynes successfully blocked all questions about the murders. By this point the vast holdings of Kendavis International were fairly well known. Asked the total sales of Kiii in 1977, Cullen replied offhandedly: "One billion, 29 million dollars, plus change." Nevertheless, Cullen's attorneys took this opportunity to fire a few verbal blasts at the opposition. Cecil Munn termed repeated attempts to question Karen Master "a disgusting cheap shot" and "outrageously distasteful." According to Munn, Priscilla's efforts to drag Karen into the mess were "nothing but an effort to heap pointless embarrassment and humiliation upon a young mother of two physically handicapped children. . . ." Jerry Loftin answered the charge in a word: "Ridiculous." The complaints were merely one more example, Loftin said, of the way that Cullen Davis expected preferential treatment. Each side accused the other of pandering to the media. True or not, hardly a day passed without some banner headline proclaiming this or that contention. DAVIS DIVORCE LAWYERS AT BOILING POINT, a headline in the August 4 *Star-Telegram* announced. By now there was no chance at all of an out-of-court settlement. Priscilla offered to settle for $20 million, and Cullen countered by offering her $5,000 a month for twenty years.

"This will be the biggest divorce trial in Texas," Donn Fullenweider predicted. "I guess everything Cullen Davis does these days is the biggest thing in Texas. And the other side claims it's bigger than we do."

"A lot of interesting things are likely to pop up," Jerry Loftin agreed. "Get your tickets early."

"Priscilla Davis knows she's going to be a wealthy woman when this is all over," said Steve Sumner, "so why not roll the dice and see if she can get some vindication?"

Hershel Payne, who had just negotiated the sale of the Willcoxson uranium property, simply shook his head as the suit headed toward what seemed to be the inevitable bloodletting. "This may be a case where nobody wins and both lose," Payne said sadly.

Overnight, it seemed, the bomb was defused. First, Priscilla's lawyers asked for another delay to examine a new document about Cullen's settlement with Bill Davis. Eidson gave them till September 18. Then both sides went privately to the judge and asked him to confine the trial to the single issue of property settlement. Eidson agreed; it would be what attorneys call a no-fault trial. No sex, no drugs, no beatings, no murders, no acts of misconduct could be introduced. What had promised to be a sensational no-holds-barred bloodletting became, in a stroke, a fairly routine property settlement.

The question was why Priscilla allowed her lawyers to request the no-fault provision. There was no easy answer to this question. Since Amarillo, Priscilla had been dead set on revenge, on using the divorce trial to vindicate herself and establish Cullen as the cold-blooded killer of Andrea Wilborn and Stan Farr. But Priscilla's lawyers had convinced her that the legal maneuver would work in her favor. The strategy was this: they would sacrifice the immediate opportunity of revenge for long-range benefits. Aultman and Loftin had already filed two civil damage suits against Cullen, one for the murder of Andrea and the other for the assault on Priscilla. Aside from the property settlement, millions were at stake in these two cases. Moreover, there were the damage suits filed by Gavrel, Jack Wilborn, and the Farr estate—each portended to be a mini murder trial. Gavrel's suit was set for trial November 6; unless the divorce trial overlapped it, this suit was almost certain to start on schedule. Aultman and Loftin convinced Priscilla that the first priority was to get at least a financial stalemate. Revenge would come in due time.

If this most recent delay dismayed Cullen Davis, he didn't show it. He went smoothly about his business. It had been almost exactly ten years since he married Priscilla, four years since he moved out of the mansion, two years since he was arrested and charged with murder; the month of August seemed to have a fatal attraction for Cullen and those around him. August in Texas is pure hell. The days are blistering hot and seem to last forever; nights offer only token relief and end too soon. August brings out the nocturnal instinct in people, and so it did with Cullen Davis, who seemed to thrive on long hours and little sleep. Instead of vacationing in some cool spot like his brother Bill, who had taken his family to Vermont, or at least hibernating in the air-conditioned comfort of the Mid-Continent Building, Cullen ranged over a wide area of the Metroplex in his air-conditioned 1975 Cadillac. In recent months he had added several new corporations to his conglomerate; it was as though he couldn't stand still, as though some primal pressure required that he keep moving, keep looking over his shoulder and moving.

One of his recent acquisitions was Jet Air. Not long after acquiring the company, Cullen did a curious thing —he hired his old pool-shooting companion David McCrory as assistant to president Arthur Smith. The job paid $20,000 a year, plus a $10,000 bonus, expenses, and a company car, not bad for an unemployed tenth-grade dropout who hadn't done Cullen any favors in Amarillo. McCrory's refusal to sign the affidavit smearing Priscilla was still a sore point with lawyers for the defense, but Cullen apparently had something else in mind for McCrory. Early that summer Cullen and McCrory met in the parking lot of Coco's Famous Hamburgers on Hulen Boulevard, not far from the mansion. It was the first of many meetings at Coco's. McCrory claimed that Cullen gave him $5,000 and ordered him to investigate Bev Bass, Bubba Gavrel, and Priscilla's attorneys, Aultman and Loftin. Specifically, McCrory said Cullen wanted to know where Bass and Gavrel "got their dope," and he wanted to know if the two lawyers paid social visits to Judge Eidson. On July 29,

McCrory and his new wife flew to Las Vegas, supposedly to launder some money for Cullen, though Cullen denied this. All through July and early August, the two men played some sort of cloak-and-dagger game. The way McCrory told it, they even used code names. McCrory left messages in the name of "Frank Johnson" and called Cullen by the code name of "Dan Edwards."

Cullen apparently had his eye on another company, Cogdell Auto Supply, owned by Jim Bradshaw, who was also serving as pro tempore mayor of Fort Worth. The mayor pro tem had met the industrialist on several occasions at the Petroleum Club or city council functions, but it was no more than a nodding acquaintance. Bradshaw was greatly surprised, therefore, when Cullen telephoned him one day in early August and arranged a business meeting.

"When my secretary told me Cullen Davis was on the phone, I thought someone was pulling my leg," Bradshaw recalled. A few days after the phone call, Cullen and Jet Air president Art Smith visited Bradshaw's office. There was some small talk about politics —Cullen wanted to know if Bradshaw intended to run for mayor—then Cullen came to the point: he wanted to do some business with Bradshaw's company. "This seemed sort of odd," Bradshaw recalled. "I ran a fairly small business by this guy's standards. Here's a man who owns an $800-million empire, and we're talking about something that might net him $2,000 a year. But I was impressed. I'd heard that's how Cullen is—100 percent business, twenty-four hours a day. Anyway, I asked him why—why would he possibly be interested in this rat race [the auto supply business]. I forget the exact figures, but Cullen said something like, 'I understand the market is $30 billion a year, and I want some of it.' He told me he might even buy my place."

Bradshaw gave Cullen and Art Smith a tour of the facilities. Like everyone else in Fort Worth, the mayor pro tem had followed Cullen's continuing saga, but until now it hadn't occurred to Bradshaw that Cullen was a genuine celebrity. "When we got to the warehouse," Bradshaw said, "all the blacks were rushing over to shake his hand and meet him. Some of the old-timers in the company, people who were set in their ways, were saying things like, 'We need a change around here. Maybe Cullen Davis is just what we need.' I mean they didn't even know what the *proposal* was."

Bradshaw wasn't the only one puzzled by the curious happenings of August. Art Smith couldn't make heads or tails out of his new assistant, David McCrory. He hardly ever saw McCrory. McCrory made the unexplained trip to Las Vegas and another to Atlanta. It was apparent that McCrory was doing something for Cullen, so Smith kept quiet.

A few days after Eidson's latest ruling delaying the divorce trial, Karen Master telephoned Jim Bradshaw's home, inviting Bradshaw and his wife, Ouida, to be their guest at the Cowboys–Houston Oilers preseason game Saturday night. Again, Bradshaw was surprised. "It was just so odd," he said. "We'd never been out with Cullen and Karen." Bradshaw knew most of the others in Cullen's party, and it was agreed they would all meet for drinks, then drive to Dallas for the game. Karen wanted Ouida and Jim to ride with them and told Bradshaw that she and Cullen would pick them up at 5:30 P.M.

Late Saturday afternoon, as Cullen and Karen were dressing for the game, McCrory called.

"My man is still here, but I can't locate him," McCrory told Cullen. "He's out."

They chatted about the game, then McCrory said, "How come you didn't invite me to that fucking football game?"

"You haven't got time for a ball game," Cullen said.

McCrory told Cullen that he needed to call him later that night. "My man is still here and he's working, and I'm trying to get ahold of him," McCrory said. "I'll contact you tonight—or probably early in the morning."

"Good deal," Cullen told him. They exchange: some locker-room talk about women and sex. Then McCrory said, "Hang loose and stay covered," and hung up.

The football game was almost secondary for Jim and Ouida Bradshaw. It seemed that the true star of the game was their host. "You could read it on everybody's lips," the mayor pro tem said. *"There goes Cullen Davis!* You could tell that Cullen kinda liked it. Total strangers would come up and shake his hand. Some people from Fort Worth came up—they didn't know me from Adam, but they recognized Cullen. During the game Cullen would get on the phone and call around to the other boxes and people would drop by. After the game we went to the Cowboy Club. Same deal . . . people shaking his hand. Later we went to a private club. Cullen didn't have his card with him, but the manager recognized him. Some fellow sent over a card and a round of drinks. We got to talking about Acapulco. I'd just bought a villa there that I'd never seen. Cullen said, 'Let's go down there next week. We'll take the Learjet.' I said OK and we made tentative plans to leave the following Thursday."

It was close to 3:00 A.M. when Cullen and Karen said good night to the Bradshaws and headed home. Shortly after they arrived, McCrory called.

"He's finished with the job and wants to get out of here," McCrory told Cullen.

"How will I know?" Cullen asked.

"I've got the proof," McCrory said. "That's no sweat."

"All that information is down at the office," Cullen told him.

"You'll have to get it," McCrory said. "I don't want to talk. I can't fake it."

"What's the matter with in the morning?" Cullen asked.

"He wants to get gone," McCrory said. "Hold on." Someone was in the room with McCrory. Cullen heard McCrory tell someone, "He wants to go to his office." Then McCrory told Cullen: "Meet me at 9:00 A.M. Don't leave me hung out on this."

Cullen said, "No, that'll work out just fine." Then he hung up and went to bed.

McCrory had parked his car behind Coco's Famous Hamburgers and was reading the Sunday funnies. It wasn't yet nine o'clock, but it was already so hot the steering wheel burned his hands. He switched off the radio when he saw Cullen's Cadillac coming fast off the Loop 820 freeway. For some reason, Cullen stopped across the street and got out to examine a van parked there. Cullen shielded his eyes and tried to look through the windows, but blackout curtains blocked his view. He rapped once on the side of the van, then returned to his car and wheeled across the street. McCrory ran his hand over the .38 hidden in the waistband of his pants and wiped the sweat from his forehead. Cullen motioned for McCrory to join him in the Cadillac. "Just paranoid." Cullen laughed. McCrory noticed that Cullen's car radio was playing soft music. He wished it was off. In an envelope in his pocket, McCrory carried Judge Joe Eidson's driver's license, two other ID cards that belonged to the judge, and a photograph of Eidson's body stuffed in the trunk of a car. What appeared to be bullet holes and blood stained the back of the judge's white T-shirt.

McCrory said, "I got some . . . hey, I got something here. I've got something here. . . ." He handed an envelope to Cullen who examined it.

"I gotta go," McCrory said. "I got problems." He sounded nervous.

After a long pause Cullen returned the envelope and its contents. "Damn," he said. "You keep it."

McCrory said: "Uh, who do you want to go next? I have never gotten ahold of him to change any plans. I've got more fucking pressure on me right now than you can imagine."

"OK," Cullen told him. "What are you going to do with these?"

"I'm going to get rid of the motherfuckers," McCrory said.

"That's good. Glad to hear it," Cullen said.

"All right," McCrory said, "who do you want next?"

"Uh, the ones we talked about," Cullen told him.

"Bubba . . ."

"The three kids," Cullen interrupted.

"Bev, Bubba . . ."

"Yeah," Cullen said.

"All right, all right," McCrory said. "I gotta go."

"OK. Uh, just a minute," Cullen said.

"You going to get in the trunk?" McCrory asked.

"Uh-huh," Cullen responded.

The two men climbed out of the Cadillac. McCrory had the envelope with him. They walked to the rear of the car and Cullen opened the trunk.

McCrory indicated another envelope in the car trunk. "Is that it?" he asked.

"Yeah," Cullen said.

McCrory opened the envelope and rippled the money through his hands. It was $25,000 in $100 bills.

"Wait a second," McCrory said, looking toward his own car parked next to the Cadillac. "Wait just a second. I'm a scared motherfucker. I don't mind telling you. When you kill a man like Judge Eidson, hey, there is going to be more heat caused than you can imagine. Hold on. Leave the trunk up."

McCrory walked to his own car and returned with something wrapped in a white towel. He peeled back a corner of the towel and showed Cullen a .22 Ruger pistol equipped with an illegal silencer.

"Goddamn," Cullen said. "Pretty!"

"OK. Now you got it. Leave it . . ."

"Look at that motherfucker," Cullen said.

"All right. But leave it alone."

"I will," Cullen said.

"Let's go. I got to get out of here."

Cullen slammed the trunk lid and climbed back into his Cadillac.

337

McCrory leaned over the door and in a nervous, shaky voice said, "Now you want . . . you want Beverly Bass . . . killed next, quick, right?"

"All right, uh . . ." Cullen said.

"Now I don't want to make another mistake," McCrory told him. "You sure?"

"Yeah."

" 'Cause he's going to operate again tonight," McCrory said. Cullen said, "Oh. Well—" but McCrory interrupted him and said, "Hey, the man is good. He's the best I've ever seen."

"Just one problem," Cullen said. "I haven't got the money lined up."

"How long will it take?"

"I'll try to get it this week. I can get it in two days."

"I don't know whether I can keep him here two days or not, Cullen."

"How far does he have to go? Halfway across the the country?"

"He's out of New Orleans, he says. Fuck, I don't know. That's just what he told me. All right, I gotta go."

The two men talked for a few more minutes, then McCrory said, "I got Judge Eidson dead for you."

"Good," Cullen said.

"I'll get the rest of them dead for you. You want a bunch of people dead, right?"

"All right," Cullen replied.

As David McCrory walked back to his car, he glanced at the van across the street. Obviously Cullen hadn't seen the FBI agents inside taking pictures with a videotape camera. McCrory had a Nagra tape recorder strapped under his shirt. He wondered if you would be able to hear Cullen's voice over the music from the car radio.

McCrory drove north on Hulen, in the direction of the mansion, but after a few blocks he made a U-turn and headed back toward Coco's. He could see the surveillance plane off in the distance, tracking Cullen's Cadillac as it headed west on Loop 820. When the other car pulled up beside him, McCrory stopped. Texas

Ranger John Hogg raced to McCrory's car and grabbed the envelope with the $25,000. FBI special agent Ron Jannings grabbed the envelope with the picture of Judge Eidson's body, then shucked off McCrory's shirt and began removing the tape recorder.

David McCrory was back at Coco's drinking milk with Ranger John Hogg when the cops popped Cullen Davis. Cullen had stopped at a telephone booth near a Kentucky Fried Chicken place. A man with a shotgun shouted that Cullen was under arrest and ordered him to put his hands on the car hood. Cullen must have been fairly certain that they weren't after him for carrying an illegal silencer on his new .22.

Two years to the day after Tim Curry's men arrested Cullen boarding his Learjet and charged him with capital murder, Davis was charged with solicitation of murder. Two years to the very hour. Specifically, Cullen was charged with hiring a hit man to kill Judge Joe Eidson, though the case was far more complex than that.

In fact, Eidson was alive and well. He had been under twenty-four-hour guard since the previous Thursday when David McCrory first went to the FBI with his incredible story. Eidson agreed to pose for the picture in the car trunk. What appeared to be bullet holes in his T-shirt were cigarette burns put there by the FBI. The dark stains were catsup. According to McCrory, the judge was only one of fifteen names on Cullen Davis's hit list. Others marked for death, McCrory told the FBI, included Priscilla, Bev Bass, Bubba Gavrel, Gus Gavrel, Sr., W. T. Rufner, Dee Davis, Judge Tom Cave, and Bill Davis. Cullen also asked McCrory to get him a pistol with a silencer.

With Bill Davis, McCrory said, the plan was to kidnap him, kill him, and dispose of the body. Kidnapping is a federal crime, and it was this allegation that allowed the FBI to pursue the case without notifying local authorities. On Friday, August 18, as McCrory and Davis met in the parking lot at Coco's, McCrory was wired for sound. On Saturday the FBI brought the Texas Rangers, the Fort Worth police, and the district attorney's investigators into the case. The FBI set up a command post in a room at the Pilgrim Inn on Fort Worth's far west side and taped the telephone conversations between McCrory and Cullen before and again after the football game. By Sunday morning there were at least a dozen law enforcement officers assembled at the command post, three more flying surveillance in a single-engine plane, and four more agents positioned in the surveillance van to film the meeting. Just before McCrory left the motel for his rendezvous with Cullen, he was again wired for sound and supplied with the key items of evidence—the photo of Judge Eidson's body, the judge's identification cards, and the pistol with the silencer that another FBI agent had made over the weekend. Both McCrory and his car were thoroughly searched to make certain that the informant carried only evidence. They made one exception: McCrory was allowed to carry a .38 concealed in the waistband of his pants. After the Sunday morning meeting, one group of officers followed McCrory and a larger group went after Cullen, following directions radioed down from the surveillance plane.

News of Cullen's latest arrest spread across Fort Worth like a flash flood down a dry creek bed. Telephone circuits were jammed with people making inquiries and spreading the news. Mayor pro tem Jim Bradshaw was watching TV on his houseboat when the bulletin flashed along the lower part of the screen, superimposed over Jack Nicklaus lining up a putt. Bradshaw rushed home to await the anticipated calls from the media. The only person who called was Bill Magnussen, one of Cullen's attorneys. Magnussen, a longtime friend of Bradshaw's, said that Cullen asked him

340

to call as a courtesy. How thoughtful of Cullen, Bradshaw told his wife. Bradshaw waited several more hours, then called the *Star-Telegram* and told a reporter about accompanying Cullen and Karen to the football game the night before. "I don't know why I called to tell you this," Bradshaw said. "I just wanted somebody to know when all this comes out."

District Judge Byron Matthews also telephoned the *Star-Telegram*. Matthews, who had known Cullen for some time and was a close friend of Judge Tom Cave, asked a reporter for details about the arrest, then offered an intriguing sidelight. "I heard he was interested in getting me killed too," Matthews said. "I heard from more than one person that Cullen cussed me and said we [Matthews and Judge Tom Cave] were in conspiracy to keep him in jail."

Tom Cave took the startling news in stride. "I'd be surprised if I wasn't on his hit list," Cave said. "I do not delude myself into thinking I'm one of Cullen Davis's favorite people."

Jack Wilborn's telephone rang all day. Wilborn told a *Star-Telegram* reporter that a caller who refused to identify himself told him: "I just want you to know this isn't the first time Cullen Davis has tried to make these arrangements. Only he's never before been willing to put up $250,000." The curious thing about this call was the figure $250,000. The news bulletins had reported the figure as *$25,000*. It was several days before the media discovered that Joe Eidson was only one of fifteen names on the alleged hit list.

In the torrent of activities that interrupted this otherwise lethargic Sunday, no one thought to conduct a public opinion poll, but almost everyone in Fort Worth had an opinion. They fell into two more or less equal categories: (1) Cullen must be even crazier than anyone thought; (2) Priscilla framed him again. "It's a goddamn frame-up!" said Kay Davis, Ken Jr.'s daughter. "David McCrory is an opportunist. If Cullen wanted to hire somebody to kill Judge Eidson, he wouldn't go to someone like David McCrory." Others felt that McCrory was exactly the sort Cullen would pick for such an unsavory assignment. Cullen wasn't renowned for his judgment of character. Those who asked *why David McCrory?* might also ask why Cullen married Priscilla or why Roy Rimmer was his best friend.

Phil Burleson was driving to his office in downtown Dallas as the cops were busting his famous client. Burleson, who had been dating Kay Davis for some months, had lunched with Cullen the previous week, and as he cruised through the sparse Sunday morning traffic, he was thinking, "I wonder what Cullen is doing?" It wasn't an unusual thought, but the attorney felt the bone-tickling chill of clairvoyance a few minutes later when Cecil Munn called and said: "I've got a case that you've got some experience with. Cullen is back in jail." All Munn knew at this point was that Cullen had been charged with solicitation of murder and that police had recovered a gun from his car. "My first thought was that someone was dead," Burleson recalled. "The part about the gun didn't make sense, unless maybe they had finally found the murder weapon." Burleson tried to telephone Mike Gibson but couldn't locate him. He called Steve Sumner, who was mowing his lawn and icing down beer for a Sunday afternoon outing on his new boat. As Burleson and Sumner sped toward Fort Worth, the first bulletins were being broadcast across the Metroplex. Writer Tom Stephenson, who had played handball with Sumner the previous day, telephoned Sumner's wife and said: "I just heard the news. I guess this means you'll be adding a swimming pool to your new house."

Racehorse Haynes was enjoying a quiet Sunday on his sailboat when he heard the news on his ship-to-shore radio. "I don't have the foggiest notion what's going on," he told a reporter who radioed. "Is this the same McCrory who was involved before?" Told that it was, Haynes said, "It's curious." By Sunday night Cullen's blue-ribbon defense team was again assembled in Fort Worth.

Cullen was jailed without bond. Tim Curry cited a new state law, approved by referendum the previous November while Cullen was on trial in Amarillo, which

342

said that a person charged with committing a felony while free on bond from another felony can be held without bond. Ironically, the referendum was one of the issues that the Amarillo jury had voted on the afternoon Judge George Dowlen recessed court for the election. The defense argued that the Amarillo acquittal invalidated the other murder charges because the evidence in the cases was substantially the same. They cited the doctrine of *collateral estoppel* and requested an immediate bond hearing.

Since almost every judge in Tarrant County had either been involved with or had commented publicly on the Cullen Davis affair, visiting Judge Arthur Tipps of Wichita Falls was called in to hear the testimony. Tipps convened the bond hearing on August 23. Armed guards ringed the courtroom. Authorities had received a number of anonymous death threats directed at Cullen Davis. The atmosphere was supercharged; if people had been shocked and tititlated by what they heard in Amarillo about Priscilla being an "other-worlder," they were stunned by the allegation that Cullen led an underground life of his own. Pam Bass, Bev's sister, was in the crowd; so was Gus Gavrel, Sr. Karen Master was escorted by James Mabe, who had helped establish Cullen's alibi in Amarillo. Dressed in a tea-party blue frock, Karen told reporters: "My side of the family is wholeheartedly behind Cullen. They have seen him with my children and see how good he is with them. We love Cullen and will stand behind him to the end. I had my family over Monday night for dinner, and they said everyone they had talked to felt it was all a Priscilla frame-up." Priscilla pointedly avoided the bond hearing. If the prosecution blew this one, she told friends, "I don't want them to be able to say 'if it hadn't been for Priscilla . . .'" Priscilla wasn't surprised by the new allegations. "After Racehorse pulled the wool over their eyes in Amarillo," she said, "Cullen was sure he could get away with murder on a big scale. Cullen doesn't think like other people. If he gets away with something, he'll try it again. That's his way. I hope people realize now that he is capable of cold-blooded murder."

The state was attempting to show that Cullen was too dangerous to be allowed out on bond. To make their case prosecutors would have to reveal their key evidence—the sound and video recordings. This would give the defense more time to prepare for the actual trial—just as had happened in the Andrea Wilborn trial—but that risk seemed small to Tim Curry compared to the risk of letting Cullen walk the streets if he indeed had a hit list of fifteen people. Besides, Curry was confident. This time they had considerable physical evidence—the fake photograph of Eidson's body, the .22 with its illegal silencer, the $25,000, and the highly incriminating recordings. Curry had so many aces he couldn't see much harm in letting Racehorse Haynes see the cards.

Almost simultaneously with the bond hearing Curry was jolted by the unexpected resignation of a key assistant, Jerry Buckner, who had beaten Haynes in the Sylvia Meek case. Chief prosecutor Joe Shannon had resigned some months earlier to enter private practice. "I'm looking for a wealthy husband who has murdered his wife," Shannon joked to other lawyers. Tolly Wilson had been elevated to chief prosecutor, and with Jerry Buckner's sudden resignation Curry had to fill the void instantly. He selected Jack Strickland, a thirty-five-year-old assistant DA, to join the prosecutorial team. All Strickland knew about the Cullen Davis case was what he'd read and heard around the courthouse, but he was a quick learner and one of the brightest lawyers on the DA's staff. Tolly Wilson would handle the burden of the bond hearing while Strickland acquainted himself with the volumes of testimony already in evidence.

On the morning of August 23, David McCrory took the witness stand and began outlining his story of the weird chain of events that preceded Cullen's arrest. Tolly Wilson opened by asking McCrory if Cullen had offered any "reward" in Amarillo for testimony beneficial to his defense. Although McCrory hadn't testified in Amarillo, Wilson's question implied that the defense had at least attempted to buy him as a witness.

"He said he'd be able to help the people who helped him when he got those bastards off his neck," McCrory replied. McCrory said he didn't see Cullen again until after the acquittal. He didn't recall the date, but he remembered that Cullen came to his home and they got drunk together. Sometime after that Cullen called and wanted to meet him in the parking lot of Coco's. "He said he had a job for me," McCrory testified. McCrory said Cullen gave him $5,000 and told him to investigate Bev Bass, Bubba Gavrel, and the two attorneys representing Priscilla in the divorce suit. McCrory began monitoring the homes of Bass, Gavrel, Eidson, as well as the mansion where Priscilla was living. The witness told of the code names Cullen selected—McCrory was to be "Frank Johnson" and Cullen used the name "Dan Edwards." On June 12 Cullen hired McCrory as assistant to the president of Jet Air. About that same time, McCrory told the court, Cullen began speaking of killing some of the people who testified against him in Amarillo.

"We started talking about the future proceedings against him," McCrory said. "He wanted to know if I knew anyone that could get rid of somebody for him and what it would cost. I asked him if he was serious. He said he wanted to know just in case. . . . He said Bev Bass was the only witness in Amarillo that the jury believed, and he wanted [McCrory to find someone who would] kill her for money."

At first he didn't take Cullen seriously, McCrory said. At another meeting at Coco's, Cullen ordered McCrory to fly to Atlanta. McCrory was apparently supposed to meet a hit man in Atlanta, but the meeting never came off. Cullen told McCrory that the trip was "just a wild goose chase." Shortly after that Cullen allegedly told McCrory that "he'd thought about it and decided to go ahead and hire someone to kill Bev Bass. And I was to do the hiring." At this meeting, McCrory continued, Cullen told him: "If you cross me this time . . . I'll have you and your wife and your whole damn family killed, and don't think I won't do it."

Tolly Wilson asked McCrory if financing Bass's murder was discussed. McCrory said it was. "He wanted to know what I thought it would take. I estimated between $10,000 and $100,000."

McCrory recalled a meeting in June in which Cullen told him he'd decided to expand the hit list. "He told me he had decided to add some names. . . . He wanted Bev Bass, Bubba Gavrel, Bubba's father, and Judge Eidson killed."

Q: Did you think he was serious in his intention?

A: I thought he was halfway serious, but not anything I couldn't control.

Q: Could you tell the substance of the conversation?

A: He said he felt very, very sure that Judge Eidson was going to try to break him. He said . . . Judge Eidson was in cahoots with—in bed with, as he said it—Priscilla's attorneys.

A few weeks later, McCrory continued, he again met Cullen at Coco's, only this time Cullen had expanded his hit list to fifteen. To the previous list Cullen added the names of Priscilla, Tom Cave, W. T. Rufner, and his brother Bill Davis. "He said he didn't want to tell me the names of the rest of them right then," McCrory recalled. "I told him it would cost so much money that even he couldn't afford it." Cullen supposedly replied that he would spend whatever amount necessary, but that he had to know the date of each hit so that he could establish an alibi.

At a July meeting, McCrory testified, Cullen brought up the subject of a pistol with a silencer. McCrory advised him such a weapon would be expensive. Then Cullen asked for specific prices for each name on his list. McCrory testified that he fabricated some prices— $100,000 for Eidson, $75,000 for Bass, $75,000 for each of the Gavrels, $200,000 for Priscilla.

"He said they were too high," McCrory said. "He said he'd pay $30,000 to have Beverly Bass killed, and he wanted it done right away."

In late July or early August, McCrory continued, Davis became more specific about what he wanted done and how.

"He told me . . . he'd come up with a solution to take the heat off him over her [Bass] being killed," Mc-

346

Crory told the court. "He said we should throw down a white substance—he suggested a sugar substitute—and break it open and throw it down wherever she was killed. He said I needed to purchase a small amount of cocaine or heroin and leave it at the scene. Then they would think it was a drug-related killing. Maybe it would be better to grab her, drop the sugar substitute and cocaine, and take her somewhere, never let the body be found, and cut her up and scatter her so nobody could find the body."

McCrory told of a meeting in early August in which Cullen suggested two ways to kill Eidson and put the blame on the Brown Berets, a militant group of Mexican-Americans.

"He said go into the house during the daytime, get his [Eidson's] wife, knock her out; then when the judge came in, kill them both," McCrory said. As an alternate plan, the killer could wait "until he comes out to turn the water on his lawn off. Then knock his head, carry him off, and be out of the area before anyone knows he's gone. He said get a Mexican-American driver's license and cap and drop them at the scene . . . then send a tape to some TV station and let the Brown Berets take the blame for it."

By the first week in August, McCrory continued, Cullen was "very unhappy" that no one had been murdered.

"He said something's got to happen. He said he was very sure Judge Eidson was going to try to break him. He knew Judge Eidson was . . . in bed with . . . Priscilla's attorneys. . . ." For emphasis, McCrory said, Cullen repeated his threats to have McCrory and his family "slaughtered." A few days later, McCrory met with FBI agent Ron Jannings.

That same day, at the FBI's request, McCrory purchased the .22 Ruger pistol from a Fort Worth sporting goods store.

Silence settled over the packed courtroom as prosecutors played the FBI tape of McCrory's Friday meeting with Cullen.

McCrory: I've got a little present for you [the gun].

347

Cullen: Well, that's nice.

McCrory: Just what you ordered. They haven't got . . .

Cullen: Just what the doctor ordered?

McCrory: They haven't got the silencer made yet, but they're working on it.

Cullen: When will it be ready?

McCrory: Just a few days. Don't point that SOB at me.

Cullen: Huh?

McCrory: Don't point that SOB at me. No, you have . . . uh, the bottom.

Cullen: Here?

McCrory: You have to pull this back. Is that sweet?

Cullen: All right!

McCrory: That is sweet. Now, do you want the . . . uh, do you want all this taken off, the numbers?

Cullen: Well, can you get 'em off?

McCrory: I don't know whether they can't ever be brought out or not, but they can take 'em off. If I was you, I would rather have it with 'em just like it is.

Cullen: Yeah.

McCrory: 'Cause that's out of the factory. You don't have to worry about it. They got to do a lot of work on the front end of it. Take all that off, make a silencer go on it.

Cullen: Huh?

McCrory: They got to do a lot of work on the front end of it to make a silencer go on it.

Cullen: They have to modify this to . . .

McCrory: Oh, yeah.

Cullen: Before the thing will go on there?

McCrory: Yeah. Uh, we got somewhat of a problem. The man is here to put the judge away. Uh, he is ready. He just found out that he was a judge, and he wants a lot more fucking money. Uh, I just threw my hands up and said look, I . . . that's the most money you can get. And he said, "Well, fuck you, that's a judge and it's gonna bring more heat." I said, well, the money's, you know, there. But he wants . . . the SOB wants $100,000 to, uh . . .

Cullen: Bullshit!

McCrory: Well, I told him bullshit too, Cullen, but goddamn, there's not anything I can do when it's in the fucking paper every day. You know, he's on TV, he's in the paper . . . what else can I do?

Cullen: I don't know.

McCrory: Well, now, Priscilla is a different story. That's . . . you know . . . he'd rather do Priscilla than the judge. I don't know. He says he can do it easy.

Cullen: Huh! Like hell!

McCrory: Well?

Cullen: Priscilla's always got somebody around her. The judge doesn't.

McCrory: Now the way . . . you know, the way we talked about doing it, he doesn't see that to be any problem. . . . You're gonna have to alibi for me for the last two days. You're gonna have to tell him [Jet Air president Art Smith] he was working for me.

Cullen: Why weren't you there?

McCrory: Well, you know, I had shit that I had to get done. You can't get this kind of shit done, Cullen, with having to be stuck under his fucking thumb twenty-four hours a day. It's impossible. Now, wipe that SOB [the gun], take the clip out and wipe it down. You handled the clip too, so wipe it down. Now, the . . . uh, does it make any difference to you what color the silencer is or you just want one with a fucking silencer, period? The Brown Beret cap? Just to drop by the judge? Shit, man, where do you find one of them motherfuckers? If you're gonna blame it on the Brown Berets, where in the fuck do you find one of their caps? There's not any.

Cullen: Beats the shit out of me.

McCrory: Give me a price on Priscilla. He says he'd rather do Priscilla than the judge so if you give me a price on Priscilla . . . I'll just lay it in his lap, unless you want to talk to the motherfucker.

Cullen: Who's that?

McCrory: The shooter.

Cullen: Yeah?

McCrory: I think you'd be making . . . well, fuck,

349

you may not. He may trust you more than he trusts me.

Cullen: You're supposed to be handling that.

McCrory: Well, I . . . fuck, I can understand your point. I'm doing the very fucking best I can, Cullen. I have had my hands tied in a lot of ways trying to do things. I mean I busted my goddamn ass working for Art [Smith]. I have really busted my ass.

Cullen: You just can't keep being absent.

McCrory: Well, fuck, I know that.

Cullen: Like that . . . I can't fade that . . , all this, and, uh, nothing's happening here either. Nothing's . . . absolutely nothing's happening. Go back to the original plan.

McCrory: What do you mean the original plan?

Cullen: Uh, get the other one, you know, who we started this out with.

McCrory: You mean Priscilla?

Cullen: No.

McCrory: Oh, Bev?

Cullen: Yeah, with . . .

McCrory: Boy, you gonna bring more fucking heat down on you, Cullen. You have that SOB killed, I promise you, you gonna have heat. Well, you know what you're doing. I'm sure you've thought it out. I'll do whatever you want done. You still want all three of them at once?

Cullen: Do it either way. Whatever is there.

McCrory talked some more about his problems with his quasi boss, Art Smith, and about the possibility that Gus Gavrel, Sr., might grab a shotgun and come looking for Cullen, and about a trip to Mexico to pick up some drugs, apparently to sprinkle around the body of Bev Bass, and about the divorce trial which had just been postponed. Then McCrory returned to the hit man.

McCrory: What if he does all three of those and just goes right on? This is the reason I told you, you may want to talk to him. He, uh, wants his fucking money, and he wants it immediately. . . .

Cullen: Immediately?

McCrory: Just as soon as he gets the job done, he wants to be paid.

Cullen: Well, I will . . . he will be.

McCrory: OK.

Cullen: You just get in touch with me any time afterwards that you want to, and it'll . . .

McCrory: Well, it's got to be immediately afterwards, that's the problem. That's the problem because I don't have the fucking money.

Cullen: You just call me and it's—you got it.

McCrory: OK, how are we gonna do that now? If he moves tonight or tomorrow night on her, what do we do? I mean how are we gonna get money exchanged? You know how much fucking spying and everything I've done on her already. I'm, you know, hot as a pistol. . . . I've got to be out of the picture somewhat when she goes, uh, down.

Cullen: Well, you know when it's gonna happen. You can always cover your . . . get yourself covered, real good.

McCrory: Uh, when are you gonna be covered?

Cullen: I'm going to—I'm covered all the time.

McCrory: You're staying covered.

Cullen: I'm staying covered. I'm not taking any chances. If I wasn't gonna be covered, I was gonna let you know. Any time that I'm not gonna be, I'm gonna let you know. That's the way we're gonna work that deal.

McCrory: Hey, now, we're friends. You're not gonna do something stupid with this fucking gun, are you?

Cullen: No, I'm gonna give it back to you right now.

McCrory: Well, I know, but I'm talking about with the silencer and all that shit . . .

Cullen: No.

McCrory: I don't know what the fuck you want with the silencer myself.

Cullen: (Unintelligible)

McCrory: Self-protection, my ass.

Cullen: You don't think I'm not going to keep on protecting myself, do you?

They talked some more about McCrory's poor at-

351

tendance record at Jet Air. Then McCrory directed the conversation back to the hit man and the first victim.

McCrory: Well, this man's good, Cullen. He's supposedly one of the best.

Cullen: Well, you just . . . whenever you need the money, whatever day that is, you just call.

McCrory: OK, you definitely want her to go down before the judge?

Cullen: Yeah, I want to . . .

McCrory: Why? I don't understand it.

Cullen: Well . . .

McCrory: I mean, I'll go along with whatever you say, but what are you gonna do if the SOB wants to do . . . you know, they're awful close together. If he grabs that judge up and puts him in his car, knocks him out and puts him in his car and takes him off, which is what he said he'd do, uh, there's gonna be a helluva stink but not near as much as if he left the SOB bloody and bleeding in his driveway. Or, walk in the house and have to blow up the judge and his wife and anybody else that might happen to be there.

Cullen: Well, he's not gonna be wandering in there if there's anybody else there. He's gonna . . . he'd know what he's doing better'n that. Do the judge, then his wife, and that would be it.

McCrory: Yes, but he ain't gonna leave any witnesses.

Cullen: Or if he . . . he might catch the judge, uh, coming in the house or something like that.

McCrory: No, the judge goes out, and remember, the judge goes out and waters his . . . turns his fucking water off. That's when he's gonna get him. Uh, but he doesn't want to leave him there. He wants to hit him, uh . . .

Cullen: What good's . . .

McCrory: . . . snatch him up and take him off.

Cullen: What good's that gonna do?

McCrory: Well, it's . . . man, there's a lot of difference. There ain't near as much heat. Uh, you know they can't prove much unless they find a body.

Cullen: Well—

352

McCrory: You know that's what he's gonna do with her. If it's her by herself.

Cullen: Let's plan to getting all three of 'em over there.

McCrory: It's a hard son of a bitch, but . . .

Cullen: It's the best way.

McCrory talked for a while about the possibility of blowing up someone (possibly the Gavrels) in their motor home; then McCrory told Cullen he would call him Saturday morning.

McCrory: All right, let's get the fuck out of here. I've got things to do, people to see.

Cullen: All right.

After some small talk, McCrory again returned to the subject of murder.

McCrory: Hey, if he works . . . if he goes to work, uh, and gets her like tonight or tomorrow night, don't leave me hanging 'cause that motherfucker will kill me, Cullen.

Cullen: I've got it. It—it's—

McCrory: OK, just don't leave me hanging.

Cullen: I won't.

McCrory: All right.

Cullen: Go back to plan, plan . . .

McCrory: Well, now, he may take a bunch of them off. That's what I want you to know.

Cullen: Hm?

McCrory: He may take a bunch of them off at once. Uh, I mean he's that kind of person, and he may just waste the shit out of a bunch of 'em and get a bunch of it over with at once.

Cullen: Well.

McCrory: If . . .

Cullen: That suits the shit out of me.

McCrory: All right. Now, there is something I need to . . . come here just a second. There's something I need to ask you. How much money is he going to get if he gets Priscilla? I mean you've got . . . man, I've got to tell him something. If you want the bitch dead, then you got to tell me how much it's . . . I mean, he says he can do 'em all, you know.

Cullen: One at a time.

McCrory: I know, but tell me something.

Cullen: Uh, I'll have to think on that one.

Pale and grim-faced, his jaws clenched, Cullen listened to the tape and watched as FBI agent Joseph Gray arranged for the videotaped scenes of Cullen's Sunday morning meeting with McCrory. There was not the slightest doubt that the voices on the tapes belonged to McCrory and to Cullen Davis. The audio and the video hadn't been synchronized so McCrory narrated as the FBI agent showed the films of the Sunday morning meeting.

"That's Cullen getting out of his Cadillac. . . . That's me getting out of my car. I have an envelope in my hand. . . . Cullen is opening the trunk of his car. He is in the process of getting an envelope out of the trunk. . . . I have picked up the pistol wrapped in a towel and placed it in the trunk of his car. We are looking at it. . . . Now we are talking. He is sitting down in his car. . . . We're still talking. . . . Now he is shutting the door of his car and I'm getting in my car. He's driving off. . . ."

McCrory testified that he had shown Cullen the Polaroid picture of the judge's body, along with Eidson's driver's license and state bar card. McCrory identified the .22 Ruger with the silencer as the weapon that he gave Davis and told of quickly flipping through the $25,000 in $100 bills that had been locked in the trunk of Cullen's Cadillac. Later the court heard the tapes of the Sunday meeting, including this exchange:

McCrory: I got Judge Eidson dead for you.

Cullen: Good.

McCrory: I'll get the rest of them dead for you. You want a bunch of people dead, right?

Cullen: All right.

Earlier in the same recording, the two men apparently talked about the killer's next victims.

McCrory: All right, who do you want next?

Cullen: Uh, the ones we talked about.

McCrory: Bubba . . .

Cullen: The three kids.

McCrory: Bev, Bubba . . .

Cullen: Yeah.

It wasn't clear who Cullen meant by the three kids, though prosecutors speculated that the unnamed third person was Dee Davis. Although Dee hadn't testified at Amarillo, she was a potential witness in any future criminal or civil action. Nor was it clear what Cullen intended to do with the gun and silencer. "A silencer is a single-purpose weapon," DA Tim Curry observed. "Its single purpose is to kill." Kill whom? The prosecutors believed that Davis planned to kill McCrory, thus eliminating the final witness to the plot. Even though the FBI had shortened the firing pin on the .22 so that it was ostensibly harmless, McCrory believed that his life was in danger. He told prosecutors that when Cullen stopped to examine the FBI surveillance van just prior to their Sunday morning meeting, he reached for the .38 concealed in the waistband of his pants. "He was scared to death," Tolly Wilson said. "He really thought he was going to have to kill Davis when Davis looked in that van. He thought Davis had caught him." When Cullen laughed and said, "Just paranoid," McCrory eased his hand away from the .38 and went on with the charade.

Though the film and tapes appeared to be devastating evidence, the flaw in the state's case was David McCrory himself. Phil Burleson noted that "his reputation is such that he couldn't even get into the Book-of-the-Month Club." As expected, Racehorse Haynes focused his cross-examination on McCrory's credibility in the same manner the defense had attacked the three eye-witnesses in Amarillo. McCrory was a proven liar; in fact, the state acknowledged in Amarillo that McCrory was "not worthy of belief as a witness." The defense was already drafting a scenario designed to show that McCrory, Priscilla, and their mutual friend Pat Burleson (Phil Burleson's distant cousin) had conspired to frame Cullen.

In quick order McCrory acknowledged that he had stolen money from Cullen Davis, had chronic problems with the IRS, and lied several times about those and other problems. Haynes avoided mentioning the incriminating film and tapes, but he appeared to be seeding the record for some future testimony. Haynes knew from experience that recorded conversations were not automatic proof of guilt. In 1973 Haynes defended Tarrant County attorney John Foster on charges of conspiring to bribe a county commissioner. The foundation of the prosecution's case was a conversation recorded while the county commissioner was wired for sound. Haynes suggested that Foster had been set up and reminded the jury that it was the county commissioner, not his client, who brought up the question of money. Foster was acquitted.

In great detail Haynes tracked the Las Vegas holiday that McCrory and his wife took in late June. McCrory had already testified that Cullen gave him $50,000 to launder. Instead of exchanging the money, McCrory admitted to Haynes, he had gambled away part of it, taken $5,000 for himself, and returned the remainder of the unlaundered money to Cullen. Racehorse stopped short of asking why McCrory hadn't laundered the money.

Haynes pounded him with long and detailed questions concerning the money, McCrory's banking practices, employment record, IRS troubles, and personal life. Time after time, McCrory replied, "I don't know" or "I don't remember." At one point he couldn't remember the maiden name of one of his ex-wives or the name of the city where they were married.

Haynes asked the witness if he ever told anyone it cost him $13,000 to rid himself of problems with Internal Revenue.

"I may have," McCrory responded. "If I did so, it was a lie. I told several stories about it."

McCrory admitted that he had not paid income taxes during the past four years and told of receiving anonymous telephone threats relating to his IRS problems while he was in Amarillo for the trial.

"They said I was going to be turned in to the IRS if I signed certain statements. Others said I would be turned in if I didn't sign the statements," McCrory said.

Haynes asked what these problems with the IRS involved.

"My problems arrived when you and Steve Sumner said you'd take care of it in Amarillo," McCrory replied.

Haynes quickly shot back, "I didn't ask you that. Has someone instructed you to say those things?"

"No, sir," McCrory said.

For the next several days McCrory entered and exited the courtroom escorted by two burly U.S. marshals. The FBI had enrolled the star witness in their Federal Witness Protection Program, which included moving his wife and family to a new location with a new identity.

The defense continued to grill McCrory about the money—the $5,000 that the informant admitted stealing from the Las Vegas money and the remainder of another $5,000 that Cullen allegedly gave him to investigate Bass, Gavrel, and the two lawyers. McCrory said that he gave part of the money to his seventeen-year-old son. "I told him if anything happened to me, I wanted him to have money to go to college," McCrory said. He gave the remaining money to his wife, McCrory said. The defense was taking the position that if McCrory actually had all that money in some secret bank account, it came from a source other than Cullen Davis. The implication was that Priscilla was paying him to help frame Cullen.

Haynes attempted to pin McCrory down on how often Cullen discussed a specific price tag for the names on his alleged hit list.

Q: How many times did you talk about how much money it would take to have someone dispatched?

A: Every time we met, I guess.

Q: And did the authorities suggest prices you should quote?

A: No, sir, I came up with them myself.

Q: Off the top of your head?

A: No, sir, I'd thought about it.

Q: But you made them up?

A: I tried to come up with a figure he couldn't pay.

Q: You already knew Mr. Davis was a wealthy man?

357

A: Yes, but he had told me about money problems he was having with his divorce.

Haynes chipped away, revealing small contradictions and probing at McCrory's relationship with Priscilla. The lawyer seemed to be attempting to confuse rather than enlighten the record. His questions were uncharacteristically awkward, and he frequently changed subjects in mid-sentence. At one point Haynes asked McCrory about a conversation he had with defense attorney Steve Sumner. McCrory said he couldn't recall all the conversation.

Q: Well, one thing you talked about was the prenuptial agreement, wasn't it?

A: I'm sorry, I don't know, Mr. Haynes. Please don't get mad at me, Mr. Haynes.

Q: Do you think I'm mad at you? Are you afraid, confused?

A: Well, not totally.

Q: Well, why would you be afraid and confused?

A: Well, if you had somebody with as much experience as you have over me, wouldn't you be scared?

With that, Haynes unexpectedly concluded his cross-examination of David McCrory. Some courthouse observers wondered if Race was losing his touch or going soft. Others merely wondered what scenario was brewing in the back of his mind. At first McCrory had refused to reveal the name of the person who put him in contact with the FBI, but under orders from Judge Tipps he admitted that it was Pat Burleson, a longtime friend of Priscilla Davis. Haynes revealed that McCrory first told his story to Burleson on Wednesday, August 16. That same day, Priscilla visited Burleson's downtown karate school. On Thursday, Burleson contacted FBI agent Ron Jannings, then visited the mansion. McCrory and Burleson met twice more that day, then rendezvoused with Agent Jannings that night. On Friday, August 18, as McCrory met with FBI agents, Burleson again visited Priscilla at the mansion.

It was a familiar song, but it wasn't enough to get Cullen out on bond. If this was another conspiracy against Cullen, as the defense contended, it apparently involved the FBI, the Texas Rangers, the Fort Worth Police Department, and the district attorney and his staff. On Friday, September 1, Judge Tipps ruled that Cullen Davis must remain in jail until he stood trial on the charge of solicitation of murder. Pale and visibly shaken, Cullen was led from the courtroom.

Kay Davis, Karen Master, and Karen's two sisters sat near the front of the courtroom, a quartet of beauties with teased blonde hair and fingers encrusted with gold and diamonds. Karen, a model of Fort Worth motherhood in her prim, high-necked cream blouse and tan Ultrasuede skirt, chewed gum throughout the hearing and from time to time whispered to nine-year-old Trey, who squirmed on the uncomfortable bench. When the judge announced his ruling, Trey crawled into his mother's lap, wrapped his arms around her neck, and cried. "OK, it's over," Karen told her son, dabbing at her own tears with a lace handkerchief. "Chin up," she said, taking the boy by the hand and leading him out of the courtroom.

Immediately after the bond hearing Joe Eidson disqualified himself from presiding over the divorce trial. Judge Tom Cave made a similar decision, though he didn't announce it for several weeks. Though Cave obviously could not preside over a case in which he was allegedly an intended victim, he had decided to move the case out of Fort Worth and was determined to rule over the change of venue proceedings. Cave was already contacting judges in other cities. To no one's great surprise, Cullen's lawyers stubbornly resisted moving the trial out of Fort Worth, and the venue hearing lasted almost as long as the bond hearing. At the last minute Cave disqualified himself and brought in visiting judge Arthur Tipps, who agreed that Davis could not get a fair and impartial trial in his hometown and ordered the trial moved to Houston.

Judge Tipps selected an old friend, Harris County judge Wallace "Pete" Moore, to hear the murder-for-hire case. Though Pete Moore was a friend of Racehorse Haynes, he was considered a hard-nosed judge unlikely to give anyone special considerations. Pete

Moore called the case "an ordinary felony" and announced that Cullen Davis would be treated like any other accused felon. And so it was that on his forty-fifth birthday, Cullen was transferred to Houston and booked into a small, stiflingly hot cell to await trial.

The incredible turn of events in the affairs of Cullen Davis attracted national and international attention and created shock waves from the Colonial Country Club to Wall Street to Caracas. Regardless of the outcome, the new trial meant that Cullen's assets would continue to be frozen for an indefinite period. A rumor circulated that Mid-Continent was experiencing a serious cash crunch and would be forced to go public. Profits at Stratoflex, for example, dropped 72 percent in 1977. With the oil industry in general experiencing a great resurgence, speculators kept a sharp eye on the Kendavis empire. Cullen's loss was certain to be someone's gain.

Fort Worth society also felt the shock waves and went quietly about its business of reevaluating its peerage. Mrs. Catherine Lipscomb revealed that Cullen's name was being dropped from the *Fort Worth Social Directory*.

"Enough is enough," Mrs. Lipscomb explained.

Judge Pete Moore was not a man to be taken lightly. He had presided over the 184th District Court in Houston for nearly ten years, and nobody had ever mistaken him for a cream puff. Moore had been a combat fighter pilot in World War II and again in Korea. He was a bourbon drinker and a chain smoker, and his soft gravelly voice carried the ring of absolute authority. He wasn't a man to be coerced or stampeded. A few years before, when an accused killer brandished a jail-made

360

knife and attempted to escape from one of Moore's bailiffs, the judge jumped down from the bench and pinned the defendant against the courtroom wall. Attorneys as well as defendants recognized the prudence of treading softly in Moore's court; the door leading to the jailhouse was a few feet from the bench, and Pete Moore was not loath to show it to any party whose behavior he found intolerable. The judge was well respected on both sides of the legal community. As an ex-prosecutor he was always able to see their point. But he was a fair man. The Texas Criminal Lawyers Association, a group that normally puts judges in the same category as hangmen, broke precedent in 1974 and named Moore the judge who most exemplified their concept of judicial fairness, the only time in history the organization had voted such an award. "Even if you're on the hurting end," said Stuart Kinard, president of the Criminal Lawyers Association, "his rulings command respect." Moore's longtime friend Racehorse Haynes agreed with this evaluation. "He's an A-number-one guy," Haynes said. "A very able lawyer and very able judge."

Moore let it be known from the start that he would not permit his courtroom to be turned into an inquisition or a circus. He meant what he said about treating Cullen Davis like any other prisoner. Prisoners were allowed only one change of clothes, so early each morning Karen Master appeared at the Harris County jail with a fresh change. Cullen was escorted to and from the courtroom just like any other accused felon. He was permitted to speak to no one except his lawyers and other officers of the court. Mike Gibson complained: "When we need to talk to Cullen, we have to go to this tiny sweatbox of a room in the basement. But that's the way they do it in Houston." Members of the press were cautioned against trying to talk to Cullen or trespassing over the audience side of the bar. No exceptions were tolerated. The gaggle of courthouse groupies who attended Cullen in Amarillo either didn't find their way to Houston or gave it up as a lost cause. As a security measure the defendant was assigned to a single-occupancy cell, but it was the same sort of cramped, dismal cell occupied by other prisoners: no telephones, no private TV, a minimum of personal effects. The sick green walls of Cullen's cell enclosed the same decor as the other cells—a tiny porcelain sink and toilet side by side at the foot of a cot. Cullen had a shelf for his files of papers and newspaper clippings. For privacy the multimillionaire fastened a pillowcase to the bars. Cullen ate jailhouse food and at the end of each day's proceedings changed his $300 suits for jailhouse whites.

Houston wasn't Amarillo or Fort Worth, and Pete Moore certainly wasn't George Dowlen. Even before the start of jury selection, Moore made several rulings that rocked the defense. There would be no irrelevant testimony aimed at assassinating the character of any witness, the judge said. To prove their conspiracy theory the defense clearly needed to question Priscilla, but when they attempted to waive their privilege against a wife testifying against her husband, Moore blocked the motion. The state had no intention of calling Priscilla as a witness, but, as the judge noted, a favorable ruling on the defense's motion would have allowed the defense "to stick it in their ear at the end and demand to know why they hadn't called Priscilla if they had nothing to hide." There was nothing in the rules to prohibit the defense from calling Priscilla, but they wouldn't be able to impeach her or ask leading questions the way they would had she been a witness for the prosecution. The defense had hoped that Moore would allow them to question prospective jurors individually and then sequester the chosen twelve, but Moore refused and ordered both sides to get about their work as quickly as possible. Moore cautioned the fifty-member jury panel to avoid any exposure to the case outside the courtroom and obey all instructions from the bench as though they were the Ten Commandments. "If you do it my way," he told the panel, "we'll all go home at night."

No one was surprised that all fifty members of the panel had heard about the Cullen Davis case. By the end of the first day of jury selection, Monday, October 30, Moore had excused twelve of the panel, either because they had formed some opinion or, in a few cases, because a lengthy trial would pose an extreme hardship. Both the prosecution and the defense told the panel that the trial could last four or five weeks, but Moore interrupted and said, "It's not going to take that long." By the end of the second day the panel had dwindled to thirty-four. Since each side would be allowed to strike ten prospects without cause, this was just two more than the minimum needed to assure a full box of twelve jurors. Both sides thought that it would be necessary to call fifty more candidates, but Moore disagreed and predicted that testimony would start the following Monday. He was right.

After four and a half days the attorneys had their jury. It had taken two months in Amarillo.

The dispatch with which the judge had moved them through jury selection no doubt handicapped the defense, as did the enormous size and diversity of the city of Houston. There was no way the defense could do the detailed jury analysis in Houston that they had done in Amarillo. Not that they didn't try. Steve Sumner's squad of investigators checked crisscross directories and public records and drove by potential jurors' homes, but it was a cursory survey compared to the study done on the citizens of Amarillo. Houston was not only big, it was a city out of control, a city without focus, a nonmalleable sprawl. It was like Los Angeles except there were no mountains to give it character and no seashore to give it relief; the Gulf of Mexico was sixty miles down the bayou, and instead of palm trees the coastal plain was jutted with the smokestacks of petrochemical plants and oil refineries. It was a city of constant movement and contradiction and classic Texas can-do mentality. Despite its distance from the sea, the port of Houston was the second largest in the nation: one out of every three dollars generated by the local economy was traceable to shipping. Some large cities like Dallas were declining or at least leveling out, but Houston grew like a monstrous vegetable in a concrete rain forest, swelling and sprawling and eating away at its environs with an appetite so out of check that nobody even bothered trying to zone it. Each month something like 3,000 newly registered automobiles joined the jam of Houston's already horrendously over-crowded freeways. The climate was worse than Calcutta's, so awful that no place on earth had more cubic tons of air-conditioning. The city thrived on contradictions: its medical facilities and revolutionary lifesaving techniques were unsurpassed, and yet few places on earth had a higher murder rate. Even as it reached up and out into the boundless skies of the Texas Gulf Coast, the city was literally sinking a few inches each year into the swamp. No one seemed especially alarmed by the contradictions; no one seemed even to notice. One thing in Cullen Davis's favor was that no twelve people in Houston were likely to share the same opinion about anything.

Racehorse Haynes had lived all his life in Houston. He didn't claim to have a fix on the city, but he did know the type of juror he wanted. His defense was going to be complicated, and so he looked for intelligence, or more accurately an ability to *conceptualize*. Since his client was forty-five, Race wanted an older-than-average jury. He wanted jurors who held strong beliefs in the value of money and material things, but who were content with their situation in life and not likely to resent a man who inherited millions. When it got down to hard cuttings, Haynes would rely on instinct, but he intended to give himself (and his client) any edge he could devise. For a time during the jury selection in Amarillo, Haynes employed the services of Dr. Margaret Covington, a psychologist who prepared profiles of prospective jurors. Dr. Covington had arrived at some broad statistical profiles common to certain professions—engineers, for example, tended to be obsessively compulsive, introverted, good with details and with logic. Covington was again invited to help with the defense of Cullen Davis. There had been speculation that the defense might also hire Bruce Vaughan, a Dallas "personologist" who claimed to be able to discern personalities by studying physiognomies, facial and body traits that were believed to reveal a person's thought

364

process. Vaughan charged $500 a day, but in the nine cases he had worked to date his record was perfect. If the defense did entertain thought of adding Vaughan to the team, they backed off in a hurry when Vaughan told a *Star-Telegram* reporter that he had studied Cullen Davis's physiognomy and concluded that "he is capable of everything he has been accused of—very capable." In particular Vaughan noted Davis's extremely flat eyebrows ("competitiveness—can't stand to lose"), his small irises ("unemotional and self-centered"), and the thin-ridged nose ("they relate to money . . . and power").

The seven men and five women finally chosen to decide Cullen Davis's fate were surprisingly homogeneous, an indication that both sides were seeking the same types. They were white, middle-class Protestants (one was Catholic) whose ages averaged close to fifty. Seven had attended college and three had degrees. Ten were either self-employed or professionals—an oil company executive, a medical technologist, a NASA space shuttle flight controller, a dealer in rare stamps. All knew Racehorse Haynes by reputation, and one of them, Mrs. Robert Carter, a strong-willed forty-seven-year-old medical secretary, was an unabashed fan of the famous attorney. "I thought your name was a household word in Houston," she told Haynes during the voir dire. The panelist who most concerned the prosecution was Frances Hambrick, who described herself as a soap opera fan and offered up the opinion that the Davis case was just like the things she saw on TV. Prosecutor Jack Strickland complained that Mrs. Hambrick "was too forthright when she said she just had a ninth-grade education and too friendly with Haynes." The prosecution offered no explanation, however, when they accepted her for the jury. The defense had serious misgivings about panelist Charles Franks, a thirty-one-year-old electrical engineer who admitted to Haynes that he would give more weight to the testimony of a policeman than he would to that of a layman. "He damned sure was an honest guy," Haynes admitted with a double-edged smile. "He can look you right in the eye and say he's got a bias." Nevertheless, Haynes argued that the court should allow the defense an extra strike in order to eliminate Franks from the jury. After satisfying himself that Franks could serve impartially, Moore refused and Franks took his seat with the others.

Prosecutors spent the weekend reviewing and revising their list of witnesses. Their case was in very good shape. The state had already decided that their star witness would be the tapes themselves, that McCrory would be presented as nothing more than a cog in the intensive and thorough investigation done by special agents of the FBI; McCrory's purpose was to corroborate the tapes, not vice versa. Assistant prosecutor Jack Strickland struck a confident pose and predicted victory, but beneath his bluster was a note of caution. "The tapes are irrefutable," he said. "If we can't convict Cullen Davis with this type of evidence, I don't think any court in the country can ever convict him of anything. If this jury turns him loose, the man will have proven that he is above the law. He'll be free to do anything he wants." Strickland had became a favorite with the media. All during the pretrial and jury selection, Strickland talked freely with reporters. His cocky, flamboyant style was a perfect counterpoint to the style of Racehorse Haynes, who was keeping unusually quiet. It seemed to chief prosecutor Tolly Wilson that Strickland enjoyed his role a little too much. An excellent lawyer, Tolly was a solemn man with a dour, plodding style; compared to his tall, lean, handsome, eloquent assistant, Tolly came across like a grumpy grandpa, irate that time had passed him by. Privately, Wilson and Strickland had already clashed over several points of strategy, including their order of witnesses. Strickland wanted to lead off with Judge Eidson, the "victim" in the charges against Cullen Davis. He felt that the allegations would be much more effective if Eidson first described that nightmarish Saturday night when he had agreed to pose as a dead man, but Wilson overruled him. Tolly's first choice was FBI agent Ron Jannings, who supervised the investigation of McCrory's allegations.

After two days of testimony from agent Jannings it

was apparent that the prosecution was off to a less than brilliant beginning. Jannings told of being contacted by Pat Burleson, who had taught him karate, and about the series of meetings with David McCrory, the tapes of Mc-Crory's meetings with Cullen Davis, the faked photo of Eidson's bloodstained body, and finally the exchange of the silencer and the $25,000. Wilson did the questioning; he was as methodical as Jannings was unemotional. In cross-examination Haynes went to work slowly and deliberately. Instead of attacking Jannings's story, Haynes used the FBI agent to outline his own scenario. He asked Jannings about the FBI investigation of the extortion letter sent to Cullen Davis shortly after the Amarillo trial and made a point of informing the jury that Davis was extremely upset over the manner in which the FBI handled the investigation. In the bond hearing and again in pretrial Haynes had brought up the name of a mysterious used-car dealer named David Binion, hinting that the defense would establish that Priscilla tried to hire Binion to kill Cullen Davis, and now he used Jannings to resurrect Binion's name for the jury. Binion had done undercover work for Jannings, but the FBI agent refused to answer questions about Binion on the grounds that federal regulations prohibited him from testifying about informants unless they were involved with the case at hand, which he assured the court Binion was not. Haynes's puzzled look told the jury that he believed otherwise. Haynes asked Jannings about the curiously timed meetings between Priscilla and Pat Burleson and between Burleson and McCrory. Jannings said he didn't know anything about these meetings. Racehorse backed off at this point.

By now the jury could identify two distinct, though perhaps interrelated, scenarios—that Cullen Davis had been framed and that he himself may have been the target of a murder plot. In an interview outside the courtroom, Steve Sumner elaborated on the defense's scenarios. It was their contention, Sumner said, that during those crucial days in August Cullen's "state of mind" was such that he believed his life was in danger and he took a cynical view of the FBI's willingness or ability to do anything about it. The extortion letter was only a part of it; the defense planned to show that there were other death threats and that Davis took extraordinary precautions to protect himself. "It'll all come out." Sumner smiled cryptically.

Something came out the following day that even Sumner didn't anticipate. Overnight Tolly Wilson had furnished Jannings with a "timetable" to refresh the witness's recollection of the events of August 16–20. When Jannings inadvertently took the notes with him to the witness stand, Haynes caught the prosecution by surprise and demanded a copy of Jannings's notes. Strickland protested that the notes were nothing more than "a work product of the state," but Texas law entitles the defense to examine notes used on the stand by witnesses, and Moore allowed the defense to copy them.

Following this unexpected break, Haynes backed Jannings into a corner and went to work with both fists. Tolly Wilson had attempted to show Jannings as a highly competent special agent experienced in complex investigations, but Haynes portrayed the agent as a bungler with a poor memory and perhaps even a vendetta against Cullen Davis. In fact, Jannings was a highly respected agent—he had supervised the investigation of convicted West Texas swindler Billie Sol Estes, among other things—but now Haynes was able to solicit a startling number of memory lapses on Jannings's part. To dozens of rapid-fire questions, Jannings could only shake his head and respond, "I don't recall" or "I'm not sure" or "I can't remember." Haynes fielded the replies with the patience of a therapist who had dedicated his life to the education of the mentally impaired. When Jannings would have trouble recalling details of the investigation, Race would pick up the agent's notes or a transcript from earlier testimony, pass slowly in front of the jury to the witness stand, lean forward, and read to Jannings in a soft, understanding voice. Then he would ask gently, "Now don't you recall that happening . . . don't you remember saying that under oath?"

In Fort Worth Jannings had testified that McCrory

had arrived alone for an August 18 meeting with FBI agents at the Ramada Inn Central, but in Houston Jannings changed the story and said he had met McCrory at a Holiday Inn and then had driven him to the Ramada.

Jannings: He was alone when I picked him up [in the parking lot] at the Holiday Inn.

Haynes (pointing to the transcript of the bond hearing): But we were talking about the Ramada Inn.

Jannings: I'm sorry.

Haynes: It's not a matter of being sorry. It's a matter of being under oath.

Jannings: You have to remember, Mr. Haynes, we were in a hurry to get things done to keep people from getting killed.

Haynes: Did being in a hurry keep you from being accurate?

Jannings: I tried to be accurate.

Haynes: In your notes you also omitted the fact that McCrory stopped at the liquor store [after the August 18 meeting with Cullen Davis] and bought a six-pack of beer, didn't you?

Jannings: Yes, sir. We were in a hurry, and we just couldn't put everything down.

Haynes: But your report was completed four days *after* Mr. Davis's arrest.

Jannings: Yes, sir.

Haynes hammered at the fact that Jannings had been selective about what information he included in his official report called a 302. For example, in his handwritten notes Jannings recorded that Cullen wanted his younger brother Bill Davis kidnapped and killed because of some "stock manipulations," and he also recorded the amounts McCrory said Cullen was willing to pay to have fifteen people killed. But the agent omitted these details when he dictated his 302.

Q: Didn't you intentionally omit them because you thought some evidence might show those statements to be inaccurate?

A: No, it was because McCrory wasn't sure.

Jannings insisted that it wasn't unusual to omit certain things from the official report because it was the practice for FBI agents to turn over their original notes along with the 302 to the U.S. Attorney's office. But later, under cross-examination, special agent Gerald Hubbell admitted to Haynes that it was FBI "protocol" to include in the 302 everything in the agent's original notes. Hubbell, who was in charge of setting up the recording devices, added that the original handwritten notes were normally filed in the agent's home office, not forwarded to the U.S. Attorney.

Haynes also riddled the prosecution's contention that Cullen Davis was willing to pay $1 million to have the fifteen people on his alleged hit list killed. At the bond hearing McCrory testified that he had seen Cullen rearranging names on the list, but that Davis had never actually given him the list. The prosecution finally had to acknowledge that there was no list, or at least they didn't have it. All they knew about the list is what David McCrory told them.

It was near the end of the first week when the state called Judge Eidson. Prosecutors had already called FBI photographer George Ridgley to introduce the photograph, and now the payoff would be the testimony of Eidson himself. The elderly judge told the court that he was first contacted by the FBI the night of August 18, after the first tape-recorded conversation. He reported to the U.S. Courthouse the following morning and listened to the tapes. "Frankly," he admitted, "I was pretty shaken up by the situation." Eidson told how he was taken to a deserted corner of a parking garage, how he removed his coat, shirt, and undershirt and watched as agents created bogus bullet holes with cigarette burns and bloodstains with catsup. The packed courtroom was dead silent as Eidson told the jury, "I got in the trunk of my car, laid down, and some photographs were taken."

As the jury examined the photograph and a sequence of twenty-two other photos taken of McCrory's meetings with Cullen Davis on August 18 and August 20, Judge Moore was deliberating on another problem. During direct examination Tolly Wilson had solicited testimony that Eidson postponed the final hearing on the divorce case just ten days before Davis's arrest, despite strong objections by Cullen lawyers. Then Wilson inadvertently posed this question to Eidson: "Prior to that time, your honor, had any attempt been made by [Cullen Davis] to remove you from the case?" It was the word *remove* that brought Racehorse Haynes to his feet—the motion filed by Cullen's lawyers the previous spring did not seek Eidson's removal from the case; it merely asked that the trial be moved from Eidson's court. Maybe it was splitting hairs, but the defense argued that the semantic difference planted the notion that Cullen wanted to "get rid of the judge" and thus tainted the jury. Haynes demanded a mistrial. Moore denied it, but he worried that the state had possibly committed an error that would be grounds for reversal.

The trial had been under way less than a week, and already the defense had forced Moore into dozens of rulings and decisions, obviously peppering the record for appeals in case Davis was convicted. Moore didn't like it, but he couldn't stop it either. The judge was already having misgivings about this case.

Before the week ended, there was one more blow for the prosecution to weather. They knew it was coming, but that didn't make it any easier. The heart of their case was the physical evidence—the tapes, the photo of Eidson's body, the $25,000, and the pistol and silencer. Yet it was possible that the most telling piece of physical evidence was the one they didn't have—Cullen Davis's fingerprints. Not on the money, not on the gun, and most damaging of all, not on the photograph that Cullen supposedly examined at the conclusion of the deal. Jack Strickland covered his eyes with his hand as agent Ridgley, the photographer, described how he had dusted the photo with fluorescent powder before sending McCrory to the August 20 meeting. The powder should have collected in the ridges of Cullen Davis's fingers and nailed shut the proverbial coffin lid, but in those dizzy hours just after the arrest something happened that's only supposed to happen in dumb movies:

unaware of the fluorescent powder, some well-intentioned Fort Worth cop did a routine fingerprint make on Cullen Davis, then ordered him to go wash his hands in naphtha. If there had been fluorescent powder on Cullen's fingers, it was gone now. Nor was there a trace of Davis's fingerprints on the photo. This demonstration of clumsiness pretty much summed up the first week of the prosecution's case.

Jack Strickland had decided to look on the bright side. Tolly Wilson had promised that Strickland would become more involved in the courtroom action. Tolly believed that the state had lost in Amarillo because they attempted to make decisions by committee—"We had too many chiefs and not enough Indians"—and though Strickland still had his own ideas about how the case should be presented, the young prosecutor had resigned himself to the role of Indian. "We're not going to let ego, tension, or fatigue get in the way of this case," Strickland said. "That would be inexcusable." When he started looking on the bright side, Strickland saw a lot of things in their favor. The defense had talked about Cullen's "state of mind" during that crucial period in August, and that was a good point. Look at it this way: what did it tell you about Cullen's state of mind when, just before the August 20 meeting with McCrory, he stopped and examined the FBI surveillance van parked across the street, then told McCrory that he was "just paranoid"? As Strickland saw it, this demonstrated a classic "guilty state of mind."

Then there was the judge. Pete Moore ran a tighter ship than George Dowlen. Moore wasn't allowing Haynes to travel with his many-tentacled conspiratorial theory. Racehorse still intended to parade a host of phantoms in front of the jury, but before he could do it, he would be required to show how the phantoms were relevant to this case. But the best thing they had going was the tapes. In Amarillo the state had had little physical evidence, but Houston was a different story. The tapes were the terrible swift sword of the case, and the time had come to wield it.

On Monday morning Joe Gray was ready for the show. Gray was the agent in charge of technical surveillance for the Dallas FBI office, and the case against Cullen Davis would either take off or sink on the merits of his latest production. The sound tape of the August 20 meeting was made from a recorder taped to McCrory's body, and the video came from a video recorder that Gray operated from the van across the street from Coco's parking lot, but since the bond hearing Gray had taken the tapes to the FBI lab in Washington and combined them into a single black-and-white motion picture. The film wasn't likely to win any Oscars, but it was damning evidence against Cullen Davis. As the prosecution prepared to call David McCrory, Gray was outfitting the courtroom with some elaborate equipment to enhance the show. Two dozen bright yellow headphones were installed so that each juror, the judge, the stenographers, and the attorneys could hear more clearly, and amplifiers were placed to boom the conversation to the audience. Four television sets were brought to the courtroom.

There was a total of five tapes—one from the Friday, August 18, meeting, three telephone conversations on Saturday, and the audio-video recording of that critical final meeting on Sunday. By far the poorest production was the August 18 tape. Parts of it were almost impossible to hear. Cullen spoke softly, and McCrory, who was closer to the mike, sometimes drowned him out.

Moore had already allowed the tapes into evidence, and now he made what was probably the most important ruling of the trial. He allowed the jurors to follow typed transcripts as they listened to the poor-quality

August 18 tape. It was a highly controversial ruling, one that could backfire, and Moore offered the defense the opportunity to present its own version of what was on the tape. The defense declined, arguing that the transcripts constituted a reversible error that they didn't intend to compound. Haynes claimed to have counted seventy-seven differences between the state's version of the transcript and the transcript from the Fort Worth bond hearing, but the changes were insignificant, usually a word repeated in a long sentence, or in the case of overlapping conversation the insertion of the editorial word *continued*.

The judge was aware that his ruling was certain to end up in the Texas Court of Criminal Appeals. Federal courts had upheld the use of transcripts in similar cases, but this was the first time they had been allowed in a state court. In a recent ruling the Court of Criminal Appeals had said that using transcripts could be a reversible error, but Moore had studied the ruling closely and noted an exception. "In that case," he said, "the jurors were allowed to take transcripts into the jury room and were not given instructions on how to handle them." Although jurors would be permitted to follow transcripts while they listened to the tape, they wouldn't be allowed to take them into the jury room, and, said Moore, "I will instruct the jury that this is just the state's version of the tapes and that the transcripts should only be considered in that light." If there was a discrepancy between what jurors heard and what they read in the transcript, they were instructed to accept what they heard on tape. Moore ruled that transcripts would be used only for the August 18 tape. The prosecution didn't protest; the other four tapes were quite clear.

David McCrory entered the courtroom dressed in a three-piece navy-blue suit and surrounded by seven deputy U.S. marshals. Moore ordered the tightest security while McCrory was on the witness stand. From the beginning Moore had prohibited cameras and recording equipment anywhere on the seventh floor of the courthouse, and now he warned courtroom artists against even sketching portraits of McCrory. As McCrory repeated much of his testimony from the bond hearing, he glanced occasionally at the jury but avoided looking at Cullen Davis.

Haynes knew that the tapes wouldn't stand alone; they would require McCrory's corroboration. However strong the tapes, Haynes was determined that the state's presentation of McCrory be as inelegant as possible. To this end he jumped up repeatedly to object to Tolly Wilson's questions—Racehorse objected nearly sixty times that Wilson was not putting his questions in time frame, and Moore sustained most of the objections. The arguments were so frequent that the jurors were soon chuckling.

But no one was laughing when McCrory testified that Cullen told him to arrange the murders of fifteen people and described the various plans for the killings. When Bev Bass and Bubba Gavrel were murdered, McCrory said, Cullen wanted the killer to spread heroin or cocaine mixed with sugar substitute at the scene, a ploy designed to make the killings appear to be drug-related. An alternative plan to kill Gavrel, McCrory said, was to "wait till he was at the cleaners—his father's store—and go in there and kill everyone there." Judge Eidson's murder was to be blamed on the Brown Berets.

McCrory had trouble remembering dates, but he said his "business association" with Cullen began when Davis gave him $5,000 to investigate some of the people who later appeared on the hit list. Later, McCrory told the jury, Cullen gave him $50,000 and told him to take it to Las Vegas and launder it. "He told me to make up some kind of story and tell people I won $20,000 or $30,000 while I was out there because he said, 'When this thing is over, you are going to have a lot of money, and people are going to want to know where you got it.'" He said Davis arranged meetings by calling Jet Air, and leaving the message that Dan Edwards called. McCrory's code name was Frank Johnson. McCrory said he played along, hoping to kid Davis out of the scheme, but finally decided to contact his friend Pat Burleson ("the best-known karate man in the

375

world"), who in turn put him in touch with FBI agent Ron Jannings. Davis also wanted a pistol with a silencer, McCrory continued, so on August 18 he withdrew his savings of $9,500, purchased a .22 Ruger automatic, and prepared to become a witness for the state.

By midweek prosecutors were ready to play the tapes. Bus drivers, lawyers, high school students, housewives, county workers, and reporters from as far away as London crammed into the dark wood-paneled courtroom. Cullen made notes as the recorded voices boomed through the room. Defense lawyers did not challenge the contention that the voices belonged to David McCrory and Cullen Davis. It was impossible to read the jurors' faces, but several exchanged sober glances when they heard Cullen say, "Do the judge and then his wife and that would be it."

Probably the most incriminating part of the twenty-five-minute conversation came near the end.

McCrory: He may take a bunch of them off at once. Uh, I—I mean, he's that kind of person. I mean he may just waste the shit out of a bunch of 'em and get a bunch of it over with at once.

Cullen: Well—

McCrory: If—

Cullen: That suits the shit out of me.

Following the playing of the August 18 tape, jurors heard tapes of three telephone calls, two Saturday and one early Sunday morning when McCrory called to tell Cullen that the first hit had been accomplished.

McCrory: The man is finished and wants to leave town.

Cullen: How will I know?

McCrory: I've got the proof. That's no sweat.

Cullen: All that information is down at the office.

McCrory: You'll have to get it. I don't want to talk. I can't fake it.

Cullen: What's the matter with in the morning?

McCrory: He wants to get gone. Hold on. [to someone else] He wants to go to his office. [to Cullen] Meet me at 9:00 A.M. Don't leave me hung out on this.

Cullen: No. That'll work out just fine.

The jurors appeared impassive as they filed out of the courtroom at the end of the day, but no one who had heard the tapes and followed the transcript could escape the gravity of what had been said. The tapes were fascinating and the transcript devastating. Whatever had been going through their minds, the two men were clearly talking about murder. In a rare burst of optimism Tolly Wilson predicted, "If Mr. Haynes gets him off this time, it will be a miracle." Defense attorneys told reporters that the curious conversations would be explained in due time, and no one doubted that they would; the tapes might be explained, but there was no way they could be denied. Veteran courthouse reporters agreed that the tapes were the most damning physical evidence they had ever heard in a courtroom.

The following morning Racehorse Haynes tried to prevent the jury from viewing the August 20 tape. Haynes called in an expert witness, John Allison, who told the court it would be impossible to synchronize audio and video recordings with the type of equipment used by the FBI. Allison, who sold both the Nagra sound recorder and the Sony video recorder used by the FBI, told the court that the video machine was the most unsophisticated machine Sony manufactured.

"The specs show it varies plus or minus 0.25 microseconds," he said.

Judge Moore thought about this, then replied, "I always thought that was close enough in government work."

The judge denied Haynes's motion and ordered Agent Gray to darken the courtroom and roll the film.

The most pertinent part of the tape came after McCrory had allegedly shown Cullen the photograph and Judge Eidson's driver's license and state bar identification card.

Cullen: OK. What are you going to do with these?
McCrory: Get rid of the motherfuckers.
Cullen: That's good. Glad to hear it.
McCrory: All right. Who do you want next?
Cullen: Uh, the ones we talked about.

McCrory: Bubba . . .

Cullen: The three kids.

McCrory: Bev, Bubba . . .

Cullen: Yeah.

On the screen the jury could see Cullen and Mc-Crory climb out of the Cadillac and walk to the trunk. Cullen opens the trunk and McCrory takes something out. On the audio track you hear the shuffling of paper, as though McCrory is flipping a stack of bills. McCrory then walks to his own car and returns with something wrapped in a white towel—apparently the gun and silencer. At this point Cullen says, "Goddamn. Pretty!" Cullen appears fascinated. "Look at that motherfucker," he says. A few minutes later McCrory tells Cullen that this man is going to operate again tonight. There is a pause, and then Cullen says, "Just one problem. I haven't got the money lined up."

McCrory: How long will it take?

Cullen: I'll try to get it this week. I can get it in two days.

McCrory: I don't know whether I can keep him here two days or not, Cullen.

Cullen: Uh, how far does he have to go? Halfway . . . across the country?

McCrory: He's out of New Orleans . . .

Cullen: Couldn't he come back?

After some conversation about Art Smith, McCrory says, "Look, this fucking murder business is a tough son of a bitch."

Cullen: Right.

McCrory: Now you got me into this . . . goddamn deal, right?

Cullen: Give me a little . . . advance notice.

McCrory: I got Judge Eidson dead for you.

Cullen: Good.

McCrory: I'll get the rest of them dead for you. You want a bunch of people dead. Right?

Cullen: All right.

McCrory: Am I right?

Cullen: All right. But I—

After some more conversation, McCrory tells Cullen that he has to go.

Cullen: Ask him about does he want to leave and come back, or do it and then wait three days for the money.

McCrory: He won't wait for the money.

Cullen: Well.

McCrory: Look. If he kills all three of those people he's going to walk.

Cullen: Yeah. Well, I don't blame him, but I just . . . I've got to get it so . . .

McCrory: OK. You talking about a lot of . . .

Cullen: It's better to leave and come back?

McCrory: You talking about a lot of . . . Yeah. You talking about a lot of money. Figure it up.

As Cullen's Cadillac is seen leaving the parking lot, McCrory can be heard saying very slowly and deliberately, "I have got the *money*. He has got the *gun*." The final voice on the tape belongs to Agent Gray, signing off: "This is special agent Joseph B. Gray of the FBI. The time is now 9:03 A.M., August 20, 1978, and I am about to remove the Nagra recorder from David McCrory that I installed earlier today."

Racehorse Haynes seemed unfazed when the lights came back on. During a recess, puffing on his pipe and cleaning his half-moon glasses on a silk handkerchief, Haynes reminded the reporters clustered about him that the system permitted both sides a turn at bat and that the defense's turn was coming. He promised that the defense would develop their conspiracy theory, linking McCrory, Priscilla, Pat Burleson, and others in an ongoing plot to ruin and possibly even kill Cullen Davis. He didn't reveal who the others might be, but a newly released list of witnesses subpoenaed by the defense included Bill Davis and Tarrant County DA Tim Curry.

"You know what they say." Haynes smiled. "The opera ain't over till the fat lady sings."

For the next five days Haynes cross-examined McCrory without once mentioning the tapes, the gun and silencer, or the $25,000. It was a hypnotic display of professional savagery, something like watching a demented dentist pull teeth with a pair of rusted pliers. Haynes asked numerous questions about McCrory's chronic financial problems, his troubles with the IRS, his well-documented reputation as a liar and a schemer. He asked about the provisions of the Federal Witness Protection Program, implying that McCrory was living off the fat of the land on $900 a month and that alone was sufficient motivation for doing the prosecution's bidding.

Haynes seemed to enjoy his confrontation with Mc-Crory, and, curiously enough, so did McCrory. The witness put great store in his own ability to jive with the masters, and McCrory seemed confident he would win the day. As he had done in Amarillo with Bev Bass, Haynes produced giant three-by-six-foot calendars and attempted to pin down exact dates and times when McCrory did the things he said he'd done. Race was working McCrory into a corner, but time after time McCrory squirmed out, answering, "I don't really remember" or "I don't have any idea." Haynes produced airline tickets showing the date McCrory and an official of Jet Air flew to Atlanta, and even then McCrory refused to admit it was the correct city or date.

Q: Doesn't that [the ticket] say you flew there on the twenty-fifth of May?

A: I can't tell for sure. It's either the thirty-fifth of May or the twenty-fifth of May.

At one point McCrory answered consecutive questions by replying "Sometime probably." Once, as Haynes was writing some response on his calendar, Mc-Crory called out from the witness stand: "Was that a question you were mumbling, Mr. Haynes? I can't hear you too well when you're over there. You need a bigger calendar." Frequent clashes between the lawyer and the witness made it almost impossible to follow the continuity of the questioning, if there in fact was one. At one point Pete Moore interrupted a squabble and said, "Let the record reflect that these two gentlemen do not like each other."

It was true. Race more than disliked McCrory. He loathed him. McCrory was the physical archtype of

380

the bully that Haynes had imagined himself fighting all his life—big and hulking, a practiced smirk on his face, flashy like the hot dogs who stood on the corner whistling at girls and looking for easy marks, and yet soft and malleable and deceptively treacherous. Haynes had never forgotten McCrory's affidavit at the close of the mistrial in Fort Worth, the way he believed McCrory had led him up an alley and thrown him to the dogs. After McCrory signed an affidavit for the prosecution, refuting everything he'd told Haynes, he made some vague claim that Haynes had promised him gifts or other considerations for his testimony. The contempt of court citation that Judge Tom Cave slapped on Haynes and Phil Burleson (which still hadn't been resolved) was easily Haynes's most humiliating moment in the entire Cullen Davis affair. The memory still pricked Haynes's ego, as did the memory of the unsavory method by which the prosecution turned his witness around with some implied threats of delivering him over to the IRS. Now the prosecution was trying to claim that McCrory was a longtime friend of Cullen Davis. Haynes believed that McCrory had betrayed Davis, not only with the unsigned affidavit, but from way back when McCrory offered sanctuary in Boston for the illicit love affair between W. T. Rufner and Priscilla. This complicity in the cuckoldry of Cullen Davis fired up the old sanctimonious impulses in the lawyer, made him detest David McCrory far out of proportion to anything McCrory might have done to Haynes himself. Haynes had no fear of David McCrory, but it's possible that deep inside he feared his own irrational hatred.

Haynes's frustration with the witness was inflamed by frequent prosecution objections that this whole line of questioning McCrory's personal life was nothing more than innuendo, and by Pete Moore's frequent admonishments for Haynes to move on to something else. The judge and the famous lawyer had clashed a number of times. At one point Haynes got McCrory to admit that he really held title to two cars he claimed to have lost as a result of being placed on the Federal Witness Protection Program, but when the lawyer coiled himself for the kill, the judge interrupted and said, "We've spent twenty minutes on this, and I don't want you sticking it in his ear." Race's long and close friendship with Pete Moore was being put to the test. The judge had made it clear he would tolerate no character assassination, and every time he thought Haynes's questions were irrelevant, Moore reprimanded him in front of the jury and said: "You're running up another rabbit trail. Now let's move on to something else."

After a couple of days with McCrory it got so that the judge started anticipating the state's objections; on one occasion Moore sustained an objection before Jack Strickland actually made it.

"I'd like to hear the counselor's objection," Haynes barked.

"I knew what he was going to say," Moore replied evenly. "I knew he wasn't just standing up stretching."

Moore allowed the defense to question McCrory briefly about his involvement in the aftermath of the 1976 murders, but when Haynes attempted to probe into McCrory's relationship with Priscilla, the judge cut him off cold. "You are entitled to ask anything that's relevant to anything in this specific case," Moore said, "but you cannot impeach the witness by attacking inconsequential matters."

In his efforts to crucify McCrory and connect him to Priscilla, Haynes tried a back door ploy, introducing some documents (their content was never revealed) in hopes they would open other doors into McCrory's past. Moore ruled the documents were irrelevant and might impeach the witness. Race tried another tack, returning to some of McCrory's earlier testimony, but the prosecution objected that now he was being repetitious. The lawyer was stuck in a vicious circle.

In the hallway during a recess Steve Sumner talked about the problem they faced. "We're trying to establish the relevance of certain questions without completely exposing the defense's case. Judge Moore is at a disadvantage because he's having trouble understanding our conspiracy theory and what all is involved. In

382

Amarillo the judge had the advantage that we were starting at the beginning. This case stretches way back and involves a lot more than just the few days before Cullen was arrested."

Was Sumner saying that the conspiracy went all the way back to the murders in the summer of 1976?

"Our position is that the 1976 incident is extremely relevant because of David McCrory's relationship to certain people over a long time."

After four days of cross-examination, McCrory still hadn't fielded a question about anything that happened on or after August 17. Over objections from the prosecution Haynes was permitted to turn again to McCrory's unexplained income in early 1978. The implication was that he'd received the money as part of the continuing conspiracy to frame Cullen Davis. McCrory admitted that he stole $5,000 of the money he claimed Cullen had given him to take to Las Vegas; then there was an additional $5,000 that Cullen supposedly gave him for investigative work. McCrory said he gave his son, Mike, $9,500 and deposited $2,900 in his own checking account in late June and early July. "I wanted to take the whole $50,000 . . . run from the whole mess and hide with it," McCrory said. Cullen, who had stopped taking notes and seemed unusually relaxed, chuckled when McCrory said Davis "ordered" him to call Fort Worth while in Las Vegas.

Unexpectedly, Haynes turned the questions to Priscilla.

Q: Did you know Priscilla Lee Davis was in Las Vegas just a few weeks before you were there?

Haynes didn't elaborate on the significance of the alleged visit, but he had more questions about Priscilla.

Q: Did you tell Cullen Davis that Priscilla Davis was going to hire someone to come shoot up 42000 Mockingbird Lane so they could claim Cullen Davis did it?

A: I told him so many stories and lies I might have.

Q: What was the biggest lie before August 1978 that you told Cullen Davis?

A: That I had gotten professional killers from Kansas City and they would get rid of his problem for him.

Q: What was your second biggest lie to Cullen Davis?

A: I told him I was doing everything I could to get people killed for him.

Q: Did you tell anyone that Priscilla Davis had attempted to hire some out-of-town hit men . . . to kill Cullen Davis?

A: No, sir.

Q: Did you ever say Priscilla tried to hire someone who looked similar to Mr. Davis . . . to come shoot up the place?

A: No, sir, not that I remember.

Q: Do you deny saying anything like that in your life?

A: Yes, sir. I do not remember saying anything like that.

A few minutes later McCrory told Haynes: "I haven't talked to Priscilla Davis in a year. I don't like Priscilla Davis."

Race appeared to be momentally dumbstruck. "You don't *like* Priscilla Davis?" he asked incredulously.

Before McCrory could reply, Moore interrupted the testimony and said firmly, "Now let's don't get into that."

Haynes asked a series of questions about McCrory's August 16 meeting with Pat Burleson.

Q: You knew at the time that Pat Burleson was a friend of Priscilla Lee Davis, did you not?

A: Yes, sir.

Q: You knew at the time there'd been some business relation between Pat Burleson and Priscilla Lee Davis?

A: Yes, sir.

At one point Haynes asked a long, ambiguous question and McCrory reworded it, saying, "I have to keep correcting you to keep the facts straight."

"*You* have to keep correcting *me* to keep the facts straight?" Haynes said sarcastically.

Again, Moore interrupted and told McCrory: "When you strap something on him like that, he's going to bite back."

At another point McCrory accused Haynes of asking repetitious and ambiguous questions for the purpose of confusing him "like you've done before."

Pete Moore didn't use a gavel, but his voice sounded like one as he ordered McCrory to quit volunteering things. "I've asked you five times this morning not to do that," Moore said angrily. "Don't volunteer *anything!*"

The judge felt he had been pushed to the limit. The defense had every right to cross-examine the state's star witness, but they were going around in circles. They were deliberately abusing the system. Moore made one more ruling that effectively put the lid on Haynes. He refused to allow the defense to ask questions about the Amarillo trial or anything that might have happened before 1976.

"If we're not going to do that," Haynes said angrily, "we might as well not do anything."

"Well, we're not," the judge told him.

Race had one more line of oblique questions before he finished with McCrory. They concerned a newspaper ad run in the August 16 *Star-Telegram* offering to sell a shotgun. McCrory said he didn't know anything about the ad. Haynes asked about the telephone number that accompanied the ad. McCrory didn't recognize it. One of the defense attorneys explained later that the question was asked to lay a predicate for some future testimony. The phone number in the ad was listed to one of Pat Burleson's karate studios. Hardly anyone noticed, but when the phone number was mentioned, a curious look crossed the face of Cullen Davis and he scribbled something on a pad.

By now the trial had consumed three weeks. Pete Moore had predicted it would be over by now, but because of the defense's protracted cross-examination they weren't even at the halfway point. It was almost Thanksgiving—almost exactly a year since the Amarillo acquittal. The state's next witness would be special agent Joe Gray who would identify Judge Eidson's stained T-shirt and no doubt take the opportunity to play the tapes again. Moore guessed correctly that this would be followed by hours of tedious and highly technical cross-examination about the fidelity of the tapes. The judge ordered a four-day holiday and sent the jurors home.

◦◦◦ • ◦◦◦

The prosecution told Moore they would finish their case the week after the holidays, and they were good at their word. As Moore predicted, Haynes's cross-examination of Agent Gray was so dull that it nearly emptied the courtroom and put several jurors to sleep. Race rambled on and on about the technical aspects of the tapes, questioning Gray's contention that the synchronization was nearly perfect, suggesting there were numerous distortions, words, maybe even whole sentences left out. Gray refused to waver. Haynes did get the agent to admit that after the August 20 meeting at Coco's David McCrory was out of Gray's sight for about five minutes, long enough, perhaps, to drive by 4200 Mockingbird and collect $25,000. This was stretching credulity pretty far, but it was the sort of innuendo that no longer surprised the prosecution. "I think I hear a cry of desperation," Jack Strickland said.

The prosecution had some surprises of its own. Their next two witnesses were two slightly bewildered and visibly uncomfortable secretaries who worked in the executive offices of Kendavis Industries. Brenda Adcock, Cullen's personal secretary, trembled as she answered Jack Strickland's questions about David McCrory and about a fat, mysterious envelope that Cullen had her lock in the office safe. McCrory started showing up around the first part of 1978, as she recalled. She had talked to him on the telephone a number of times. Once when he called, McCrory identified himself as Frank Johnson, but only once.

She said that Cullen handed her the white envelope in early August and asked her to lock it in the safe. The only people who had the combination were Brenda Adcock and Ken Davis's secretary, Mary Ann Carter. On August 19, the day before Cullen's arrest, Adcock left for a vacation in Acapulco. When she returned to work ten days later, the envelope was gone.

As Mary Ann Carter took the witness stand, it was obvious that Strickland was implying that the mysterious envelope contained the $25,000.

Mrs. Carter testified that on Sunday morning, August 20, she was awakened by a call from Cullen Davis shortly before 8:00 A.M. He asked for the combination to the safe. She told him it was written on a piece of paper in her desk drawer.

Q: Did he say anything to you to indicate he was at the office?

A: No.

Q: Did he say anything like, 'Wait a minute. I'll see if I can find it'?

A: Yes.

Q: Did he come back to the phone and say he'd found it?

A: Yes.

Q: So he would have been at the office?

A: Yes.

Q: Did you tell him anything else?

A: Just if he had any trouble to call me back.

Q: And did he call you back?

A: No.

Except for the one phone call from McCrory that Brenda Adcock mentioned, neither secretary recalled any messages from a Frank Johnson. McCrory had testified that he used the code name frequently when calling Cullen Davis, and Phil Burleson rammed this point home in his cross-examination. Burleson also got both secretaries to say that McCrory frequently sounded "frustrated" when he couldn't reach Davis, contradicting McCrory's claim that he had easy access to Cullen during the months before the arrest. Nevertheless, the secretaries' testimony about the fat envelope clearly

387

damaged the defense's case. Brenda Adcock smiled weakly and gave her boss a tiny wave of her hand as she left the courtroom. Cullen remained impassive, but his jaw gyrated as though he were chewing on a tough piece of meat.

The state's remaining witnesses were law enforcement officers who told about the arrest and the search of Cullen's Cadillac.

Rodney Hinson, an investigator for the Tarrant County DA's office, told of conducting a superficial search of the car immediately after Davis was taken into custody, then following the car to the police garage and waiting several hours for a search warrant before opening the trunk. Moore sent the jury out of the courtroom while Haynes argued that the first, superficial search was illegal and therefore "tainted" the later search. Haynes asked the judge to suppress Hinson's testimony about finding the Ruger with the silencer in the Cadillac trunk, but Moore denied the motion, and Hinson was allowed to tell the jury what he found.

Another DA's investigator, Morris Howeth, gave a vivid account of Cullen's arrest a few minutes after the August 20 meeting with McCrory. Cullen had taken a circuitous route after the meeting, "washing his trail" in case he was being followed, but the investigator explained to the jury that the white-on-blue Cadillac was actually being tracked by an FBI spy-in-the-sky plane that radioed his route to the officers on the ground. Cullen was emerging from a telephone booth outside a Kentucky Fried Chicken place when the cops closed in.

"By the time we pulled in beside his car, Mr. Davis was coming out of the phone booth," Howeth said. "He put his hands up to his face like this. . . ." The investigator demonstrated by bowing his head and covering part of his face with his hand. "I called out to him, 'Cullen, you're under arrest. Put your hands on the car.' "

While Morris Howeth was testifying, a frumpy middle-aged woman in the back row began mumbling, "He's not guilty . . . not guilty I tell you." A bailiff quietly removed her from the courtroom, but later the woman returned, unnoticed. The woman apparently thought the DA's investigator was David McCrory because suddenly she jumped up, pointed a finger at the witness, and cried out, "McCrory's lying. . . . He's lying!" As two bailiffs hustled her out a rear door, the woman continued ranting that she was going home to get a gun and kill McCrory. "They're framing Cullen Davis!" she shrieked. "They ought to hang the prosecutors!" As the woman's shrill voice trailed off down the hallway, Judge Moore told the jury: "I don't know what that was, but it had nothing to do with this case. She was either drunk or not wrapped too tight." The only thing surprising about the outburst was that it hadn't happened earlier. The Cullen Davis case was bound to attract more than a fair share of nuts, and it occurred now to everyone involved how easy it would be for someone to walk in and blow any one of them away. After that, bailiffs kept a close eye on spectators. One of Cullen's lawyers privately admitted that he'd moved his chair a little farther away from the defendant just in case.

The state introduced its final piece of evidence, the $25,000 in $100 bills, then called its final witness, Texas Ranger John Hogg. The sandy-haired, ruddy-faced Ranger was an imposing figure sure to impress any Texas jury by his mere presence. Rangers are part of the state's history and mythology—every schoolchild in Texas has heard the story about the riot and the single Ranger who answered the call for help. "Only one Ranger?" someone is supposed to have said, to which the Ranger replied, "You only got one riot, ain't you?" Ranger John Hogg was cut from the classic hard-scrabble mold, and when he spoke, it was like listening to a blue norther thundering through the chaparral. Hogg told of sleeping in the back seat of his car the night before the alleged payoff and corroborated the testimony of other officers who said McCrory and his car were thoroughly searched before the meeting with Cullen Davis. Hogg cut hard at the defense's contention that McCrory was out of sight for five minutes or longer after the meeting. Hogg, who was the first officer to see the $25,000, said that he caught up with McCrory about "two minutes" after the meeting concluded. Then the thunder in his voice subsided, and Hogg's face seemed to sag with compassion as he described McCrory's emotional state.

"He was visibly shaken, his cheeks wet with tears," Hogg said. "He was just plain driven up."

Hogg's testimony was the first indication that McCrory was anything except Mr. Cool during the setup, and several jurors appeared moved.

Asked for his reaction to the Ranger's testimony, Phil Burleson said, "I nearly puked."

It was a calculated risk, but Racehorse Haynes went after Ranger Hogg like a band of Apaches. His voice edged with fire and sarcasm, the lawyer tore apart the written report Hogg submitted after the arrest, forcing the suddenly beleaguered Ranger to admit the report was marred by hearsay, errors, omissions, and oversights. Tolly Wilson remarked later that he'd never heard a witness, much less a Texas Ranger, handled so roughly, though of course he had if he'd been listening. Ranger Hogg apologized repeatedly for the obvious inconsistencies and inaccuracies, but Haynes cut him off and barked: "Don't apologize. Just answer the questions!"

When Hogg stepped down, the prosecution rested its case. Haynes had done his best in cross-examination. Except for the technical questions he had not even mentioned the tapes, the prosecution's strong point, but his brutal questioning of the state's first and last witnesses, Jannings and Hogg, made the police work look haphazard and sloppy, and he had made McCrory look like something less than a model citizen. Still, when the defense's turn came, Haynes would have his work cut out for him: the tapes were such powerful evidence that Cullen's future looked bleak.

While Racehorse was finishing his assault on the Ranger, Karen Master sat on a bench outside the courtroom answering Cullen's fan mail. Something like fifty letters a week were being delivered to Cullen's cell, all of them positive, and Karen answered each one in a flowing hand on personalized letterhead that said KAREN AND CULLEN. One letter said, "Cullen, keep that sweet smile . . . don't ever lose a positive thought and you will win." Many of the letters had religious overtones. Some asked for money or other types of assistance. A nineteen-year-old wrote that it was his ambition to be a millionaire by age twenty-one, but it was going to be hard to do without Cullen's assistance. Karen was trying to phrase her refusal so as not to stifle the young man's ambition.

"There are so many wonderful people out there who want to help Cullen," she said. "Total strangers willing to do anything they can. I just wished I could meet them."

She was about to get her wish. A lot of totally strange people were about to come forward in behalf of Cullen Davis.

~∽ • ∽~

The first two witnesses for the defense, Priscilla Davis and Pat Burleson, were strange only because they were so obviously hostile toward Cullen Davis. Haynes would have loved having both under cross-examination, but after the experience in Amarillo the state was not about to call Priscilla, and Pat Burleson had only a peripheral connection to the case in the opinion of the prosecution. So if Haynes wanted to question them, he would have to call them himself; though he chafed under the court ruling that he could not impeach his own witnesses, Race had no choice. He needed them to lay the groundwork for his conspiracy theory. "We've got to let the jury see them," Mike Gibson said.

Priscilla had selected a stark black high-collared outfit with pearls and a diamond cross for her appearance, and as she walked from the hotel to the courthouse, traffic stopped and some winos who had wandered up from the bayou saluted her with a bottle of Swiss Colony Black Port. A young woman across the street called out, "Mrs. Davis, Mrs. Davis, I admire your guts." Priscilla smiled, waved, and walked on, flanked by attorney Ron Aultman and her brother, David Childers. A man removed his cowboy hat as she stepped into the elevator, and when she emerged on the seventh floor, reporters swarmed toward her.

Priscilla took a pastel cigarette from her purse, changed her mind, then changed her mind again. "I don't have to please anyone, do I?" she said as a reporter lighted her cigarette. Priscilla had some sort of skin infection, and the makeup on her face was thick as an orange peel. She waved to Karen Master across the hall, but Karen didn't wave back. "I read in the paper she's going to marry my husband," Priscilla said. "They remind me of Adolf Hitler and Eva Braun."

Inside the courtroom Racehorse Haynes was already preparing the jury for her appearance. In his opening statement he straightened them out on something: McCrory wasn't a friend of Cullen Davis, he was a friend of Priscilla Davis. Priscilla was a greedy and scheming woman who would stop at nothing to get Cullen's fortune. Priscilla had acquired large amounts of cash shortly before McCrory claimed to have got the $25,000 payoff from Cullen. Even as the feds were moving in on Cullen, Priscilla was having clandestine meetings with McCrory and Pat Burleson and others. Haynes also reminded the jury that Cullen Davis had told the FBI a year before that the author of the extortion letter used the initials D.M.R., which brought to mind the name David McCrory. "Things are not what they may seem," Haynes concluded.

An elderly woman seated in the front row clutched her Bible as Priscilla was sworn in, and behind her fifty teenage Bible school students squirmed in their seats, preparing themselves, perhaps, for a contemporary recitation of Sodom and Gomorrah. If so, they were disappointed. Pete Moore had already made it clear that he wouldn't allow the defense to assault its own witness,

392

and every time Haynes strayed into some lurid area of Priscilla's life, the judge told him: "You're walking on real thin ice now. I don't want all this irrelevancy in the record." Haynes had to content himself with establishing Priscilla's relationship to McCrory and Pat Burleson.

Priscilla admitted that on August 18, the day McCrory first approached Pat Burleson, she went to Burleson's karate studio. She met Burleson again the next morning at the mansion, at roughly the same time McCrory had his first contact with the FBI. She was with Burleson on Sunday morning even as Cullen Davis was being arrested. But she denied any advance knowledge of what McCrory was doing and confirmed McCrory's story that they hadn't talked to each other in at least a year. She told the jury that all the meetings with Burleson had to do with security measures for the divorce trial. Priscilla freely admitted that she had borrowed $47,000 in 1978; in fact, the reason she met with Burleson was because she was nearly broke and could no longer afford to pay for security guards.

"He was the only one I could ask for help," she said. "I couldn't borrow any more money. The divorce was running longer than I anticipated . . . court was just a little more than two weeks away, and I knew I couldn't afford the police officers."

Haynes wanted to explore the details of her relationship with Burleson dating back nearly ten years, but Moore stopped him. He tried to make a full-scale inquiry into the divorce suit, and Moore stopped him again. Priscilla admitted being in a Fort Worth restaurant in July and seeing David McCrory across the room, but she flatly denied that they spoke or in any way communicated. Haynes tried to force her to diagram the seating inside the restaurant, but Moore stopped him. The defense had subpoenaed telephone records of Priscilla, Bill Davis, McCrory, and several others, but when Haynes attempted to explore them, Moore ruled that he would first have to prove they were relevant. As he had with McCrory and would later with Pat Burleson, Haynes brought out his giant calendars and took his witness over an hour-by-hour account of her activities, but one juror slept through the whole tedious process and several others stifled yawns. If the defense intended to establish its conspiracy theory, it would be done without Priscilla's assistance. Aware of this, Haynes now had David Binion brought into the courtroom and asked Priscilla if she recognized him.

"I've never seen him in person." She smiled. "I've only seen him on the TV, on the news." Priscilla was referring to a press conference called by Binion to deny Haynes's allegations.

Haynes knew that he had at last won a small victory—Binion had already told defense lawyers about visiting the mansion—but the look on Racehorse's face as he passed the witness said it was small indeed.

In cross-examination the prosecution took the opportunity to play the tapes for the fifteenth time. Priscilla trembled, and tears came to her eyes as she listened to her own murder being plotted.

McCrory: And now Priscilla is a different story. Uh, that's . . . you know, he'd rather do Priscilla than the judge. He says he can do it easy.

Cullen: Huh! Like hell!

McCrory: Well.

Cullen: Priscilla's always got somebody around her.

McCrory: Now the way . . .

Cullen: The judge doesn't.

The jury didn't hear it, but Priscilla told reporters later: "I think Cullen has considerable firsthand information on how hard I am to kill." She shivered slightly as she said it. "It's all very frightening," she said. "I can't hide that."

When all five tapes had been replayed, Tolly Wilson asked Priscilla, "Did you conspire with Pat Burleson to get your husband to say any of the things he said on that tape recording?"

"No, I did not," she said firmly.

"Did you conspire with David McCrory to get your husband to say any of the things he said on that tape recording?"

"No, I did not."

What remained of Priscilla's testimony was all done outside the presence of the jury. Moore allowed the defense to make a bill of exception for the record, but even then the lawyers were prohibited from asking questions about her relationship with W. T. Rufner and others. Steve Sumner insisted that the defense could prove that Burleson and Priscilla had a long-standing love affair and that David McCrory had been Priscilla's "agent" for at least ten years. Only they weren't going to get the opportunity to prove it. Not with this judge. Sumner also revealed one key segment of their case— they would contend that McCrory used his *own* $25,000 to frame Cullen. Was he saying that the defense had reversed its course, that they were no longer saying the $25,000 came from Priscilla? "Bear with us." Sumner smiled.

The defense hadn't expected to get much further with Pat Burleson than they had with Priscilla, and this judgment was correct. Racehorse Haynes appeared uncharacteristically awkward as he produced his latest set of giant calendars and led Burleson through a tiresome interrogation of his activities prior to Cullen's arrest. To Haynes's chagrin, Pat Burleson proved to be a very able and patient witness; it was Haynes who appeared obstinate and unsure of his direction. About the best Haynes could do was establish that Burleson wasn't positive about the exact times he met with Priscilla and McCrory. In the bond hearing he said a meeting took place at 10:00 A.M., but now Burleson was telling the jury it took place at *mid-morning*. "Well," Haynes grilled him, "which was it?" Burleson looked at the jury, sighed, and said, "I guess mid-morning."

Haynes did establish that the telephone number in the August newspaper ad offering to sell a shotgun was the business number for one of Burleson's karate studio franchises. This was to be a key piece of evidence, the defense maintained, but for the moment its significance was a mystery.

All along the defense had been trying to suggest a sinister familiarity among Priscilla, Burleson, and McCrory. Now Jack Strickland's brief cross-examination of Burleson offset hours of questioning by the defense. Burleson had told how McCrory called him in the early morning hours of August 16 and asked Burleson to meet him in front of a 7-Eleven store. When Strickland questioned him about the meeting, Burleson said: "He related to me that he was in a lot of trouble, that the company he worked for was owned by Cullen Davis, and his problem related to Cullen Davis. I told him I didn't want to hear about it, and I chastised him for being involved with Cullen Davis again. I was sick and tired of these problems with Cullen Davis."

Q: How did Mr. McCrory react to this?

A: He hung his head.

Q: And what was his demeanor?

A: He was completely scared, totally to death.

Q: What leads you to that conclusion?

A: The pallor on his face, the rash on his hands, and he was shaking.

Strickland softened his tone as he inquired about Burleson's longtime relationship with McCrory. Burleson had gone to high school with McCrory's older brother, Big Moose; after Big Moose was killed in a car wreck years ago, Burleson had looked on McCrory as a sort of hapless younger brother who always seemed to have his shirttail hung on someone else's picket fence.

Q: Did you run around a lot together?

A: No, I knew his older brother better than I knew David.

Q: Is it true, Mr. Burleson, that Mr. McCrory has often sought your advice?

A: Constantly.

Q: It is true, isn't it, that your relationship is very much like that of an older brother to a younger brother?

A: It's been a very hectic relationship. . . . I don't find the words to describe it.

Q: Is the way you perceived it this time that "Here's David in another jam again"?

A: That's how I saw it exactly.

Q: And you attempted to get him out of that jam?

A: I attempted to do what I thought was right.

Burleson told the court that he contacted Ron Jannings, an FBI agent who had trained at one of his studios, and arranged for McCrory to meet with the agent. That was the extent of his involvement, Burleson testified.

Racehorse had been promising that he would produce solid evidence that a conspiracy against Cullen Davis existed, and on December 7 he made his first attempt to do it. He called David Binion, the mystery man he had introduced during cross-examination of Ron Jannings. Though Jannings refused to answer questions about Binion, it was fairly clear that Binion had done undercover work for the FBI.

Binion was a muscular, balding slightly seedy man of middle age; he was a used-car salesman, but he could have passed for a hit man, which is what the defense claimed he did. Whether they would get to assert their claim was the subject of several hours of wrangling with the jury excused. Binion admitted he had worked as a paid informant for a number of law enforcement agencies and that he had built a reputation as an underworld character. In the fall of 1977 and again in the winter of 1978, Priscilla attempted to contact Binion. After her third telephone call, Binion visited the mansion. Binion claimed that he "thought it possible" that Priscilla wanted him to kill Cullen Davis; in fact, during their twenty-minute meeting he tried to steer the conversation in that direction. Nothing came of it. A Houston lawyer named Jewel Lemmon later delivered Binion to Haynes; Binion volunteered the opinion that if Priscilla hadn't been so "messed up" on drugs, he felt she would have "popped the question." He also told the defense that a man named Guerrero told him that a man named Rodriguez was claiming that Priscilla offered him a contract to kill Cullen. There was no way that Judge Moore was going to allow this double hearsay in his courtroom, and the prosecution argued that Binion's whole story was irrelevant. Binion was saying flat out that Priscilla never mentioned killing or harming Cullen Davis; in fact, Binion had told Haynes that it had never happened—the only reason for calling Binion as a defense witness was to impeach Priscilla, who claimed she'd never seen him. Haynes said this wasn't the case at all, that the defense only wanted to "demonstrate another witness's error on a certain point." Moore agreed that Binion could tell about the visit to the mansion and ordered the jury returned to the courtroom.

It took the lawyers considerably less time to question Binion than it had to argue about the admissibility of his testimony. Haynes used the blackboard to impress on the jury the dates leading up to Binion visiting the mansion, but Binion remained unflappable when Haynes tried to get him to talk about murder.

Q: Did Priscilla Davis say to you that "he [Cullen] will get his"?

A: No.

Q: What did she say, exactly?

A: I can't remember exactly. It was in a religious sense, a religious manner.

Q: She didn't call you up there because you were a preacher, did she?

A: No, sir.

Q: She didn't call you up there to buy a used car?

A: No.

Q: Did she say that Cullen Davis would get killed?

A: No. I already told you that.

Q: Well, what did she say?

A: She said God would take care of these things, and he'll get what's coming.

Q: God would take care of things?

A: I think you and I are taking the conversation in a different light.

Haynes got Binion to acknowledge that Priscilla appeared "messed up" on drugs during the meeting, but in cross-examination Tolly Wilson scored some points by exploring this a little more. Binion said that Priscilla seemed slghtly confused, groggy even. She stayed in bed during the conversation. She didn't seem to recognize him or recall that she'd asked him to come to the mansion. "Did you ever see anybody recovering from a gunshot wound?" Tolly asked before the defense could object. Tolly knew that he was drifting into a gray area—there wasn't supposed to be any mention in the jury's presence of the shootings at the mansion, but he had slipped it in anyway. Haynes also objected strongly when the prosecutor asked his next question, but Moore permitted it.

Q: You reported the fact that Priscilla Lee Davis had not asked you to get a hit man to kill her husband to Mr. Haynes before this trial, did you not?

A: Yes, sir.

Wilson had inadvertently given Haynes an opening. Since Binion had been allowed to tell part of what he told the defense before the trial, Haynes argued that the witness should be allowed to tell all of it. Moore refused to allow Haynes to ask questions about the man named Guerrerro, but he permitted this line of questioning:

Q: You do recall, do you not, that you thought she was calling you because of your reputation as someone to hire someone to kill someone?

A: I thought it was a possibility, yes.

Q: What did you say to me about her being . . . messed up . . . and whether or not, if it had not been for that, she would have . . . popped the question.

A: I don't recall what I told you.

Haynes also got across the fact that the Tarrant County DA's office had made some "deal" with Binion regarding the dropping of certain charges against him. At the conclusion of Binion's testimony, both sides claimed victory. "I think David Binion makes a great hit man," Jack Strickland said. "He came in here and fired the fatal shot at the defense."

Strickland's report that the defense was dead soon proved to be greatly exaggerated. The defense had a biggie waiting in the wings. After calling a series of baby-sitters, maids, and Kendavis secretaries to refute McCrory's claim that he was constantly in touch with Cullen Davis, the defense ushered Dorothy Neeld to the stand. Mrs. Neeld, a receptionist for a company that shared a building with Jet Air, said that in mid-July she watched McCrory leave for lunch and climb into a "burgundy Mercury or Lincoln" with three other people. She recognized the woman with platinum hair and sunglasses as Priscilla Davis and later identified the driver as Pat Burleson. She didn't recognize the third party, a man, but Priscilla's lawyer, Ron Aultman, drove a 1977 burgundy Lincoln.

Dorothy Neeld was the nearest thing the defense had to a bombshell witness at this point. In fact, the defense didn't even know she was a potential bombshell when they called her to Houston. She was originally called as one of almost a dozen secretaries and receptionists whose cumulative testimony would establish that while McCrory called Cullen Davis frequently, Davis seldom returned his calls. But a few days ago she'd almost casually told Steve Sumner about the mid-July incident. "I just thought it strange that McCrory would leave with Mrs. Davis when he was an employee and friend of Mr. Davis," the receptionist said. She didn't even think the incident was important, but it was easily the most important testimony the defense had: for the first time a witness had challenged the unanimous testimony of Priscilla, Burleson, and McCrory that they were never together at the same time.

Tolly Wilson couldn't shake her story in cross-examination, and his efforts to discredit her with a tiresome series of questions about her background went nowhere. Jack Strickland called her testimony "incredible," and Tolly Wilson stopped just short of calling it perjury. If Neeld really had seen what she said she saw, the prosecutors asked, why had she waited until this week to mention it? "She testified that the reason she walked over to the window and watched McCrory drive away was because she was curious," Wilson noted. "How can a woman with that kind of curiosity keep something like that a secret for so long . . . for five months in fact?" Strickland had another question: "If they were plotting against Davis, why wouldn't McCrory walk two blocks down the street and avoid being seen there at a Davis company?" The prosecutors could only hope jurors were asking themselves the same questions.

Contacted in Fort Worth, Priscilla was outraged.

"It's not just innuendo, it's a downright lie!" she told reporters. Attorney Ron Aultman said Neeld's testimony was a "ridiculous insinuation." He added that "I had never seen Pat Burleson until this week in court, and the only time I've ever seen McCrory was in the hospital after Priscilla was shot. They have never been in my car, I can assure you."

Whatever the truth, the defense claimed a major victory, their first, in fact.

∽ • ∾

However powerful the evidence against his client, Racehorse Haynes had one undeniable advantage: he didn't have to prove Cullen's innocence, just plant the seed of reasonable doubt as to his guilt. For the next two weeks, Haynes scattered seeds like a berserk farmer. Haynes stepped up the pace of the defense partly because he hoped to finish up by Christmas, only two weeks away—and partly because speed itself, with its attendant confusion, was his ally. Over the next two weeks Haynes would call more than a dozen witnesses. If he did it right, Cullen would be eating Christmas dinner at home and the prosecutors would be back in Fort Worth licking their wounds once more.

Their leadoff witness was Mary Ramsey, wife of the Mid-Continent Supply Company sales manager, who testified that she accidentally ran into Priscilla in Las Vegas on June 13, 1978. Priscilla had sworn she hadn't been in Las Vegas in 1978, but Mary Ramsey recalled in detail having a thirty-second conversation with Priscilla in the casino of the Aladdin Hotel. She didn't say what they talked about. In cross-examination Strickland got Mrs. Ramsey to admit that she sometimes gets "lost on time," and when he asked her why she hadn't told this story to law enforcement officials, the witness replied that the only way she would have told them was if they'd come after her with a court order. Ramsey's loyalty to Cullen Davis went unmatched. There was no apparent significance to Ramsey's testimony except to refute Priscilla's statement—June 13 didn't coincide with the dates McCrory had visited Las Vegas. But Steve Sumner reminded reporters that "Las Vegas is a very good place to hide money. Someone could have dropped it there, and McCrory could have picked it up." *Could have* was a very important part of any good defense.

For example, David McCrory could have been the mysterious D.M.R. who mailed the extortion letter to Cullen Davis two weeks after the Amarillo acquittal. The semiliterate typewritten letter, which arrived at Karen Master's home on December 7, 1977, was now read in court. It said:

"I have a contract to see that you don't live to see Xmas. If you don't want this contract filled, get 10,000 dollers in twenty doller bills together, run a ad in the Star-Telegram in the personal section reading DMR call home and a phone no. Do this right, no cops and I will see that you live and also tell you who put out the contract on you."

FBI special agents James Acree and Bobby Oakley conducted a two-and-a-half-month investigation but never tracked down D.M.R. The defense was claiming that the agents did a poor job in their investigation, including ordering the removal of a tracing device from Karen Master's telephone without informing Cullen or Karen. Karen Master had speculated that the author of the extortion letter might be her ex-husband. It was claimed now that Cullen suggested that the agents check out David McCrory, but Acree denied this. Besides, Acree said, when they checked a latent fingerprint on the letter, it proved not to belong to McCrory. But as far as Cullen Davis mentioning McCrory as a suspect, Acree said, that never happened. The defense didn't pursue this line of questioning. From their point of view, Agent Acree had already served his purpose.

Then came the strangest witness of all. One Larry

Gene Lucas, two-time loser, shocked and momentarily paralyzed the prosecution by testifying that David McCrory offered him $20,000 to kill Cullen Davis. The offer was tendered, Lucas said, at the Sylvania Bar and Billiards Club in Fort Worth, at a time most crucial to the defense's case—in June or July 1978. Lucas, a seedy, gray-faced man with tufts of flaxen hair and a Hawaiian blue print shirt flaring open under his iridescent green suit, recalled that McCrory was big-timing it that night at the Sylvania Bar and Billiards. McCrory was talking a lot and strutting about in a $300 suit and $100 shoes. Lucas was fairly sure it was a $300 suit because he'd shoplifted several just like it.

Lucas recalled that things went down this way:

McCrory sashayed into the Sylvania in his new duds bragging that he'd won $5,000 playing backgammon. Lucas said he was really glad to hear that because now McCrory could loan him $10. McCrory whipped out the $10, then observed: "You obviously need to earn some money. Let's go outside and talk about it." Lucas said he was shocked when McCrory offered him $10,000 to kill Cullen Davis. "I said, 'You're crazy. The man has more security than the president.'" At that point, Lucas continued, McCrory jumped his offer to $20,000. "I told him, 'David, I've never known you to have $20, much less $20,000,' and he said, 'The money's there.' I said the money could stay there. I wouldn't touch it with a ten-foot pole." Lucas recalled that McCrory then followed him over to a car where Lucas's pal Joe Espinoza was waiting. Both Lucas and Espinoza claimed to have heard McCrory say, "We're going to get him one way or another." Joe Espinoza had already been subpoenaed by the defense.

Lucas's testimony stunned the prosecution. Even before Lucas stepped down from the witness stand, DA's investigators in Fort Worth were hauling in assorted characters and paying surprise visits to underworld hangouts. Lucas had to be lying, the prosecution believed; and the prosecution had better prove it. At the rate Racehorse was moving, they might not have much time. That night two investigators called at the home of Lucas's common-law wife, Mary Weir, and visited with Joe Espinoza and other regulars at the Sylvania Bar and Billiards.

Lucas's testimony was a weird development, but things were going to get weirder. The following afternoon, while the seventeen-year-old son of David McCrory was telling how he stashed $9,500 of his father's money in a safe deposit box, W. T. Rufner rippled into the courtroom carrying a suitcase and a six-pack. "Hello there, Mr. Davis!" Rufner called out. Bailiffs tripped over one another in their haste to get T-man out of the courtroom, and when the defense called him to the witness stand later, the bailiffs reported that Rufner couldn't be found. That's because he was in the fourth-floor press room treating the media to eggrolls and beer and trying to hawk a new issue of T-shirts bearing the image of a chimpanzee dressed to look like Racehorse Haynes. WHAT PRICE JUSTICE? said the caption, and the chimp puffed his pipe and looked down his half-moon glasses and answered: "One million dollars." High school girls crowded around Rufner, seeking his autograph and admiring his red felt cowboy hat and the belt buckle that spelled out "I bring joy to women." T-man said he wasn't sure why the defense wanted him to testify—he hadn't seen Priscilla in at least a year—but since he was technically in Houston as Cullen Davis's guest, it was his intention to make the best of things. "I hope they keep me here a couple of days," he said, popping a ten-milligram Valium and washing it down with Scotch. "I'll drink a couple of hundred dollars' worth of Scotch tonight and get some $200 hookers instead of those $25 jobs up in Amarillo."

Rufner didn't get a chance to steal the show in Pete Moore's court. There was some fearsome wrangling outside the presence of the jury, but Rufner's actual testimony was limited to a few routine questions that advanced the case not at all. According to a forthcoming defense witness, Bob Brown, who worked for one of Cullen's companies and was married to Rufner's ex-wife, T-man called the Browns in June or July and told them that someone was coming to town that weekend to kill Cullen. But Rufner denied making the call and unless the defense could come up with something more substantial, that was the extent of his testimony.

Bob Brown followed Rufner to the stand and recalled the telephone call in late June or early July. Rufner was very cryptic, Brown said, and gave him this warning: "Something big is coming down." The line had the familiar ring of Sandy Myers's recollection in Amarillo—that Priscilla had told her "something heavy is coming down."

"W. T. said there was a man coming into town that weekend to take care of Mr. Davis," Brown told the jury. "He said it wasn't going to be clean and fast because they wanted to see the son of a bitch suffer." Brown added that he immediately relayed this information to Steve Sumner, who at the time was heading up the investigation for Cullen's long-awaited divorce trial.

On cross-examination, Brown said he was "shocked" by Rufner's revelation.

"Why is it that you were so concerned . . . but didn't call police?" Jack Strickland asked the witness.

"To be really honest about it, I didn't think it was that important at the time . . . until I discussed it with my wife."

"Oh," Strickland said, shooting a glance at the jury. "So that's when you called police?"

"I never did call police," Brown replied.

What was Racehorse Haynes doing? To the prosecution and many of the spectators, it appeared that the master was calling up anyone who might have anything at all to say about the Cullen Davis affair. With Lucas, Rufner, and Brown, the lawyer seemed to have bottomed out. But Haynes wasn't done. To his growing list of people who conspired to frame Cullen Davis, Haynes now added the Tarrant County DA's office. And to support this claim, the defense called three prison inmates to testify that the DA's office had offered them "deals" to testify falsely that Davis had hired them to kill Priscilla. Race said this was an example of the

DA's "longtime, ongoing effort to get Cullen Davis."
The three inmates were highly unsavory types; this,
Haynes said, demonstrated the depth of the DA's
depravity, though some people thought it showed the
depth of Haynes's desperation.

Judge Moore wanted to hear what the convicts had
to say before admitting their testimony, so he kept the
jury out of the courtroom. First to the stand was Randall Craig, who was serving a ten-year sentence for
burglary. Craig testified that on August 17 DA's investigator Don Evans asked if Cullen Davis had ever tried to
hire him as a hit man. Craig said he denied it; then the
investigator told him: "It's a shame you can't remember
Cullen asking you that. I'm going to put you back in jail
and you think about it." Craig added that the investigator told him that if he thought of anything to help nail
Cullen Davis, the DA would drop the burglary charges.
On cross-examination, Craig, who was in his mid-twen-
ties, admitted that he had been convicted of burglary
in 1972, 1975, and 1978, but there was a reason for
it—he was a drug addict.

Then came John Florio and his nephew Salvador
Florio, two people right out of central casting telling another amazing story of malfeasance. Sal Florio, who
talked with a nasty north Jersey accent, had been in
and out of prisons all his life and was currently serving
twenty years for an aggravated robbery conviction in
Tarrant County. He said that members of the Tarrant
County DA's staff visited them in prison in May. "They
told us they'd gotten an anonymous letter saying John
and I had been hired to kill Priscilla Davis," Sal testified. "I laughed at them and said I didn't even know
Cullen Davis." Sal testified that the DA's men offered
them some kind of unspecified deal if they would say
Cullen tried to hire them as hit men. "They wanted
us to come up with some ideas that would be strong
enough to frame Davis," Sal said. His Uncle John, who
was doing sixty years for the same crime and admitted
previous convictions of armed robbery, robbery, and
unlawfully obtaining narcotics, backed up Sal's story.

Tolly Wilson, surprisingly calm for a lawyer who had

just been accused of suborning perjury, pointed out that the Florios had their story "a bit backwards." It was true that the DA's office received an anonymous letter, Tolly said, and when investigators went to the state prison in Huntsville to check it out, the Florios said they had pictures and tapes to prove that Cullen once tried to hire them. "I didn't believe the Florios from the very beginning," the prosecutor said, "but we had to check it out." At the Florios' suggestion, two investigators were sent on a wild goose chase to New York, but they never found the pictures or tapes. As for the letter, "John Florio finally admitted he wrote it himself."

At the end of the day Judge Moore issued an unexpected ruling. He said that Craig and both Florios could testify in front of the jury. "It's the defense's theory," he said. "If they put them on, they got to fly with them." But the defense was already having second thoughts about the three convicts. Mike Gibson admitted that the defense was "reevaluating" the testimony, and for the time being the three witnesses were returned to jail. A few days later, after several other witnesses had testified, the defense did call Sal Florio. By then the defense had pulled in its horns, and Florio's testimony amounted to very little. But the battle over the convicts' testimony had its effect nonetheless. The trial Pete Moore thought would take three weeks was dragging on, and both sides were getting testy. It wasn't long before they were downright angry.

There was considerable speculation by now that Cullen Davis himself might take the witness stand; the belief was intensified ten days before Christmas when Karen Master testified. Karen had furnished her lover's alibi in Amarillo, but it was going to take more than an alibi to free Cullen this time. The tapes had gone unchallenged, and only Cullen could explain all that strange language about murder.

The defense was hammering at the theme that because of the manner in which the extortion letter was handled, Cullen Davis would not have trusted the FBI or other law enforcement agencies but instead would have handled things his own way if he felt he was being

407

threatened or framed. Karen supported this theme. She testified that a tracing device placed on her telephone to track the mysterious D.M.R. was removed without explanation while she and Cullen were on a skiing trip from December 17 through January 2, 1978. On January 9, she continued, D.M.R. made contact. As soon as he hung up, Karen told how she followed the procedure outlined by the FBI. To her shock and dismay a telephone company executive told her that the call could not be traced.

"And what reason did they give you that the call could not be traced?" Haynes asked.

Her voice breaking as she told her story to the jury, Karen Master said a telephone company executive informed her the FBI had ordered the device removed. "I cannot *believe* the FBI told you to have the tracing device off after they had been emphatic about us keeping it on!" Karen told the phone company executive. Karen told of then calling agent Jim Acree and complaining bitterly that the FBI was acting free and easy when Cullen Davis's life was being threatened.

Turning and smiling at the jury, Karen also confirmed the defense's theme that from January to July Cullen *emphatically* refused to answer David McCrory's repeated phone calls. Then she dropped the bomb. On July 13, McCrory called her home and Mr. Davis agreed to speak with him. Karen didn't reveal the reason for the sudden reversal, but she remembered that shortly afterwards Mr. Davis went to meet McCrory. When he returned home Mr. Davis had an envelope stuffed with money. The next morning Mr. Davis took the envelope to his office.

There was more—Karen reinforced the theme that after the extortion letter Cullen mistrusted the FBI and took precautions to protect his own life, including wearing a bulletproof vest—but it was the mysterious envelope of money that caught everyone's attention. Karen couldn't come right out and say that Cullen claimed McCrory gave him the envelope. That would be hearsay. But she was laying the groundwork for Cullen's own version.

408

The defense was no longer predicting they would be finished before Christmas. It was about to be a whole new ball game, Jack Strickland believed. He was sure now that Cullen Davis was coming. It was only a matter of when. "I thought they might try to prove up their case through Karen," Strickland said. "That's why we fought to keep her from telling her hearsay conversations with Cullen." The defense had called more than forty witnesses at this point, but their case amounted to a bunch of dangling innuendos that only Cullen Davis could tie in sequence.

For example:

• Karen testified outside the jury that in March Cullen refused a call from McCrory and told her, "I don't ever want to talk to that nut." But only Cullen could tell the jury he said that. Karen told of her own strong dislike for David McCrory, but the jury had no way of knowing that it was because of the unsigned affidavits in Amarillo. Karen said that McCrory told her that he had to lie—"I had to! I had to!"—in Amarillo; otherwise the DA's office would turn him over to the IRS.

• On the advice of one of his private security men, Harry Knieff, Cullen started wearing a bulletproof vest in April. Knieff told the jury that he had information that Cullen "was in danger," but Moore wouldn't allow Knieff to relate his exact conversation with Cullen.

• Karen testified that on the twenty-third of May Cullen told her he had decided to hire McCrory, but the court wouldn't let her say why.

• In June, Karen said, McCrory told her: "Karen, I have some information that I think you should know. I know that Priscilla Davis and Gus Gavrel, Sr., have a contract out for Cullen's life and I think that you and your children should stay low." She added that "Mr. Davis had already told me something similar."

• In August a man who identified himself as an FBI agent called Karen Master's home and asked to speak to Mr. Davis. The defense contended that the caller was an impostor who told Davis that there was a conspiracy to frame him, then advised him to go along with it until the plot could be exposed. If Cullen actually believed the caller was an FBI agent, it might explain why he said all those things to McCrory that were now part of the record. Was it possible that the whole plot was a strange refraction of reality, that in fact *Cullen* had set out to trap *McCrory?* It was hard to believe, but no more so than the claim that the $25,000 actually belonged to McCrory, that Cullen was just keeping it for him as a favor.

In the final hours before the Christmas break both sides forgot Cullen and Priscilla and went instead for each other's throats. They came like two biblical armies whose only common ground was an absolute conviction of their own righteousness. Pete Moore normally disdained wearing a robe on the bench, but he wished privately for a striped shirt and whistle.

First the defense accused the DA's office of conducting a midnight raid on the home of one of their star witnesses, Larry Gene Lucas, of sweeping down on the small mobile home in Fort Worth at a time when they knew Lucas was still testifying in Houston, of putting the arm on Lucas's old lady, a known prostitute, and tearing the mobile home apart looking for something to impeach Lucas. The DA's staff replied that Lucas was lying about this too. His wife, which the lady of the house denied being, let their men inside the house, in fact led them to an incriminating letter Lucas had written her telling how he was going to make some bucks with his timely story about David McCrory. The mobile home, in fact, didn't even belong to Lucas, though he occasionally visited there; the last time he visited there, the lady recalled, he put a pistol in her ear and had his way with her. Moore told the warring parties of lawyers that anything that happened in Tarrant County was out of his jurisdiction unless or until it was brought up in court under the proper rules of evidence.

Next, the defense maintained that the DA's office had condoned and probably gained information from a private investigation financed by Bill Davis and supervised by former prosecutor Joe Shannon. This charge not only brought Bill Davis and Joe Shannon into the conspiracy, it claimed one financed it and the other masterminded it, using a law firm in Denver as a cover. The alleged investigation was directed not at Cullen Davis but at his lawyers and investigators, who, it was claimed, had been under surveillance for some weeks now. Bill Davis had been under subpoena since October, but nobody had been able to serve him papers. The defense blasted the prosecution for dirty tactics, and the prosecution sniffed that the pot was calling the kettle black, though the DA's office denied knowledge of any such investigation.

District Attorney Tim Curry had taken pains to stay out of the Cullen Davis fray, sensing, no doubt, a feeling among certain powerful factions in Fort Worth that the DA had a personal vendetta against the millionaire. But after the Florios were permitted to smear his office and good name, Curry charged that Racehorse Haynes and his cohorts had violated the legal code of ethics. Curry threatened to haul the whole bunch of them before the State Bar Grievance Committee to explain their disgraceful display with the Florios and Randall Craig.

Cullen Davis anticipated a Christmas present from Austin, where the Texas Court of Criminal Appeals was reviewing his bond. Cullen had figured on being out of jail long before now and had recently expressed his impatience and displeasure to his attorneys. "Everyone is having fun but me," Cullen complained. The lawyers believed they'd have Cullen out for Christmas, but now the Court of Criminal Appeals ruled that the defendant wouldn't be eligible for bond until December 30. Even then the question of bond would depend on "circumstances." One of the circumstances could be a jury verdict. If Cullen was acquitted before that date, the question of bond would become moot; if he was convicted and sentenced to more than fifteen years, he would be sent straight to prison pending appeal. In the event the trial lasted past December 30, another circumstance regarding bond would be the opinion of Judge Pete Moore. When Cullen heard the odds, one attorney revealed, he demanded to take the stand himself.

Haynes hadn't wanted to put Cullen up. He wasn't sure Cullen would make a good witness—he was too cool, too arrogant. Karen Master could melt a jury's heart with her sweet demeanor and ready smile, but Cullen, thin-lipped and proud, could freeze it again in an instant.

Cullen *was* proud, and perhaps that pride is the reason he did take the stand. No one knows what was going on in his mind in those days before Christmas. Cullen, of course, knew for certain whether or not he was guilty. He must also have known that the case against him was formidable and sensed that Haynes was having trouble making headway in Pete Moore's strictly ruled courtroom. As the holidays approached, he must have felt his imprisonment with a special force. He had been in jail since August, and before that, awaiting his first trial, he'd spent nearly fifteen months behind bars. He had never been one to lie in the sun, but his face had an awful prison pallor, and there were circles under his eyes. He must have been lonely too; he shared the defense table with his lawyers, and Karen sat just a few feet away in the courtroom, but there was no time or place to just sit and talk, to operate in the ways he was used to operating, to be with friends or share moments with his lover.

Most of all, Cullen was impatient. All the temper tantrums Priscilla had accused him of, the night-long math lessons with Andrea, the time at the Steeplechase Ball when he scattered everyone's keys in the mud, all of this testified to a man who wanted things done in a hurry. Cullen wasn't the type just to sit there day after day while others dickered with his future. It was his life, and Cullen was sick and tired of waiting for it to resume.

At a Christmas party thrown by a group of well-known Houston lawyers in honor of Racehorse and his team, Mike Gibson looked like a man who'd just played Santa for a pack of fat, sticky kids. There were circles under his eyes too, and sometimes he caught himself staring off into space, his mind completely blank. All the lawyers were dog-tired. Days were long and getting

412

longer—for several weeks now the jury had decided to start each morning at eight (instead of nine), shorten recess and lunch breaks, and work until nearly dark. Nights for Gibson and Steve Sumner consisted of grabbing a sandwich, then interviewing the next day's witnesses until midnight. Gibson and Sumner were still young, but they were getting old in a hurry. This was harder than Amarillo, much harder. And much different. It was late in the game, and the defense lawyers weren't at all confident of the outcome.

Gibson looked at his empty glass and shook his head and said something that must have been in the minds of all the defense lawyers. He said, "I think we'd all settle for a hung jury right now."

Two days after Christmas a slightly apprehensive Cullen Davis was sworn in and directed to the witness chair. The public already knew the essence of what he was about to say. Someone from the defense leaked it to the press three days earlier, just about the time the twelve jurors would have been lifting their cups of eggnog and chatting with family and friends. The media leak got wide play all over Texas. No one could say for sure that any of the jurors heard the story, but this certainly wasn't out of the question.

The foundation of their counterconspiracy theory was this—Cullen would testify that on August 10 he received a telephone call from a man who identified himself as FBI special agent Jim Acree. The agent supposedly told Cullen that McCrory and others were involved in a plot to frame him and advised Davis "to play along." "In his mind he was taking no chances," an unidentified source for the defense told the Associated

Press. "He thought that all in all, someone from the FBI was there [when the murders were discussed] and everything was OK." The defense wouldn't attempt to prove that an agent from the FBI actually made the phone call, only that Cullen *believed* the caller to be Special Agent Acree. The scenario recalled Racehorse's description of the classic defense: "You sue me, claiming my dog bit you. My defense is this. First, my dog was tied up that night, and second, in the alternative, my dog doesn't bite. Third, I don't think you even got bit. And fourth, *I don't have a dog*." You had to wonder why they'd waited for eight weeks to call Cullen to the stand (he was the forty-seventh defense witness), but maybe Haynes's dog-bite story explained it—maybe this was the fourth choice.

Before Cullen took the witness stand, the judge warned attorneys to avoid all questions that might resurrect the Amarillo trial, an order that greatly frustrated Tolly Wilson. Neat as a department store mannequin in his powder-blue sit, Cullen fidgeted and stuttered occasionally when he first took the stand, but he appeared to relax and gain confidence as Racehorse Haynes methodically directed him through the first six hours of incredibly complex testimony. Cullen spoke precisely, with an economy of words, and his recollection of dates and events was extraordinarily sharp. Race claimed it was Cullen's "engineer's mind" being publicly demonstrated for the first time. Cullen spoke of his stormy marriage to Priscilla, though not in detail, and of his casual, "not very friendly" relationship with David McCrory. Cullen said he didn't see McCrory much after his breakup with Priscilla. They couldn't talk about the Amarillo trial, but Haynes skipped the questions ahead to January 16. That was the date, Cullen said, when McCrory appeared at his office without an appointment and forced a meeting.

"He said he wanted to be friends with me and he wanted a job," Cullen said, turning and offering the jury something like a smile. After that, Cullen said, he refused calls from McCrory for the next three months. Even though Cullen had his number changed, Mc-

Crory continued to call. Finally, on May 1, Cullen agreed to meet McCrory in the parking lot at Coco's. "He said he was broke and didn't have a job," Cullen continued. "We discussed the fact his wife was a prostitute and he had been pimping for her. He started to cry. He volunteered to help with my divorce case if I would give him a job."

By June McCrory was employed as a $20,000-a-year salesman at Jet Air, but not because of his qualifications as a salesman. McCrory had information that he needed, Cullen said, information about Priscilla, drugs, and sex. "I was motivated [to hire him] mainly by the fact that he was going to help me in my divorce, particularly in matters pertaining to Priscilla."

"Priscilla and another party?" Haynes prompted.

"Yes."

Cullen recalled that he met McCrory twice in June. On both occasions McCrory revealed threats against Cullen's life and said he was still "seeing Priscilla Davis." McCrory claimed he had some information from old friends that "there were going to be some things perpetrated by Priscilla that they were going to try to blame on me." At one of the meetings, Cullen said, McCrory showed him a gun equipped with a silencer and offered to give him one "as a present."

On July 13, Cullen testified, McCrory gave him $25,000 and asked him to keep it in his office safe. Cullen denied McCrory's story that he'd sent McCrory to Las Vegas to launder $50,000. Cullen said he had no idea McCrory had been to Las Vegas until McCrory gave him the $25,000, which he claimed to have won gambling. After the July 13 meeting, Cullen said he didn't see McCrory again until August 11. On August 10 he received an "unusual" call from a man identifying himself as FBI agent Jim Acree.

"He said he had information that McCrory was involved in an extortion plot. He said, 'We think you are the victims. We want you to play along. That's the only way we can catch him. Follow his suggestions.'" The next day McCrory called and asked for another meeting at Coco's.

At this point Cullen revealed yet another twist in the plot, one that would become indispensable to his story. McCrory showed up for the August 11 meeting carrying a small Norelco *tape recorder*. The four lawyers at the prosecution table were dead silent as Cullen made this revelation, but you could almost hear gears meshing. A juror who had been dozing snapped suddenly to attention. Cullen explained that he'd been told that Priscilla had hired some people "to bump me off." If Cullen could prove that, it would help his divorce case enormously. McCrory said the killers would talk, but only if they were convinced that Cullen wouldn't double-cross them. A tape was to be their insurance: with a recording of Cullen making incriminating statements, they could hold Cullen to the bargain. That's why Cullen agreed to make a tape, that plus the fact that he believed he was helping the FBI trap McCrory.

"I was doing what I thought the FBI agent had told me to do," Cullen said. "McCrory did most of the talking about my wanting to kill Priscilla and Judge Eidson and Beverly Bass, and I would say yes. I would steer him away from Priscilla. I would not say how much money I would be willing to pay; it would be sticking my neck out."

After the August 11 meeting, Cullen continued, he called the number that Agent Acree had given him and reported what had happened. Cullen testified that the voice on the other end that he assumed to be Acree told him: "That's fine. You keep playing along, and we'll be back in touch."

About a week later, McCrory called and arranged another meeting at Coco's. McCrory supposedly told Davis they needed another taping session because the August 11 tape "wasn't good enough." Cullen agreed to play along again. The date was August 18, the same meeting in which the FBI made its first undercover tape with a secret recorder fixed to McCrory's body. While McCrory held his small Norelco, Cullen told the jury, they sat in the car and talked about murder plots. The conversation was roughly the same one they'd had on August 11, he added.

"McCrory said I was going to have to say more if I was going to convince his people. He said if he asked me for a figure, I was to say $25,000 or something like that." One might suppose that this taping session would have started with some preliminary discussion, maybe even a review of the August 11 tape to illustrate places where Cullen could improve on the dialogue. If this had been the case, the warm-up talk would have been caught on the *second* tape recorder hidden under McCrory's shirt. Curiously, the prosecution never got around to asking about that. Maybe there was an explanation, maybe not. There was no explanation at all why the FBI didn't find a Norelco when they searched McCrory and his car both before and after the August 18 meeting.

But the mysterious Norelco was to furnish yet another twist to the plot, this one more important than any other single piece of testimony in the defense's case. Cullen said that he'd promised to return McCrory's $25,000 any time McCrory wanted it, and when McCrory called him at 3:00 A.M. on August 20 and Cullen said, "That information is down at the office," *information* was a code word for the $25,000. Six hours after that phone call Cullen met McCrory again at Coco's. And here was the clincher: it wasn't a picture of Judge Eidson's body that McCrory flashed that morning, Cullen told the jury. It was a pair of mini cassettes made at their previous taping sessions. Then Cullen revealed something else. He said McCrory opened his shirt and pointed to something on his chest.

"He didn't say what it was," Cullen testified, "but I guessed. It looked like a bug." And so, Cullen said, he continued to feign responses to McCrory's talk of murder.

At the end of Cullen's first day on the stand, Jack Strickland stood shaking his head at the maze of absolute contradictions just placed before the jury. "I've seen my eight-year-old son come up with better stories. I'm having a real hard time following the story line. There's a little something in it for everyone." Phil Burleson begged reporters to please "understand what Cullen was trying to do." What was that? "He was trying to find out who did the killings at the mansion," Burleson said. When Tolly Wilson heard Burleson's comment, he said: "That's a switch. Cullen never lifted a finger before to find out who killed Andrea, but of course he already knew."

Before turning his client over for cross-examination, Haynes stole some of their thunder by playing sections of the tapes and asking Cullen to explain. It was the moment everyone had been waiting for, and nobody appeared more interested (or relieved) than Pete Moore when Cullen acknowledged that the tapes were accurate. Since his early ruling allowing the jurors to follow along with transcripts, Moore had wondered if he'd made a reversible error. But now the defendant himself was concurring. As Cullen explained the tapes, almost everyone in the courtroom except Strickland was taking notes; Strickland sat back in his chair and didn't once take his eyes off Cullen Davis.

August 18 tape—McCrory says, "The man is here to put the judge away . . . but he wants $100,000." Cullen replies, "Bullshit."

Cullen's explanation—"I'd never told McCrory I would pay any amount of money to do anything." Cullen indicated that the profanity was directed toward the whole plan, not the extra fee.

August 18 tape—McCrory says, "Priscilla is a different story. . . . He says he can do it easy." Cullen replies: "Huh! Like hell! Priscilla's always got somebody around her. The judge doesn't."

Cullen's explanation—"He brought her up in a similar fashion in our August 11 meeting. I didn't want to be talking about Priscilla in case he turned on me again."

August 18 tape—After further discussion of a "price" on Priscilla, Cullen tells McCrory to "go back to the original plan." McCrory asks what plan, and Cullen says, "You know, who we started this out with." McCrory says, "Oh. Bev?" and Cullen replies, "Yeah."

Cullen's explanation—"That related to the fact he wasn't producing what we were having the meetings for.

I wanted to get the show on the road. And he kept wanting to make tapes. There was no plan to kill anybody. The original plan was to get Priscilla's people over to my side."

August 18 tape—McCrory says, "You still want all three of them at once?" Cullen replies: "Do it either way. Whatever is there."

Cullen's explanation—"He had told me the conversation about killing people is how we would convince Priscilla's people I wouldn't turn on them."

August 18 tape—Cullen says, "Do the judge, and then his wife, and that would be it."

Cullen's explanation—"I was going along with him, just like I thought the FBI wanted me to do. I was just following his cue. We weren't really talking about killing people. I was just trying to get his people to come around to my way of thinking. And I was just doing what I thought the FBI wanted me to do."

August 18 tape—Cullen says, "I'm covered all the time. . . . I'm staying covered."

Cullen's explanation—"I was worried about four different sources of threats on my life. I wanted to stay covered." Cullen added that he told McCrory he would pay $25,000 for help from Priscilla's killers. "I was willing to play along, and if it worked, I'd pay for it."

August 19 tape—On the telephone McCrory tells Cullen: "My man is working. He's out." Cullen replies, "You'll be uppermost in my mind."

Cullen's explanation—"The man here working didn't make sense to me. I knew shooting wasn't going on. I thought people would be listening in."

August 19 tape—McCrory calls again at 3:00 A.M. and tells Cullen the job is finished and the man wants to get out of town. Cullen asks, "How will I know?" and McCrory tells him he has proof. Cullen says, "All that information is down at the office."

Cullen's explanation—The word *information* referred to the $25,000 he was holding for McCrory. Cullen used the code word because Karen was in the room at the time. He said McCrory had instructed him to bring the money whenever money was mentioned. "I

419

had told him to call any time, but I didn't think he would call at 3:00 A.M."

"I didn't know what he meant by somebody being finished with the job. I did not believe someone had been killed. I didn't know what he was going to do."

August 20 tape—Cullen arrived with the money six hours later. Before joining McCrory at Coco's parking lot, however, he stopped across the street and walked around the FBI surveillance van. His first comment to McCrory was, "Just paranoid."

Cullen's explanation—Cullen told the jurors that he first thought the van belonged to one of his investigators. Then it crossed his mind that "maybe that's the FBI." Whatever the case, he saw no harm in carrying out his meeting with McCrory.

August 20 tape—McCrory tells Cullen he's got "something" for him; according to McCrory, he then handed Cullen the phony photograph and identification cards of the dead judge. Cullen asks what McCrory intends to do with them, and McCrory replies, "I'm going to get rid of the motherfuckers." Cullen says, "That's good. Glad to hear it."

Cullen's explanation—"He pulled out a white envelope, opened it up, and there were a couple of mini cassettes in it. I thought they'd come from his tape recorder, from our first attempts at making tapes. That's what I was referring to." Cullen denied seeing a photograph of Eidson's body or the judge's credentials. He offered no explanation of why he was glad McCrory was going to get rid of the tapes; ostensibly they were made for Priscilla's killers to keep.

August 20 tape—McCrory asks Cullen whom he wants as his next victim "because he's going to operate again tonight." Cullen responds: "Just one problem. I haven't got the money lined up."

Cullen's explanation—"I was trying to stall him at that point. I couldn't get the money anyway without Priscilla, her lawyers, and the judge finding out about it. I didn't know how much money he meant anyway."

August 20 tape—McCrory says, "I got Judge Eidson dead for you," and Cullen replies, "Good."

Cullen's explanation—"I was just going along with his conversation. I believed his conversation was just the way he talks. I had no reason for wanting Eidson dead. I didn't think there was going to be anybody who would kill anybody."

By now Haynes had been asking questions for nearly twelve hours, and Cullen appeared nonchalant, almost bored. But Haynes was coming to the key question about the August 10 phone call from the bogus FBI agent.

Q: How many times have you talked to agent Jim Acree face to face?

A: One time.

Q: How many times have you talked to him by phone?

A: A couple of times.

Q: You heard Agent Acree testify in this courtroom. Can you now testify under oath that the voice who called you on August 10, 1978, was the same Agent Acree who testified here?

A: I feel very certain it's not the same person.

As Haynes fed him questions, Cullen went on to say that he was also sure the August 10 voice did not belong to Bill Davis, David McCrory, or Pat Burleson. "Right now I don't have any idea who called me and said he was Acree," Cullen admitted. *But* he had heard something else in this courtroom that was highly significant. He had heard the *telephone number* that the bogus Acree gave him, the number he had called to inform Acree about the August 11 and again about the August 18 meetings with McCrory, the number he was in fact trying to call as the police moved in on him that Sunday morning.

Q: Did you hear that number in this courtroom during the course of this trial?

Q: Yes, I heard it.

Q: Was it during the period of time Pat Burleson was on the witness stand?

A: Yes.

The number Cullen now claimed to have heard, the number that jiggled his memory and supposedly explained things, was the number in the classified ad for the shotgun, the phone number of one of Pat Burleson's karate franchises. Although the school was shut down in late July or early August, Burleson had installed a forwarding device to transfer calls automatically to another number.

At a recess Jack Strickland said he wasn't surprised by this revelation. "They'd been dangling the phone number in front of the jury. We were taking bets last night that it would turn out to be Pat Burleson's home number. We were in the ball park." Now that Cullen acknowledged that he had been duped, that it wasn't actually Agent Acree he had talked to those several times but some impostor trying to frame him, one more question begged for an answer. It was this enormous contradiction—if Cullen mistrusted the FBI as both he and Karen Master had testified, why was he so willing to follow the bogus Acree's advice to play along and make those highly incriminating tapes? Why had he waited until now, eight weeks into the trial, to make known this startling discovery? You might suppose that as soon as the cops had moved in on him that Sunday morning, Cullen would have said something like: "Wait a minute! There's been a big mistake! Somebody get Acree on the phone. He'll explain all this terrible mix-up." But he didn't. These were questions that Racehorse Haynes didn't ask, and strangely enough, neither did the prosecution.

Haynes concluded his direct examination with this question: "Are you guilty of conspiring with Charles David McCrory . . . to cause the death of Judge Joseph Eidson?"

"As God is my witness," Cullen replied, "I certainly am not."

Tolly Wilson had dreamed not of Christmas sugarplums but of the day a-coming when he would finally be able to cross-examine Cullen Davis. Tolly had been the designated cross-examiner in Amarillo, he'd spent hours prepping for the big moment, and when it didn't come, Tolly took it hard. No one felt the essence of Cullen Davis's guilt, felt the righteousness of the prosecutor's wrath the way Tolly felt it—no one saw the full extent of the man's malevolence or the absolute necessity of ending it here and now. It was more than a mere feeling; it was an obsession with Tolly.

At first Tolly seemed to be directing his cross-examination toward the main discrepancy in Cullen's story —the inconceivability that a man who was angry with and mistrusted the FBI would then allow himself to be used like a trained seal. The prosecutor asked questions about Cullen's work, about the highly complex and important decisions that a man of his stature made daily.

Q: Decision making is not a new thing to you, then?

A: That's right.

Tolly asked about the extortion letter and about a bomb threat to one of Cullen's companies in 1976, and about the $100-million settlement with Bill Davis, but instead of leaning on the heart-of-the-matter contradiction Tolly switched to another one. He was skeptical of Cullen's claim that he made the tapes in order to convince Priscilla's killers that they should come over to his side.

Q: It was David McCrory's idea to talk about killing people to prove to them you wanted them to work for you and you would work for them?

A: This was to be their assurance that I wouldn't turn on them.

Q: How could you turn on them if all they were going to do was testify [in your divorce trial]?

A: I'm not sure. It wasn't my plan.

Q: Did David McCrory represent that these people were fine, upstanding citizens?

A: No.

Q: Did he represent that these people were the type that wouldn't turn on you?

A: I took it they might go to the highest bidder. If they were willing to turn on Priscilla to help me, they might turn on me if Priscilla offered them more money.

Q: Did you really expect they would come in and testify that they were available as hired killers?

423

A: I was skeptical of the whole program. That's why I wouldn't put any money into it.

Q: But you thought enough of it that you were willing to make a tape . . . to lay your whole self in their hands with that tape?

A: I thought I'd be safe if I didn't consummate a deal or agree to kill anybody.

Q: The thought didn't occur to you that they might take those tapes and blackmail you for the rest of your life?

A: Yes. That's why I was being a little bit careful.

For the next several hours Tolly took the witness almost line for line over the tapes, pausing to write the most incriminating parts on a blackboard.

THE MAN IS HERE TO PUT THE JUDGE AWAY.

Q: Did you understand that meant killing people?
A: No.
Q: Did you consider that [statement] damaging to you?
A: No, I didn't.

To each of more than a dozen incriminating statements Tolly asked the same two questions and Cullen gave the same two answers. No, he didn't think they were actually talking about killing people. No, he didn't consider the statements damaging so long as he didn't consummate the deal. Cullen revealed now that he had been relying on the advice of attorney Hershel Payne, his close friend and business associate. Early in the game, Cullen testified, he spoke of these problems with Hershel Payne.

"I told Hershel that David was wanting to talk about killing people," Cullen testified. "I said, 'Can David and I be prosecuted for it?' Hershel told me, 'If you don't intend to do it and you don't consummate the deal, no law is broken in this state. People talk about killing people all the time with no intention of doing it. There's no law against it.'" The attorney warned him, however, to be wary of a blackmail plot. Cullen added that he'd told Payne about other things—about McCrory giving him the $25,000 he claimed to have won

424

gambling and about McCrory offering him a gift of a gun and silencer. Cullen said the attorney advised him that possession of a silencer was legal if it was registered with Alcohol, Tobacco and Firearms agents. Cullen thought he also told Hershel Payne about Priscilla's hired killers and at least two other possible threats on his life. But by far the most important thing he told his friend Hershel Payne was about the August 10 phone call from FBI special agent Jim Acree. Cullen told Payne that Acree had urged him to play along with McCrory, that he and McCrory had made an incriminating tape; he'd even given Payne "all the names we discussed on the tapes . . . Priscilla, Beverly, Bubba, Mr. Gavrel, Sr., and Judge Eidson."

This was a startling revelation, and the only thing Tolly Wilson could think of to ask was why Davis called on Hershel Payne instead of one of his many regular criminal lawyers when he was seeking advice on all these matters.

Jurors giggled when Cullen replied wryly, "Because Hershel doesn't charge me when I call him."

Throughout the ordeal, Cullen Davis appeared every inch the high corporate executive, coolly deliberate, in control, terse, even frugal. In his testimony Cullen frequently fell back on the contention that he himself never once offered to put up a cent of his money to finance McCrory's crazy scheme. He was prepared to pay for *results,* nothing less. McCrory had even offered to put up his own $25,000 against a "bonus" from Cullen if he could in fact deliver Priscilla's hired killers to Cullen's team. Like a good executive, Cullen had sought the advice of attorney Hershel Payne before he decided to play along. Cullen seemed pleased when Tolly Wilson asked if he had counted the $25,000. Yes, he said. He counted it when McCrory gave it to him, and he counted it again when he returned it to McCrory. Asked if it bothered him that McCrory didn't count it on August 20, Cullen said, "No. That was his problem." When Cullen told the prosecutor that the tapes were "just making conversation . . . there's no law against that," his voice was tinged with arrogance.

One reason for his arrogance was that Cullen expected to be released on bond as soon as the jury was excused for the weekend. This was Friday, December 29. Technically, Judge Moore couldn't rule on bail until the following day, but the judge had already told attorneys to be prepared for a hearing Friday afternoon. Phil Burleson carried a large cashier's check in his coat pocket. Cullen Davis had spent nineteen of his last twenty-eight months behind bars, but he planned to celebrate the new year a free man. And then, suddenly, with no explanation at all, the defense withdrew its bond motion. Nobody would say why, except that the unexpected retraction concerned an unspecified legal matter. It was almost a month later when Pete Moore revealed the real reason—the judge tipped off Cullen's attorneys in advance that he would not grant bond. In fairness to the defendant, Moore didn't want to surprise the defense by reciting in open court his reasons for not granting bond; someone might have taken it as a comment that in his opinion Davis was guilty. Defense attorneys could have gone ahead and filed the motion, but they backed off in fear of the bad publicity in the final stages of the trial.

The only thing Cullen Davis observed on New Year's Eve was the end of his 588th day of confinement since his first arrest in August 1976. While the other prisoners in the Harris County jail voted on what football bowl games they would watch on their community TV, a new and no doubt frightening dilemma was churning in the stomach of Cullen Davis. Several reporters had telephoned Hershel Payne in Fort Worth, and Hershel was slightly astonished by Cullen's testimony.

"Some of it is accurate, but a lot of it isn't," Payne said. "I'm under subpoena, so I'd better not comment any further."

When court resumed on the second day of the new year, the defense had two surprise witnesses. One was Cullen Davis, who had "reflected" over the weekend on his previous testimony and wanted an opportunity to clarify certain parts of it. Not surprisingly, they concerned two key pieces of testimony about his conversations with Hershel Payne.

Cullen now recalled that the only person he'd told about the August 10 call from Agent Acree was Karen Master. He'd been mistaken when he testified seven days earlier that he also told Hershel Payne about the call and about the FBI agent's advice that he should play along with McCrory. Cullen also recalled now that he hadn't told Payne the identities of the people he and McCrory had discussed killing, nor had he mentioned making any tapes. "I don't think I said that," Cullen testified. "If I did, I didn't mean that."

Ostensibly, the jury had no way of knowing that Cullen changed his story after newspaper accounts told of Hershel Payne's denials. The retraction did give the prosecution an opportunity to question Davis concerning anyone else he might have told about his agreement with Acree—the cops, for example. Until now prosecutors had shied away from attempting to demonstrate anything Cullen might or might not have said at the time of his arrest, before he was advised of his Miranda rights. Now Tolly Wilson asked the defendant if he'd yelled for the arresting officers to contact Acree. Cullen admitted that he had not. Tolly didn't pursue the contradiction. Instead, he tried to introduce into evidence a list of names and phone numbers confiscated from Cullen at the time of his arrest.

Cullen had testified that the first of two phone calls

427

he made just before his arrest was to the number "Acree" had given him. There was no answer. His second call was to one of his own investigators, but Cullen explained that the line was busy. The prosecutor wanted to point out to the jury that the list included the phone numbers of McCrory, Ken Davis, Steve Sumner, and investigator Harry Knieff, but it did *not* include the supposed FBI number. Judge Moore refused to allow the list into evidence.

The defense's second surprise witness was a Fort Worth used-car dealer named James Stephens, who had a potential dynamite revelation for the court. Somewhere around noon on either August 17 or August 18, Stephens said in a beer hall drawl, he was fixing a flat tire in front of the Holiday Inn on University Drive when he saw David McCrory, Pat Burleson, and Priscilla Davis emerge from the motel. Stephens slumped in the witness chair and regarded the jury through sunglasses as he recalled telling a companion: "There's Priscilla Davis, the TV star. There's Pat Burleson with them." Dorothy Neeld had linked the three alleged counterconspirators together in front of Jet Air in mid-July, but until now no one claimed to have seen them together during the crucial period just before Cullen's arrest. Stephens acknowledged that he'd first contacted the defense several weeks earlier. Stephens claimed he was reluctant to testify, and he started to tell the jury why: "It wouldn't be safe. Too many dope heads that Priscilla Davis . . ." At that point the judge cut him off. Stephens claimed that a few days after Cullen's arrest he told his story to a Tarrant County sheriff's deputy and to a DA's investigator. He preferred not to divulge their names. Stephens added that the DA's investigator warned him, "It'd be best if you don't get involved."

Stephens's potential bombshell was quickly defused when Pete Moore ordered him to tell the names of these two law enforcement officers. Stephens shrugged and said he couldn't remember their names. The judge shot a glance at Tolly Wilson, inviting the prosecution to request that Stephens be cited for contempt of court. Tolly Wilson decided this wasn't necessary.

"You say you can't remember their names?" Wilson asked the witness. "Is that just as true as the rest of the testimony you've given here?"

"Yes, sir," Stephens said.

"No further questions," Wilson snapped.

Later, after the judge had instructed Stephens to make some long-distance phone calls and refresh his memory, Stephens changed his story. Now he remembered that it wasn't a DA's investigator who'd advised him not to get involved, it was deputy sheriff D. K. Dunlap. But when investigators contacted Dunlap, the deputy said he hadn't seen Stephens in two years. Stephens finally said, "I don't remember one day to the next. I wish I hadn't got involved."

The following day the defense called Hershel Payne. Both sides already knew what he was going to say. The initial shock had subsided, but after the long ordeal of waiting, Hershel looked and felt like a Halloween pumpkin left too long in the heat. A friend had asked Hershel what he was going to do, and Hershel had said, "Do what's right, I guess." Since Cullen's falling out with Roy Rimmer, Payne had probably been Cullen's closest friend. No one had to remind him that a very valuable friendship was in jeopardy.

Payne took the stand and corroborated Cullen's story that he'd told the lawyer that David McCrory had mentioned hired killers and offered to give Cullen a silencer. But Payne said any suggestions he offered were as a business partner and friend, not as a lawyer. "I told him it appeared from looking at the statutes that it was legal to own a silencer as long as it was registered and approved in advance by the federal government. I told him it was no crime to talk about killing people as long as he didn't intend to do it and didn't consummate the deal." Payne confirmed too that Cullen had told him McCrory gave him "a substantial amount of money" for safekeeping, but he denied that Cullen ever mentioned the sum $25,000.

In cross-examination Jack Strickland had the witness

recount four conversations in which Cullen Davis mentioned McCrory or silencers. Each conversation began with talk about their uranium stock, Payne said, then drifted "almost incidentally" to the matters now before the court. In January or February, Cullen first mentioned David McCrory. "I told him he should stay away from David McCrory," Payne recalled. "He kind of laughed and said, 'Don't worry. I wouldn't trust David.'" In late May or early June, Cullen told Payne: "Hey, David McCrory has been talking to me again, and this time he says he can have people killed for me if I need him to. They can't have me arrested or put in jail for talking about it with David, can they?"

Payne explained: "I thought Mr. Davis was not serious about it, and he didn't think McCrory was serious about it. I didn't get the impression Mr. Davis intended to enter into any agreement with David McCrory. It was more an incidental discussion. If I thought there was a serious plot to take anyone's life, I would have advised the district attorney's office."

Sometime in July, Payne continued, Cullen again inquired about silencers. The conversation went like this:

Payne: Why do you want to know?

Cullen: Don't worry, I'll let you know.

Payne: I hope you're not asking for yourself because you don't need a gun of any kind, especially one with a silencer.

Cullen: Oh, don't worry about it, Hershel.

Payne: If you're really serious about this, you better talk to someone who knows more about it.

Later in July, Cullen mentioned that McCrory had given him a substantial amount of money. "I told him to give it back," Hershel said. "He said, 'Oh, don't worry. I'll take care of David' or something like that." At no time, the lawyer testified, did Cullen Davis tell him about any tapes, the FBI, any threats or extortion schemes, bulletproof vests, or plots to kill Eidson. Specifically, Payne said that Cullen never mentioned an August 10 phone call or the name Jim Acree. "I never heard the name Acree until this trial started," he said.

The witness also contradicted Cullen's story that he called Payne after the August 11 taping session with McCrory.

Strickland asked the witness, "Did you feel that in some way you were being set up to provide an alibi for Cullen Davis?"

A: I don't think my friend of ten to twelve years, Cullen Davis, would set me up, no, sir.

Q: Have you not, in fact, said that you don't want to be number sixteen on his hit list?

After Haynes angrily objected to the question, Strickland glanced at the jury and phrased it another way.

Q: You do not *think* your friend Thomas Cullen Davis would set you up or manipulate you to provide a cover, but in fact, has that thought crossed your mind in the last five or six months?

A: I guess it may have crossed my mind, when I've seen the sequence of events.

Q: Have you been able to discern this pattern of asking you, not a criminal lawyer, about matters which might appear to be violations of criminal statutes?

A: That needs to be put in context. I may be Cullen's closest personal friend. With that in mind, yes, sir.

Q: Without drawing any conclusions or making any judgment as to what this chain actually meant, you are able to see this chain of events, are you not?

A: I think all I can do is recount these events. The facts are the facts.

Strickland was working up to what he considered the most damning question of all. The prosecutor directed Payne's attention to the morning of August 21 when he visited Cullen's cell. It might be argued that the reason Cullen didn't call for Agent Acree at the time of his arrest or during the interrogation that followed was that he didn't trust the authorities who were holding him, but surely he trusted Hershel Payne. Strickland asked the witness if Cullen had brought up the name Acree that Monday morning or told his old friend "this is all a terrible misunderstanding . . . I've been working for the FBI."

431

"No, sir," Hershel Payne said. "That wasn't mentioned."

It was with enormous trepidation that Hershel Payne visited Cullen late that evening. He couldn't imagine what Cullen might say. What Cullen said was, "Thank you, thank you very much." It was Cullen's impression that Hershel Payne greatly assisted in his defense. Tolly Wilson had no doubt that Payne aided in Davis's prosecution. "I think that blew them out of the water," Tolly told reporters. "I was really proud of my profession today when Hershel Payne testified. You know that testimony was damaging to him financially, as well as damaging to a friend. But he told the truth. That's all we have to rely on in our profession."

Some thought it was an act of desperation or at least an attempt to draw attention away from Payne's testimony, but Cullen's defense immediately threw its total energies into exposing a bizarre subplot that Racehorse Haynes termed "the creeper peeper conspiracy." Haynes resurrected his charge that Bill Davis was financing the entire conspiracy against Cullen and told Judge Moore they were prepared now to prove it. Payment for the operation was concealed with checks written by a non-existent company in Laramie, Wyoming, Haynes contended. The money was funneled through a Denver law firm that had represented Bill Davis in the past, and then down to ex-prosecutor Joe Shannon, who hired a team of investigators to, among other things, "surreptitiously intercept phone calls" between Cullen and his attorneys, his attorneys and witnesses, and between the attorneys themselves. Racehorse told the judge that electronic "bird dogs" were attached to cars and that defense attorneys and witnesses were being followed all over Houston. The lawyers' living and working quarters were also under surveillance, Haynes charged. Finally, Haynes said he could produce evidence tying the secret investigation to Priscilla, Pat Burleson, and David McCrory.

At this late stage in the trial Pete Moore felt he had no choice. Haynes was permitted to call a whole new batch of witnesses, though only a few of them were heard by the jury. When they testified, it turned out that there was a basic flaw in Haynes's contention: whatever Shannon's investigators were up to, they didn't begin work until after Cullen's arrest on August 20.

Pete Moore had had it. He must have been knocking off two packs of cigarettes a day by now, and at times it appeared all that smoke was coming out of his ears. His face was the color of Tabasco sauce and his voice the texture of new lava as the judge finally called for a showdown with his old friend Richard Haynes.

"I think the whole system of justice is being abused, and I don't like it!" the judge told Haynes.

Racehorse swelled up like a blowfish and retorted, "I want to know who paid these people, who would go to the trouble to investigate us, and why!"

"Who cares?!" Moore said in a mild roar. "I don't! This is a complete waste of time. I don't see how an investigation in October has anything to do with what happened before August 20."

Haynes must have got the message. Two days later the defense called its final witness, a former Las Vegas cocktail waitress who testified that in 1975 David McCrory questioned her at great length about the benefits of the Federal Witness Protection Program, with which she was most familiar. The defense was apparently implying that McCrory concocted the whole story so that he would be eligible for a federal handout.

After five weeks on center stage, the defense rested, and the prosecution immediately called rebuttal witnesses to repair the damage. Both sides speculated that the case would go to the jury in another week, but no one really knew who was winning. Houston bookies were laying two to one for acquittal. All that really indicated was that more people were betting on Cullen's millions and Racehorse Haynes's charm and expertise than were betting on the tapes. Some weeks earlier, before the defense got in high gear, Fort Worth police raided a bookie joint that was quoting seven to five for guilty.

If it got down to bottom dollar, one gambler said,

the smarts would bet on Cullen. He could reach deeper. He didn't have a choice.

It was possible the case could boil down to bottom *nickel*. Some people missed the significance, but one of the state's first rebuttal witnesses demonstrated that the contents of Cullen Davis's pockets on the morning of his arrest proved he was lying on at least one vital point. Cullen testified that he made two calls from the phone booth just before his arrest. One no answer, and one busy. Cullen said specifically that he put twenty cents into the slot and got it back after each unsuccessful call. When police searched him, Cullen was carrying $1,122 in bills but only *fifteen cents* in change. How could that be? Logic suggested that Cullen either reached someone whom he lied about talking to, or he called no one. Or Ma Bell cheated him out of twenty cents, and he lied about that. Whatever the case, there was unsurpassed irony in speculating that the richest man ever brought to trial in Texas might lose for lack of a nickel.

Monday, January 8—this was supposed to be the final week, but even a casual glance at the headlines told everyone it wouldn't be: DAVIS WITNESS JAILED FOR PERJURY. The accused was Larry Gene Lucas, who was slapped in the Harris County jail on $100,000 bond after a sealed indictment charged him with aggravated perjury. The grand jury had actually handed down its indictment on December 20, and prosecutors had intended to keep it secret until the conclusion of the trial, but two rebuttal witnesses refused to testify as long as Lucas was walking the streets. When word spread over

Houston that Lucas was in jail, Racehorse Haynes exploded.

One of the grand jury witnesses who helped put Larry Gene Lucas in the slammer was Joe Espinoza, whom Haynes had counted on to support Lucas's story. Another was Kimberly Vandiver, sister-in-law of Lucas's common-law wife, Mary Weir, and still another was Mary Weir herself. They all testified that Lucas lied to the jury on December 11 when he said David McCrory offered him $20,000 to kill Cullen Davis.

Kim Vandiver introduced a letter written by Lucas to his lady friend Mary Weir. The letter was postmarked November 13, less than a month before Lucas hit the witness stand, and though the language was semiliterate, the implication was profoundly clear. The letter read in part:

"Hi, Baby: I want you to call Bill Morris, a bail bondsman. . . . tell Bill that your my wife. And that I was approached by David McCroy to wipe Kullen Davis. Tell him I know David for 14 years. I can prove that he talked to me. Also tell him that I'll have to have enough money to leave the country. Because the FBI will be so hot I won't be able to stay here. If he thinks my information might be important, then get in touch with me . . . now do this because there . . . could be some good money in it.   Love, Gene.
          P.S. Now do this whether you want to or not."

Larry Gene Lucas was no stranger to the inside of a jailhouse, but from the way Racehorse Haynes was spitting hot nails, you might have thought Lucas was a martyr to the Inquisition. Haynes bellowed that the prosecution had deliberately leaked word of Lucas's arrest in order to prejudice the Cullen Davis jury and demanded that Pete Moore declare a mistrial. Moore refused. Haynes demanded that the judge question each juror to determine if the news of Lucas's misfortune had permeated the jury box and then to sequester the jury for the remainder of the trial. Moore refused, but he did instruct the jury to disregard anything they might have heard or read about any witness. But Race wasn't satisfied. He took it as a personal affront and demanded that the court investigate the media leak.

Moore refused, but he allowed Haynes to question Tolly Wilson under oath.

Haynes asked the chief prosecutor how word of Lucas's arrest leaked to news reporters, and Wilson said, "The first reporter that phoned me said he had received an anonymous tip."

"The old anonymous tip, eh?" Haynes said, his voice dripping with sarcasm.

"I'm sure you're quite familiar with that," Wilson sniffed.

"Do you think *I* placed the anonymous tip?"

"I don't think you did," Wilson replied. "But I believe you could have had it done."

"Are you suggesting that *I* had it done?" Race asked incredulously.

"Yes, sir!"

"Is that the result of some recent illness?" Haynes inquired, his voice dangerously close to cracking.

"Are you *dethroned of your reason,* Mr. Haynes?" Tolly responded in a voice that shook with indignation.

"That's the most asinine thing I've ever heard," Haynes said.

Terry Wilson, a Harris County assistant DA who had been assisting the prosecution, was on his feet now, shaking his finger at Haynes. Race clenched his fist and took a couple of menacing steps toward Terry Wilson, saying, "Don't point your finger at me like that again!" Terry Wilson, who was about a head taller than Haynes, repeated the gesture. This time Race turned to the bench and told Moore, "He's not *big* enough to make threatening gestures!" At this point assistant DA Paul Gartner, who is five foot four, leaped to his feet and said, "Who is Mr. Haynes to talk about not being big enough?!"

"All right, let's get on with it," Moore said, meaning the trial, not the brawl. But Haynes wasn't through. Now he elicited testimony from Moore about when the judge first learned of Lucas's indictment (December

21 or 22) and put into the record that the defense was not advised of the indictment or the arrest.

Tempers flared again while Tolly Wilson was questioning Mary Weir. Haynes accused the prosecutor of "a rank insubordinate tactic . . . in bad faith." Tolly belched, "Let Mr. Haynes get petulant on his own time, not on this jury's time."

"Gentlemen," Moore warned the lawyers, "I'm not going to have any more of this."

Several jurors giggled; they had been a long time without laughs.

Mary Weir, a tall, washed-out woman in her late thirties, told the jury that she had lived with Lucas from time to time since her husband died in the late 1960s. Shortly after Cullen Davis's arrest, she said, Lucas began formulating his plan. "He said he knew McCrory and felt like if McCrory could get in on a good deal like that, there's no reason he couldn't be of help to Cullen Davis. He was going to say McCrory offered him money to kill Davis. He was going to say [this discussion] happened in late December or early January." The night before Lucas testified in Houston, Weir continued, he and Joe Espinoza came to her mobile home. "Gene wanted me to come down to Houston to back up his statement and say I was with him when he talked to McCrory. He thought I'd be a more credible witness than Joe." The following night Lucas called her from Houston and said he'd changed the date from winter to summer. That's when she contacted the Tarrant County DA's office, Mary Weir said. They visited her that night, and she gave them Lucas's letter.

Haynes began his cross-examination by establishing that Mary Weir was a prostitute who was probably lying about her marriage to Larry Gene Lucas in order to cheat on her Social Security benefits. Mary Weir acknowledged her unsavory past, but she didn't waver on her testimony that Lucas lied under oath.

Haynes: Are you telling this jury that Larry Gene Lucas told you he hadn't seen David McCrory at all?

Weir: That's what I'm telling them.

Haynes: Are you telling this jury he said he was going to make up a story and be a witness?

Weir: That's what I am telling the jury.

Then why didn't she go to the police? Haynes asked. Weir said she didn't think anyone would take Lucas seriously. Well, why didn't she call police that time that Lucas rammed a pistol in her ear and had his way with her pretty flesh? Weir acknowledged that she wasn't on very good terms with the police. And yet she wanted the jury to believe that she had *called* the DA's office and volunteered Lucas's letter?

There was a hint of desperation in Haynes's style as he continued to maul the witness. Some thought he was intentionally stalling the course of the trial. "That's an old tactic when you're playing for a hung jury," Tolly Wilson suggested. Pete Moore tended to agree. Moore had watched Racehorse Haynes at work on other occasions, "but that was before he developed the technique of asking the same questions seven different ways." You could tell that Moore greatly admired Haynes as a lawyer, and when this was all over, they might still be friends. What seemed lost was the *respect*—certainly a lawyer was supposed to fight for his client, but Moore had the uncomfortable feeling that this time Race was fighting for his own ego. Lawyers and reporters who had followed Haynes's career, especially those who had watched the two Cullen Davis trials, thought they saw in Haynes something more than just a tireless defender of a man he no doubt believed innocent; was it *justice* that drove Haynes, or was it his own out-of-control egomaniacal competitiveness? Did Haynes really see a conspiracy in which half of Fort Worth was attempting to frame Cullen Davis, or did he see the terrible apparition of his own vulnerability? Haynes had been a star in Amarillo, but he hadn't been a zealot. Now the battlefield was Houston, the place where his character was molded, the home of his absolute peers. The biggest case of his career, the peak. "Who knows?" one Houston lawyer speculated. "He might be fighting just as hard if it was Joe versus Blow. The important thing is winning." Race might not have agreed. The important thing at the moment was *not losing*.

The state had a few more cleanup witnesses before it rested. One of them was FBI agent Jim Acree who denied that he'd talked to Cullen Davis in August but testified that he *had* given Cullen his phone number eight months earlier. He'd given him *four* numbers, in fact, along with explicit instructions that Davis not meet with any extortionist unless Acree knew about it in advance and arranged for surveillance.

The state's final witness was David Childers, Priscilla's brother. Childers was called to shoot holes in the testimony of Mary Ramsey, who claimed to have seen Priscilla in Las Vegas on June 13. Childers, who was living in Ohio at the time, had documents to prove that he visited Fort Worth from June 10 to 16. On June 13, Childers told the jury, he was with Priscilla in Fort Worth until 5:00 P.M., and he talked to her by telephone again that night at the mansion.

By midweek when the state finally rested its case, tempers had calmed and an uneasy peace existed in the courtroom. It didn't last long. The defense's first rebuttal witness, a golf hustler named Harold Sexton, came forward with an astonishing story. Sexton grew up in Arlington, between Dallas and Fort Worth, but now he lived in Anaheim, California. Two weeks ago, Sexton told the jury, he'd read in one of the Los Angeles papers about Cullen's testimony that he "played along" with McCrory because of a telephone call from a man he believed to be an FBI agent. Sexton suddenly recalled a chance meeting with David McCrory the previous summer when he was home on vacation. Sexton couldn't remember the date, but it was several weeks before Cullen's arrest. Sexton, who hadn't seen McCrory in several years, ran into him at Sambo's restaurant on East Lancaster in Fort Worth. They talked about old times for a while. "David came to the conclusion that things hadn't been going good for me in the past year or two," Sexton told the jury, "and he asked me if I would like to make some money. He said, 'We need someone to place a phone call to Cullen and represent himself as a police officer.'" Sexton added that he assumed *Cullen* to be Cullen Davis, though there was no other reference to Davis in the conversation. "I asked no questions at all about it," Sexton said. "I didn't want to know."

Caught off guard by this eleventh-hour witness, Tolly Wilson hammered away with questions designed to raise doubts about Sexton's motives, asking why he refused to talk with state investigators and pointing out his suspicious financial status. Sexton exhibited a highly selective memory. He couldn't recall the names or addresses of people he'd stayed with while on vacation (except his mother), but he clung firmly to the story that he'd met McCrory at Sambo's restaurant on East Lancaster. DA's investigators worked most of the night trying to find something to rock Sexton's credibility, but all Tolly had come up with the next morning was the suggestion that Sexton was acquainted with known gamblers in Fort Worth.

There was a basic flaw in Sexton's story, however, and some enterprising reporters found it Thursday night: Sambo's on East Lancaster burned on May 20 and did not reopen for business until September 20.

Sexton was accompanied by a lawyer when he appeared in court Friday morning. Again, the defense used newspaper accounts to grab the initiative. Before the prosecution had a chance to parade their own witnesses to show that the Sambo's on East Lancaster had burned two months before Sexton claimed to have had coffee there with McCrory, Haynes asked his witness to return to the stand and describe his route on the morning in question. On reexamination, it turned out that Sexton was talking about *another* Sambo's, this one on Division Street in Arlington, seven miles from the place he'd first described.

Sexton claimed he just made a mistake—Division in Arlington and East Lancaster in Fort Worth are both part of U.S. Highway 80. "Highway 80, Division, Lancaster—hell, they all run together," Sexton said. "They're one and the same." Maybe it sounded that way to a jury in Houston, but it was almost inconceivable that anyone who grew up in Arlington would mistake the two streets. Division started at the east city limits and ran to the west city limits of Arlington, where it became simply Highway 80. Then came a four- or five-mile stretch of undeveloped land. At the Fort Worth city limits just past the Handley Drug Store, the street widened into a boulevard and became East Lancaster. Sexton admitted he had traveled the road many times.

"Don't you know if you were trying to float this story in front of a bunch of Fort Worth or Arlington people they'd laugh you out of the courtroom?" Wilson asked.

"I've been laughed at before." Sexton shrugged.

The witness denied that newspaper and radio accounts of the fire at Sambo's prompted his reappearance on the witness stand.

"To this day, you never heard that until I told you?" Wilson asked in his inscrutable style.

"No," Sexton said coolly.

"Out of the woodwork they do come," Tolly Wilson groused after the witness had been excused. Pete Moore was less charitable. Some long-dormant prosecutorial instinct was boiling inside the judge, who admitted he had a difficult time keeping his mouth closed during the cross-examination of Sexton. "My blood pressure must have gone up to about 3,000," Moore sad later. "Hell, I live in Houston, and I know that highway better than Sexton. Highway 80 is Davis in Dallas, Main in Grand Prairie, Division in Arlington, then there's a long open space before it becomes Lancaster." This wasn't the first time that Pete Moore had been incensed by the prosecution's inability to shake a witness's already shaky story. Tempers on both sides were badly frayed. Later that day Moore intervened to stop what would have been a fist fight between Tolly Wilson and Racehorse Haynes. "I'm going to put this case before the jury Monday morning if there is any way," the judge told attorneys outside the presence of the jury. "I'm going to land this monster if I have to blow out every tire in the courtroom." At the end of the day Moore

441

told the jurors to bring their toothbrushes Monday; he was going to sequester them.

The defense used its final batch of witnesses to establish that Bill Davis had taken considerable effort to avoid testifying. One final witness, a Houston travel agent, brought airline time schedules to prove that Priscilla could have flown to Las Vegas on the night of June 13 and still returned to Fort Worth before her brother saw her again the next morning, though this didn't explain how David Childers had been able to phone Priscilla that night at the mansion.

It was all over now but final argument and jury deliberation. Both sides claimed their cases were in good shape. Jurors had heard more than one hundred witnesses in eleven weeks, but it really boiled down to a simple liar's contest—who would they believe, Cullen or McCrory? If the defense had been obliged to prove their conspiracy theory, the case would have been thrown out of court weeks before. Of the more than sixty witnesses called by defense, only a handful emerged as credible: one had been indicted for perjury, another had barely escaped a perjury indictment, and at least five had been forced to hire lawyers in their own defense. One Houston lawyer compared the defense's strategy to juggling hand grenades. The prosecution had made many mistakes, but in the final analysis it could turn on the tapes and ask, Is that the voice of a man "playing along" or a millionaire buying murder? And yet, as Mike Gibson pointed out, "we only have to convince one juror." Someone asked Pete Moore what he would do in case of a hung jury. Moore said he would probably slash his wrist, turn, and walk away.

Virtually the entire cast was assembled for closing arguments. On the right side of the courtroom, in a section reserved for the defense, Ken Davis and his family sat with Karen Master and her family. Except for the austere surroundings it might have been the Jewel Charity Ball. Cullen's women appeared uniform—teased blonde hair, jewels, furs, Ultrasuede. Even the lawyers' wives appeared blonde and bejeweled. The left side of the room was reserved for the prosecution and could have passed for a local party caucus. Judge Joe Eidson sat front row center, a few feet from the jury box. W. T. Rufner and friends sat near the back, giggling occasionally and passing what appeared to be a joint. In the middle, like so many strangers in a lifeboat, sat the press, and behind them, in what seats remained, the public.

Terry Wilson, the prosecutor on loan from the Harris County DA's office, led off, coaxing a few laughs from the jury as he assumed the role of Cullen Davis and attempted to demonstrate the absurdity of Cullen's story. "According to Cullen Davis's scenario," Wilson told the jury, "David McCrory was so broke he couldn't even afford to go to Las Vegas, much less win $25,000. Yet you're supposed to believe that he came back from Las Vegas and gave all that money to Cullen Davis for safekeeping?" As Terry Wilson reviewed the evidence, he backed away from the jury box, moving closer to where Cullen Davis sat stone-faced and motionless. When Wilson came to the part about the mysterious Norelco tape recorder that Cullen claimed McCrory had on August 18, the prosecutor looked at Davis, then at the jury, and asked: "What *happened* to that tape recorder? It wasn't on McCrory or in his car when the FBI searched him before the meeting. It wasn't there after the meeting. Where did it come from? Where did it go?" The prosecutor snapped his fingers in Cullen's face. "It just appeared!" He snapped his fingers again. "And then . . . it was gone. Wonderful!" And what about the mini cassettes Davis claimed McCrory showed him on August 20? Disappeared, just like the tape recorder. Wilson reminded the jury that Cullen claimed he was making the tapes to show the divorce judge how Priscilla was squandering her money on hit men, admitting at the same time that he might be forced to buy them back. "The judge is gonna be mad if I say I want to kill Priscilla but not if I say I want to kill him!" the prosecutor said, doing a bad imitation of Cullen's voice. Leaning across the table until his face was a few inches from Cullen's, Wilson shouted: *"I got Judge Eidson dead for you!* . . . and from the cheering gallery . . .

443

good!" Finally, the prosecutor walked to the stand and assumed the role of witness. "Well, Judge," he said, "I'm one of Priscilla's killers. I make my living killing folks. I just want you to know how Priscilla spends her money!"

Three defense attorneys used their allotted four hours arguing that the evidence was not sufficient to convict Davis on the two charges drawn up by the court, solicitation of capital murder and criminal conspiracy to commit capital murder. Both charges carried a possible life sentence. The jury would have to either acquit Cullen or choose one of the two charges.

"The only thing they have is the tapes," Mike Gibson reminded the jury. "And since there are two versions of why the tapes were made—one credible and one incredible, that's McCrory's—there is not enough evidence to convict Cullen Davis."

Phil Burleson invited the jury to consider the situation if the roles had been reversed, if Cullen was the star witness and McCrory the defendant. "Let's think if that *had* been Jim Acree [on the telephone] and we were now in a U.S. District Court and the case was the United States versus Charles David McCrory. And the witness called in support of the tapes was Thomas Cullen Davis. If he told you exactly the same thing he testified to here and then McCrory got up on the witness stand and testified just as he did here, I can assure you the U.S. Attorney would tell you Thomas Cullen Davis was telling the truth.

"It is hard in a sterile courtroom to understand why someone would do the things Cullen Davis did," Burleson continued. "But it is not unrealistic to think that when a person of authority calls and asks a concerned citizen for help, he goes along without asking for the person to come out and show him his U.S. Department of Justice identification card."

It was generally agreed that Racehorse Haynes's closing argument was "remarkable"; most remarkable was the fact that no two people who heard it agreed on what was said. It was as though Race were talking two simultaneous, harmonious, completely unrelated languages. The lawyer had a head cold that was developing into a case of flu, but he talked for two hours, alternately raging and dropping his voice to a pitiful whisper. After a while tears came to his eyes. Mostly, it was an attack on McCrory and on Priscilla Davis. "McCrory . . . the opportunist . . . the man who had information Cullen needed . . . who listed on his application form at Jet Air: sales of all things." McCrory sold Priscilla, then sold Cullen, then sold the FBI, and now he was trying to sell the jury. Several times Race spoke of the *sequence of events,* starting with Priscilla's demand for a $20-million divorce settlement, known as Priscilla's "gamble" . . . the extortion letter . . . "the FBI's cavalier attitude" toward the extortion letter . . . Cullen's admittedly "bad judgment" in hiring McCrory . . . McCrory's unabashed envy of rich people . . . Cullen's state of mind, the enormous pressures of his business and his personal life . . . (Haynes's voice softens) the $20-million gamble "that failed because Charles David McCrory wouldn't betray his trust to Priscilla Lee Davis [almost a whisper now]. *I suspect she'd a lot rather be contesting her part of the estate as a widow, knowing her* [voice rising]" . . . Jannings's sloppy 302 . . . the fact that some FBI agents weren't called to testify . . . "Charles David McCrory, *the man who sells all things. . . ."*

The jurors' faces showed not the slightest indication whether or not they were following Haynes's "sequence of events." Mary Carter, the forty-seven-year-old medical secretary who had told Race his name was a household word in her family, seemed mesmerized, as though she were eyewitnessing Judgment Day, watching the exorcism of demons she didn't know existed. Frances Hambrick, who was five years younger than Mary Carter but looked five years older, dozed from time to time. This wasn't the first time Haynes had put Mrs. Hambrick to sleep. During voir dire she expressed great respect for Haynes and giggled as she admitted she had only a ninth-grade education. Frances's hobby was watching soap operas, and Racehorse seemed to find that amusing. Frances said she didn't see anything

445

amusing about real life. Jack Strickland had observed that "Haynes insulted her . . . I mean really talked down to her." It was this observation that convinced the state she would make a good juror. Charles Franks, the engineer Haynes had tried to eliminate because he attached too much credibility to the testimony of police officers, appeared impassive as he tried to follow Racehorse's sequence. So did most of the jurors. Impassive, or maybe bored.

By law the prosecution has the final word. Jack Strickland reminded the jurors that the case was unique because they were actually "eyewitnesses" to the crime. "There is no guesswork involved in this trial," he said. "You don't have to guess if Cullen Davis said 'good' when told that this man right here [pointing to Eidson in the front row] was *dead*. What in God's name could be the explanation for a statement like that? You may not want to believe it, but you know what David Mc-Crory said, and you know Cullen Davis's response." The only answers the defense had for the tapes, Strickland told the jury, were "gossip, innuendos, character assassination," and theories that might be described as "ABC—*Anybody But Cullen.*"

Earlier, when he was alone in his hotel room outlining his final remarks, Strickland thought about ramming the jury with the hardest fact of all—there sat *Cullen Davis,* a man of immense power and wealth and arrogance, a man accused of plotting the murders of fifteen people. If this jury turned him loose, *they* would bear the consequences of any future criminal acts, *they* would risk becoming accomplices to murder. But Strickland backed off; he felt that this was a challenge better left unspoken. Instead, he pointed to Davis and said in a soft voice, "The only thing standing between this man and anything he might want to do any time he wants to do it . . . is *you twelve people . . . you* are the aggrieved parties."

Tolly Wilson finished up by explaining that everyone in the courtroom had just watched a classic example of how to hang a jury. "Keep them here long enough. Make them irritable and divide them. Make them forget

446

what testimony they heard eleven weeks ago. Sooner or later you'll get to a point where *no* verdict is possible. I'll leave it to your consideration if that's what happened here." Tolly wondered out loud why the defense went into such great detail challenging the validity of the tapes when the defendant himself admitted they were basically correct. "Don't you know he told his attorneys this fact from the very beginning? That man *there* [pointing at the defense table in general] has just taken eleven weeks out of your lives." Tolly said he shuddered at the thought of having to try the case again, but if the jurors couldn't reach a unanimous verdict, he'd by God do it. The chief prosecutor thanked the jury for its time and patience and sat down. Everything else that needed to be said would be said in the jury room.

～๑ • ๑～

In the late afternoon of Tuesday, January 16, the seven men and five women who would decide Cullen's fate retired. They deliberated only thirty minutes before recessing for the night; in retrospect the key decision was probably made in that first half hour when the jury elected Mary Carter foreman. A woman of strong opinions and a sense of civic duty, Mary Carter had told the lawyers in voir dire that she was between jobs as a medical secretary and thought serving on the Cullen Davis jury would be a constructive way to occupy her time. She clearly exercised some leadership over some of the other women jurors, though not over Frances Hambrick, who had little in common with Mrs. Carter.

By Wednesday night the jury had deliberated more than ten hours without reaching a verdict, and as each succeeding hour went by with no sign of agreement, the specter of a hung jury seemed more probable. After nineteen hours, lawyers were already talking about the ordeal of having to try the case again. The mere thought of having to review 15,000 pages of transcript was enough to suggest that perhaps the Tarrant County DA's office might have had a bellyful of Cullen Davis. The cost to the taxpayers had been enormous—the bill for the Houston trial was in excess of $150,000; counting Amarillo, the tab was more than a half million dollars, by far the most the county had ever spent to try a single person. Junior members of the DA's staff were referring to the Cullen Davis affair as "Tim Curry's Vietnam—he keeps sending in men and money and he never gets anything back." Already a petition was being circulated in Fort Worth demanding that Tim Curry abandon his pursuit of Cullen Davis; simultaneously, other citizens were starting to mail in their quarters and dollars to assist the county in pursuing Davis to the bitter end.

Even before the Amarillo trial Tim Curry had called the Cullen Davis case "a no-win deal for me," but that didn't mean the DA was ready to give up. Curry was absolutely convinced that Cullen was guilty both of murder and of solicitation of murder, and when taxpayer groups complained and budget supervisors tore at their garments, Curry reminded them firmly, "Cost is no justification for giving a man a free ride." If Pete Moore was forced to acknowledge that the jury was deadlocked and declare a mistrial, there was not the slightest doubt Curry would come after Cullen Davis again. Getting him would be a different matter: Cullen's lawyer would probably be able to delay a second trial for at least a year, and, as Steve Sumner noted, a lot can happen in a year. That's what worried Curry and a lot of others. Judge Joe Eidson, who had remained in the courthouse throughout the long jury deliberation, told reporters that he wouldn't feel safe until Cullen Davis "is broke or dead."

Pete Moore had no doubt at all what he would do in the event of a mistrial. He'd walk away from the case. "This has been the worst experience of my career," Moore said. "Haynes took the trial away from me the first week and I haven't got it back yet." Moore was more than willing to see Cullen tried again but not in *his* court.

By noon of the second full day of jury deliberation it was possible to speculate on what issues divided the jury. Mary Carter sent a note to the judge requesting that the tapes be sent to the jury room. Moore refused, but he brought the jury back into the courtroom for a replay. "That's a good sign for us," Mike Gibson thought. "It means at least some of the jurors are not accepting the tapes as evidence of guilt."

Although she had heard the tapes at least thirty times by now, Mary Carter seemed to be agonizing over the interpretation. She closed her eyes and pressed the headphones to her ears, leaning forward in her chair as the voices spoke of murder. Helen Farmer, a forty-eight-year-old housewife and another acknowledged fan of Racehorse Haynes, smiled and studied the faces in the gallery. Several other jurors listened halfheartedly, but Frances Hambrick leaned her head against the wall and massaged her eyes, and James Morrison, a fifty-year-old medical technologist, looked at the ceiling and at his watch.

Over the next several hours the jurors sent a number of notes to the judge, requesting that the court read back selected pieces of testimony.

One note implied that some of the jurors might be formulating their *own* theory, as juror Karl Prah had in Amarillo when he concocted his "coincidental conspiracy theory" to explain how two women running in opposite directions could tell the same story. It was a theory so bizarre that the defense hadn't dared try it, yet it was a major factor in Cullen's quick acquittal. Now the Houston jury sent in a question about Art Smith's testimony that McCrory was officially "terminated" from Jet Air on August 15. That was the last date McCrory reported to his office, and it seemed clear that the termination was retroactive from the day after Cullen's arrest. Nevertheless, someone on the jury seemed to be wrestling with the notion that McCrory might have framed Cullen in revenge for being fired.

The jury had still other questions.

Q: What did Hershel Payne say Cullen told him about the FBI calling?

A: Payne said Cullen never mentioned it.

Q: What did Karen Master say about the August 10 telephone call?

A: She said the voice "sounded familiar." It could have been either Agent Acree or Agent Oakley. She didn't inquire how the FBI got her unlisted phone number.

Q: Why did Cullen say he was making the tapes, and what was the first date he made a tape?

A: Cullen claimed the first tape was cut on August 11. The purpose was to "turn the tables on Priscilla. If I could pay them more than she could, they'd work for me." Cullen had added that he wanted the killers to give him information that would be helpful in his divorce trial.

Finally, the jury asked the judge for a more specific definition of the charge of solicitation of murder. Moore replied that he had already given them all the law applicable. The law didn't permit him to be more specific.

Friday afternoon the jury sent a note to the judge saying it was hopelessly deadlocked. After twenty-five hours of debate the jury had taken six ballots, and the vote hadn't changed. It had been eight to four all the way. The jury didn't say which way it was leaning, but even the defense assumed that the eight were voting guilty. They immediately asked for a mistrial. "It's in Cullen's best interest to assume the majority is for conviction," Gibson said. Moore denied the motion for mistrial and told the jury to keep trying.

The judge didn't have to be told that he was operating on thin ice. Haynes was already accusing him of "coercing" the jurors by forcing them to continue deliberations. "This goes right to the heart of the system," Haynes said. "Each juror is entitled to his or her independent judgment and should not be coerced under

450

conditions such as fatigue when they are in the minority." Racehorse's high-blown proclamation about the system was totally self-serving. Pete Moore noted that the law said a jury should continue deliberating "a reasonable length of time," leaving the judge to decide what was reasonable. "You can't sequester a jury for longer than it took to try the case." Moore smiled. *Eleven weeks?* The judge was just kidding. But he knew this: if he discharged the jury too soon, it would subject Davis to double jeopardy and prohibit a retrial. Pete Moore wasn't about to make that mistake.

Moore considered the possibility of a dynamite charge used sometimes in federal cases—the judge could remind the jury of the time and expense, advise them that another jury couldn't be expected to have an easier time, and urge that they settle their differences, if possible. This was also a dangerous course of action. A dynamite charge would have to be worded very carefully so that it would in no way coerce the jury or comment on the evidence. If the split had been ten to two, Moore might have entertained it, but under the circumstances he felt constrained to keep his mouth shut.

The jury worked all day Saturday, but the only thing that moved were the hands on the clock. People in the hallway or the nearly empty courtroom napped or read or just stared into space. The jokes were stale, and so was the conversation. W. T. Rufner was trying to explain how he'd broken his hand in a pool game, but nobody listened. Pete Moore chain-smoked and wondered if he'd ever get around to repairing the frozen pipes in his country house. Two reporters shared a plate of cold Chinese food, and an artist sketched Jack Strickland as he slept on a hallway bench. At noon Sunday the jurors took a break to watch the Super Bowl, and the courthouse emptied. Jack Strickland had lost his appetite for football. Instead, he took a solitary walk along the bayou, oblivious to the cold gray drizzle and the petrochemical smaze that seeped in from the ship channel. People were going to say they'd lost. Maybe they had. It occurred to Strickland that maybe it was impossible to convict Cullen Davis of any crime, impossible to find any group of twelve who could look at Cullen Davis, be apprised of his wealth, education, and family background, be subjected to the charm and expertise of Racehorse Haynes and the ordeal that enormous wealth could foist on a trial, and still reach a unanimous verdict of guilty. Maybe there would always be one or two or three or four jurors who would hear the evidence, search their souls, and conclude that Cullen Davis was not *capable* of the things they said. Maybe Cullen Davis *was* above the law. Strickland had taken an oath to uphold the system, but right now he was sick of it. Sick of watching Racehorse Haynes twist and torture it, sicker still of Haynes's sanctimonious proclamations. In a speech to the state bar association Haynes referred to himself as "a trustee of liberty." You had to admire his candor. He was certainly the trustee of Cullen Davis's liberty, a tiny law unto himself. Jack Strickland wouldn't always be a prosecutor. He had ambitions. Other lawyers had watched him work and predicted he might someday be a Racehorse Haynes. Strickland stopped beside Allen's Landing where more than a century ago the first steamship had docked and proclaimed Houston the headwater of navigation, the state's passage to the sea. It was a ridiculous claim, yet here it was, *Houston*, the nation's second largest seaport. The city that pioneered *can-do*, the birthplace of Richard "Racehorse" Haynes. Anything was possible, Strickland told himself, but he wondered if it was worth it.

On Monday, January 22, after forty-four hours of debate and fourteen ballots, the jury still stood eight to four for conviction. Shortly before 4:00 P.M. Cullen Davis entered Judge Moore's courtroom for the last time, pale as a man who had passed his own ghost but ebullient and smiling at the assembled jurors. Pete Moore polled the jury, asking each member if further deliberation might produce a verdict. All twelve had the same answer: "Never!" Haynes gripped the lapels of his suit and in a strong, trembling voice asked once more for a mistrial.

The judge told Cullen Davis to stand. "Your attorneys have asked for a mistrial," Moore said. "I need your consent."

"You have my permission, your honor," Cullen said. Cullen started thanking the jury, but Moore told him to sit down. Phil Burleson leaned across and whispered something in Cullen's ear, and both men smiled. Burleson carried in his coat pocket a cashier's check for $30,000. Cullen was about to walk the streets again.

Juror James Morrison, one of the eight who voted all the way for conviction, confirmed what a lot of people had already decided—that the jurors who voted for acquittal couldn't find any way to convince themselves that a man of Cullen's wealth would lower himself to having a judge killed. "Subconsciously, I know some of them were thinking that this man could never have done this because he's rich and owns a bunch of companies," Morrison said. Morrison identified the four holdouts as Mary Carter, Helen Hill, Vera Miller, and Charles Franks. "They believed Davis's story per se," Morrison said. "I thought his story was pure fantasy . . . next to nothing."

Frances Hambrick called the entire defense "an insult to our intelligence."

Juror Frank Digenova said that the jurors who voted for acquittal harped on that fact that the defense needed only to plant a reasonable doubt in the jurors' minds. "There were constant reminders that there only needed to be reasonable doubt," said Digenova, who had none himself.

Mary Carter refused to say how she voted, but she was clearly speaking for the minority when she said, "Some of the twelve felt, even with the tapes, the prosecution did not present a strong enough case . . . even if the defense had presented nothing."

Mary Carter was infuriated by suggestions that she was awestruck by Cullen's wealth or by Haynes's charm. Her arguments in the jury room had closely paralleled Racehorse's opening remarks that *things are not as they appear*. The foreman thought that the testimony of Karen Master and Harold Sexton sufficiently supported Cullen's story about the phone call

453

from the FBI and explained the curious conversations on the tapes.

"I saw the tapes and heard them," Mary Carter said firmly, "but I still do not know the *reason* the tapes were made. Was David McCrory telling the truth when he went to the FBI about Davis wanting people killed? There's nothing to substantiate his story. Or was Cullen Davis telling the truth when he testified that a representative from the FBI called and told him to play along with McCrory? I believed Davis's version. . . ."

Helen Farmer freely admitted that she was charmed by Racehorse Haynes. "He has gorgeous eyes," Mrs. Farmer said. "Do you know how old he is? He really *cried* during the final arguments. I nearly gave him a Kleenex. He's a wily fox, a really superb lawyer." Farmer failed to explain, however, why she voted all the way to convict Cullen Davis. How she voted and why was her business, she said with a smile.

Racehorse had dried his tears, but he was still trembling as dozens of reporters and cameramen clustered about him. "They didn't get us, did they?" Race grinned fiercely. When someone brought up the contention that Cullen Davis had *bought* his freedom, the grin became a mask of defiance. "Those who say that are bitter, dissident, irresponsible people who have no experience as to how it feels to be poor or wealthy," Haynes said. "They don't know that both the very rich and very poor are vulnerable targets in this country!" So far Haynes hadn't made much of a mark defending the very poor, but he perhaps intended to. He could afford it. Rumor was that he had jacked up his fee considerably since Amarillo. A million in front and another $2 million to be paid over a number of years. It was a victory for the system, Race said, a great victory.

Pete Moore disagreed. It was the judge's opinion that Haynes had just brought the system to its knees. "I think the entire system has been abused by this case, and I don't like it," Moore told reporters. "If it had taken half as long to try, I think the jurors could have reached a decision. They had to have all the first part of the testimony reread. They were confused. Obviously, they couldn't recall the testimony they heard back in early November."

Fifty or sixty reporters were waiting at the basement jail entrance when Cullen Davis appeared. Cullen was on his way to a small victory party—nothing like Amarillo, of course, but then neither was the victory. Cullen said he wasn't bitter, just disgusted with the conspirators. In Amarillo someone had asked him what he learned from his experience, and Cullen told them he learned that no matter how rich a man is, it's not always possible to make bond. What had he learned in Houston? "Not to listen to the FBI," Cullen said. Someone asked him about the next trial. Cullen took Karen by the arm and said he hoped there wouldn't be one. Karen had a funny look on her face, and the reason was W. T. Rufner, who was pushing through the mob with something in his hand. It was one of his WHAT PRICE JUSTICE? T-shirts, and he shoved it toward Cullen without comment. "Thanks, W. T.," Cullen said. "I appreciate it."

A black limousine came around the corner and stopped abruptly outside the jail entrance. Phil Burleson climbed out and held the door open for Cullen and Karen. Cullen waved one final time, then disappeared into the damp, cold Houston night.

The news that Cullen Davis was back on the streets came as no surprise to Fort Worth.

Jack Wilborn thought it was dangerous, but he expected it. "It's extremely difficult to convict a person if the person has unlimited resources," Wilborn said. "But I wouldn't trade places with Cullen Davis for all the money in the world. He'll be looking over his shoulder from now on. Justice will come. It may be when he dies a natural death, but it will come."

Bubba Gavrel wasn't commenting on the verdict, and Bev Bass's mother said that Bev had been "sent away for a little while."

A winter storm was barreling toward Fort Worth, and the mansion at 4200 Mockingbird winked through the dust like something blowing in time. Priscilla had just come from the cemetery. She had placed flowers on the graves of Andrea, who would have been fifteen that day, and Stan Farr, who would have turned thirty-four. It could have been a nice birthday, she thought. Maybe it would yet, some other year. A group of reporters followed Priscilla down the long, opulent main hallway, past the baby grand that no one had ever played, to the living room with the painting of Cullen and Priscilla. Nothing had changed, she said. Nothing had ended. There would be another time. She'd testify again. "I may have to dye my hair and put on my granny glasses to get them to listen, but I'll do it." Priscilla posed in front of the painting in her white knit turtleneck, holding her cat Stanford to her breast. The fear would always be there, she said, but she wasn't alone anymore. Joe Eidson knew how she felt. So did a lot of people. They all had to be patient. Cullen would strike again. She was positive of that.

"Just watch," she said cheerily. "Just watch him work."

Epilogue

The marriage that shocked Fort Worth society and triggered the incredible chain of events described in *Blood Will Tell* was officially dissolved April 20, 1979. It ended with a whimper, albeit a multimilion-dollar one. The big bang, the final resolution of the murder-for-hire charges against T. Cullen Davis, was still to come.

By mutual consent, the divorce was tried as a no-fault lawsuit, meaning that the court would tolerate no bloodletting but would limit issues simply to the division of property. Still, it wasn't easy. Priscilla was now demanding $50 million and Cullen was offering $400,-000. The trial consumed more than one hundred hours of highly complicated testimony and very nearly consumed the patience and fortitude of two judges. Visiting judge John Barron, who practiced in the small central Texas town of Bryan, heard the first few weeks of testimony, then proclaimed that he'd had enough and walked out. Barron had failed to reckon with the hoopla and pyrotechnics that had become back alley habit to the regulars in the Cullen Davis affair. Barron had reservations from the very beginning, when he found himself guarded around the clock by not one but *two* Texas Rangers—"one more than it takes to quell a riot," courthouse wags, observed. Back home in Bryan, the judge sometimes resolved such bitter disputes with a little old-fashioned jawboning, making off-the-record visits to the homes of the warring parties where they could sit on porch swings, sip lemonade and maybe reason together. When the judge secretly invited Cullen to meet with him privately in his hotel suite, the media treated it like a major scandal. The last straw, though, was when prosecutors from District Attorney Tim

Curry's office unexpectedly subpoenaed and seized divorce court records, even as testimony in the suit continued. Barron announced that he would not put up with such "arbitrary actions of a wet-eared, fool prosecutor." He declared he was withdrawing from the case and going "back to Bryon [to] hunt rabbits."

A mistrial at this point would have put everyone back at ground zero. Fortunately, it didn't come to that. District Judge Clyde Ashworth, appointed to replace Barron, checked the books, then ruled that the two parties could pick up where they left off. A few weeks later, Ashworth issued a Solomon-like decree dissolving what was surely the most litigated marriage in Fort Worth history, and allowing both Priscilla and Cullen to claim a measure of victory. Cullen was allowed to keep the mansion and the bulk of his fortune. Priscilla was awarded $3.4 million, tax free. After a mandatory thirty-day waiting period, Cullen and Priscilla were at last free from their nuptial vows.

A few minutes after midnight on May 24 the waiting period expired and Karen Master became the third Mrs. T. Cullen Davis. Only a handful of relatives and close friends attended the private ceremony. There was a short honeymoon, then Davis returned to Fort Worth to again face charges that he had attempted to arrange for the murder of the original divorce judge, Joe Eidson.

Both sides knew this would be the final round. It was time to play the hole card, if either side still had one. By now, the case had been returned from Houston to the court of District Judge Gordon Gray who, it was assumed, would follow the pattern and move it to another city. Gray was in the process of trying to find an out-of-town court when the defense played its first card. Racehorse Haynes announced that he opposed a change of venue. Cullen demanded to be tried in his hometown. This move didn't come as a complete surprise to District Attorney Tim Curry, who was counting on his own hole card—Judge Gray. "If the defense thought Pete Moore was tough in Houston," one lawyer said, "wait 'til they meet Gordon Gray." If Cullen insisted on being tried in Fort Worth, he would have to take Judge Gray in the bargain.

Racehorse Haynes also had his doubts about Judge Gray, but as to the part about Cullen being unable to receive a *fair* trial in his hometown, the Houston lawyer had yet another perspective: it was Haynes's opinion that, if anything, a Fort Worth jury would be less than fair to the *prosecution*. In a sense it was the *prosecution* that was on trial. Rivals were already nipping at Tim Curry's heels in this election year. Many voters believed that the county had already spent too much time and money on Cullen Davis. For some convoluted reason voters couldn't seem to separate the two alleged crimes, the murder of Andrea Wilborn and the attempted murder of Judge Eidson. In the public mind Cullen's troubles seemed to be a two-headed mutant, growing from the same legal root.

Conspiracy is a term reserved almost exclusively for the prosecution, but in this particular case it had been preempted by the other side. Cullen, the accused, was perceived to be the victim. From the beginning, the Cullen Davis affair had defied custom and tradition and in this respect nowhere was convention more twisted, more unorthodox, than in Fort Worth, where the normal roles of accused and victim had run together and intertwined like so many miles of highline disappearing into the horizon. It seemed inconceivable to Haynes that any twelve people in Fort Worth could agree on Cullen's guilt. Certainly Cullen could survive another hung jury, but the prosecution couldn't. "It's a no-lose proposition for ol' Racehorse," one lawyer said. "If the judge plays it straight, they got a hung jury. If he leans toward the state, they got a reversal. Either way, Cullen walks."

Curry had one more ace to play. He retired chief prosecutor Tolly Wilson to administrative duties and appointed young Jack Strickland to head the team. Strickland didn't have Racehorse Haynes's experience, but he had the same style, the same dash and imagination and gut instinct, the same willingness to charge and, if necessary, bluff his way through uncharted wilderness. Strickland's first order was to authorize the unprecedented expense of a computer to collect and correlate the tangles of evidence. He hired an expert from the University of Texas at San Antonio to design giant cardboard "flow charts" that he hoped would simplify the evidence for the jury. Then he proceeded to pick what had to be the strangest jury in the history of Tarrant County prosecution. He picked precisely the type of jury that the *defense* would normally pick. Prosecutors almost automatically strike members of minorities for fear that they will resent the state for perceived persecutions of the past. This jury included two blacks and an Hispanic. It was by far the youngest of the three juries to try Cullen Davis; five were thirty-one or younger. Instead of strong, stable pillar-of-the-community types, Strickland went out of his way to select jurors who had themselves been victims of prejudice or character assassination. He refused to strike a man who was an admitted gossip about the Davis case, or a man who had quit his job to sit on the jury, or another man who divorced his wife and quit his job because he was tired of driving to work. One woman on the jury panel told lawyers that all she knew about the case is what she'd read about Priscilla. Strickland approved her, too.

The defense approached jury selection with the belief that an acquittal was a virtual impossibility, that their best bet was to play for a hung jury. Dr. Margaret Covington, the psychologist who had helped Haynes on previous occasions, observed that the inseparable deadlock in Houston could be attributed to the strong, independent personalities of the jurors. This time the defense tried to pick jurors who could work together. "A cohesive group," as Dr. Covington described them. This, too, was a calculated risk. The state had a strong case: maybe this cohesive group would decide their man was guilty. On the other hand, they might *agree* on reasonable doubt.

The retrial took fifteen weeks, but what was billed as the third act of the Cullen Davis saga was more like a reprisal. There were a few new twists, but mostly it was the same old songs, the familiar low comedy and duplicity and evangelical sideshowing underscored by the same haunting theme that someone had left a few pages out of the script.

As usual, the groupies clustered about Cullen like adoring aunties. Like a bit player who by some metamorphosis emerges as the central figure, Cullen no longer appeared as the little boy wronged, but as the man in charge. For reasons never made completely clear (rumor said he'd experienced a "religious conversion"), Racehorse Haynes seemed uncharacteristically gloomy, even petulant, dodging the spotlight and grousing about media coverage. Race insisted from the start that Judge Gray take a hard line and issue a gag order prohibiting lawyers and witnesses (and the judge himself) from mingling with members of the media. But Cullen more than took up the slack. People brought him flowers, food, lucky charms. The richest man ever to be tried for murder posed for countless pictures, graciously holding the sticky-faced grandchildren of total strangers in his lap and trading quips with reporters. Cullen was usually the first one at the courthouse and the last to leave. At lunch, Cullen and his entourage took over Duffy's Restaurant on the second floor of Tandy Center near the courthouse. Friends, followers and believers called out and Cullen waved and usually greeted each by name. Cullen never seemed to question that now, at last, he was riding the inevitable winning streak, that he had kept pushing out chips until the odds changed, until he was at last playing with the house's money. If Fort Worth had been Las Vegas, they would have called him a *striker: Keep your eye on that feller, mama, he's gonna own this place before he's through!* Maybe it was because he'd spent six hundred twelve days in jail that this freedom to come and go and control the pace here in his own hometown seemed so delicious.

And, still, there was the current of expectation in the courtroom, as though the Great Hand of Justice might at any second intervene and take off the roof and sail it over the river. The trial *started* with a three-week delay because the defense couldn't locate one of its key witnesses, Pat Burleson. The man that defense attorneys had alleged to be one of the three conspirators who set out to frame Cullen Davis had been devastated by the experience in Houston. He'd lost his wife, his family, his business, his respect and finally he had vanished so that even the force of investigators working for Cullen Davis couldn't find him. Defense attorneys hinted darkly that this time they would present foolproof evidence that Burleson had been in Priscilla's pay throughout. Stories circulated among reporters that Cullen's investigators had located "boxes of treasure" buried behind Burleson's cabin in the mountains of southeast Oklahoma. The boxes were said to contain jade, silver and ivory carvings secreted from the mansion.

Expectation crackled like spring lightning during one afternoon recess when armed guards pushed through the crowd carrying two very heavy, badly rusted, mud-splattered Army ammunition boxes. The "treasure chests" contained a broken jar, some brown liquid that looked like tobacco juice, and a note warning that whoever disturbed the contents of the boxes would die a hideous death from a poison for which there was no available antidote.

"Just when Judge Gray declared that he wouldn't allow his courtroom to be turned into a circus," wrote Fort Worth *Star-Telegram* reporter Carolyn Ondrejas, "they brought in the elephants." Ondrejas learned that the boxes had once contained some foreign coins and Oriental karate statues that Burleson had collected during his travels in the Navy. No one ever presented evidence that the boxes contained anything else, and Judge Gray refused to admit them into evidence. The defense finally located Pat Burleson, then changed its mind and never called him to the witness stand.

In late September, the trial was delayed another two days when a woman juror broke her leg during a weekend shopping trip. Gray ruled that the trial would continue with only eleven jurors, which is permissible under Texas law. Not long after that, the judge fell off his horse, breaking two ribs and his collarbone. With the aid of a body brace the judge and the trial continued.

Just as the state had simplified its case with a computer and flow charts, the defense streamlined its witness list, trimming from more than sixty in Houston to about twenty-five. A number of the less credible witnesses, such as Larry Gene Lucas and the Florios, were never recalled. Neither was Harold Sexton, whose story about meeting informant David McCrory at a Sambo's restaurant that had already burned down was likely to amuse rather than impress a jury in Tarrant County. The defense did recall James Stephens to repeat the story of how one day as he was nursing a hangover and changing a flat tire he happened to see Priscilla, McCrory and Pat Burleson coming out of a motel. Again it was the only piece of testimony that put the three "conspirators" together in one place at the same time. But this time the prosecution's trusty computer had the answer. The computer coughed up a contradiction that the state had overlooked in Houston: records showed that at the exact moment Stephens recalled seeing Priscilla she was in fact being examined by her doctor miles away. The only witness who offered additional support to the defense's conspiracy theory was an ex-convict named Larry Francis, who testified that David McCrory was flashing an envelope containing one hundred dollars two days before the arrest of Cullen Davis. The fact that Francis admitted six state felony convictions and one federal conviction did not improve his standing as a witness.

"Of course, you don't have any hard feelings against the Tarrant County District Attorney's Office for sending you to the pen three times, do you?" Jack Strickland asked caustically.

"Just doing their job." Francis shrugged.

The defense was slowly, subtly, shifting emphasis, not exactly abandoning its contention of conspiracy, but putting much more weight on the conventional alibi defense Cullen couldn't have been trying to kill fifteen people because he was doing something *else.* He was working for the FBI, or so he thought. The defense no longer tried to establish that the Tarrant County DA's office cooperated in the conspiracy, or that it was being secretly financed by Cullen's brother, Bill Davis. There was one part of the familiar formula that Racehorse Haynes clung to, maybe from habit. He again attempted to paint Priscilla as Typhoid Mary. Judge Gray harnessed these attempts, however, ruling that the entire line of questioning concerning Priscilla's morals was irrelevant and immaterial. "It's trash," the judge lashed out, threatening to cite Haynes for contempt if he persisted.

What saved Cullen in Houston was his own surprising explanation of what the conversation on the tapes really intended. That he was merely *playing along* with McCrory, that he never *intended* to have anyone killed, that he was only following what he *thought* were FBI orders. The defense had lost the element of surprise, but Haynes decided to offset the loss by bringing in an expert witness to support the story. The defense's key witness in Fort Worth turned out to be Dr. Roger Shuy, professor of linguistics at Georgetown University and president of the American Association of Applied Linguistics. Armed with charts and graphs, Dr. Shuy testified that he had spent more than fifty hours listening to and analyzing the tapes and that in his expert opinion Cullen never intended to kill anyone. Cullen was just "playing along," Shuy said, repeating Cullen's exact phrase. Shuy, who charged the defense more than $10,000 for his expertise, repeatedly challenged the state's interpretation of the conversation between Cullen and McCrory, introducing the jury to such esoteric terms as "shared reference, internal cohesion and conversational strategy." He claimed to have found one hundred twenty-five discrepancies between the state's transcript and what he heard on the tapes.

In cross-examination, Jack Strickland asked the linguistic expert to explain why they kept talking about hit men if they didn't mean to kill anyone. Shuy said that he wasn't familiar with the term *hit men*.

"They're hired killers," Strickland said evenly. "People who kill for money."

"I don't know about things like that," the linguistic expert replied.

Shuy agreed with the prosecutor that the subject matter on the tapes did not conform to ordinary conversation. "It's hard to tell what the subject matter is," Shuy argued.

"After fifty hours of listening . . . after fifty hours . . . you can't tell this jury that the subject matter concerns killings, guns, silencers?" Strickland asked incredulously.

Strickland had warned jurors that his adversary was a "master illusionist" and late in the trial Haynes petitioned the court for permission to attempt perhaps his greatest illusion. From the defense's standpoint, the *key* piece of physical evidence was the so-called *second* tape recorder that no one could produce, the one Cullen claimed McCrory held in his lap as they discussed hired murder. The cassettes from this phantom recorder were supposed to be "insurance" that Cullen wouldn't betray Priscilla's "hired killers." In fact, it was the cassettes, not the photograph of Judge Eidson's body or the judge's ID cards, that Cullen claimed to have seen the morning after the faked murder. Haynes hadn't been able to produce the phantom recorder or the phantom cassettes in Houston, but now he asked the court to give him a chance to demonstrate how the FBI's search of McCrory's car could have *overlooked* these key pieces of evidence. Judge Gray surprisingly agreed and the jury reconvened in the courthouse basement where the defense demonstrated that cassettes could have been hidden in the air-conditioning vent, or in the rear seat ashtray. The prosecution countered by demonstrating that the two hiding places were smaller than a normal man's hand, far too small, in fact, for a hand the size of David McCrory's. It was like stuffing a ham through a mail slot. Nevertheless, the jury seemed impressed. It was as though they had just watched Blackstone saw the pretty lady in half.

Both sides had a final surprise for the jury. The prosecution produced a witness who contradicted a crucial element of Cullen's story, the time and place of two of his meetings with McCrory. Gale Helms testified that McCrory was with him in Oklahoma City June 9, 1978, the day Cullen claimed McCrory first told him of the plot to kill him. Haynes's antagonistic cross-examination failed to shake Helms's story, but a few days later the defense produced hotel records that proved that Helms and McCrory hadn't checked into the Holiday Inn in Oklahoma City until *June 10.*

When the testimony was completed and it was time to give the case to the jury, Defense Attorney Phil Burleson turned to his client and asked the same question he had asked in Amarillo and again in Houston: "Is there anything else we could have done? One more witness, *anything* to make you more satisfied with your defense?"

In the two previous trials Cullen had considered the question with much apprehension. Surely there was something. Somehow the defense had never been able to package it and tie it with a ribbon. Now in Fort Worth, Cullen looked at the silver-haired defense attorney and said in his ice cold corporate voice, "No, this time you did it right."

So after fifteen exhausting weeks, the fate of Cullen Davis rested with eight men and three women who, in the imperfect if ostensibly egalitarian view of the criminal justice system, would now act as his peers. It was the first week in November 1979. It had been almost exactly two years since the acquittal in Amarillo. The eleven members of the panel retired to the jury room, said a silent prayer and elected Robert White, an ex-Marine who plays classical guitar, as chairman. Mary Gross, a meticulous woman with an interest in the use of language, was named secretary. Mrs. Gross maintained detailed notes of the jury's activities, which she dutifully destroyed fifteen hours later at the end of the deliberations. A few members of the panel wanted to vote right away, but White decided they should move slowly, methodically reviewing the many pieces of evidence and the testimony of the long list of witnesses. "We tried going down the list," said juror Jack Grable, "but everything kept coming up *David McCrory and Cullen Davis.*" Although they had heard the tapes dozens of times by now, they listened to them again and again and again, backing and repeating the tapes anytime anyone had a question.

Several jurors were troubled by the .22 revolver and silencer that FBI agents confiscated from Cullen's car. Mary Gross asked to examine the weapon and it was delivered to the jury room. One juror took the gun apart, removed the silencer, pulled out the clip and opened the chamber. Juror Jack Grable, who knew something about weapons, thought the silencer was *inoperative*. "All it does is bolster the state's case," someone said. "Maybe that's the reason they gave it to him," someone else said. Cullen had looked at the gun and silencer: on the tape you can hear him say, "Damned pretty!" Grable said that he could see how Cullen chose those particular words. "I have an obsession for a *machine gun*," Grable said. "I have no use for one, but I've always wanted one. I can see where it would be nice to have it laying around. It's something nobody's got."

One juror was bothered by McCrory's hasty retreat from the August 20 meeting with Cullen. Why did McCrory leave without waiting for instructions from the FBI? McCrory had answered that question in the courtroom: he left when Cullen left to avoid raising Davis's suspicions. But juror Ed Dennis, who operated the recorder, wanted to hear the last part of the August 20 tape again. "We replayed the part where McCrory starts the car and leaves the scene," Dennis said. "To me, that just blew McCrory." It indicated to Dennis and others that McCrory, not the FBI, was running the show.

And what about McCrory's role in *all* of this? Dr. Shuy, the linguistics expert, had pointed out how McCrory dominated the conversations. Didn't that support Cullen's claim of a frame-up?

Twelve hours into deliberation the jurors approached what ultimately became their moment of truth. Although no one had mentioned it during fifteen weeks of testimony, the jurors themselves began to notice an odd *rattling* noise in the tape about the place where McCrory is supposed to be showing Cullen the photograph and ID cards of the dead judge. What *was* that noise? "It doesn't sound like paper," juror Darryl Cremer said. "It sounds more like little plastic cassettes knocking together." Grable dropped the photograph and Eidson's ID cards in an envelope and shook it. Everyone strained to listen. He shook it again. There was no sound. Then Grable knocked two pieces of plastic together. "That's more what it sounds like," the juror said.

Foreman White said: "I think it's time for a vote."

When word reached the courtroom that the jurors had a verdict, prosecutors requested a brief meeting to discuss the punishment phase of the trial. Both sides took the notice of verdict to mean a notice of guilty. It was now Friday morning and Judge Gray announced that he would hear testimony in the punishment phase Monday morning. As the jury filed into the courtroom, Haynes placed his head on the defense table. Steve Sumner put his arm over co-counsel Mike Gibson's shoulder. "What do you think?" he asked Gibson. "Guilty," Gibson said. At the prosecution table Jack Strickland was smiling broadly. Sumner watched the jurors find their chairs. There was no eye contact. The women weren't carrying their handbags as they usually do when it's over and they're ready to leave. Worse. "What do you think?" Cullen asked. "I don't know," Sumner said. Cullen was like stone.

Judge Gray opened the verdict, read it to himself, blinked and read it again. He stumbled over his words as he announced: "The jury has found Thomas Cullen Davis not guilty."

"Thank the Lord," Racehorse Haynes said as spectators rushed forward and the hugging, kissing and back-slapping began. Cullen was close to tears as he thanked the jurors and invited them to his victory party at Duffy's, where they had been stocking champagne for two weeks in anticipation of victory.

Jack Strickland was crushed. "I can't believe it," he said. "I can't believe eleven decent citizens would vote to turn him loose. I don't care what happens next . . . if that's the kind of conduct people want to approve in this community." Strickland walked away before he said something he would regret. It was no secret that the young prosecutor had his eye on the DA's office. But Cullen Davis was academic. In a few hours, Tim Curry announced that all charges against Davis would be dropped. A number of civil suits were pending, but this ended Cullen Davis's criminal problems.

The victory party at Duffy's was comparatively subdued. After three record-length trials and twelve million dollars in legal fees, what's left to toast? Someone delivered flowers and there were tears and speeches and maybe even some second-guessing, although everyone agreed it was vain and petty and self-serving to second-guess victory. Racehorse was unusually quiet, barely sipping his drink. There was a mighty roar, however, when one of the jurors showed up at Duffy's.

Tempa Davis Hooper broke into tears as Cullen stepped forward and hugged her.

"We took the first vote this morning," the sixty-year-old Sears saleswoman told Cullen.

"Then what were you doing all that time?" Cullen asked.

"Cullen," she said, her voice wobbling, "we were clearing our conscience. We have to live with ourselves."

Cullen nodded that he understood.

"I felt sorry for you," Mrs. Hooper added. "It would have been the same if we'd voted the first day."

"A toast for Mrs. Hooper," the crowd cheered. Haynes bent from the waist and kissed her hand.

Mrs. Hooper seemed more composed now. She told Haynes, *"You* couldn't find the cassettes, but we think we found the damn things. You could hear the cassettes clinking together on the tape. We heard the clinking sound. That was the crucial turning point of the trial."

The look on Racehorse's face said it all. *Incredible!* You spend a career studying juries, analyzing evidence and postulating theories, then something like this appears out of God's own sweet blue heaven. It was like juror Karl Prah's unsolicited "coincidental conspiracy" theory in Amarillo. Blue world stuff. *Amazing!* A seemingly inconsequential rattling noise on a tape of almost

469

insurmountable complexity, muddled sounds and tell-tale lapses, curses and randomly scattered seeds of destruction. One little background noise that all but went unnoticed. *Remarkable!* Race wouldn't have thought of it in a million years! But for twelve million dollars, he probably should have.